A CULTURAL HISTORY
OF SEXUALITY

VOLUME 5

A Cultural History of Sexuality
General Editor: Julie Peakman

Volume 1
A Cultural History of Sexuality in the Classical World
Edited by Mark Golden and Peter Toohey

Volume 2
A Cultural History of Sexuality in the Middle Ages
Edited by Ruth Evans

Volume 3
A Cultural History of Sexuality in the Renaissance
Edited by Bette Talvacchia

Volume 4
A Cultural History of Sexuality in the Enlightenment
Edited by Julie Peakman

Volume 5
A Cultural History of Sexuality in the Age of Empire
Edited by Chiara Beccalossi and Ivan Crozier

Volume 6
A Cultural History of Sexuality in the Modern Age
Edited by Gert Hekma

A CULTURAL HISTORY

OF SEXUALITY

IN THE AGE
OF EMPIRE

Edited by Chiara Beccalossi and Ivan Crozier

B L O O M S B U R Y

LONDON • NEW DELHI • NEW YORK • SYDNEY

Bloomsbury Academic
An imprint of Bloomsbury Publishing Plc

50 Bedford Square	1385 Broadway
London	New York
WC1B 3DP	NY 10018
UK	USA

www.bloomsbury.com

Hardback edition first published in 2011 by Berg Publishers, an imprint of
Bloomsbury Academic
Paperback edition first published by Bloomsbury Academic 2014

British Library Cataloguing-in-Publication Data
A catalogue record for this book is available from the British Library.

ISBN: HB: 978-1-84788-804-4
PB: 978-1-4725-3919-9
HB Set: 978-1-84520-702-1
PB Set: 978-1-4725-5480-2

Library of Congress Cataloging-in-Publication Data
A catalog record for this book is available from the Library of Congress.

Typeset by Apex CoVantage, LLC, Madison, WI, USA

CONTENTS

PREFACE

A Cultural History of Sexuality is a six-volume series reviewing changes in sexual attitudes and behavior throughout history. Each volume follows the same basic structure and begins with an outline account of sexuality in the period under consideration. Academic experts examine major aspects of sex and sexuality under seven key headings: heterosexuality, homosexuality, sexual variations, religion and the law, medicine and disease, popular beliefs and culture, prostitution, and erotica. Readers can choose a synchronic or a diachronic approach to the material—a single volume can be read to obtain a thorough knowledge of the body in a given period, or one of the seven themes can be followed through time by reading the relevant chapters of all six volumes, providing a thematic understanding of changes and developments over the long term. The six volumes divide the history of sexuality as follows:

Volume 1: A Cultural History of Sexuality in the Classical World (800 B.C.E. to 350 C.E.)

Volume 2: A Cultural History of Sexuality in the Middle Ages (350 C.E. to 1450)

Volume 3: A Cultural History of Sexuality in the Renaissance (1450 to 1650)

Volume 4: A Cultural History of Sexuality in the Enlightenment (1650 to 1820)

Volume 5: A Cultural History of Sexuality in the Age of Empire (1820 to 1920)

Volume 6: A Cultural History of Sexuality in the Modern Age (1920 to 2000)

Julie Peakman, General Editor

SERIES ACKNOWLEDGMENTS

This series has been a long time in the making, mainly because it is not an easy task to bring together fifty-four international scholars, even when we were all willing and eager. Every one of us had other commitments—to our universities, other books, and/or to our families. I therefore appreciate those who came together to create this special project. I want to thank the editors of all the volumes; Peter Toohey and Mark Golden, Ruth Evans, Bette Talvacchia, Ivan Crozier and Chiara Beccalossi, and Gert Hekma for their sterling efforts in the face of my continual demands, and for helping to keep their contributors on track, especially when the occasional one dropped out with little warning. Huge thanks also go to all the contributors who freely committed their time and efforts. I also want to thank Tristan Palmer at Berg for all his support and Catherine Draycott from the Wellcome Trust Picture Library for making available the Wellcome images.

Julie Peakman, General Editor

ILLUSTRATIONS

CHAPTER 1

CHAPTER 2

CHAPTER 3

CHAPTER 4

CHAPTER 5

CHAPTER 6

CHAPTER 7

CHAPTER 8

CHAPTER 9

CHAPTER ONE

Introduction: The Cultural History of Sexuality in the Nineteenth Century

CHIARA BECCALOSSI AND IVAN CROZIER

An entertaining essay might perhaps be written on the sexlessness of historians; but it would be entertaining and nothing more: we do not know enough either about the historians or sex.

Lytton Strachey, 1931, p. 177

The discipline of the history of sexuality emerged largely from discussions of nineteenth-century sex. The ceaseless wonder of historians tittering at modestly clothed table legs, Prince Albert's penile piercing, and Queen Victoria's inability to conceive of the physical details of lesbian lovemaking—all fabulous myths about the period—have of course dissipated. So too have all notions of the absence of desire in the long nineteenth century that lay at the heart of Lytton Strachey's important characterizations of the time.[1] Today, the period is constantly exploited as a fecund site for understanding the forging of modern conceptions of sexual practices, knowledges, and ideologies. No longer are the Victorians sexless moral beasts haunting the obscure pages of history, their alter egos acting on every depraved word of the mountains of Victorian pornography as if performing a choreographed version of Walter's *My Secret Life*.

Now we know that the Victorians were fully engaged with coming to terms with the issues raised by sexual desire. In this volume, a number of these problems will be addressed in detail.

Given the range of feasible topics for discussion in a collection of essays about Victorian sexuality—possibilities spanning everything from autoerotism to zoophilia, both nineteenth-century concepts—this introduction and the chapters that follow aim to sketch out a number of important problems, organized thematically. The volume contains chapters that touch upon (in more or less detail) homosexuality, heterosexuality, medical knowledge, erotic writing, "perversions," pornography, child sexuality, sexual regulation, erotic imagery, and prostitution. All these topics are well situated in historical research. Thus, this book aims to act as something as a guide to the breadth of this important historical field. This introduction will not discuss the chapters in any detail but instead surveys the scope of the historiography of nineteenth-century sexuality in all its variety, situating many of the questions that are given scholarly attention within.

SOURCES FOR SEX IN THE NINETEENTH CENTURY

One of the key problems for historicizing intimacy in the past is the source material. It is hard enough to verbalize the erotic release of a sexual encounter in the present; to discover this precise yet mercurial intensity in historical detail is impossible. Nevertheless, traces of sexuality—representations, repressions, and codifications, but not experiences[2]—are present in the archive. As the chapters in this volume—and the work of the rest of the history of sexuality—show, sex can be found in all sorts of places. These writings are a testament to Michel Foucault's observation that discourses around sexuality proliferated in the very century that was supposed to be so anxious about repressing sex.[3]

As the rhetoric of the nineteenth century is so focused on regulation, it is perhaps best to start with mention of the two main sources of such control: law and medicine. The burgeoning interest among historians in nineteenth-century sexuality allowed for the sexual exploitation of various records, including court reports, other judicial statements, and newspaper articles reporting crime. Through these documents we can uncover the details of sordid sex scandals or the facts of homosexual affairs or the specificities of unfortunate individuals who were sexually abused. The regulation of sexuality through the prohibition of sexual knowledge and contraception also provides us with a sense of the ways in which the state struggled to maintain control over aspects of sexuality.[4] Many of these details are to be found in legal documents and in the reporting of sex scandals in newspapers (which of course give a whole range of opinions and ideologies regarding the subject of sexuality). New resources, such as the Old Bailey Online, further provide historians with an amazing source of charges tried in the central criminal courts in London, with a large proportion of sex-related crimes recorded.[5] There is much scope for more research into legal sources, especially where a longitudinal study would be more easily achieved by tracing the analysis of a concept through the legal system.

Also prominent in their use by historians have been medical discourses, as sexuality is a significant constituent of medical history. Medicine often has addressed aspects of sexuality, from the control of venereal disease, with its descriptions of prostitution and syphilis, to the pathologization of pleasure in psychiatry, which produced so many of the sexual categories that are with us today in the *Diagnostic and Statistical Manual of Mental Disorders*. Forensic medicine has described the corporeal ramifications of sex, and there are detailed discussions on the detection of rape and the signs to be found on a sodomized anus.[6] Furthermore, writings about contraception, on the radical fringes of nineteenth-century medicine, supply us with details of how the Victorians thought of conception, as well as providing political and ideological arguments about the control of intimacy.[7] In all these sources, it is possible to access ideas about what people did for sex. The historian must be careful, however, to avoid treating this material at face value. It is not possible to read a sexual case history as a pure or realistic representation of sex that was actually experienced. Medical sources were and are still written—in the main—for other doctors, and case histories are selected because they exhibit some special point.[8] Nevertheless, these medical sources allow us to see the limits of the nineteenth-century conceptions of sex.

Allied to these medical discourses were other forms of advice literature, such as the billowing industry in the control of spermatorrhea, the incessant leaking of seminal fluids as a result of unbridled masturbation.[9] Such advice literature, and associated tracts about the cultivation of muscular Christianity and other species of masculinity, portrays sexuality through its control.[10] A similar point can be found in the literature about neurasthenia.[11] In such discourses we perceive the construction of the body in relation to sexuality as well as gender roles. Many historians of sexuality have thus exploited these texts in order to describe sexual anxieties in the period, especially in their wider ramifications in culture.

Cultural historians have not only raided such official sources from sites of power like the law and medicine. They have also done much to trace ideas

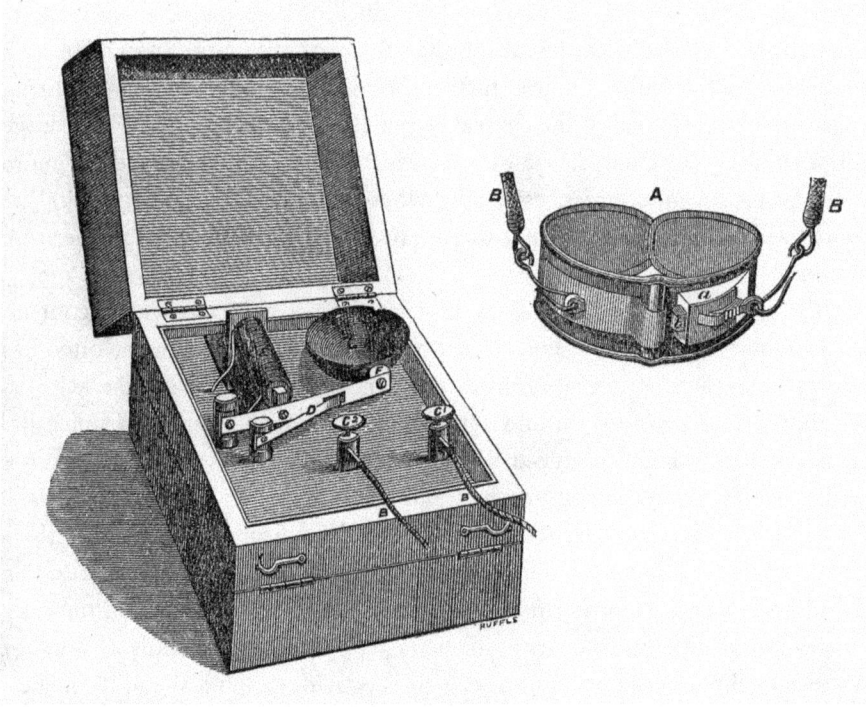

FIGURE 1.1: The electric alarm for the treatment of masturbation, nineteenth century. In John Laws Milton, *On the Pathology and Treatment of Spermatorrhoea* (London: Henry Renshaw, 1887), 132. Wellcome Library, London.

about sexuality in literatures of all varieties, from the novels of Charles Dickens to Walter's pornographic texts, and from Algernon Swinburne's poetry to that of Coventry Patmore. Examining the constructions of sexuality in this literary source material is key to situating sexuality in culture. These new cultural histories carefully deconstruct representations and codifications of sexuality in extremely nuanced ways, often reading between the lines for the tensions fueled by erotic desires, but unable to be engaged with in writings that were not to be proscribed. Using literature as source material, scholars historically reconstruct texts to place sexuality in context. Of course, arguments can be presented that suggest that a tendency to slip easily between genres, or to fail to adequately take into account social and political contexts, mars some of these texts. The point nevertheless remains that literary sources are a viable and important place to examine sexual ideologies and representations.

The analysis of erotic imagery is another facet of cultural history that has significantly shaped the variety of sources the historian may draw upon. Lynda

FIGURE 1.2: A Sicilian boy posing naked by a door-
way, holding a sprig of leaves, Taormina, Sicily.
Wilhelm von Gloeden, Taomina, August 1, 1900.
Wellcome Library, London.

Nead's discussion of Victorian representations of the prostitute serves as a
good example of this use of visual sources.[12] Other studies, including the Tate
Britain catalog of the *Exposed: The Victorian Nude* show from 2001, explore
the way in which representations of the naked body had to skirt around issues
of sexual propriety at a time of increasing censorship. Reliance on classical
art forms gave some credence to what were in many cases representations of
highly sexualized bodies.[13]

This brief discussion of sources hopes to illustrate the ingenuity that historians of sexuality of the nineteenth century have had to employ to locate the
materials with which they work. Sexuality, it appears, was everywhere over
the course of the century, permeating all manner of documentary sources, leaking out of discreet categories into the general populace. Given the huge scope
for sources in which sexuality can be uncovered, depending on the mind and
method of the historian, it is worthwhile to trace the major developments in this

field, as such a task also serves to illustrate the breadth of Victorian sexual issues that are further explored in this book.

VICTORIAN SEXUAL HISTORIOGRAPHIES

Early Writings

The history of sexuality did not spring from Clio's forehead, ready made for post–sexual revolution acolytes to enjoy. Before twentieth-century historians of sexuality began their investigations, nineteenth-century men were already pursuing this. It was a common belief shared by late-nineteenth-century European medical writers obsessed with notions of national and cultural degeneration that ancient Rome collapsed because of sexual immorality, and while indulging in titillating descriptions of ancient sexual habits, they warned contemporary society about the danger of sexual indulgence.[14] Quite often anecdotal histories, their investigations of changing attitudes toward sexual customs indicated a certain degree of cultural relativism in dealing with sexuality. In 1883, the literary critic John Addington Symonds published privately *A Problem in Greek Ethics*, in which he invited medical and legal experts to look at ancient Greek culture as an example of a great and highly developed civilization that not only tolerated same-sex passions but held the spiritual value of such passions in high regard and used them for the benefit of society.[15] In 1891 Symonds again published privately *A Problem in Modern Ethics Being an Inquiry into the Phenomenon of Sexual Inversion*, in which he contrasted contemporary society with ancient Greek and Roman cultures (Symonds was notoriously pro-Greek and anti-Roman in his tastes and values, preferring Plato's noble philosophical homoeroticism to the unbridled lust of the Roman bathhouse). In this work he argued that Christian nations, in separating themselves from ancient paganism, introduced a new sexual morality with regard to homosexual passions, enforcing legal prohibitions.[16] In 1885, the ethnologist Richard Francis Burton, famous, among other things, for having translated *The Arabian Nights* into English, addressed the issue of "pederasty." As part of his ten-volume translation, he included a "Terminal Essay" addressing a number of interpretative questions, which included the famous section devoted to pederasty.[17] This essay represented one of the earliest modern efforts to collect and inform readers about both cross-cultural and historical knowledge of homosexual passions, including lesbian love.[18] Other ethnographic works, such as American ethnologist H. H. Bancroft's five-volume study of the *Native Races of the Pacific States* (1874) and German Hermann Ploss's *Das Weib* (1885) and the London School of Economics–based Finn Edvard Westermarck's *History of Human Marriage* (1891, reworked substantially in 1901), also utilized the history of sexual customs in order to relativize contemporary understandings of sexuality. The same uses of history are often found in sexological writings of the period. The well-known sexological work *Sexual Inversion*, co-written by the psychologist of sex Havelock Ellis and Symonds, contained an introduction with a historical overview of how homosexual practices had been interpreted in different ways in various cultures.[19] Similar nineteenth-century investigations into sexual "problems" such as prostitution (starting with Alexandre Jean Baptiste Parent-Duchâtelet's study *La prostitution dans la ville de Paris*, 1836) situated their work historically. Other sexologists, such as Berlin dermatologist Iwan Bloch, offered much more expansive analyses of historical material, also adopting a relativistic stance.[20]

FIGURE 1.3: Prostitution: Dicterion Grec. In Pierre Dufour, *Histoire de la prostitution chez tous les peuples du monde: Depuis l'antiquité la plus reculée jusqu'à nos jours,* vol. 1 (Brussels: Librarie Encylopedique de Perichon, 1851), opposite 134. Wellcome Library, London.

These essays into historicizing and relativizing sexuality were all important forebears of the works of Steven Marcus (*The Other Victorians*, 1966), Alex Comfort (*The Anxiety Makers*, 1967), and Robert Pearsall (*The Worm in the Bud*, 1969), and other texts that, riding the waves of the sexual revolution, sought to show that received sexual ideologies about the nineteenth century were problematic.[21] Similar works, such as Paul Robinson's investigation into the history of sexual knowledge (*The Modernization of Sex*, 1976), also began to open up paths for the history of sexuality, albeit by ahistorically criticizing psychiatrists (or, in the case of Ellis, praising him ahistorically). Such paths were much expanded when Michel Foucault developed the lectures he had been giving at the Collège de France into the first volume of his *History of Sexuality* (1976).[22] Understanding the modern cultural history of sexuality requires attention to Foucault's work.

Foucault and His Interlocutors

The study of cultural attitudes to sexual customs throughout history is not a twentieth-century novelty, nor can it been thought of as Michel Foucault's creation; nevertheless, any investigation of nineteenth-century sexuality leads to his *The Will to Knowledge* (*La volonté de savoir*, 1976), introduced by a chapter entitled "We 'Other Victorians.'" Here Foucault undermines the widely held belief in Victorian repressiveness by showing that in the nineteenth century there was a proliferation in discourses concerning sex. At the same time, he argues that sexuality as we think of it today (as an integral part of the way we define ourselves) is an invention of the late-eighteenth century and nineteenth century. This is because sexuality, according to Foucault, is a result of distinct techniques for extracting confession. Through confessional practices the Roman Catholic Church instigated detailed self-examination, questioned desires, and produced rules for interpreting and classifying what was unveiled. Thus, Foucault saw the historical roots of the phenomenon of "institutional incitement to speak about sex" in religious confessions.[23]

Foucault devoted a considerable part of *The Will of Knowledge* to arguing that, as a result of the declining authority of the church in modern culture, the influence of scientific knowledge increased throughout the nineteenth century.[24] *Scientia sexualis* focused on the so-called sexual pathologies, and sexologists increasingly subscribed to the view that, in many cases, irregular sexual activities (non-uxorious, non-monogamous, non-procreative, etc.) were not immoral choices or sins but symptoms of innate characteristics.[25] According to Foucault, at the transition between the eighteenth and nineteenth centuries, sexual activity ceased being a matter of acts (sanctioned or sinful), and through the emerging field of sexology, sexuality became a key way of categorizing individuals.[26] Sexologists crystallized principal perversions into distinct types, each with its own unique symptomatology and psychology. This did not disclose the hidden truths about sex but rather produced sexuality as a new category of knowledge, a historically specific field.[27]

Opening areas of inquiries that historians are still exploring today, Foucault charted the way in which complex discourses about sexuality operated throughout the nineteenth century: the "hysterisation of women's bodies," the "pedagogisation of children's sex," the "socialisation of procreative behaviour," and the "psychiatrisation of perverse pleasure."[28] First, while women were ideally seen as devoted mothers who cared for the home and offspring, deviations from this image were increasingly portrayed in the form of nervous women whose sexually saturated bodies required medical treatments (everything from clitoridectomies and the use of mechanical vibrators to more benign tonic treatments for nervousness).[29] Second, children's bodies were placed under surveillance to avoid masturbation (and such practices were institutionalized in schools and in the middle-class home), with various nasty cures available for the boy who could not control himself (e.g., electric alarms placed around the penis that went off when he became erect in his sleep, implements with sharp edges placed around the penis, cauterization of the urethra with caustic substances). Third, reproduction was increasingly linked to discourses of moral responsibility while, at the same time, the economic considerations of Thomas Malthus were taken seriously. Fourth, "normal" manifestations of the sexual instinct were separated from the "pathological," and the latter became the objects of various attempts at medicalization. The hysterical woman, the masturbating child, the Malthusian couple, and the perverse adult epitomize the way in which discourses about sexuality have constructed Western bodies.[30]

The extent of Foucault's impact on the history of sexuality is incalculable. Even now—more than thirty years after the first publication of Foucault's work, and twenty-five years after his death from AIDS, there is scarcely a publication in this field that does not cite his work, either to laud it, to criticize it, or to make some kind of historical genuflection in its introduction. Only perhaps Freud's work has a similar place in its specific field. Foucault's interlocutors have nevertheless extended his analyses in significant ways, both within and outside the history of sexuality. Two stars in this crowded constellation include Ian Hacking, who now occupies the position Foucault held at the Collège de France, and Arnold Davidson of the University of Chicago. Both scholars have picked up on the strand of Foucault's work called historical epistemology,

FIGURE 1.4: Demonstration using the vibrator, 1891. In C. H. Liedbeck, *A Description of the Vibrator (Engl. Pat. 1890. No. 4390) and Directions for Use* (Stockholm: P. A. Norstedt & Söner, 1891), fig. 35. Wellcome Library, London.

and both have shown the fruitfulness that such detailed analyses of concepts provide in their specific historical context.[31] The insights of Hacking, Davidson, and the countless historians who have followed Foucault, not always slavishly, have shown in incredible detail the extent to which sexual practices, ideologies, cultures, and identities can be historicized. Statements about the truth of sex are inherently problematic in this field, even if the details of Foucault's historical investigations have been nuanced, challenged, or reified by two generations of historians.[32] But this is of course not to say that we cannot proceed in the historiography of this subject. Rather, we can examine ways in which sexuality can be historicized, in full cognizance that we are "other Foucauldians."

SEXUAL PROBLEMS OF THE NINETEENTH CENTURY

Sexual Respectability

The Western world of the nineteenth century was characterized by, among other things, intensified urbanization, a solidification of class and gender structures, the growth of a consumer culture, an increased interest in the health and well-being of populations shown by both the governing elites and the general populace, expanding colonialism, and the mounting cultural influence of the town-dwelling middle classes through institutions (schools, hospitals, prisons, etc.) that had become central to the modern nation-state. As the middle classes extended their cultural authority, their sexuality became an object of extensive historical analysis. There is a general agreement among historians that despite differences among countries and among the middle classes themselves, nineteenth-century bourgeoisie promoted a morality based on sexual respectability.[33] According to the historian George Mosse, the European middle classes felt the need to tame a society that seemed to be on the brink of chaos. They perceived the cities as seething cauldrons of crime, anxiety, and wild sexual passion. Sexual vices were thought to lead to illness, and some conditions, especially alcoholism and venereal diseases, were a source of shame because of their roots in an immoral life.[34] In order to contrast contemporary unruliness, the bourgeoisie promoted a lifestyle based on frugality, devotion to duty, and the restraint of passions—in opposition to the assumed feckless values of the lower classes and the purportedly dissolute values of the aristocracy. There was a general consensus among the professional classes that decorum ought to be protected.[35] Morality had to be guarded through the promotion of a sexual specific morality, by approval of laws to regulate sexual conduct, and by censorship of images and publications. By way of example, in 1857 the French writers Gustave Flaubert and Charles Baudelaire were put on trial for their work, which had supposedly outraged morality and religion. Flaubert was acquitted, Baudelaire condemned.[36] Starting the same year in England, a series of obscenity laws, the Obscene Publications Acts, established what tended to "deprave and corrupt" and therefore governed what could be published in England and Wales. In 1888, Emile Zola's publisher, Henry Vizetelly, was sentenced under the act to three months in jail for selling an expurgated translation of *La terre*.[37] In 1873, the American Comstock Law forbade the mailing of obscene art and literature and all material about controlling sexual reproduction.[38] Given the heavy-handed efforts at repression, it is little wonder that the nineteenth century earned a reputation for sexlessness.

The family, as the symbol of order and stability, became the foundation of the social order and of the state; its role in social control was crucial. Fathers had to be able to provide for their families. The accepted role of middle-class women (and those harboring such bourgeois aspirations) was that of passionless good mothers and wives. Celibacy dovetailed with family status. Officially, sex was confined to marriage, but men were justified if they did transgress

A NIGHT HOUSE.—KATE HAMILTON'S.

FIGURE 1.5: A night house—Kate Hamilton's. In Henry Mayhew, *London Labour and the London Poor* (London: Griffin, Bohn, 1862), opposite 217. Wellcome Library, London.

because 'natural' sexual needs drove them to look for sexual intercourse outside marriage, typically by making clandestine excursions into the urban demimonde. Although the Victorians were promoting an ideology of sexual respectability, what they were really doing in bed was another issue.[39] While women faced social reprobation if they indulged in sexual intercourse outside marriage, men consorting with prostitutes and mistresses were silently accepted by what has come to be called the double standard.[40] Since Steven Marcus's *The Other Victorians*, historians of sexuality have shown that in the nineteenth century, bourgeois sexual morality and respectability were the thin covering of an underworld of ebullient eroticism. Pornography, prostitution, degeneration, and sex crimes were the unsettling reverse images of nineteenth-century public culture.[41]

Feminism

The bourgeois ideology of sexual respectability reinforced the separation between the male and female spheres. This separation was also formulated in terms of biological difference. While the Enlightenment had promoted ideas of equal rights between human beings, nineteenth-century scientific theories underpinned the elaboration of differences between the sexes, which in turn justified the continuing inequality of rights between men and women. Biological "facts" were used to demonstrate the intellectual inferiority of women: in anthropology this gave rise to the idea that the smaller size of the female signified lesser intellectual ability.[42] Different evolutionary theories inferred explicitly or implicitly that women had reached a lower rung of the evolutionary ladder than men.[43] Scientists agreed that maternity was the biological lot of women, who, it was argued, found their fullest expression in the family. Medical and biological writers fostered ideas that women were sexually passive and naturally submissive, while men were active and naturally aggressive.[44] Women's subordination to men was reinforced by law. During the nineteenth century different legislation in Europe and Britain dealt with sexual conduct. By way of example, both the Napoleonic Code and English common law reinforced a double standard within marriage: in the Napoleonic Code a man's adultery was not considered enough to grant a divorce unless he brought his mistress home; however, a woman's adultery could land her in jail for up to three months and was certainly grounds for divorce.[45] In England, the 1857 Matrimonial Causes Act made divorce more widely accessible, but while any husband could divorce his wife for adultery, a woman had to prove not only the adultery of her husband but an additional "matrimonial offence" such as cruelty, desertion, bigamy, or incest.[46] Sex within marriage, as the radical doctor George Drysdale made clear in his anonymous *Elements of Social Science* (1854), was all about property rights.[47]

While the nineteenth century was marked by increasingly active women's rights movements that campaigned to change unequal laws, to obtain political rights, and to improve educational opportunities, women and radical groups increasingly contested the accepted male sexual morals. In England in the 1870s, social purity feminists began contesting the sexual double standard, pornography, and the Contagious Disease Acts of 1864, 1867, and 1869. These acts allowed the compulsory examination of women suspected of working as prostitutes in garrison towns and ports, while not only tolerating male clients but leaving them free to spread venereal contagions. The campaign for the repeal of the Contagious Disease Acts exposed women to public discussion of sexual matters. Feminists, who fought the assumption that prostitution was necessary because of the particular nature of male sexuality, believed that the male sexual urge was a social, not a biological, phenomenon. Led by the charismatic Josephine Butler, women attacked the acts while claiming the right to promote wider moral reforms within society and arguing for a single, rather than a double, moral standard.[48] Butler's campaign was based on a manipulation of Victorian ideals of femininity. Taking up the model of the American temperance movement, with its vigils, during which genteel women clad in white would stand outside brothels and make clear the private damage wrought by public vice, Butler also engaged in the symbolic use of feminine purity.[49] While the campaign challenged male privilege, it promoted an idea of femininity as pure, thus echoing the medical ideal of female sexuality.

While most Victorian and Edwardian feminists sought to protect women from sex, a second generation of feminists and other radical campaigners advocated women's right to sexual pleasure and to sexual freedom. The socialist writer Edward Carpenter saw sex as a vital force that would created a healthier and more equal new bond between men and women. Havelock Ellis sought to address this problem in his wartime pamphlet *The Erotic Rights of Women* (1918), as well as in his many comments on the subject in his sexological writings. Such had been a central aim of the Fellowship of the New Life (founded 1883), which included in its membership advocates of sexual expression such as Olive Schreiner, as well as Ellis and Carpenter. Later, feminists such as Stella Browne sought to liberate women from Victorian prudery, campaigned for birth control, and defended abortion,[50] while Mary Stopes began writing sex advice books and promoting birth control. Her *Married Love: A New Contribution to the Solution of Sex Difficulties* (1918) went through numerous editions over the next forty years. Stopes included explicit advice about sexual acts, such as the need for a husband to arouse his wife and the need for a woman to achieve sexual orgasm.[51]

Pioneering historical analysis of the complex relations between nineteenth-century sexual morality and women appeared in the 1970s.[52] Since the 1980s, historians have paid extensive attention to how Victorian social purity movements related to the legal and medical regulation of sexuality.[53] Since then, self-proclaimed feminist scholars have sometimes portrayed Victorian women as docile creatures subjected to an apparently transhistorical male dominance.[54] In the 1990s, feminist historians such as Susan Kingsley Kent and Lucy Bland documented the extent to which nineteenth-century women actively participated in public debates about sexual matters and the extent to which they criticized the sexual double standard and male sexuality, which they represented—picking up on Victorian ideologies—as an uncontrolled and brutal force.[55] More recently, historians such as Lesley Hall have provided nuanced accounts of the complex interaction between nineteenth-century feminists and male discourses about sex.[56]

Lesbianism

In the main, three types of love relationships between women in the nineteenth century have been explored: so-called romantic friendships, the relationships of cross-dressing women who passed for men, and relationships within female communities. Within the ideology of sexual respectability, which assigned women to the domestic sphere and fostered the idea that respectable middle-class women were without sexual passion, romantic friendships between women were largely acceptable. While many female romantic friendships were asexual, historians have documented the complex ways in which such relationships could involve various degrees of sexual activity. By way of example, Anne Lister (1791–1840), a Yorkshire gentlewoman who was very conscious of her homoerotic desires, recorded her passions and sexual activities with other women in her coded diaries.[57] In the last decades of the nineteenth century, women's romantic relationships increasingly became associated with feminism. Some middle-class women, especially students, teachers, and office workers, began to gain more economic independence by accessing higher education and

FIGURE 1.6: Sarah Ponsonby (left) and Lady Eleanor Butler, known as the Ladies of Llangollen, outside with a dog. Lithograph by J. H. Lynch, 1830s, after Mary Parker (later Lady Leighton), 1828. Wellcome Library, London.

entering professions. Some of these women adopted a more masculine lifestyle, from their dress to their pastimes. Educated, independent, unmarried, and feminist, the so-called New Women became associated, quite often negatively, with female homosexuality. Novelists, sexologists, and even radical campaigners wrote about this association. In 1886, the Anglo-American writer Henry James published *The Bostonians*, in which he described a marriage-like relationship between two New Women. Havelock Ellis associated female homosexuality with the growing independence of women and feminism,[58] as did his friend Edward Carpenter in his work on the "intermediate sex," in which he dealt extensively with same-sex love.[59]

Women who were adopting male dress or who were successfully passing as men in their everyday lives were also associated with female homosexuality. In a society where women did not have many opportunities outside family and marriage, passing as men enabled them to escape from social expectations and to take up job opportunities usually reserved for men. While not all cross-dressing women had sexual relationships with other women, some of them did, and in rare cases women even managed to marry other women.[60]

Finally, in the nineteenth century, small lesbian subcultures appeared. In the middle of the century, the well-known American actress Charlotte Cushman (1816–1876) traveled to Rome with her partner, Matilda Hays, and some friends. In Rome, Cushman created a woman-centered community stressing unity with other women and emancipation from men. From 1852 to 1868, her salon for her friends and lovers became a magnet for unconventional American and English women.[61] However, at the end of the nineteenth century, no other city was as famous for its lesbian subculture as Paris. The salon of the rich American heiress Natalie Clifford Barney was at the heart of a lesbian community from the 1890s to the 1930s.[62] Settled permanently in Paris in 1900, Barney published love poems to women, promoted women's writing, and caused scandals because of her visible relationships with women, among whom were the poet Renée Vivien and the painter Romaine Brooks. She opposed monogamy, had various overlapping relationships, and rejected traditional nineteenth-century sexual conventions.[63]

In the mid-1970s, lesbian-feminist historical scholarship began to pay attention to love between women in the nineteenth century. Much of the historiographical debate has focused on the nature of female romantic friendships and their pathologization by late-nineteenth-century sexologists. In 1975, Carroll Smith-Rosenberg wrote an influential essay, "The Female World of Love and Ritual," in which she contended that before the "invention" of homosexuality as a pathology in the late-nineteenth century, emotional and erotic intimacy between women were accepted as part of normal female domestic life. Following Smith-Rosenberg, other historians such as Lillian Faderman have suggested that before sexology emerged, both men and women were allowed a broad range of physical and emotional relationships with members of their own sex. From the late-nineteenth century on, however, medical authorities started to stigmatize such relationships,[64] and medical interest in female homosexuality has been interpreted as a reaction to the fear of the rise of women's education and the feminist New Woman.[65] The historian Martha Vicinus has called for a reorientation in the study of the relationship between sexology and female homosexuality. She has recommended that rather than labeling sexological descriptions misogynistic, historians might learn more from them about both contemporary lesbian mores and women's attitudes.[66] More recently, Vicinus has also shown that many of the relationships that Faderman had previously identified as platonic and "innocent" were actually imbued with sexual activities.[67] Finally, other historians such as Laura Doan have suggested that for lesbians the greater dissemination of sexual knowledge made possible new paradigms for self-understanding, paving the way for subculture formation.[68]

Homosexuality

Alongside the emergence of a male homosexual subculture in urban spaces, male homosexuality became the object of legal reform, moral control, and sensational reporting in newspapers. It was also an emerging medical topic. In their analysis of sodomy, the French physician Claude François Michéa (1849) and the German forensic doctor Johann Ludwig Casper (1852) noticed that the preference for members of the same sex was often innate and involved femininity in men.[69] A more comprehensive formulation of such a development occurred almost twenty years after these first insights, in 1868, when Wilhelm Griesinger, a leading German psychiatrist, associated sexual desire for one's own sex with congenital "neuropathic" conditions. Griesinger underlined that often such diseased states expressed themselves only in the psychological realm.[70] In the following year Griesinger's student Carl Westphal published the first psychiatric article on what he called *conträre Sexualempfindung* (contrary sexual feeling). Westphal's article dealt with two case studies, one of which, the longest, was of a woman who, from an early age, had desired other women, shown an aversion to men, and felt that she had a man's nature. According to Westphal, this case revealed a psychopathic condition.[71]

Similar ideas about the inborn nature of same-sex desires were put forward by non-medical writers such as Karl Heinrich Ulrichs, a Hanoverian lawyer who published a series of books between 1864 and 1879 that aimed to change the legislation that punished male same-sex sexual acts. Ulrichs argued that same-sex passions, which he called "uranian" love, were natural and innate, and he believed that "Urnings" were born with a female sexual drive in a male body and constituted a "third sex."[72] While these ideas were not restricted to medical writers, *conträre Sexualempfindung*, or "sexual inversion," became a fashionable medical subject in the last two decades of the nineteenth century. After Westphal, the study of sexual inversion was addressed by the Austrian psychiatrist Richard von Krafft-Ebing in 1877,[73] by the Italian forensic doctor Arrigo Tamassia in 1878, and finally by the French neurologist Jean-Martin Charcot and the French psychologist Valentin Magnan in 1882.[74] Following Wesphal's text, Continental doctors began collecting case studies of sexual inverts whose main psychological characteristic was gender-inverted behavior. By the 1890s, "sexual inversion" entered the psychiatric nosologies of the major German, French, and Italian treatises. In turn, such terminology and the concept that same-sex desires were innate were taken up by self-identified homosexuals, quite often in an attempt to argue that same-sex sexual acts must not be punished by law, as it was a natural phenomenon, not the result of vice or immoral choices.[75]

Homosexuality became a topic in newspapers through sexual scandals. In Britain, one of the most famous homosexual panics in mid-Victorian times was that of Fanny and Stella (aka Ernest Boulton and Frederick Park), who were arrested on a charge of "public indecency," then of buggery, for being dressed in female clothes outside the Strand Theatre in 1870.[76] However, it was impossible to prove that they were doing anything more than masquerading. The trial, with its details of shared beds and ladies' silk panties and the most exposed medical examination of the defendants' anatomy, has been relied upon by a number of historians to reconstruct gay lives and attitudes toward them in Victorian London.[77] The so-called Cleveland Street Scandal of 1889, involving a male brothel in London that was reported to support the vices of a number of members of the British aristocracy, is another example of sexual scandal that has allowed historians to uncover homosexual subcultures.[78] The prosecution of Oscar Wilde is doubtlessly better known. In 1895, the Wilde trials became critical in creating a public image of and for the homosexual as decadent, effeminate, artistic, and upper class and caused public attitudes toward homosexuality to become harsher and less tolerant. According to some historians, before the trials there was a certain pity for those who engaged in same-sex passion, whereas after the trials, homosexuals were seen more as a threat.[79] People with close same-sex relationships grew anxious about doing anything that might suggest impropriety. Mercilessly punished under English law in 1895, Wilde is commonly held to be the iconic victim of Victorian puritanism.[80] Continental Europe was also shocked by homosexual scandals. In 1902, the German Friedrich Alfred Krupp, probably the wealthiest armaments manufacturer and trader of that time, was accused by German newspapers of having engaged in orgies with young men on the island of Capri in Italy. The resulting international humiliation eventually led to his suicide. A few year later, between 1907 and 1909, a series of scandals involved Kaiser Wilhelm II's entourage, which was accused of homosexuality. Phillip (prince of Eulenburg-Hertefeld) and General Kuno Graf von Moltke were accused of same-sex sexual acts, along with other close friends of the kaiser. These accusations by the journalist Maximilian Harden resulted in a series of courts-martial and five regular trials, and the obvious international scandal.[81]

MR. OSCAR WILDE.

FIGURE 1.7: Portrait of Oscar Wilde. In *Illustrated London News*, 1892. Wellcome Library, London.

Historiographical debate about nineteenth-century male homosexuality has been particularly vigorous since the late 1960s. In 1968, the sociologist Mary McIntosh suggested that homosexuality was primarily a social category rather than a medical condition.[82] McIntosh's work paved the way for thinking of homosexuality (and sexuality) as a social construction, as Jeffrey Weeks does in *Coming Out* (1977). In this work, Weeks paid attention to the changing ways in which society named homosexuality and the way homosexuals had seen themselves since the nineteenth century.[83] At the same time Foucault, in his *The Will to Knowledge*, identified nineteenth-century sexological works on sexual inversion as pivotal in the emergence of the modern way of thinking of homosexuality. Copious scholarship has since been dedicated to refining Foucault's analysis and to examining the details of the appearance of homosexuality as a sexual medical category and a modern sexual category.[84] Since the 1980s, historical accounts of nineteenth-century male homosexuality have been dominated by a social constructionist approach. In these studies some historians have moved to focus on how a male homosexual identity developed independently from medical accounts of sexual inversion, as in the case of George Chauncey's work on American gay culture.[85] More recently, some British historians have revised gay history and criticized Foucauldian literature on nineteenth-century homosexuality that focuses on the influence of medico-legal arguments in the formation of homosexual identity. Historians such as Matt Cook, Harry Cocks, and Sean Brady have shifted their attention to how homosexual identity was shaped by a variety of cultural pressures, including religion, spirituality, social status, and class. Moreover, according to Sean Brady, British society in the nineteenth century displayed a marked reluctance either to clarify or to control sexuality between men in any explicit sense, and in particular, he shows how British culture, including medical writers, was characterized by a resistance to Continental sexological ideas.[86]

Sexual Crime

As is evident from issues already raised in this introduction, regulation of sexuality remains an immense undercurrent of the nineteenth century, a fact that is nowhere better illustrated than in the laws of the period, and in the varieties of prosecution that historians have examined in order to reconstruct sexual cultures. Legal provisions for the control of sexuality in the nineteenth century included the various rape and sodomy acts. Along with these laws came forensic medical discussions of such crimes and their detection, eventually leading the way toward the psychological construction of sexual types who were involved in such crimes (the homosexual, the sadist, the kleptomaniac, etc.). The construction of the rape victim in these legal and medical sources is particularly of interest, as she is seen to be the innocent victim of crime. Signs of struggles, bruises and scratches and other lacerations on and around the genitalia, and in the case of young (unmarried) women and girls evidence of an obliterated hymen became the features sought under forensic examination in order to sustain the innocence of the victim as much as to prove the guilt of the accused assailant. The absence of such features cast some shadow over the integrity of the victim.[87] These attitudes were embodied in the legal definitions of crimes such as rape, where the idea of the struggle (except in cases of drugging or coercion through other threats) was codified.[88] Such ideologies about women being attacked by strangers

Le vieux Séducteur.

FIGURE 1.8: A corrupt old man tries to seduce a woman by urging her to take a hypnotic draught in her drink. Color Lithograph 1820s Charles Etienne Pierre Motte, Paris: Chez Martinet R. des marais. Wellcome Library, London.

of course carry the most famous of nineteenth-century narratives of sexual crime—the case of Jack the Ripper.

Regulation of sexual crimes, though, is in some ways best considered through the various methods for controlling prostitution, or at least for keeping it under strict surveillance. The English Contagious Diseases Acts, which controlled women suspected of soliciting in eleven barrack towns, are a prime example of this tendency,[89] although of course most European countries had some significant form of regulation of prostitution.[90] Under these laws and other forms of regulation, women who sold sex were specifically targeted, while their customers were generally ignored.

Related to the regulation of prostitution was that of sodomy. Although countries that had adopted the Napoleonic Code did not criminalize sodomy in private, other countries, such as Britain, did. The 1885 Law Amendment Act raised the age of consent for girls from twelve to sixteen and strengthened the legal prohibition of sodomy and bestiality to designate acts such as two men masturbating together in private as an "indecent act" carrying the penalty of two years' penal servitude with hard labor.[91] Oscar Wilde was the most prominent victim of this legislation. The 1885 act also prompted the collaboration between Havelock Ellis and John Addington Symonds, whose *Sexual Inversion* can be seen as a direct response to this law.[92] Likewise, the unification of Germany in 1871 prompted the criminalization of same-sex sexual behavior under the adopted Prussian legal code (para. 175), which outlawed homosexuality.[93] In France, a negotiation of homosexuality in relation to the law is also evident.[94] It is impossible to think about homosexuality before the sexual revolution of the 1960s outside these legal strictures. The very legal constraint of homosexuality did, however, create space for various sexual scandals, often involving blackmail or libel.

As mentioned, the other notorious sexual crime of the Victorian period is the unsolved murders of five East End prostitutes in the late 1880s. Jack the Ripper in many ways embodies the fears surrounding urban life that characterized the nineteenth century. The extent to which such pervasive anxiety about the dangers of the city crossed different strata of society is displayed by the wide range of writings addressing this issue. Violent sexual assaults attracted the popular imagination not only through newspaper accounts but also through early psychological writings about *Lustmord*, algophilia, and other constructions of sadism that rely upon the details of sexual cruelty.[95] This coming together of violence, illegal sex, and murder, the sheer brutality of which was not only shocking but made public through depictions in the *Illustrated Police News* and involved a significant use of forensic photography of the mutilated prostitutes' bodies, has been too much for a number of amateur historians—self-styled "ripperologists" to whom the case of Jack the Ripper is the most significant of the nineteenth century. Of course, it isn't. Many other cases of sexual violence exist.[96] But the way that Jack the Ripper's case has become emblematic of the sexual underbelly of one of the major metropolises of the nineteenth century remains significant. This conflagration of crime and sexuality is just as fascinating now as it was in the period.

NEW CULTURAL HISTORIES OF SEXUALITY

The study of homosexuality—still a dominant aspect of the history of sexuality, along with feminist historiography—has changed somewhat since the formation of medical arguments about sexual psychopathologies, as they were then seen. Historians are increasingly asking questions about what "the people" actually did, and less about what doctors liked to tell their readers. Of course, much of this new writing still addresses medical case histories of sexual practices in the nineteenth century, but these sources are exploited precisely because they have the kinds of sexual details that are sought about erotic experiences.[97] Despite what some might consider the naive use of such medical sources, historians can profitably exploit such details in order to at least gain a sense of the sexual potential that existed. While there might not be the same kind of details about what happens in S&M clubs or autobiographical narratives about erotic piercings that a historian of the late-twentieth century could exploit from the vast array of blogs on such topics, these nineteenth-century texts certainly do provide a sense of the limits of sexual thought in the period. The extent of historical studies of sexuality—especially in the realm of other "perverted" sexual practices, such as non-heterosexual and homosexual practices, such as masochism, cross-dressing, necrophilia, bestiality, autosphyxiphilia[98]—has seen remarkable growth in these cultural historical studies, further emphasizing the usefulness of a huge variety of source material.

An especially fruitful source that historians have used is the plethora of erotic imagery and writing that exists. The Victorian pornography industry, which portrayed and described (and, one might hypothesize, encouraged) a variety of sexual acts, has long been noted for its novel use of new media. At the birth of photography, or mass-circulation printing, and even of film, devotees of pornography were there to exploit the potential of such new media. The result has been a series of studies of pornography that stretch at least as far back as Steven Marcus's groundbreaking study.[99] Pornographic sources are useful. They exhibit the forms of the erotic imagination in ways that would otherwise be difficult to access. Through such sources, we can learn a variety of facts, from what Victorian attitudes were toward pubic hair (they were for it)[100] to the exact mechanisms of restraint used in nineteenth-century bondage and spanking practices. Emphasizing the material in such ways is precisely the method used by cultural historians to reconstruct the past.

Another fertile area of research in the culture of sexuality in the Victorian period is the rise of urban history and historical geography in the historiography of sexuality. Taking from Foucault the idea that space both constrains and fuels possibility—and we take this to include the possibility of desire—urban histories of sex let us know where people were doing it, and how they met their partners.[101] Of particular note here is the work of Matt Houlbrook, whose research into the gay history of London allows us to appreciate the way that the city created a context in which people with shared desires could meet while managing to use the anonymity of the city to construct a private sense of self that was not compromised in many cases.[102] We also are privy to the spaces in which sex took place—from public toilets, theaters, and private clubs to Hyde Park. London, in many ways, made it possible for men to meet. Of course, research into the history of prostitution had already furnished us with many of these insights into urban history. Alain Corbin, Judith Walkowitz, and Frances Finnegan all alerted us to the ways in which the city is a space where sex can be bought and have described in detail the ways in which the portrayal of the prostitute as dangerous can be interpreted as the expression of anxieties about the city itself.[103] Other studies, such as the study of the Foundling Hospital in Coram Fields by Françoise Barret-Ducrocq, also allow us to reconstruct how the city made possible everyday sexual encounters without requiring participants to face legal penalty.[104] From the accounts of women who found themselves pregnant and had to abandon their children, we can reconstruct how and where such women were able to have sex. The city, once again, provided spaces for such encounters, thus blurring the once-hardened distinctions between public and private spaces that earlier historians used to argue formed the basis of gendered divisions in society. Private moments, it would seem, could take place in the back of a cab, or under a bridge, or in the darkness under the trees of public parks in urban centers. Sex is everywhere in urban culture; all one needs to do is look for it.

The history of sexuality, as it now stands, is a strong discipline with its own journal (and there are many others more than willing to publish in the area). It has produced hundreds of books, many of which have helped us appreciate the emergence of new ways of thinking about sexual practices, representations, and theories, and forms a substantial aspect of contemporary historiography involving some of the more interesting theoretical developments since the 1970s—from Foucault to queer theory. While there are still a number of sexual practices that deserve much fuller historical attention, the achievements of the field to date are very substantial. This introduction, which has only touched upon some aspects of this field, demonstrates that the field of the history of sexuality is growing from strength to strength—as the chapters in this collection demonstrate.

CHAPTER TWO

Heterosexuality: An Unfettered Capacity for Degeneracy

CHAD PARKHILL AND ELIZABETH STEPHENS

During the great nineteenth-century categorization of sexual types, practices, and subjectivities—undertaken within the context of sexological case studies, police photographic archives, and anthropometric medical records—the term "heterosexuality" and the identity of the "heterosexual" remained one of the least examined.[1] As historians of sexuality have subsequently recognized, the terms "heterosexuality" and "homosexuality" were coined at the same historical moment—by the Austro-Hungarian poet and translator Karl Maria Kertbeny in 1868.[2] Yet while the term "homosexuality" was quickly taken up and used within medical and psychiatric discourses, the term (and thus idea of) "heterosexuality" was subject to much less investigation. Such an oversight is consistent with the tendency Michel Foucault identifies in the first volume of *The History of Sexuality*, in which he argues that whereas those who are pathologized or marginalized by normative discourses about sexuality are forced to provide an account of themselves, and are seen to require diagnoses and treatment, those understood to be "normal" are accorded the privilege of silence and invisibility:

> The legitimate couple, with its regular sexuality, had a right to discretion. It tended to function as a norm, one that was stricter, perhaps, but quieter. On the other hand, what came under scrutiny was the sexuality of children, mad men and women, and criminals; the sensuality of those who did not like the opposite sex; reveries, obsessions, petty manias, or great transports of rage.[3]

It is a characteristic and privilege of norms to tend toward silence, as Foucault recognizes here. And it is precisely for this reason that, while those who would come to occupy the space of the sexual margins were increasingly eroticized, pathologized, or criminalized during the nineteenth century, heterosexual monogamy was able to maintain a modest and discretionary silence about itself. This chapter, then, seeks to do two things: first, to trace the emergence and significance of the term "heterosexuality," subjecting its circulation to the same attention long accorded that of "homosexuality," and, second, to consider the function of this normative idea of heterosexuality in structuring discourses of sexuality from the late-nineteenth century onward.

It is interesting and yet not surprising to note that the first published incidence of the term "heterosexuality," while understood to refer to "normal sexuality," focuses on its potential for excess and perversity:

> Both [heterosexual men and women] are driven by their nature to opposite-sex intercourse in so-called natural as well as unnatural coitus. They are also capable of actively or passively giving themselves over to same-sex excesses. Additionally, normally-sexed individuals are no less likely to engage in self-defilement if there is insufficient opportunity to satisfy one's sex drive. And they are equally likely to assault male but especially female minors who have not reached maturity; to indulge in incest; to engage in bestiality and the misuse of animals; and even behave depravedly with corpses if their moral self-control does not control their lust. And it is only amongst the normally-sexed that the special breed of so-called "bleeders" occurs, those who, thirsting for blood, can only satisfy their passion by wounding and torturing.[4]

Although Kertbeny focuses on heterosexuality's *potential* for perversity, the term "heterosexuality" does not name here a specific perversion. As this passage demonstrates, for Kertbeny heterosexuality is normal, although he clearly feels moral indignation at what some "normal" heterosexuals might be driven to in order to achieve sexual gratification. By comparison, for Kertbeny, homosexuality in men is at most morally neutral: in his classificatory scheme, the vast majority of homosexuals are "mutual" homosexuals who practice "manustupration," while the remainder are divided into active and passive "pygists," as well as "Platonists," who "do not touch each other's genitals, indeed sometimes even do not have an erection, keeping themselves far from frivolous and unchaste thoughts."[5] Of these subgroups of homosexual men, the only ones to attract moral censure are the "super-virile" active pygists, one of whom, Valerian Schober, Kertbeny describes as "a true monster."[6]

These moral considerations reflect the extent to which Kertbeny's own use of the terms "heterosexual" and "homosexual" varies from the way the terms would come to be used in the twentieth century. In Kertbeny's system, heterosexuality and homosexuality are not oppositional categories, but categories of persons organized on a hierarchy of sexual virility, which "increases from onanists to homosexualists to normally-sexed individuals respectively."[7] Thus Kertbeny could claim that certain historically infamous libertines such as Marshall de Retz and the Marquis de Sade, whose texts describe a range of sexual acts between men and who thus might appear themselves to be homosexuals, were in fact "normally-sexed":

> Were these men somehow homosexual, even though they had more than enough men, youths, and boys whom they misused horribly? No, they were firm, resolute and very potent normally-sexed individuals, for they went through hundreds and hundreds of young girls, women, and, yes, even old ladies.[8]

Any understanding of heterosexuality and homosexuality thus construed would soon collapse under the weight of its own internal contradictions. Indeed, Kertbeny's theory complicated his own avowed position as a "normally-sexed individual," which has led some historians, particularly Jean-Claude Féray and Manfred Herzer, to examine whether or not Kertbeny was a closeted "homosexualist."[9] Such considerations are immaterial to a genealogy of the terms "heterosexuality" and "homosexuality"—we need merely note that Kertbeny's own taxonomy of sexuality was riven through with contradiction. The promulgation of the term "heterosexuality" was therefore only successful insofar as the term's circulation loosened Kertbeny's own definitional grip on it.

The late-nineteenth century was a site of a great proliferation of (often-competing) sexual terminologies and taxonomic systems. Thus the fact that we now customarily divide the sexual world into the heterosexual and homosexual must be understood not merely as the result of the invention of new forms of categorization but also the triumph of those forms of categorization over other competing forms, such as the medico-juridical formulation "pederasty" (*Päderastie*) favored by the German forensic doctor Johann Ludwig Casper.[10] More specifically, the terms "heterosexuality" and "homosexuality" were created in direct response to the theory of "Urnings" and "Dionings" proposed by Karl Heinrich Ulrichs, a Hannoverian legal clerk who has posthumously been dubbed "the first theorist of homosexuality."[11] Ulrichs began his career as a theorist of sexuality during protracted legal debates surrounding the potential inclusion of section 143 of the Prussian penal code, which strictly forbade male-male anal sex in the unified German penal code (within which it eventually appeared with little modification as section 175).[12]

FIGURE 2.1: Karl Heinrich Ulrichs. In Hubert Kennedy, *Karl Heinrich Ulrichs: Pioneer of the Modern Gay Movement* (San Francisco: Peremptory, 2002).

At the same time, medical authorities such as the French physician Claude François Michéa and forensic expert Ambroise Tardieu began searching for the biological signs of pederasty, with Tardieu developing a theory that located these signs in the genitals: active sodomites, he claimed, had long, "thin penises shaped like [those of] dogs."[13] It was against this background of legal conflict and the anatomization of sodomy that Ulrichs developed his theory of the Urning.

In a series of twelve books he began to publish in 1863 under the pseudonym Numa Numantius, Ulrichs outlined his theory of *mannmännlich liebe*, or man-manly love. Ulrichs saw himself as a member of "the third sex," or, in his terminology, an Urning, which he defined as *anima muliebris virili corpore inclusa*—a female psyche in a male body.[14] This creature was defined specifically against the "Dioning," or "real man." Ulrichs posited the existence of embryonic germs or seeds (*Keime*) to explain the phenomenon of uranism: the human fetus contains both a mental germ and a physical germ that determined sex; in most cases, mental sex lines up with physical sex, but in the case of the Urning there is a mismatch.[15] Ulrichs thus cast same-sex attraction as a form of mental hermaphroditism, and so the signifiers of uranism would not be physical (like Tardieu's pointed penises and infundibuliform rectums) but behavioral, such as an interest in female pastimes, especially in childhood: "The Urning shows as a child a quite unmistakable partiality for girlish activities, for interaction with girls, for playing with girls' playthings, namely also with dolls," he wrote.[16] The Urning's future same-sex attraction was thus based on an explicit narrative of developmental psychology. We must note, however, that Ulrichs's concept of uranism was developed in, and informed by, the context of legal battles. At the time that Ulrichs began composing his books, he lived in Hanover, where consensual male-male sex acts were legal, if not socially acceptable. In 1866 Hanover was annexed by Prussia and so came under Prussian law. Ulrichs protested this turn of events and was imprisoned twice before being expelled from Hanover.[17] After this experience his chief aim became legal reform on the basis of his theory of psychic hermaphroditism, and it was in this capacity that he appeared before the Congress of German Jurists in Munich in 1867 to protest against section 143.[18]

It is against Ulrichs's theory of *anima muliebris virili corpore inclusa* that Kertbeny constructed his own theory of homo- and heterosexuality. The two terms first appear in a letter dated May 6, 1868, from Kertbeny to Ulrichs, alongside two other terms that did not survive past the nineteenth century, "monosexuality" and "heterogeneity," which refer to masturbation and bestiality, respectively.[19] Although Kertbeny and Ulrichs corresponded, there can be little doubt that their relationship was strained. Kertbeny, for his part, wrote in a confidential letter of 1869 that he believed the term "Urning" "was invented by one of the most unclear heads from their [i.e., the Urnings'] ranks."[20] Ulrichs claimed that he felt his ideas "from the outset attacked" by Kertbeny[21] and, possibly in response to Kertbeny's letter of 1868, wrote that "K's letter, which was supposed to bridge the gap between him and me, has (for the time being at least) entirely failed its purpose."[22] This animosity is reflected at the level of theorization. Whereas Ulrichs's theory of *anima muliebris virili corpore inclusa* is entirely consonant with later characterizations of the homosexual as "invert"—particularly Carl Westphal's later and more famous understanding of *conträre Sexualempfindung* (contrary sexual feeling) as "the feeling of being alienated from one's own sex in one's whole inner being"[23]—Kertbeny's own theory tellingly does not construe homosexual men as androgynous in either physique or mentality. Indeed, "Kertbeny's lists of famous homosexuals from history ... emerge as a means of showing that homosexualism is a matter of real and actual men who only in one respect, due to a 'riddle of nature,' are different than other men."[24] Kertbeny in effect took the mental-physical distinction that Ulrichs had made and specified it further: "homosexuality" in his work refers only to the choice of sexual object, not to the subject's own gender identity. Only later on in his chapter written for Gustav Jäger's 1880 book *Die Entdeckung der Seele* (*The Discovery of the Soul*) did Kertbeny posit

FIGURE 2.2: Karl Maria Kertbeny. In Hubert Kennedy, *Karl Heinrich Ulrichs: Pioneer of the Modern Gay Movement* (San Francisco: Peremptory, 2002).

some kind of connection between male homosexuality and effeminacy.[25] We may characterize the distinction between Kertbeny's and Ulrichs's theories of homosexuality by recourse to Eve Kosofsky Sedgwick's terminology: Ulrichs's theory is "gender transitive," "seeing same-sex object-choice … as a matter of liminality or transitivity between genders," whereas Kertbeny's theory is "gender intransitive," seeing same-sex object choice "as reflecting an impulse of separatism—but by no means necessarily political separatism—within each gender."[26]

Despite these salient differences between Ulrichs's theory and Kertbeny's, the triumph of Kertbeny's terminology over those of Ulrichs, Casper, and Westphal remains a curious historical contingency. To begin with, Kertbeny only used the terms in two anonymous pamphlets of 1869 protesting section 143, both of which were published months after Westphal's article defining *conträre Sexualempfindung*.[27] Kertbeny himself was at this time supposedly at work on a full-length manuscript entitled "Sexualitätsstudien," or "Studies on Sexuality," yet despite several pleading letters from his publisher, the volume was not forthcoming.[28] The terms "heterosexual" and "homosexual" thus appear to have dropped out of public discourse entirely until 1880, the year that Jäger published his *Entdeckung der Seele*. Jäger's book manuscript included a chapter penned entirely by Kertbeny (under the pseudonym "Dr. M.") about homosexuality; according to a letter from Jäger to Kertbeny, this chapter had to be removed at the insistence of the publisher after it had been typeset. Although Jäger promised Kertbeny that the chapter would appear as a stand-alone supplement, this did not occur until 1900, eighteen years after Kertbeny's death, when it appeared in Magnus Hirschfeld's journal *Jahrbuch für sexuelle Zwischenstufen*.[29] Despite the removal of Kertbeny's chapter, Jäger adopted his terminology, and it was from Jäger's book that Richard von Krafft-Ebing appropriated the term "homosexuality" for the case notes in the second edition of his own *Psychopathia sexualis* (1887), as Krafft-Ebing acknowledged in the text.[30] Krafft-Ebing's text is the source of the first known deployment of the term "heterosexual" in the English language, in an article by James G. Kiernan that appeared in the *Chicago Medical Recorder* in 1892.[31] In that article, "heterosexuality" does not describe "normal sexuality" (however morally problematized) as it does for Kertbeny and Krafft-Ebing[32]; instead, it is a form of "psychical hermaphroditism" that belongs to a list of "sexual perversions proper."[33] For Jonathan Ned Katz, therefore, the most salient aspect of the term "heterosexuality" is its movement from pathology to norm as it is transcribed from the world of specialized medical discourse into the "big world of

American mass media," in which "the heterosexual idea moved from abnormal to normal, and from normal to normative."[34]

We have thus far traced the emergence of the term and category of "heterosexuality" from its appearance in a highly idiosyncratic taxonomy of sexual expression in 1868 through to its entrance into medical discourses in the late-nineteenth century and its proliferation at the beginning of the twentieth century. Yet it is not at all clear that this kind of historical work on the conditions in which the *term* "heterosexuality" emerged constitutes a genealogy of the *concept* or of its practice. Heterosexuality, perhaps more than any other sexual category, is still popularly understood as something without a genealogy, invoked across a wide range of discourses as natural, normal, necessary, and above all transhistorical and transcultural. After all, evidence can readily be found to show that, in any given cultural epoch, men and women cohabited, had genital contact, and thus reproduced. In such a worldview, these acts, now identified under the rubric of heterosexuality, are not so much practices whose incidence and significance are a product of their particular historical context as they are the very condition of possibility for history as such. Under such a naturalized transhistorical understanding of heterosexuality, the invention of the term "heterosexual" in 1868 becomes a trivial matter at best warranting a footnote: it becomes construed as the first instance of a term that is currently used to describe what most people were already doing, even if they had a different name for it, or perhaps no name at all.

The relationship between tracing the genealogy of the word "heterosexuality" and tracing the history of practices and identities that modern readers might be inclined to describe as heterosexual raises the same questions discussed in histories of homosexuality, most influentially by Foucault in the first volume of *The History of Sexuality*. As Foucault has famously argued, the idea of homosexuality coalesced what had previously been understood as a wide range of sexual practices into a fixed and stable identity:

> As defined by the ancient civil or canonical codes, sodomy was a category of forbidden acts; their perpetrator was nothing more than the juridical subject of them. The nineteenth-century homosexual became a personage, a past, a case history, and a childhood, in addition to being a type of life, a life form, and a morphology, with an indiscreet anatomy and possibly a mysterious physiology. Nothing that went into his total composition was unaffected by his sexuality. ... It was consubstantial with him, less as a habitual sin than as a singular nature. ... The sodomite had been a temporary aberration; the homosexual was now a species.[35]

While subsequent historians of homosexuality such as David M. Halperin have shown that recognizable forms of what we would now call homosexuality existed prior to the mid-nineteenth century, it is the invention of the word "homosexuality" that allows a wide range of sexual practices and identities to be newly understood as part of the same thing, thereby reorganizing the way such practices, and the people who undertake them, are understood.[36] Such an understanding of the historical distinction between same-sex acts and homosexual identities lends itself to a vigilant critique of the anachronistic application of the term "homosexual" or "homosexuality" to historical material prior to 1868. By his own admission, Halperin's early work is "priggish" in its "insistence on the alterity of the Greeks," in its efforts "to get historians of sexuality to adhere unfailingly to neat, categorical, airtight distinctions between ancient pederasty and modern homosexuality, as if any admission of overlap between the two could *only* be disadvantageous."[37]

Halperin's early priggishness may be one of the dangers in conceiving of the invention of the terms "homosexuality" and "heterosexuality" as a radical epistemic break, and his later work deploys a much more nuanced understanding of both historical continuities and ruptures. Yet what we find interesting is that, for all the emphasis placed on homosexuality's historical novelty, the term "heterosexuality" seems uniquely *resistant* to the kind of historicizing that Halperin insists is necessary for the term "homosexuality." One example we can draw from the small field of critical heterosexuality studies is the work of Chrys Ingraham, who, in her *White Weddings: Romancing Heterosexuality in Popular Culture*, claims that "historically, weddings have served as one of the major events that signal readiness and prepare heterosexuals for membership in marriage as an organising structure of the institution of heterosexuality."[38] Yet no more than nine pages later, Ingraham cites Katz's *The Invention of Heterosexuality* as providing proof that the term "heterosexual" was invented in 1868.[39] If weddings existed prior to 1868—as, demonstrably, they did—then they cannot by virtue of that fact have *historically* served as one of the major events that prepare heterosexuals to partake in the institution of heterosexuality, unless we are to understand the sweeping rhetorical force of the adjective "historically" to be restricted, in this instance, to the period of 1868 until the present day. What we might argue, more precisely, is that the rise of a particular norm or ideal of marriage—as companionate—transformed its cultural significance. It is during the nineteenth century that marriage acquires its defining role within the new configurations of sexuality, gender, and the family also emergent at this time.

FIGURE 2.3: A young woman
in her wedding dress holding flowers. Engraving by J.
Cochran after A. E. Chalon.
Wellcome Library, London.

The anachronism that is often found within histories such as that of marriage, whereby particular practices are seen to derive from and to support an
"institution of heterosexuality" before its historical emergence as a conceptual category, can be found even in the most careful historical work. Thomas
Laqueur, who is otherwise exemplary in his scrupulous avoidance of pre-
sentism in his histories of the sexual(ized) body, nevertheless refers to the
kind of sexual intercourse described by Hippocrates, Aristophanes, Shake-
speare, Ambrose Paré, and Richard Carlile, among others, as "heterosexual."[40]
Foucault, for his own part, describes a form of "heterosexual monogamy"
(*monogamie hétérosexuelle*) circulating prior to the seventeenth and eighteenth
centuries in a passage that directly precedes his famous historicization of the
homosexual as a new species.[41] Even Monique Wittig, whose rigorous anti-
essentialism is so pronounced that she considers biological sex a construct
violently inscribed upon the body, also claims that "the social contract ...
is heterosexuality," despite her acknowledgement on the very next page that
"as a term it was created as a counterpart to homosexuality at the beginning
of this century [i.e., the twentieth]. So much for the extent of its 'it-goes-
without-saying.'"[42] This vacillation between heterosexuality as construct and
heterosexuality as transhistorical norm allows Wittig to claim that Aristotle
founds the necessity of heterosexuality in his *Politics*, ignoring her own earlier comments about the term's more recent creation.[43] Our point here is not
to chastise others for not being sufficiently rigorous in their recognition of the

historical specificity of heterosexuality as both a term and a social institution, but to highlight the fact that heterosexuality continues to operate as a silent norm to such an extent that one can discover traces of this operation in the very texts that provide the theoretical apparatus best suited to exposing the mechanisms of this operation.

One of the main reasons for this is that where the term and concept of "heterosexuality" have come under closer consideration—especially in the work of contemporary theorists and historians of sexuality—it is almost always in relation to its constructed opposite, homosexuality. According to Sedgwick, the binary opposition of hetero- and homosexuality that emerges in the nineteenth century has now become so culturally central that "an understanding of virtually any aspect of modern Western culture must be, not merely incomplete, but damaged in its central substance to the degree that it does not incorporate a critical analysis of modern homo/heterosexual definition."[44] The reason this opposition has had such a profound cultural impact, argues Sedgwick, is that it served to broaden an earlier binarization of gender (in which all subjects were culturally and legally assigned a male or female gender) into a new cultural domain: that of sexual orientation. As a result, "New, institutionalised taxonomic discourses—medical, legal, literary, psychological—centering on homo/heterosexual definition proliferated and crystallised with exceptional rapidity in the decades around the turn of the century."[45] This new emphasis on sexual orientation, on the distinction between the terms "heterosexuality" and "homosexuality," produces, as Foucault argued, the modern idea of sexual subjectivity, which in turn represented a move away from an earlier focus on the significance of sexual acts. In so doing, the increased dominance of this newly binarized understanding of sexuality served also to eclipse both their internal differences and any similarities evident across these categories—not to mention ignoring other taxonomic types such as bisexuality, intersexuality, and transsexuality that blur the binary nature of the heterosexual-homosexual divide itself. As a consequence, when particular sexual practices between persons of different genders—such as masturbation; oral, anal, public or group sex; sadomasochism; prostitution; and so on—come under critical or public scrutiny, it is almost invariably within the context of a historical or cultural examination of masturbation, sadomasochism, or prostitution rather than of heterosexuality per se. This is amply demonstrated by the proliferation of nineteenth-century discussions of prostitution in literature as well as medical and legal writing. Although nineteenth-century prostitution involved predominantly male clients and female service providers, and although it was widely condemned as a major social problem and threat to health and family, it was

FIGURE 2.4: A well-dressed client inspects the prostitutes at a brothel, 1884. In Léo Taxil, *La prostitution contemporaine* (Paris: Librairie Populaire, 1884). Wellcome Library, London.

rarely contextualized as a consequence of the new social structures emergent at this time around changing ideas about sexuality and sexual subjectivity. Heterosexuality itself, the assumed invisible norm, has an entrenched and enduring capacity to remain quarantined from the practices and identities that would trouble its normativity. This is in distinct contrast to the way, for instance, the gay club scene of the 1980s was invoked in the popular press to denounce the "promiscuity" of homosexual men in general—an argument that was especially forceful during the AIDS crisis of this period.[46]

This difference is indicative of the powerful cultural effects and consequences of the binarization of hetero- and homosexuality, and it is on this issue that the majority of contemporary theorists and historians of sexuality have accordingly focused. For Sedgwick and Halperin, the significance of the conceptual pairing of the terms "homosexuality" and "heterosexuality" resides in the way the cultural privileging and legitimization of heterosexuality has functioned to marginalize and pathologize homosexuality.[47] In *Saint Foucault*, Halperin argues that this makes the term "homosexuality" the "supplement" to that of "heterosexuality." In so doing, Halperin draws on the theorization of supplementarity found in the work of Jacques Derrida, which describes the paradoxical relationship between the dominant and marginalized terms of a binary opposition—seen both as opposites, hence exterior to each other, but also structurally and semantically dependent on each other, and hence inextricably interwoven.[48] As Halperin argues:

> Homosexuality and heterosexuality do not represent a true pair, two mutually referential contraries, but a hierarchical opposition in which heterosexuality defines itself implicitly by constituting itself as the negation of homosexuality. Heterosexuality defines itself without problematising itself, it elevates itself as a privileged and unmarked term, by abjecting and problematising homosexuality. Heterosexuality, then, *depends* on homosexuality to lend it substance—and to enable it to acquire *by* default its status *as* a default, as a *lack of difference* or an *absence of abnormality*.[49]

As Halperin here recognizes, the term "heterosexuality" asserts its privileged status largely in respect to its function—by "abjecting and problematising homosexuality"—while itself remaining "unmarked" and largely unspecified in its particularities. Heterosexuality is therefore defined negatively, "as a *lack of difference* or an *absence of abnormality*."

Such a poststructuralist understanding of the relationship between terms in a binary opposition leads Halperin to assume, explicitly, that any historicization of one of the terms in the binary—in this case, "homosexuality"—will automatically historicize its paired opposite. Thus he writes in *How to Do the History of Homosexuality* that his "purpose in historicizing homosexuality [in his earlier book *One Hundred Years of Homosexuality*] was *to denaturalize heterosexuality*, to deprive it of its claims to be considered a 'traditional value,' and ultimately to destroy the self-evidence of the entire system on which the homophobic opposition between homosexuality and heterosexuality depended."[50] Yet, as we have noted, the peculiar resistance to historicization that seems to inhere within the category of the heterosexual opens up the question of how, exactly, a rigorous and detailed study of Athenian pederasty is going to achieve the laudable goal that Halperin set himself in *One Hundred Years of Homosexuality*. The asymmetry of scholarly interest between the terms "homosexual" and "heterosexual" within the field of the history of sexuality—vastly more material has been written about the former—carries its own implicit dangers. As Leo Bersani argues in *Homos*, such constructionist analyses, "while valuable, can have assimilative rather than subversive consequences. ... [They accomplish] in [their] own way the principal aim of homophobia: the elimination of gays."[51] Given the fact that homosexualities are frequently construed within Western culture at large as somehow derivative of or secondary to heterosexuality, it is unlikely that a non-sympathetic reader of Halperin will make the cognitive leap required to apply his constructionist analysis to heterosexuality itself. Clearly, then, the historicization of homosexuality calls for, rather than accomplishes de facto, the historicization of heterosexuality.

It is against this background of a political necessity that historians of sexuality have turned to interrogate heterosexuality itself and to draw attention to the specificity and contingency of the term. Katz's book *The Invention of Heterosexuality* is exemplary in this regard. In it, Katz presents a historical narrative of epistemic rupture: he wishes to emphasize the alterity and novelty of the notion of heterosexuality, and its impact upon its arrival in the United States of America. Katz's thesis is that "heterosexuality" names a nascent different-sex erotic ethos that emerged prior to 1892 but was not legitimate or legitimated.[52] This erotic ethos was centered not around a telos of procreation, but around sexual pleasure—or, as sexual moralists of the time called it, "conjugal onanism" or "fraud in the accomplishment of the generative function."[53] Heterosexuality's triumph is, for Katz, the manner in which it has become normalized as *the* transhistorical sexuality par excellence, as we have outlined here. The preface to *The Invention of Heterosexuality* makes explicit the work's political intentions, which are to "provide a startling new view of a previously invisible, taken for granted, 'normal' social universe coexistent with the more deeply pondered 'deviant' world—perhaps even unsettle forever our idea of norm and deviance."[54] In his conclusion, he argues that "if a specifically heterosexual system didn't exist in the past ... it doesn't have to exist in the future."[55] Thus its focus is not on the conditions of possibility for heterosexuality's emergence in the specific context of late-nineteenth-century Germany, but on the prevailing conditions in the United States that allowed heterosexuality to swiftly adopt the status of a norm in that country. This is reflected in the selective, non-chronological order in which he presents his research: his account opens, after a lengthy prologue, with the first deployment of "heterosexuality" in the North American context in May 1892[56]; only thirty-three pages later does the reader encounter the German invention of the term in 1868.[57]

One problem with the order in which Katz presents his historical data is that it underdetermines the role of the term's invention in a specific cultural, juridical, and medical context and overdetermines the role of its reception in another context. Although this is undoubtedly the product of another invisible norm—the norm that constructs North American history as "history" proper while relegating the histories of other geographical, cultural, and temporal regions to the realm of specific histories—it has damaging effects in his conception of the path that the term "heterosexuality" took in becoming a norm. One way we can think through this is to employ the distinction between "perversion" and "perversity" as it appears in Krafft-Ebing. For Arnold I. Davidson, these two notions are what differentiate homosexuality and sodomy in Krafft-Ebing: homosexuality is a "perversion," whereas sodomy "was a vice, a problem for morality and law, about which medicine had no special knowledge."[58] Perversion is thus a disease, perversity a crime; the whole personality of the pervert becomes subject to medico-psychiatric treatment, whereas the perverse act remains subject to juridical interdiction. That the concepts of perversion and perversity should coexist at the end of the nineteenth century should not surprise us; their coexistence confirms Sedgwick's critique of Foucault and Halperin's "unidirectional narrative of supersession," in which "the superseded model ... drops out of the frame of analysis."[59] The opening up of a medical discourse regarding same-sex object choice does not, of course, settle the legal question of whether or not homosexual acts ought to be punished and, if so, through what means, although new medicalized understandings of same-sex attraction clearly can be deployed in juridical battles, as both Ulrichs's and Kertbeny's theories demonstrate. Importantly, though, for Kertbeny homosexuality is a fundamental orientation toward a same-sex object choice, thus fulfilling the structural requirements of a "perversion," although not a perversion that can be described as an illness; heterosexuality, on the other hand, names not a determinate perversion of the sexual instinct toward an inappropriate object, but rather "an unfettered capacity for degeneracy," or a perversity.[60] As we have seen, Kertbeny's heterosexuals are capable of a number of sexual acts that would now disbar them from the presumptive status of heterosexuality in twenty-first-century Western culture: "giving themselves over to same-sex excesses," assaulting "male but especially female minors," and engaging "in bestiality and the misuse of animals."[61] By foregrounding heterosexuality's (mis)construal in Kiernan's paper of 1892, Katz constructs a narrative of the term's shift from an unproblematized perversion to a contested term with normative force: in short, a version of heterosexual history that follows in its broadest contours, albeit over a much shorter period of time, the constructionist history of homosexuality.

As such, and as we have seen here, the history (and historiography) of heterosexuality largely bears out the claims made by recent theorists and historians of sexuality: that the significance and cultural function of hetero- and homosexuality are closely interconnected and conceptually interdependent. At the same time, insofar as heterosexuality has occupied the place of a transcultural and transhistorical norm—the "it goes without saying" of sexuality, in Wittig's terms—we must also recognize the specificity of its emergence, both as a term and as a set of sexual practices. In one of the most important distinctions between the histories of hetero- and homosexuality, the former has proved adept at separating itself from those practices that trouble its claim to occupy the space of sexual normality, primarily defined as reproductive marital monogamy. Nymphomania, frigidity, BDSM, masturbation, polyamory, and other such practices are usually treated as distinct from (or perversions of) heterosexuality itself. For this reason, while a critical history of heterosexuality may derive from—and remain interconnected with—that of homosexuality, the same historiographic tools cannot necessarily be used, or used in the same manner. However, as we have sought to show in this chapter, when subjected to the same scrutiny as the histories of more marginalized and yet also more visible sexualities, heterosexuality reveals itself to be just as semantically volatile, and equally historically contingent.

CHAPTER THREE

Homosexuality: European and Colonial Encounters

SEAN BRADY

Until the late 1960s, the systematic study of sexuality—and homosexuality in particular—remained firmly the domain of biologists and psychologists. As Jeffrey Weeks states, until the 1970s, the notion that sexuality has a history would have been regarded as "absurd."[1] Since then, however, historical studies have demonstrated that homosexuality and sexuality per se are mutable categories. Homosexuality, far from being a fixed and determined psychological and biological category, changes over time and space. In other words, homosexuality is historically and culturally specific. To be sure, the range of possible sexual acts between men and between women is a constant. But the implications and meanings attached to these acts, and attitudes toward the perpetrators of these acts, change from society to society, and in different historical periods and contexts.

The "age of empire" is generally taken by historians to refer to the era of Western colonial expansion in the late-nineteenth and early-twentieth centuries. The age of empire was also the period when the term "homosexuality," along with other quasi-scientific labels for same-sex sexuality, were coined by scientifically minded men to identify and categorize same-sex sexual behaviors and lives. Homosexuality, in particular male homosexuality, was developed into a scientific category that implied a separate species of being that was pathological, and contrary to the normal.[2] Sex between men had long been regarded in Western Judeo-Christian culture as an abominable and unmentionable vice and sin—though attitudes and punishments varied considerably over the centuries. But in the age of empire, same-sex sexuality was given an existence and a life of its own through scientific discourse. In this chapter, we shall see that the ideas that influenced the heterosexual-homosexual scientific binary created by psychiatrists and sex psychologists such as Carl Westphal, Richard von Krafft-Ebing, Havelock Ellis, and Sigmund Freud were not disconnected to prevailing Western attitudes toward non-European societies in imperial territories. Also, these new scientific ideas of sexual categorization were informed by prevailing concepts of acceptable gender behavior and the legality of sex between men and between women.

Late-nineteenth-century medical discourses contributed to the construction of a vilified, pathologized, and criminalized conception of the male homosexual. Since the 1970s, scholars have shown the extent to which late-nineteenth-century sexologists might be represented as the patriarchal pathologizers who, at a particular point in time, crystallized the notion of the homosexual in Western culture and thinking. Undoubtedly, the difficulties that homosexual and homophile campaigners encountered for social and legal rights in the mid- to late-twentieth century were to a considerable extent the result of the association between pathology and criminality in "the homosexual" in many Western societies. Arguably, many of the historians who first looked at homosexuality as a historical category were as much concerned to refute the authority of science that had been given to the pathological category of the homosexual in their present context as they were to discern the history of same-sex sexuality in the nineteenth century.

Today, pathologization of same-sex desire is the preserve of the charlatan and has no authority in current medical scientific thinking.[3] This chapter is reflective of more recent historical scholarship in this field. It examines the often-uneasy existence of the early discipline of sex psychology in the social and cultural context of Europe before the First World War. It looks at the extent to which the new discipline of sex psychology exerted an influence upon the lives of men and women who desired members of their own sex, in Europe between the mid-nineteenth century and the First World War. This chapter also brings together these themes in an examination of European attitudes to sexual difference in other cultures in the territories of the British and French empires.

Homosexuality as a pathological category was undoubtedly a powerful and institutionalized form of pejorative social labeling until the early 1970s, particularly in societies where the ideas of the sex psychologists had suffused

A GROUP OF SEXUAL PERVERTS (ELMIRA).

FIGURE 3.1: "A group of sexual perverts (Elmira)." In Henry Havelock Ellis, *The Criminal* (London: Walter Scott, 1901). Wellcome Library, London.

the disciplines of psychology and psychiatry in the mid-twentieth century, such as the United States.[4] But an examination of sexuality between men and between women in the age of empire reveals that the ideas of the early sex psychologists were regarded by many homosexuals themselves as liberationary.[5] In addition, broader social attitudes toward the ideas of sex psychologists on homosexuality ranged from ambivalence to outright hostility and proscription. Sexology was a radical and new form of thinking in this era. In many respects, these thinkers based their ideas upon the milieu of homosexuals that could be found in the period. For many "homosexual" men and women, their fashioning of their sexuality was not influenced by the "sexologists"—but their sexualized desires and lives became part of a new discourse in the quest by radical and often-marginal thinkers to classify the natural world around them as they saw it.[6]

SEXOLOGY AND HOMOSEXUALITY

The term "sexology" was first coined with reference to medical science at the beginning of the twentieth century and is used retrospectively by historians today to describe the outpouring of scientific writings on sexual disease in the late-nineteenth and early-twentieth centuries.[7] The quest of the first sexologists was to provide a distinctly scientific explanation for a variety of sexual phenomena. These medical writers developed complex systems to classify and describe a range of sexualities, such as bisexuality, heterosexuality, and homosexuality. Sexology also undertook the systematic investigation of various forms of sexual desire, such as fetishism, masochism, and sadism.[8] Quasi-scientific concerns about what was regarded as sexually abnormal, such as "perversion" and masturbation, long predated the late-nineteenth century.[9] Julie Peakman argues that perversion existed as a moral category associated with sex as early as the late-seventeenth century.[10] But in the quest to develop greater critical insights into sexual phenomena, the investigation of sexuality underwent a distinct semantic shift in the nineteenth century. Sexual perversion was defined from the 1830s most often as a form of "moral insanity," a disorder of the emotions, instincts, and will caused by neurological or other organic problems.[11] Ivan Crozier suggests that this association of perversions with moral insanity made sexuality an obvious concern for the newly emergent profession of psychiatry in the nineteenth century.[12] The new science of sexology posed questions of sexual deviance in novel ways. As Arnold Davidson demonstrates, sexology grappled with sexual deviance as a psychic identity rather than with the assessment of sexual practices or physical signs. This shift away from the description of sexual behaviors was consistent with a broader transfer of interest in the nineteenth century from the consequence of acts to their causes, and a general preoccupation with impulses that drive behaviors.[13]

Part of the reason for this shift in thinking, was the difficulties associated with linking pathological anatomy with sexual deviation. For example, Ambroise Tardieu's study *Etude médico-légale sur les attentats aux mœurs* (1857; *Medico-legal study of Crimes against Morals*) claimed to detect homosexuality in males through physical signs in the genitals and anus. Tardieu, through examination of male prostitutes arrested in Second Empire Paris, claimed that the penis showed certain specific signs of physical change and shape caused by repeated acts of anal sex (giving it the appearance of a canine penis with a pointy tip). Habitual passive anal sex altered the shape and look of the anus and rectum, he argued, inducing an "infundibuliform" appearance.[14] Tardieu's obsessive pursuit of physical signs was recognized as ludicrous by German scientists by the late-nineteenth century. Even Tardieu had to recognize that not all male homosexuals could be identified thus, and that many "sexual perverts" had no incriminating signs at all.[15] Nonetheless, Tardieu's study remained in print, in France at least, for much of the nineteenth century. Realizing that the pursuit of physical signs of sexual perversion was a chimera, physicians looked to the brain as the anatomical key to the origins of perversion.[16] Nonetheless, the quest for neurological signs proved to be as unsatisfactory as were physical signs in providing answers. The idea of sexual instinct was created as a method of circumventing the problems of physical signs of perversion while at the same time creating the impression that sexual desire and its anomalies could be located in the body.[17] Sexologists such as Westphal were influenced by the concept of "psychophysical intermediacy" put forward in the work of the Karl Heinrich Ulrichs, a homosexual German jurist and campaigner, for the rights of the "Urning," or homosexual. The latter, in turn, had adapted

Charles Darwin's theory of biological gender mutability as an explanation for homosexuality in nature.[18] Scholars tend to agree that this new "psychiatric style of reasoning" was an epistemological break with the past, although there are considerable disagreements about the direct effects of this development.[19]

Carolyn Dean cautions that although this semantic shift in reasoning was undoubtedly a powerful one, it was also symptomatic of the failure to define "anomalies" of desire in older and more familiar terms. As Dean states, "it has never fully replaced the older model, nor as it ever been completely coherent."[20] For example, Krafft-Ebing's *Psychopathia Sexualis*, published in Germany in 1886 and the model for all treatises of its kind in its wake, sought to determine in each case study "whether the individual suffered from perversity (a disease of the *moral will*) or perversion (a disease of the *body*)."[21] Significantly, Krafft-Ebing's diagnosis of perversion absolved the individual concerned of any culpability. As Harry Oosterhuis argues, Krafft-Ebing's formulations on perversion described "diseases" such as masochism and sadism "on a graded scale of health and illness that explained aspects of normal sexuality."[22] For Krafft-Ebing, "perversions" such as masochism and sadism were inherent in

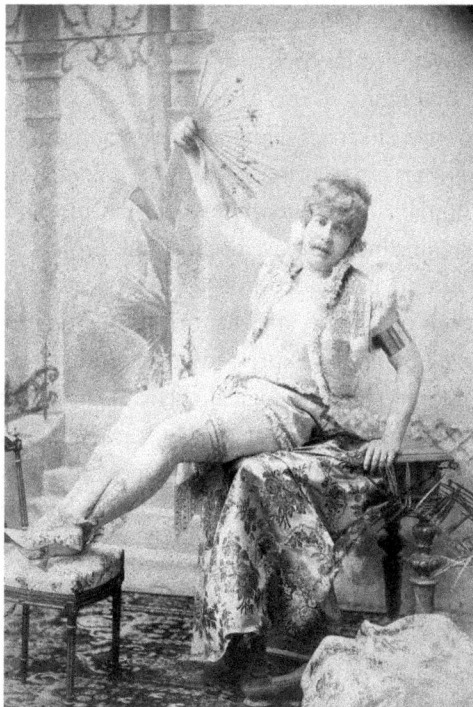

FIGURE 3.2: Postcard, c.1896. Krafft-Ebing collection. Wellcome Library, London.

normal male and female sexuality—masochism being an extreme extension of women's natural passivity, and sadism an extreme extension of men's natural aggressiveness.[23] A distinct tension existed between older moral models of deviance and new biological and compulsive ones, even within the same text. Sexual drive remained elusive, and the sexologists were unable to locate sexual drive definitively within the body. This tension remained problematic in sexological works by Albert Moll, Iwan Bloch, Havelock Ellis, and others.[24]

The jumble of corporeal and moral markers of homosexuality with the psychic markers of the new psychology is apparent in most sexological texts of the late-nineteenth century. Buttressed to this, argues Siobhan Somerville, were notions of race—indeed, most of the significant sexological texts were written in a context of intellectual upheaval in notions of race and new imperialism.[25] Havelock Ellis's *Sexual Inversion*, the first extensive scientific study in English of the phenomenon of homosexuality, mixed the notion of race with nation and ancestry in describing the backgrounds of the homosexuals used for his case studies, who were predominantly British, with a few Americans, Germans, French, and Portuguese. Somerville notes that Ellis's ambiguous use of the term "race" was not uncommon in scientific thinking at this time, when it might refer to groupings based on geography, religion, class, or color. In many respects, the "techniques and logic" of late-nineteenth-century sexologists reproduced the methodologies developed by comparative anatomists, who sought corporeal evidence for sexual ambiguity in the African body. Sexual ambiguity served to delineate the boundaries of race.[26] This did not go unnoticed at the time. John Addington Symonds's privately printed essay *"A Problem in Modern Ethics"* (1891) is the first humanist critique of sexology and its methods and conclusions. Symonds is significant not least because the project of *Sexual Inversion* was his brainchild, and he persuaded Ellis to collaborate on the matter, lending a scientific authority to his literary and historical investigations on male homosexuality. In the essay, Symonds expressed considerable alarm at the inherent Eurocentricity of much of the sexological theories that were available on the Continent. If the sexologists looked at non-European races at all, evidence of "homosexuality" was read as male members of these societies yielding to primitive instincts. "Sodatic" or Arab and African (and, in some circumstances, southern European) sexuality had no place in modern Christian European society.[27]

Symonds noted that sexologists such as the Frenchman Paul Moreau de Tours placed European Christians as a species distinct from and above all other races. He observed wryly that the Frenchman or the Englishman who indulged in sex with another man was considered diseased, whereas the Persian or the African was simply responding to the primitivism of his race.[28] Symonds had little difficulty in refuting these arguments. But his was a lone voice in this period.[29] Theories of race and sexual anomalies rooted in physical differences were gradually replaced in the first quarter of the twentieth century by psychoanalytic interpretations of "abnormal" sexual object choice.[30] Even Ellis, who was sympathetic, up to a point, with Symonds's historicist and culturally-relativistic interpretation of homosexuality, generally ignored his criticism of other sexologists in this respect. This should not be entirely surprising. Symonds died in 1893, and Ellis felt duty bound to include aspects of his work in *Sexual Inversion*. But Ellis was keen to tone down the literary contributions of Symonds and keep the text in line with current scientific thinking on the matter on the Continent.[31] Additionally, "the concepts within racial science were so congruent with social and political life ... as to be virtually uncontested from inside the mainstream of science."[32] This notwithstanding, Ellis's publication of *Sexual Inversion* was banned by the British authorities as a work of obscene libel in 1898.

The banning of *Sexual Inversion* in Britain brings us to another point in the scholarly debates about the formation of the modern homosexual in this period, and sexology's role in creating this identity. Although *Sexual Inversion* indubitably was a form of scientific discourse, very few people in Britain got the opportunity to read the work until 1936, when it was republished as part of Ellis's *Studies in the Psychology of Sex*. Since Michel Foucault's highly influential and groundbreaking analysis in *The History of Sexuality*, scholars have followed the tendency in his thinking that the modern (male) homosexual was a product of scientific discourse. The medico-legal argument that legislation and taxonomic classification and pathologization of sex between men "produced" sexual identities and subcultures is highly problematic.[33] Historians in this field have tended to promulgate a rather mechanical notion of the ability of a scientific discipline or a legislative body to "produce" the sexualized identities of individuals throughout society. Sociological studies conducted in the early 1980s highlight the fact that most elderly British gay men had never heard the term "homosexual" until the 1950s.[34] If this finding is juxtaposed with the marked reluctance of British psychiatry to engage with sexological theories until the mid-twentieth century, then the irresistible conclusion to be drawn, using the medico-legal analysis, is that there were no "identities" or communities based on same-sex desire between men in Britain before the 1950s. This is clearly a problematic historical claim. Studies have shown that there were more venues available in eighteenth-century London for men to meet for the purposes of sexual liaison than in London in the 1950s.[35] Also, nineteenth-century British society was remarkable in Europe for the intensity of its hostility toward sex between men to the point that public discourse on the matter was intolerable—as we have seen, Ellis's *Sexual Inversion* was banned. At the same time, there is much evidence of knowledge of the types and coteries of men who indulged in this passion. One could argue, using a Weeksian analysis, that coteries and communities predating late-nineteenth-century sexological taxonomy were not "homosexual." Historians such as Weeks and David Halperin argue that before the taxonomy of homosexuality was created, sex between men cannot be regarded as "homosexual."[36] But George Chauncey in his study *Gay New York* (1995) argues that queer lives and a thriving "gay" subculture existed independently of the taxonomy of sexology in New York City of the 1920s, long after the supposed watershed of the 1880s. Chauncey places the dominance of "a world in which men were divided into 'homosexuals' and 'heterosexuals'" as late as the 1940s and 1950s.[37]

HOMOSEXUALITY IN CONTEXT

Homosexuality, far from being a monolithic Western construct in this period, varied considerably from society to society in the West, both in terms of its visibility, particularly in discourse, and the difference in attitudes toward sex between people of the same sex. Each of the societies and regions of Europe had, on close examination, a bricolage of contradictions and differences in attitudes toward homosexuality, even among scientists.[38] Thoroughgoing comparative studies of homosexualities in differing European societies in the age of empire remain to be researched and written.[39] Nonetheless, the scholarship within national contexts for this period is well developed enough to provide here a survey synthesis of context for the legal, moral, and medical differences between European societies in this respect. It must be stressed that this survey concentrates in particular upon the social and cultural context of male homosexualities. Female homosexualities have an even more ambivalent place in the historical record for this period. Part of the reason for this was the general lack of criminality associated with sex between women, and therefore a lack of court cases for the historian to interrogate. Also, for reasons of gender relations and notions of masculinity prevalent during this period, sex between men preoccupied the attentions of the sexologists more comprehensively than did sex between women.[40] In an era that had firmly identified the sexually dangerous gender as male, aberrations in sexual normativity had wider social ramifications when the perpetrator was male.

Historians of homosexuality in France have recognized a cultural specificity to social, legal, and medical attitudes toward homosexuality in this period. As Antony Copley argues, representations of homosexuality in scientific discourse were much more prevalent, prominent, and sophisticated than in England.[41] As we have seen, publication of such scientific discourses on homosexuality was nigh impossible in Britain in the period in question. This notwithstanding, French scientific treatises proved "remarkably provincial" and neglected more subtle modes of analysis being developed by sexologists in Austria, Germany, and Italy in the late-nineteenth and early-twentieth centuries. In one fundamental respect, the debates in France were differentiated from those in Britain, the German states, and Austria; acts of sex between consenting adult males were legally tolerated. The Code Napoléon had ensured that since 1805, acts of sex between men in private were not criminal offenses. Nonetheless, local statutes and regulation of offenses against public decency, particularly after 1848, ensured that acts of sex between men in public places, such as urinals and parks, and male prostitution were criminalized, and that male homosexuality in the late-nineteenth century became heavily associated with criminality and moral degeneracy. As Robert Nye argues, the French penal system enshrined a sharp legal distinction between the public and private spheres, and the state had no business in regulating private sexuality or the rules of conduct in private. Only dangerous public manifestations, such as sex acts between men in public or male prostitution, were punishable.[42] Indeed, France was often the locus of exiles from ostensibly harsher legal regimes toward male homosexuality, Wilde's sojourn in Paris after his release from Reading Gaol being just one example. But the basic legal tolerance afforded by the Code Napoléon has fostered, suggests Copley, the lack of development of a self-conscious homosexual movement in modern France.[43] As Nye points out, the legal tolerance of male homosexuality in private was more than counterbalanced in France during this period by a discourse of cultural norms supported by the authority of science and medicine. In spite of the sharp legal divide between public and private morality, legal impotence in this respect was negated by "censorious norms, and the obsessive linkage of love with procreation." Nye emphasizes the relative uniqueness of France in this respect.[44]

French scientific writings on homosexuality in the late-nineteenth and early-twentieth centuries are notable for their censoriousness of tone. Nye places the cultural specificity of the harshness of French scientific writings on male homosexuality (and other sexual aberrations) in the context of the sociopolitical situation in post-Revolutionary France. New civil codes reinvented the patriarchy of the ancien régime in specific ways. They gave legitimacy to principles of masculine management of "family assets, encouraging a man to maintain a tight control over both his material and biological capital, and to think about inheritance literally as a mode of self-perpetuation."[45] This made social phenomena such as adoption unthinkable. Adultery and production of a bastard by a wife challenged directly a husband's patrimony. Conversely, a husband's adultery was excused by the codes, and paternity suits were banned. High premiums were placed on careful management of biological capital, to the extent that France experienced an early and rapid decline in the birth rate. People in France had much better access to artificial contraceptive methods than in other European societies.[46] Nonetheless, the drop in the fertility rate led to a proliferation of organizations concerned with examining some of the causes of infertility. It is in this context, argues Nye, that the discourse of French sexology "favoured biological metaphors of pathology and norm with respect to the survival of the French 'race.'"[47] Sexology in France was influenced predominantly by theories of degeneration. Degeneracy theory promoted ideas of society as an organic body, as well as the idea that its inevitable decay was rooted in each human body in that

FIGURE 3.3: A lesbian brothel, where jealousy has caused two women to come to blows. In Léo Taxil, *La prostitution contemporaine* (Paris: Librairie Populaire, 1884). Wellcome Library, London.

society.[48] Male homosexuality, among other "perversions" such as masturbation, was characterized pejoratively as an "egoistic" and "sterile" sexuality, and as "the 'shame' of *honnêtes gens*."[49] Marriage and marital love became highly eroticized and celebrated in French culture as a counterpoise to the ambivalence represented by phenomena such as homosexuality and the general spread of syphilis. These attitudes toward homosexuality remained, however, more or less a bourgeois preserve in this period. The eroticization of married life and marital sexuality did little to affect patterns of sexuality among the urban working classes. Casual unions remained common (as young women had little in the way of means to compel partners to marry). Additionally, homosexual men and their relationships were tolerated, and Nye highlights the large proportion of stable lesbian relationships to be found within the large communities of prostitutes in Paris among both regulated and unregulated prostitutes.[50] Leslie Choquette argues that the "lesbian" subculture in late-nineteenth-century Paris was notable for its overlapping and intersection with the world of theater and that of prostitution, rather than its distinctiveness and separateness. Lesbianism was "visible" among actresses, singers, dancers, and other women of the theater world, many of whom were indistinguishable from the courtesan in this period.[51]

HOMOSEXUALITY AND EMPIRE

Many ideas on male homosexuality in France were shaped, not least by homosexual men themselves, through engagement with France's imperial possessions, in particular its North African possessions. In many respects, argues Robert Aldrich, the place of empire holds a particular fascination for French homosexual writers, both in the period in question and during the twentieth century. Writers such as André Gide, François Augiéras, and Jean Genet explored homosexual encounters with North Africans in novels, plays, travelogues, and autobiographies.[52] France's North African possessions had long held sway as the eroticized "other" in French imaginations. For most, North Africa represented "irregular pleasures," and the belief was widely held that Arab masculinity was synonymous with homosexuality. The writer Gustave Flaubert, writing in 1850 of his encounters in Egypt, commented that:

> Here it's quite well accepted. One admits one's sodomy and talks about it at the dinner table. Sometimes one denies it a bit, then everyone yells at you and it ends up being admitted. Travelling for our learning experience and charged with a mission from the government, we see it as our duty to give in to this mode of ejaculation. ... It is practiced in the baths. One reserves the bath for oneself ... and one takes one's boy into one of the rooms.[53]

The legal tolerance in France of sexual acts between men in private meant that in the French colonies, prosecutions were only enacted if sex between men involved offenses to public decency, abuse of authority, or violence. Nonetheless, army doctors in the French army worried about the deleterious effects of homosexuality among French soldiers in North Africa and commented in censorious and pathological terms about the effect of the French presence in Algeria on national morals. Soldiers, it was argued, "could not resist imitating the ways of indigenes, and soon their bad reputation for having 'African morals' had reached France."[54] It was feared that sodomy, like the plague, would "spread from the army to civilian society, from military camps to cities, from the colonies to motherland."[55]

One army doctor, Dr. René Jude in a remarkable text from 1907 on "degenerates" in the French *bataillons d'Afrique*, relayed an almost pornographic description of the behavior among soldiers in Tunisia. The so-called Bat' d'Af had been established in 1832 and was made up of men who had been twice convicted of crimes in civilian life or after conscription. Dr. Jude reported that in spite of the ready availability of women prostitutes, out of eighty men he observed, only one or two men visited them. The rest had sex with each other. Jude observed "households of male couples with a clear division of roles," both domestically and sexually, in the tented battalion.[56] In many cases Jude remarked upon the intensity of attachments between these men. He attempted a physigonomical assessment of whom he perceived to be the active and passive partners in these "households." He was particularly concerned with those soldiers not in a "household ménage," who lived and slept on their own. These men, called "Moroccans" by the other soldiers, were coerced into, or in some cases enjoyed, performing fellatio on their comrades.[57] Jude was not alone in his observations. Two years after the publication of his book, Dr. Paul Rebierre conducted a study of homosexuality in the Bat' d'Af. Some soldiers' tents, observed Rebierre, became "theatres of violent orgy." Male prostitution of a kind flourished, though one of Rebierre's subjects refused to use his rectum for this purpose in the army, "in order to preserve [his] capital for civilian life" when demobilized to France.[58] What is remarkable about these medical texts is that they were freely available in metropolitan France, with full and lurid details of homosexual sex life, promiscuity, intense passionate attachment and love, and male-only households in the nation's imperial battalions. Although they were intensely pejorative and hostile in tone, the French doctors spared the reader none of the details of the "degeneracy" they observed.

For some sexological theorists in this period, the risks to morals at home posed by contact with exotic and imperial territories were less than the challenge to moral continence created by European civilization itself. In the quest to categorize a "well-ordered sexuality," theorists disagreed upon the effects of "nature" and "civilization." "Ordered living, moderation, and willpower" were considered crucial to a healthy and moral life in the realms of sexual instinct, as well as other aspects of behavior and personal habits. "Nature" was considered problematic by some theorists. Civilization "subdued the human potential for wildness, the primitive animalism so pervasive in nature."[59] For others, modern civilization, particularly modern urban culture, was the corrupting factor creating decadence and sexual aberration; in such thinking, "moral and physical adjustment to an unspoiled natural order" was the surest method of keeping sexual aberrations such as homosexuality at bay.[60] Sexual degeneracy was associated with the primitive. Equally, the European Christian civilization of the nineteenth century, regarded by many contemporaries as the "higher evolutionary development of humanity" in the world, made sexual activity more dangerous than ever before as concerns about civilized lifestyles

FIGURE 3.4: A male brothel, where boys from the street are made available to clients, in this case one man is passionately kissing a boy's foot. In Léo Taxil, *La prostitution contemporaine* (Paris: Librairie Populaire, 1884). Wellcome Library, London.

and urban living coalesced within new notions of mind and body. "Degeneracy" might have been associated with "primitivism," but the condition required the advances of modernity to give it cause and definition. Even Krafft-Ebing's theories, often intimately tied to a biological interpretation of sexuality, targeted the European city and its temptations as a root cause of sexual aberrations such as homosexuality. Primitive peoples, argued Krafft-Ebing, lacked shame but were more or less free from the "perversions" created by civilization and modern urban living.[61] In Krafft-Ebing's formulations, human morality had become possible because of the advent of modern European Christian civilization; in other words, morality was the preserve of European Christians, but modern living had forced individuals from simple, stable communities and exposed them to novel stimuli, leading to moral and sexual degeneration.[62]

An example of the tensions surrounding civilization, homosexual desire, and the exotic "primitive" in imperial territories is highlighted in Anne O'Brien's work on missionary masculinities in late-nineteenth- and early-twentieth-century Northern Australia. O'Brien analyzes the writings and missionary activities of the Englishman Gilbert White, the first Anglican bishop of Carpentaria in North Queensland. In no sense could White be construed as a sexually active homosexual. However, the passions with which White imbued his male friendships in the near-exclusive homosocial environments in which he thrived would have been "decreed ... pathological" by contemporary medical thinking.[63] Although White was unlikely to have been exposed to the writings of sex psychologists, not least because these were either available through the pornographic black market only or banned outright in British publishing markets, the culture of masculinity and severe moral and criminal opprobrium accorded to male homosexual activity in Britain would have provided considerable incentives in maintaining a chaste homoeroticism, even in the far-flung corners of the empire. White found himself in an outpost where women were conspicuous by their absence. He was himself a committed bachelor at a time when religious missionary organizations were aware of the potential for homosexual scandal and arranged marriages for male missionariess.[64] In his writings, he valorized the men he encountered and often described them in close physical detail. The male white settlers, also bachelors by and large, impressed him, particularly when these "bearded and sinewy" men gathered for his church services held at water tanks and stations in this wilderness. White's admiration for most of the men he encountered through his mission was based on their taciturn natures, which matched his own sense of reserve.[65]

Nonetheless, in some of the tin-mining communities, where some townships were exclusively male, White wrote critically of Saturday night activities where the men ran races in "primeval garb," or semi-nudity, and his mission was to "inculcate more conventional methods of dress and demeanour."[66]

O'Brien argues that White did not wholly condemn the custom—he may have found it entertaining—but he clearly saw it as his business to civilize the men he encountered. White moved in a society where the "boundaries between homoeroticism, homosociality and homosexuality were likely to have been particularly porous," but at no point did White attempt to intervene in the masculine culture he encountered: in fact, he admired it.[67] White's attitude toward and interest in the male body was highlighted most specifically in his meetings with Aboriginal men. Nudity in white men fostered mild admonishment, but among the Aboriginal men, he regarded nudity as their "natural state." This made White unusual in his time, particularly among British religious missionaries, in his attitudes to indigenous peoples and their cultures. He described groups of Aboriginal men wearing "only a narrow loin-cloth," "danc[ing] and jump[ing] about with much gracefulness, playing and jesting with one another." For White, the naked beautiful Aboriginal male was the epitome of the "noble savage."[68] He commented that "his dark chocolate-coloured body, kept clean by constant swimming in water-holes or lagoons, shines with the glow of health and good condition. ... The colour of his body is such that he does not seem to be naked even though quite unclothed."[69] This was a most unusual view at this time, though his views accorded indirectly with Krafft-Ebing's view of the "primitive"; in fact, White was one of the few imperial religious missionaries in the period to advocate Aboriginal rights and preservation. However, to White, the archetypal Aboriginal was always male. Other sympathetic missionaries expressed concerned with the plight of Aboriginal women and pointed out the ill treatment of these women at the hands of both white male colonists and their own menfolk.[70] White was detached from their plight. O'Brien highlights that although White noted colonial settlements where Aboriginal women were suffering from sexual diseases, he offered no sympathy, "nor does he denounce the sexual practices of white men."[71] O'Brien argues that although White's casting of the Aboriginal male indirectly assisted the Aboriginal cause, his indifference to Aboriginal women, and women in general, elided discussion of the oppression of these women, who were "used and abused as sexual partners" in this heavily masculine population.[72]

HOMOSEXUALITY AS "OTHER"

Encounters with imperial territories formed a crucial source of influence in the homosexual self-fashioning of men such as Edward Carpenter (1844–1929). Carpenter was a pioneer English socialist and is remembered today predominantly for his homosexuality and his activities as a campaigner for reform of attitudes toward homosexuality. He has tended to be regarded by historians as forming his homosexual identity through contact with the ideas of sexology.[73] To be sure, he was intimately involved with Ellis and Symonds's project *Sexual Inversion* in the 1890s, particularly after Symonds's death in 1893. Following this event, Ellis was reliant on Carpenter for "case studies" for *Sexual Inversion*, and their extensive correspondence after Symonds's death "must have been a buoy to Ellis" in completing the project.[74] But Carpenter's sense of self and understanding of his sexual desires, and especially his highly esoteric views on socialism, had been formed some years before his encounters with sexology. Recent historians detect a bricolage of influences in the self-fashioning of educated upper-middle-class homosexual men in this period, including religious experiences and their accommodation of their desires to the overriding expectation in this period for them to marry.[75] Oscar Wilde and John Addington Symonds, both homosexual and central to the historiography of homosexuality, were married men with families. Carpenter never married and isolated himself from society, living in the north of England, and working as an itinerant lecturer with the university extension movement. He had been an Anglican cleric but sued for his own defrockment in 1874 and eschewed traditional Christian beliefs in his quest for a millennial vision of socialism, which found expression in his influential 400-page poem *Towards Democracy* (1883), and his "ethical socialist experiment" on his isolated farm, Millthorpe, in North Derbyshire, which Carpenter described as being in a "happy valley [with] ... no resident squire of any kind, nor even a single villa."[76]

Carpenter's main influences in his vision of socialism and ultimately in his vision of homosexuality were the notions of masculine comradeship inherent in the American poet Walt Whitman's *Leaves of Grass*, although Whitman always vehemently denied any homosexual overtones or inspiration in his work. Carpenter's socialist vision, which centered on the politics of the personal and a sense of sexual liberation, was a fusion of the ideas of Whitmanite comradeship and the Hindu philosophical text, the Bhagavad Gita. His exile from his own class left him emotionally isolated from other men, and in the 1870s and 1880s he sought emotional solace through travel through the Orient and the examination of Asian belief systems.[77] Many of Carpenter's contemporaries had a passing knowledge of the beliefs of subject peoples, and after the creation of the Crown Imperial of India in 1876, knowledge of Indian beliefs was considered necessary for the English gentleman in the Indian civil service.[78] Carpenter's exposition of Hindu philosophy was quite different, however, as he used it as a source of inspiration in realizing his own desires for other men, which were valorized in this scripture.[79] Parminder Bakshi argues that Carpenter's affinity with Indian scripture and his sexual explorations with native men in Ceylon (Sri Lanka) were a particular form of Orientalism. The "homosexual predicament" in nineteenth-century Britain was one of the most extreme and compelling examples of the Western tendencies to draw exaggerated boundaries between Europe and the Orient. As Bakshi argues, "against the context of social and religious intolerance, homosexuals invariably turned to places and ideas outside English society that accommodated love between men."[80] As Ronald Hyam states in *Empire and Sexuality: The British Experience*, empire unquestionably gave European men an "enlarged field of opportunity" for sex. In many places, "local girls would offer themselves; or boys, especially in Ceylon. The white man's status put him in a strong position to get his way."[81] Carpenter's journey to Ceylon was undoubtedly a spiritual quest. He visited the Gnai Ramaswamy, a guru with whom he was to maintain a correspondence for many years. Sheila Rowbotham, in her biography of Carpenter, describes the exhilaration he felt at witnessing a Hindu festival at Tayapusam in Ceylon. The procession consisted of "hundreds of men and boys, bare-bodied, barehead and barefoot, but with white loin cloths all in a state of great excitement."[82] These encounters left him with the impression that this "primitive" culture felt no guilt about the body, and that spiritual energy was suffused with sexual energy.[83] Carpenter had a sexual affair with a young Singhalese man named Kuala. The combination of spiritual enlightenment and sexual fulfillment that appeared free from local censure left a powerfully enduring impression on him.[84]

For homosexual men with means, exotic imperial territories (and even some parts of southern Europe) formed a primitive "other" where sexual fulfillment could be found. Carpenter used his experiences rather differently in that he was inspired to live more openly as a lover of men back home in Britain. On his return from Ceylon, Carpenter met George Merrill, a working-class man whom he described as "bred in the slums quite below civilization."[85] The two men became lovers in 1891, and after 1898, much to the consternation of Carpenter's enlightened inner circle of friends, they lived together at Millthorpe. This was an extraordinary step for him to take in the extreme censure in Britain against such relationships, and of course in light of its illegality; undoubtedly his isolation on his remote farm protected him from prosecution.

Carpenter's esoteric reinterpretation of the exotic sexuality to be found in Britain's imperial territories was highly idiosyncratic. However, the notion of exotic sexually ambivalent relations between men, and exotic sexually ambivalent relations generally, suffused the writings of English novelists such as E. M. Forster and Joseph Conrad and explorers such as Sir Richard Burton.

For many in Britain, the empire "was inconsistent with morality."[86] Concerns were expressed in the late-nineteenth century that the half-million personnel, mostly male, involved in maintaining the empire were at risk of "falling to the level of the immoral heathen" and forming "immoral relations with natives."[87] In Britain, social purity campaigns aimed at promoting sexual continence in men did so in the name of promoting racial purity and maintaining Britain's moral fitness to govern its empire.[88] As Hyam argues, by 1914, the concept of masculinity had been thoroughly redefined as signifying sexual restraint and "cleanliness," partly in the name of empire. It is significant that after the 1880s, moral and sexual continence were promoted in English public schools, as these provided the bulk of senior personnel for imperial governance.[89] In a society that promoted marriage as the only acceptable expression of sex, irrespective of class, and promoted British masculinity as the moral exemplar in a rapidly transforming world of competing imperialism with other European powers, most notably France, male homosexuality had no place. Even pejorative scientific recognition was anathema, for fear of advertising its existence.

European ideas on homosexuality in the age of empire were, in some significant respects, shaped through increasing levels of contact with exotic imperial territories. European homosexual men, especially British and French homosexual men, regarded the cultures of masculinity they encountered in imperial territories as sexually liberating, particularly in light of the social restrictions and opprobrium at home. Empire, in many respects, was a thoroughly masculine affair and in the late-nineteenth century attracted committed bachelors seeking adventure, including sexual adventure with men. Nonetheless, in the British Empire, the use of imperial territories for exploring sexual peccadilloes became less easy, particularly when legislation criminalizing sex between men (such as the Criminal Law Amendment Act of 1885) was not only exported to imperial territories but increasingly enforced during the twentieth century. In fact, the present-day illegality of male homosexuality in India is a consequence of this piece of British legislation remaining on the Indian statute books after independence, whereas in Britain, this legislation was dismantled from 1967 onward.[90] In Carpenter's affair with a young Singhalese man in Ceylon, the apparently idyllic setting for this relationship, "free from local censure," was illusory. Hector Macdonald, commander-in-chief of the army in Ceylon, shot himself following his exposure as a pederast by a white colonial tea planter in 1903. He was caught in a railway carriage engaging in acts of communal masturbation with four Singhalese boys. Macdonald had been promiscuous with Singhalese boys to a considerable degree, and this did not escape the attention of the white settlers, who disliked him intensely.[91] Interestingly, the story was kept out of the Ceylon newspapers, but when the story made the *New York Herald*, Macdonald killed himself—much to the relief of the British authorities, as this saved them from conducting a highly embarrassing trial. To be sure, Ceylon had its traditions of catamites at the temples and the "ubiquitous nude bathing boys on the beaches" who would offer themselves for sex.[92] Pejorative British attitudes toward male homosexuality, however, not only

FIGURE 3.5: Male nude, c. 1905. Photo of male nude posing with drapery from behind. Second prize winner for "Beate Plastique," Adrien Deriaz as featured in the magazine *La Culture Physique*, 1905. The nude's pose is based on "Perseus" by Canova and was featured in the chapter titled "Notre Concours de Beaute Plastique." Wellcome Library, London.

was pervasive among the increasing number of white settlers but also began to change the sexual morality and culture of masculinity of native peoples in imperial territories in the twentieth century.

Notions of race, civilization, and the separateness and superiority of white European Christian societies suffused the writings of the new discipline of sexology in the age of empire. Although serious differences between sexologists existed on the role civilization played in creating "perversions" such as homosexuality in men and women, all serious scientific thinkers regarded European civilization as the developmental epitome of human evolution. Sexologists attempted biological and psychological analyses of the homosexuals they found in the milieu of the city and created a new pathology of homosexuality. Homosexuality was a symptom either of civilization itself or of degeneration from the moral state to a form of "primitive" state in modern society, or simply through contact with the "primitive." With the exception of Symonds's clandestine and unpublished historicist and culturally relativist critique of scientific thinking, homosexuality as pathology in the white European male was considered in Eurocentric isolation, resulting in the treatment of the white European as distinct from the rest of humanity. Where non-Europeans were considered at all, either perversions were supposed to be absent in "primitives" or these "racially inferior" people were regarded simply as yielding to primitive quasi-animalistic instincts.

CHAPTER FOUR

Sexual Variations

LISA DOWNING

It is commonly acknowledged, after Michel Foucault's *The Will to Knowledge* (*La volonté de savoir,* 1976), that the nineteenth century is the epoch that produced, via the science of sexology, the construction of the normal and abnormal sexual subject, and that cataloged with taxonomical zeal the series of variations that so-called abnormality might take. Most often discussed in contemporary sexuality studies, given the predominance within this interdisciplinary field of the subdisciplines of gay and lesbian studies and of queer theory, is Foucault's assertion that the nineteenth century created the "personage" of the homosexual, defined in contradistinction to the heterosexual. This construction of a binary organization of sexual subjects based on the biological sex of object choice is, however, only one facet of sexual science's project of erotic nomenclature. Indeed, Foucault states that the nineteenth century was "the age of multiplication: a dispersion of sexualities, a strengthening of their disparate forms, a multiple implantation of 'perversions.'" He concludes: "Our epoch has initiated sexual heterogeneities."[1] One only needs to glance briefly at the table of contents of what is often considered to be the bible of nineteenth-century sexology, Richard von Krafft-Ebing's *Psychopathia Sexualis* (1886) to see this point amply borne out. Even homosexuality is not a single category here, as it comprises various subcategories, including "acquired homosexuality," "simple reversal of sexual feeling," "congenital homosexuality," and "Urnings," a term devised by Karl Heinrich Ulrichs (1825–1895), which itself is subdivided into types. And alongside this anatomy of forms of same-sex desire are found such perversions as masochism and sadism, fetishism, "violation of statues," rape and "lust-murder," and necrophilia.

In this chapter, my aim will be twofold. First, I shall consider the idea of variation alongside the underlying logic of binary thinking in sexology, since nineteenth-century medicine and its surrounding culture understood sexuality in terms of both organizational parameters (binary thinking on the one hand, multiplicity on the other). I will pay attention to the complexities and contradictions inherent in this system that held the logic of "either/or" in tension with multiplicity. Second, I want to demonstrate that medicolegal discourses alone were not responsible for constructing the variety of types and typologies of sexual practice and personage that emerged in the textuality of the nineteenth century. The producers of literature and art, as well as the compilers of medical texts, were preoccupied throughout the nineteenth century in Europe with describing, cataloging, and understanding sexual variations. As Mario Praz writes in his canonical study of the erotic imagination of the nineteenth century, "in no other literary period, I think, has sex been so obviously the mainspring of works of imagination."[2] Several studies show the influence of nineteenth-century medical models of sexual and gender variation on the work of creative writers of the nineteenth and early-twentieth centuries.[3] As well as discussing the ways in which some literary writers in the nineteenth century attempted to provide fictional case studies that would stand as equivalents of those case studies presented in sexological texts (the most obvious example, perhaps, being French naturalist Emile Zola [1840–1902], who corresponded with doctors about the psychosexual character sketches in his work), I shall look briefly at how other nineteenth-century literary texts offer alternative or parallel—rather than simply derivative or imitative—interpretative accounts of the meanings of sexual variation to those presented by medicine, especially Zola's near contemporary, the Decadent French female writer Rachilde (pseudonym of Marguerite Eymery [1860–1953]). In my exploration of some literary, as distinct from scientific, exegeses of sexual variation, it will become clear that forms of sexual knowledge and anti-knowledge were produced variously for attempts at edification, for satirical critique, and finally for resistant political strategies—what a Foucauldian would call "reverse discourse." Equally, the reactions of sexual science to this attempt on the part of creative writers to contribute to and expand knowledge and ideas about sexual variation will be considered. My aim, then, is to demonstrate the necessity of understanding the nineteenth century's conception of sexual variation as the product of a range of disparate discursive fields—dominant and dissident—and as a trope in a variety of textual and political strategies, rather than as the output of any single or authoritative disciplinary voice.

TWO OR MANY? SEXUAL VARIATION AND BINARY LOGIC IN RICHARD VON KRAFFT-EBING'S *PSYCHOPATHIA SEXUALIS*

The coexistence of a logic of binarism and a logic of multiplicity in the sexological understanding of sexuality is explicable if we take into account the fact that nineteenth-century sexologists operated using strictly dualistic categories of healthy/unhealthy, natural/unnatural, and normal/perverted, into which the vast range of sexual symptoms and behavioral phenomena with which they were presented were organized. Broadly, while certainly giving discursive currency to variation (listing a whole array of sexual practices and desires; subdividing these practices and desires into smaller and more precise variations within a theme; exhorting patients to confess at length the smallest and strangest details of their varied fantasies and pleasures, such that a given patient could end up falling under numerous diagnostic labels), nineteenth-century sexology had extremely limited ideas about what behaviors could fit on either side of the healthy-unhealthy, normal-perverted divide. That is to say, the attempt to expand the linguistic and imaginative lexicon of sexual variety was seldom identical to an attempt to broaden the scope of what could be considered to fall under the definition of sexual "normality." Even a homosexual liberationist like Ulrichs used his Platonic theory of Urnings (beings in whom the soul of one sex was supposed to be trapped in the body of the other) to argue—normatively to our contemporary mind, but strategically given the punitive legal culture of his time—that homosexuality was an innate abnormality that should not be punished by law but rather be explored by medicine. Ulrichs's work has been criticized for promoting the idea of inversion as intrinsic to homosexual identity,[4] that is, for suggesting that the model of desire operating between members of the same sex is derivative of heterosexuality, as the male Urning is one in whom the soul and body are of different sexes, and who is therefore making a heterosexual object choice in desiring a person whose sex is the opposite of that of his own inner soul or nature. This contributed to the persistent and damaging essentialist stereotypes of the effeminate homosexual man and the "butch" lesbian. It seems that the assumption of the natural inevitability of attraction between the two sexes was so ubiquitous in the nineteenth century that Ulrichs would have been hard pressed to conceptualize desire otherwise, even while expanding the range of variations on how covert hetero-desire might be made manifest.[5]

Arnold Davidson has shown that the introduction of the concept of perversion with reference to sexuality in nineteenth-century medical circles was
predicated on the dominant understanding of the human sexual instinct
as identical to the drive for reproduction, ensuring the preservation of the
species.[6] This understanding of the sexual instinct as reducible to the drive for
reproduction (obviously a legacy of theology, as much as an interpretation
rooted in biology or psychology) can be found in the work of the French
doctor Paul Moreau de Tours (1844–1908) and in Krafft-Ebing's *Psychopathia Sexualis*, which was heavily influenced by Moreau de Tours' *Des
aberrations du sens génésique* (1877), considered the first psychiatric work
on perversion.[7]

According to this narrow and somewhat utilitarian understanding of
the functioning of sexual instinct (always pulling toward the opposite sex,
because always seeking propagation of the species), everything except penetrative heterosexual intercourse would logically come under suspicion as

FIGURE 4.1: Richard von Krafft-Ebing. Pho-
togravure. Richard von Krafft-Ebing Collection. Wellcome Library, London.

abnormal or contra nature. Krafft-Ebing develops, from this basic principle, four classifications of sexual "anomaly": (1) sexual anesthesia, in which the desire for sexual activity is entirely lacking (e.g., frigidity); (2) hyperesthesia, in which the intensity of sexual desire is excessive (e.g., nymphomania); (3) paradoxia, in which the sexual instinct is present at an inappropriate (non-reproductively viable) age, (i.e., in infancy or very old age); and finally (4) paraesthesia, in which the sexual instinct does not lead to a reproductive act but instead turns aside (is "perverted") in the direction of some other act. Homosexual acts and perversions would both come under this category, given the narrow understanding of the "proper" nature of sexuality as always already reproductive.[8]

The result of employing these rigid definitional parameters around normality is the constitution of a self-fulfilling prophecy. It produces as an apparently observable fact the hypothesis of human sociosexual life that the sexologists most feared: abnormality, in taking so many forms, in being everything that is not the one thing that is "correct," appears to be everywhere endlessly proliferating and out of control. The *Psychopathia Sexualis* is, as the name suggests, a textbook about sexual malady, not sexual health. However, in excluding so much from the potential remit of "health" (an idea that is collapsed, as we shall see, onto ideas of moral virtue), it gives the unwitting impression that sexual pathology is more pervasive than sexual normality. This sleight of hand can be understood along the lines of Canguilhem's analysis of the concept of normality in early forms of modern medical and social science.[9] According to Canguilhem, "normality" was supposed to describe a hypothetical statistically "average man," what Vernon Rosario has called "a demographic construct rather than any particular person."[10] However, this construct soon came to be used not as a descriptive fiction but as a *pre*scriptive one, accruing moral weight. "Normality," in short, moved from meaning the most commonly occurring, or the statistical average, to meaning the ideal, with all the material impossibility suggested by the Platonic overtones of the term.

The introductory section of *Psychopathia Sexualis*, called in different translations of the German text "A Fragment of a Psychology of the Sexual Life" (translation of the seventh edition by Chaddock) and "Fragments of a System of Psychology of Sexual Life" (translation of the tenth edition by Rebman), is a programmatic account of ideal sociosexual behavior.[11] Krafft-Ebing opens with a eulogy to the strength and power of the instinct to reproduce: "The propagation of the human species is not committed to accident or the caprices of the individual, but made secure in a natural instinct which, with an all-conquering force and might, demands fulfillment."[12] However, he goes on to expand upon this as a potential problem:

> In coarse, sensual love, in the lustful impulse to satisfy the natural instinct, man stands on a level with the animal; but it is given to him to raise himself to a height where this natural instinct no longer makes him a slave: higher, nobler feelings are awakened which, notwithstanding their sensual origin, expand into a world of beauty, sublimity, and morality. On this height, man overcomes his natural instinct.[13]

The "height" of civilized feeling to which Krafft-Ebing refers finds its proper place in the religious and social institution of marriage, which is held up as the only appropriate domain for sexual expression. In this, Krafft-Ebing is very clearly paying lip service to religious discourses, perhaps in an attempt to overcome the suspicion of immorality that accrued to early sexual science owing to the nature of its object of investigation.[14] Sexuality here is seen as an ethical project, then, an achievement of civilization, that in and of itself stands at odds with the other idealizing discourse whereby a "normal" sexuality would approximate a "natural" sexuality.

The flawed logic of this extract is immediately obvious. It makes the following assertions: (1) the "natural instinct" to propagate the species is all powerful in all living beings; (2) human morality can enable "man" to behave differently from animals in the realm of sexuality; (3) healthy modern social sexuality is a triumph of culture overcoming natural instinct; and (4) natural instinct is therefore bad and must be converted to something good in marriage. If this message were not mixed enough, Krafft-Ebing's ambivalence with regard to the virtue of being "natural" is put in the shade by the evidence he himself then goes on to present to contradict his grandiose opening statement. The "problem" that his whole book sets out to address is precisely that of those sexual subjects in whom the powerful "natural" instinct to propagate the species seems to have been turned aside, leading them to seek out very different outlets. Given that he is using Moreau de Tours' model, whereby sexuality *is* the *instinct génésique* (reproductive instinct), rather than leading *to* it, a definitional and logical problem is intrinsic to Krafft-Ebing's discussion of sexual perversion. He nevertheless persists with it throughout, even when the fit between this understanding and the phenomenon described is obviously a poor one.

The manifestations of sexual variation that stand in the strongest tension with this narrow assumption about sexuality are those in which the content and object of the pleasurable act or fantasy are entirely dependent on an inanimate object (fetishism) or on an eroticized desire for destruction and death rather than for reproduction. Where some elements of perverse or abnormal behavior occur alongside the desire for, and ability to perform, coitus, this is seen as less of a problem, leading to the definition of sexual perversion that would run from nineteenth-century sexology through psychoanalysis to late-twentieth-century so-called progressive and constructionist sexual science, such as that associated with the late John Money (1921–2006). Namely, sexual variation is acceptably normal if it accompanies heterosexual coitus. If it replaces it, however, a problem occurs. The problem, I would argue, is of the order of epistemology and definition and is felt as such by the sexologist, not by the abnormal sexual practitioner. This is seen in abundance in Krafft-Ebing's text. Some milder forms of (male) sadism, for example, are seen as unfortunate side effects of man's nature, given the assumed inevitable aggressiveness of the masculine sexual instinct and the predatory behavior to which it may lead: "under pathological conditions, man's active *role* of winning woman may become an unlimited desire for subjugation."[15] Fetishism, similarly, may be a part of "normal" desire, as elements of fetishism can determine attraction, an idea suggested by French psychologist Alfred Binet, who coined the term "amorous fetishism" in 1887 and who is subsequently acknowledged by Krafft-Ebing for this contribution: "Binet deserves great credit for having studied and analysed in detail the fetichism [sic] of love. ... Thus one is attracted to slender, another to plump beauties, to blondes or brunettes."[16] Krafft-Ebing even goes so far as to use fetishism as an rationale for monogamy, as it may "explain the individual sympathies between husband and wife; the preference of a certain person to all others of the same sex."[17]

In perversions such as necrophilia (the eroticization of dead matter, or sexual contact or intercourse with a corpse) and lust-murder, however, both of which Krafft-Ebing discusses, the instinct for reproduction would at first seem to be completely absent from the acts performed. Krafft-Ebing performs tautologous logic here. He does not submit his definition of sexual instinct as the instinct to reproduce to interrogation, nor does he consider whether some of the acts he describes are appropriately cataloged under the remit of "sexual" aberrations. Instead, he attempts to make the variations fit the norm. When faced with a case of necrophilia in which a man killed a woman he was attempting to rape and then violated her corpse, he opines that "in certain cases there may be nothing more than the possibility that unbridled desire sees in the idea of death no obstacle to its satisfaction."[18] So overwhelmingly potent, then, is the natural instinct demanding the propagation of the species that sometimes it fails to take account of inherent stumbling blocks to the achievement of its aim (such as the death of the sexual object). So far, so good, perhaps. However, Krafft-Ebing also discusses cases of necrophilia in which the object has been so long dead as to effectively debar the plausibility of the act being in the service of the reproductive instinct. An example is the case of the infamous Sergeant Bertrand, the "vampire of Montparnasse," brought to trial in France in 1849, who sought out "preexisting" corpses rather than killing victims during sexual attacks and spoke during clinical interviews of erotically valuing those corpses precisely for their quality of deadness.[19] Krafft-Ebing concedes that in such cases as this, "there is undoubtedly direct preference for a corpse to the living woman."[20] Since this does not fit the description of sexuality he is working from, Krafft-Ebing can offer no consistent interpretative comments on this form of sexual variation, other than to say that power must play a part in the psychological aspect of the practice, as the corpse represents the ultimately passive object that cannot resist the necrophile's advances (persisting with the idea that necrophilia is an extension of sadism, a perversion that is understandable within the definition of "normal" male sexuality). *Vampirisme: Nécrophilie, nécrosadisme, nécrophagie,* a French medical thesis that appeared in 1901 by Alexis Epaulard, a student of French criminologist Alexandre Lacassagne, divides the perversion of necrophilia (as is the sexological wont) into a set of practices and fantasies exhibiting increasing degrees of violence, from "funerary fetishism," in which the pervert would be content merely to be surrounded by dead and funereal objects, through "necrophagy," where part of the corpse would be ingested, to "necrosadism," involving destruction of the body. Despite this finely differentiated set of necro-erotic behaviors, Epaulard, like Krafft-Ebing, is directed in his theorization by the belief that reproduction is the true unacknowledged aim of the behaviors he studies. He comments, "The instinct impels the subject toward coition, even with corpses,"[21] and calls these behaviors (even those that do not include genital penetration) "vampirism of genital origin."[22] German sexologist Albert Moll later corrected the tendency in much early sexological writing to overstate the proximity of sexual sadism and necrophilic perversions, pointing out that because a dead object is beyond the point of feeling pain or distress, the motivations of sadism appear to be inappropriately ascribed to erotic interaction with the dead.[23] In the example of necrophilia, as indeed of fetishism proper, and of "violation of statues," which are also discussed by Krafft-Ebing, the urge to propagate the species at all costs, which, as we have seen, is the working definition of sexuality for the time, seems to be patently absent—indeed irrelevant—leading us perhaps to a Foucauldian insight regarding the necessity to question the epistemological foundation for labeling so many disparate phenomenological, psychological,

FIGURE 4.2: Postcard. Richard von Krafft-Ebing Collection. Wellcome Library, London.

and physical manifestations of human behavior under the umbrella term "sexuality." For if sexuality really is no more than *instinct génésique*, why does Krafft-Ebing not create a new category in which to group the practices detailed in his nosography? This highlights how the field of knowledge constituted as sexuality in the nineteenth century is both fraught with ideology and riven with internal contradiction.

As well as organizing a range of pleasurable modalities around the problematic, narrowly defined, and uneasily overlapping criteria of normal/abnormal and natural/unnatural, the *Psychopathia Sexualis* also organized its gamut of perverse sexual acts around another contentious binary system—that of sex and gender. In the "Fragments" chapter, Krafft-Ebing makes a series of comments about the difference between (healthy) males and females who betray confusion with regard to the roles of nature and culture similar to that we saw in his description of civilized man's ethical duty to tame the reproductive instinct by giving it free rein only within the strictures of marriage. Krafft-Ebing makes it clear that the "natural instinct" for reproduction (that is, as we have seen, identical to the sexual instinct) is natural only for men in his schema. Woman's "nature," on the other hand, inclines toward romantic love that is "more spiritual than sensual,"[24] leading to monogamy and the wish to bear a child in wedlock, since "if she is normally developed mentally and well bred, her sexual desire is small. Were this not so the whole world would become a brothel."[25] It is hard to ignore the neat conflation of distinct biological and social ideologies in this statement. Mental and physical female nature are attenuated by the class-bound idea of upbringing, and the notion of good breeding implies not only "proper" socialization into the female role, but also birth into a family free from the taint of degeneration—as the ideas of heredity and degeneration dog the pronouncements of nineteenth-century sexology on sexual and gendered health and illness.[26] Whereas Krafft-Ebing's abnormal or unnatural male subject obstructively fails to obey the *quidditas* of (male) sexuality (the reproductive instinct), the abnormal or unnatural woman would be the one who has too much desire or a desire that is inappropriate to her sex (for which the twentieth century would read "gender role"). Women, then, are the guardians of male morality in this system, since "the weakness of men in comparison with women lies in the great intensity of their sexual desires,"[27] and since "base" sexual urges only become "civilized" when man mates with a monogamous partner in marriage. To wit, in marriage, "to the barbarous sensual feelings of sexual desire the beginnings of ethical feeling are added."[28] Because of women's assumed passivity and desire to submit to men, the presence of masochism in women is like that of sadism in men—an unfortunate extension of their nature that needs to be tempered by civilized morality, but that does not lie outside the natural order of things: "under pathological conditions [masochism may] become a perverse, pleasurable desire for subjection to the opposite sex, which … represents a pathological degeneration of the character (really belonging to woman) of the instinct of subordination, physiological in woman."[29] Masochism, in moderation, is so appropriate to the feminine role that unless it is extreme in kind or takes the form of a woman actively and promiscuously seeking out the sadistic services of another, it barely deserves the label of "variation" or "abnormality," though many feminist commentators have pointed out that, as the notion of sexual instinct in nineteenth-century sexology is so obviously based on the assumed model of male desire, the very idea of female desire would already constitute a deviation from the norm. The women who pose the biggest problem for the nineteenth-century taxonomist, then, are those whose perversion is not merely an inappropriate *extension* or intensification of the nature of their sex (masochism) but a deviation from it and an inappropriate encroachment on the masculine. Similarly, those men who fail to live up to the imperative of active, aggressive masculinity are presented as aberrant problems. This is in ample evidence if we note that whereas (in the tenth revised edition) Krafft-Ebing discusses twenty-seven case studies of male masochism, only two cases of female masochism are documented. Sadism and masochism are paradigmatic of the ways in which logics of binarism and variation coexist in sexology—they operate as a set of deviant fantasies and practices, each subject to infinite variation, but also as a complementary pair, as reciprocal perversions—what Krafft-Ebing calls "perfect counterparts"[30]—just as male-female desire is assumed to be. The extent, in fact, to which these perversions are to be understood as adumbrating heterosexuality can be seen in Krafft-Ebing's basic definition of masochism as always already heterosexual: "the distinguishing characteristic in masochism is certainly the unlimited subjection to the will of a person of the opposite sex ... with the awakening and accompaniment of lustful feeling to the degree of orgasm."[31] As in the logic of inversion for Ulrichs, forms of deviation from heterosexual coitus can only be understood with reference to or by analogy with it, as the yardstick of sexuality proper.

TEXTUAL/SEXUAL VARIATION: LITERARY COUNTERPARTS AND COUNTEREXAMPLES

The extent to which sexology and psychoanalysis make reference to literature as a source of knowledge about sexual proclivities, fantasies, and practices has been widely commented on in histories of these respective disciplines. An oft-cited example of this is the fact that the names of literary authors Donatien-Alphonse-François (the Marquis de Sade [1740–1814]) and Leopold von Sacher-Masoch (1836–1895) are inscribed in sexological manuals as the terms for the perversions of, respectively, sadism and masochism. However, where Freud argues that literature can tell us much about the workings of the unconscious and has therefore contributed to literary studies from a psychoanalytic critical perspective, sexologists such as Krafft-Ebing were often suspicious of literary creativity in its more avant-garde or explicit forms. About Sade's copious writings he remarks in a footnote to *Psychopathia Sexualis* that "fortunately it is difficult to-day to obtain copies."[32] There is a certain irony here, since a Sadeian text such as *The Hundred and Twenty Days of Sodom* (*Les 120 journées de Sodome ou l'école du libertinage*, 1785), which catalogs a series of sexual variations ranging from the merely bizarre (e.g., fetishizing the flatulence and feces of a prostitute) to the violent and eventually murderous, resembles nothing so much as the structure and contents of Krafft-Ebing's manual of sexual medicine. The purpose of the two texts may be ostensibly very different: Sade's to titillate and to illustrate a nihilistic philosophical treatise, the sexologist's to edify, taking care not to titillate by rendering particularly shocking details in Latin to make them incomprehensible to the non-educated layman. However, the fact remains that it is the convention of ascribing generic difference to texts—another function of the taxonomic imagination—that constructs the distinction between these two works, both of which are characterized by enumeration and descriptions of varied sexual practices. Foucault comments that while Sade was writing in the eighteenth century and in the broad tradition of libertinage (though taking this to previously unknown extremes of brutality), his taxonomic imagination is resolutely modern, making his work a bridge between eighteenth-century libertine conventions that celebrated the art of plural sexual pleasures and the nineteenth-century fashion for proliferating sexual pathologies and forms of knowledge about them. In this way he "holds sway precisely on their frontier."[33]

FIGURE 4.3: *Justine*. Frontispiece illustration. Marquis de Sade, *Justine ou les malheurs de la vertu* (Libraries Associes Hollande, 1791). Frontispiece Collection, Rare Books. Wellcome Library, London.

The naturalist school of writing in France in the late-nineteenth century sought to overcome this tendency to differentiate between works of fiction and works of science. Zola was a keen reader of contemporary medical theses. In particular, he was fascinated by French and German sexology, by the degeneration theory of Max Nordau (1849–1923), and by the attempts of Italian criminal anthropologist Cesare Lombroso (1835–1909) to classify and catalog inborn criminality and deviant moral, psychological, and sexual nature by means of anthropometry (or reading physical characteristics as revelatory of psychological ones).[34] Zola's novel *La bête humaine* (1890) sketches case studies of a lust-murderer, Jacques Lantier, named after Jack the Ripper,[35] and of a woman, Flore, who has inappropriately active "masculine" traits and a pathological sexual jealousy that leads her to kill. Zola sent the novel to both Lombroso and Nordau, with very different results. Delighted to have a novelist popularizing his theories, Lombroso wrote approvingly of the physiognomical characterization of Zola's dramatis personae. Noting that Zola's anti-hero is described as a "handsome boy with a round and regular face marred only by a jutting jaw,"[36] he remarked that "Jacques Lantier certainly has some anatomical characteristics of the inborn criminal."[37] Lombroso even carried out a study of Zola's own cranium in an attempt to better understand the exceptional figure of the imaginative genius.

Nordau, meanwhile, felt that naturalist literature was a cause of degeneration, not a means of enlightening the population about it, and Zola's novels were among those that he condemned most forcefully. Nordau strongly believed that degenerate art, as he termed naturalism, was rooted in the "sexual psychopathology" of its creator. In the context of a system in which artists and writers were seen to bear strong resemblances to the mentally ill, Nordau was able to write of novelists that, like "all persons of unbalanced minds," they "have the keenest scent for perversions of a sexual kind."[38]

Zola's study of Jacques Lantier faithfully pursues the belief in the *instinct génésique* as the definition of all sexuality that we have already examined in Krafft-Ebing. Here too even a practice as deviant as lust-murder is understood by reference to the yardstick of intercourse. Just as Krafft-Ebing explains the psychology of lust-murder as "the sadistic crime alone becom[ing] the equivalent of coitus,"[39] so Zola provides the following account of Jacques Lantier's erotic development:

> Kill a woman, kill a woman! This refrain rang in his ears, from his earliest years, with the increasing, maddening fever of desire. As others, at the onset of puberty, dreamed of possessing a woman, he was excited by the idea of killing one.[40]

Zola only deviates from conformity to the accepted medical understanding of the motivation for this perversion once, but Lombroso is quick to point it out in what is otherwise an admiring study of Zola's work. He notes that Zola's portrayal was not thoroughly psychologically accurate, as the "real" murderer with a hereditary predisposition to lust killing would never be able to enjoy sexual intercourse with a woman without feeling the need to kill her, as Jacques is shown doing in his early encounters with his lover, Séverine.

We can argue that Zola makes this decision for reasons that are purely literary. (Novelistic generic conventions demand an *amour fou*.) He effectively sacrifices psychological "accuracy" here, then, in favor of a dramatic plot device. This highlights, perhaps, one of the ways in which literature's function may force its author to deviate from that of science cum social theory, however determined that novelist may be to represent faithfully the theories in question. Moreover, the fact that Zola is operating in a literary rather than purely scientific genre allows him to imagine the possibility of complex sexual subjects that we do not often find in sexological manuals. Flore, the masculine woman, "virgin and warrior, contemptuous of the male,"[41] is also a fetishist of bloodshed with sadistic tendencies, somewhat like Jacques: "she had a fascination with accidents."[42] Zola draws a portrait of the traditionally feminine woman, Séverine, as a counterpart to the inappropriately masculine and active woman, Flore, and their natures are narratively confirmed by their destinies: Séverine will be Jacques Lantier's murder victim, while Flore will commit suicide by walking in the path of an oncoming train—like a warrior going to battle—after having committed mass murder.

However, while Flore is presented as an unnatural, masculine woman, she is not constructed as a lesbian, uncoupling, perhaps, the idea of masculinity in a female from that of attraction to other women; indeed, the object of Flore's attraction is Jacques. This is perhaps surprising, as in a letter to Dr. Laupts on the nature of the homosexual, Zola recapitulates Ulrichs's notion of homosexuality as the soul of one sex in the body of another and reproduces the caricatures of the homosexual that issue from an understanding of sexual inversion: "the effeminate, delicate, cowardly man; the masculine, violent, insensitive woman."[43] The fact that this is Zola's idea of a female invert suggests that he has somehow got Flore's orientation wrong. A different way of interpreting this "getting it wrong" is to pursue the idea that literature can do more subtle things with conventional contemporary understandings of sexual variation, using metaphor, and may even correct some assumptions in the science to which it alludes. It is possible to argue that Flore's desire parallels a homosexual orientation, even while she is not defined as homosexual according to the sex of her object choice. If she is to be understood as having the soul of a (masculine) warrior in the body of a woman, Flore's desire for bloodthirsty inborn killer Jacques Lantier may complicate the sexological understanding of the invert. Flore desires someone whose body is other to hers, but whose soul is of the same kind (violent, sadistic). One active sadistic agent desires another, *regardless of* bodily sex, it seems, suggesting that desire for the same may be a valid model for imagining orientation, even as the dominant contemporary understanding of homosexuality bases it, as we have seen, on heterosexual principles. Thus, the paradigm of sexual difference is displaced by the model of activity/passivity, retaining a problematic binarism, but uncoupling it from ideas of natural masculinity and femininity. So, while adhering as closely as possible to the orthodox tenets of sexology, degeneration theory, and criminology, Zola's literary license allows sometimes for more imaginative models of deviant desires and genders than we would find in Krafft-Ebing.[44]

If these deviations from medical orthodoxy are accidental or unconscious results of the creative process in Zola, Rachilde constructs models of sexual excess and deviation that are deliberately contentious, especially in their determination to challenge reactionary ideas about the meanings of the gender and sex binarism. Rachilde was a self-proclaimed Decadent writer, where Decadence was an aesthetic and philosophical badge, rather than a pathologizing ascription by the medical profession of moral decay to certain forms of fin-de-siècle art and writing. If the medical sciences feared the deterioration of morals and the threat to civilized society that they believed degenerate phenomena to pose, Decadent writers celebrated those very threats.

The only female writer in the French Decadent movement, Rachilde was excluded from the canon of literature and from serious scholarly study until about thirty years ago. Since the efflorescence of critical interest in this author, she has often been considered, like Zola, to be writing texts that seek to approximate sexual science. Her biographer, Claude Dauphiné, wrote in 1991 that her works should be considered "literary illustrations of manuals of sexual psychopathology."[45] This understanding—I would argue misunderstanding— presumably issues from the fact that Rachilde's texts take as their primary subject matter sexual variations such as same-sex desire, cross-dressing, fetishism, sadism, lust-murder, and necrophilia. However, her textual strategies are very different from Zola's, and—one can argue—the politics of her textuality set her apart from the naturalist project to approximate science and constitute instead a complex resistance to normalizing discourse that, while politically ahead of its time, is aware of, and plays with, the ideas of the day regarding the nature of men, women, and sex itself.

The titles of Rachilde's novels suggest the kind of games with sexual knowledge that she wishes to play. Many of these focus on gender inversion. So, *Monsieur Vénus* (1884), a novel banned on publication in Belgium for obscenity, ascribes the attributes of the goddess of love to a biologically male character. It depicts a beautiful, effeminate young man who is the love object of a powerful, wealthy, dominant female aristocrat. The novel closes with the death of the young man, a death that—in a gesture that references and mocks the cases of fetishists and necrophiles discussed by Krafft-Ebing—provides no stumbling block to the all-powerful determination of the heroine's passion, as she commissions a life-size sex doll of her love object, into which she incorporates his real hair and nails, that she visits nightly for carnal pleasure. Here, the subject possessed of the sex instinct so strongly that obstacles such as death cannot stand in the way of its pursuit is a female—a possibility that would be unlikely to occur to the normative and one-dimensional stereotype of the woman in

FIGURE 4.4: A woman riding a man, on all fours, like a horse. Sexual role play. Photograph c. 1880s, Richard von Krafft-Ebing Collection. Wellcome Library, London.

sexology texts. Similarly, the titles of other works such as *La marquise de Sade* (1887) and *Madame Adonis* (1888) demonstrate Rachilde's reliance on a mechanism of inversion (not to be understood as identical to inversion as homosexuality, but as the disturbance of the supposedly inevitable and correct relationship between biological sex and gender roles). The inversion of expectations of gender within sexual interactions and desires occurs in Rachilde's writing, however, not so much to question whether "natural" sexuality exists as to *celebrate* the idea of the unnatural that Decadence prized as superior to the natural.

In the novel that is perhaps the most referential (and the most mocking) of sexual science and contemporary medical discourse, *La marquise de Sade*, Rachilde imagines the *education sentimentale* of a young woman, Mary Barbe, who grows up with a sadistic and murderous sexuality. The difference between Zola's intentions and Rachilde's is exemplified by the fact that where Zola seeks approval from doctors for his portrayal of sexual perverts, Rachilde targets doctors in her novels as objects of mockery and, indeed, presents them as far from exempt from sexual perversion themselves. Mary's uncle, Dr. Barbe, for example, is fascinated by the similarity between Mary's thumb, which reaches the top joint of her next finger, and that of the hand of a murderer cut from the gallows. This feature, thought to reveal inherent criminal tendencies—a nod to Lombroso's anthropometry—should awaken consternation in the good doctor but instead causes him to become enamored of his niece, revealing him to have incestuous as well as rather macabre sexual preferences. The black humor and satire of this episode are an attempt, perhaps, to reveal the fallacy of the moral rectitude and incorruptibility of medics—a belief demonstrated by the common fact of describing salacious details in sexology manuals in Latin, making them comprehensible only to the educated.

La marquise de Sade is also concerned with dethroning assumptions about women's natural desire for marriage, monogamy, and children. On her wedding night, Mary Barbe announces to the husband she will subsequently poison that reproduction will have no place in their marriage: "Louis, I have decided not to give you an heir. ... I don't want to get ugly, or to suffer. And what is more, *I am sufficient*, JUST BY BEING. And if I could make the world end with me when I die, I would do so."[46] The solipsism and self-possession of the perverse woman is at odds with anything seen in texts of medical science. Rachilde ensures that Mary's stance is not explicable as a form of frigidity—about the business of sexual intercourse, we are told that Mary "had neither the prudishness of a young girl nor the tastes of a prostitute, but rather an indifferent nonchalance."[47] Rachilde thus expresses something that is contrary to the very foundations of nineteenth-century sexual medicine—the idea that sexual intercourse may simply be a matter of disinterest to a given psychosexual subject, neither the object of the single-minded instinct as it is described for men nor the necessity to which women submit, despite their lesser sex drives, given their "natural" desire for a baby. Rather, Rachilde's perverse characters refuse the idea that desire and pleasure have anything at all to do with *instinct génésique*—whether as a "turning aside" from it in perversion or as an attempt to replace it with something else (as in Jacques Lantier's instinct to kill, which stands in place of the instinct to procreate).

Finally, the extent to which Rachilde's textuality can be seen as an example of reverse discourse is found in the closing chapter of *La marquise de Sade*, which details the now-widowed Mary's descent into a Decadent underworld. The chapter is rich with intertextuality, paraphrasing a passage from Sade's "Français, encore un effort" in *La philosophie dans le boudoir* (1795), which concerns young men who dream of killing their mothers as soon as they have raped them.[48] But as well as referencing Mary's eponymous namesake, Rachilde lists a series of her perverse recreational activities, activities that could be taken directly from texts by Nordau or Krafft-Ebing as symptoms of the degenerative society and individual. And, tellingly, these include, alongside reading sensationalist reports of murder trials and visits to the morgue, "naturalist novels."[49] That Rachilde should cite the kind of writing that Zola produced as likely to stimulate her protagonist's murderous appetites demonstrates an acute awareness of the suspicion felt by Krafft-Ebing and Nordau of literature—and mocks, perhaps, the attempts of Zola to ingratiate himself with the German physician and social critic. In its self-awareness and its irreverence, then, Rachilde's writing constitutes a kind of queering *avant la lettre* of the medical discourses of sexual variation that surrounded her and influenced the thinkers and writers of her epoch.

CONCLUSION

The dogmatic claims about the truth of healthy sexuality and its plural unhealthy counterparts made throughout the nineteenth century can, when carefully read, be shown to contain tensions, contradictions, and logical problems. When Krafft-Ebing writes that love transforms the brutal, lustful feelings that are (man's) natural instinct toward the woman, he adds that at this point "the instinct is intellectualized."[50] A "natural," "primitive" instinct turns in the direction of sociable impulses and becomes part of the cement of civilization through its subjugation to the institution of marriage. What Krafft-Ebing is unable or unwilling to see, however, is that the same argument could be made—harnessing his own obvious ambivalence about all that is "natural," given its proximity to animality—for the moral superiority of the perversions in all their variety. The capacity of human Eros to adapt itself to individualistic narratives and talismans of desire that have no apparent natural or productive value could equally be understood as the mark of a non-animal sexuality. This is the kind of idea that we see emerging in the work of Rachilde, whose *Überfrau* Mary Barbe rejects the imperative of reproduction as banal in comparison with the imaginative thrills of Decadence. The capacity of the instinct for pleasure to detach itself from the aim of reproduction and find a myriad of unrelated forms might, then, through a different ideological lens and with a different argumentational aim be interpreted as a most advanced achievement of human evolution.

I am not seriously suggesting that this is a valuable way of viewing sexual variation, that perversions should be thought of as higher up on the scale of evolution than reproductive sexualities. Indeed, these very value judgments about the use to which sexuality *should* be put, and this Platonic discourse of the ideal/the spiritual, as opposed to the bodily/the base, that disturbingly haunts ideas about human sexuality in the nineteenth century and after, are the target of my critical reading of the ways in which sexual variation is treated in the sexological texts of the nineteenth century. I merely allude to this possible reading against the grain of nineteenth-century arguments about what sex is, which oppose Krafft-Ebing's politics but push his logic to its own extreme limit, in order to show that the statements made in texts such as the *Psychopathia Sexualis* could, with a little tweaking, be used to make a very different political argument about "normal" and "abnormal" sexualities. To acknowledge this, of course, also involves an acknowledgement of the very prominent role of politics and ideology in informing the so-called scientific and neutral assertions about sex that proliferated in the Europe of the nineteenth century and, indeed, that continue to influence the theorization of non-normative sexualities in the social sciences and sexual medicine more than a century later.

CHAPTER FIVE

Sex, Religion, and the Law: The Regulation of Sexual Behaviors, 1820–1920

LOUISE A. JACKSON

In July 1902, representatives of sixteen Western nations met at the Foreign Office in Paris to draw up an international agreement to tackle the problem of the "white slave trade." Vociferous campaigner William Coote described it as the launch of "a holy crusade against the vice of men who would, in their selfish interest, besmirch the purity of the womanhood of the world."[1] Collaboration among governments, police forces, and voluntary bodies would involve the surveillance of railway stations and ports for evidence of sex trafficking, the exchange of information about "foreign" prostitutes and pimps, and the "rescue" of vulnerable young women and children. The campaign against white slavery illustrates how sexual continence had come to be viewed as a key marker of the extent of civilization and social progress by 1900 within Western public discourse. It is also indicative of the continued significance of religion in the regulation of sexuality. Finally, it shows that understandings of sexuality were based on social categories, including those of gender (assumptions about feminine purity), of "race" or ethnicity (whiteness required protection from the eroticized lure of the foreign), and of age (youth as a time of innocence). These understandings dramatically shaped responses and interventions, showing the extent to which lawmaking and law enforcement are culturally situated, and reflecting social values and assumptions.

This chapter will offer an overview of the mechanisms through which sexual behaviors were policed within Western nations and their empires, charting key shifts in the period 1820–1920.[2] It includes discussion of the formal institutions of the state (the law and enforcement agencies) as well as religious and voluntary societies and associations, but it also deals with the continued significance of informal community and neighborhood sanctions. The term "regulation" is used here to encompass the strategies of prohibition and punishment, containment, prevention, social condemnation, and circumscription. While the criminal law itself requires careful scrutiny, the social, economic, and political contexts that shaped it will be considered, as well as limitations on its effectiveness. Recent historical research has drawn attention to the relationship between strategies of sexual regulation and the organization of space and place.[3] Differences between urban and rural areas, the dichotomy of public and private as separate structuring concepts, and the relationship among local, national, and colonial agendas will all be touched upon. Regulation involved judgments as to specific sexual behaviors that were permissible between specific categories of people, often in relation to specific types of places. In terms of the criminal law and the delineation of sexual offenses, the legacy of the nineteenth century was significant, since it shaped the parameters of a legal system that in many cases were not challenged until the 1960s.

SHOCK CITIES

Existing histories of nineteenth-century sexuality tend to foreground the growth of the "modern" institution of the bureaucratic nation-state in western Europe and, in particular, its development in response to industrialization, urbanization, and population growth. By 1890 the population of London (the largest city in the world) had grown to over four million, New York had topped two-and-a-half million, and the population of Paris followed closely behind. The first half of the nineteenth century had seen significant urban expansion in Britain as "the first industrial nation," while the later decades of the nineteenth century produced steep increases in North American populations as a result of migration from Europe.[4] The problem of how, exactly, to manage increasingly concentrated masses of people through the organization and regulation of city space was a matter of concern for local as well as national and, ultimately, colonial governments. Where small rural communities were associated with social familiarity, it was soon assumed by contemporary commentators that the growth of cities was leading to anonymity and the loss of traditional ties and moral influences for a younger generation who had migrated for work. The early-nineteenth-century lack of sanitary and planning controls resulted in overcrowded living conditions, poor housing stock, and the spread of contagious diseases such as cholera, which was widely assumed until the 1850s to be airborne. From the 1830s onward social commentators linked the slum dwelling, deprivation, and disease they saw in Europe's largest cities with incest and sexual corruption. This medico-moral framework assumed that immorality, like disease, was contagious.[5] According to the French social scientist Eugène Buret, writing in 1840, "in the heart of the very busiest centres of industry and trade, you see thousands of human beings reduced to a state of barbarism by vice and destitution."[6] Governments were afraid "lest formidable dangers may some day burst forth from amid these degraded and corrupted people."[7] The prevalence of common lodging houses, in which strangers rented dormitory bed spaces for the night, also received regular criticism. For Friedrich Engels the "shock city" of Manchester, England, was a warning of what was to come for other less developed industrial centers. Despite his anti-capitalist analysis, he repeated rumors that linked poverty with sexual transgression, describing the city's common lodging houses as "the scene of deeds against which human nature revolts, which would perhaps never have been executed but for this forced centralisation of vice."[8] With the emergence of a bourgeoisie, or middle class, that identified itself closely with respectability and, in particular, the impeccable moral status of women, sexual incontinence was mapped onto a decadent aristocracy and an idle poor through the language of both class and race. Moreover, by the 1880s references to degeneracy were commonly used by social commentators to construct the poor as atavistic, depraved, and biologically distinct.[9]

Yet the bourgeois fear of the "great unwashed" who formed the mass of the urban poor led to little in the way of direct state intervention, although attempts by voluntary organizations to rescue and rejuvenate street children reflected an environmentalist approach that aimed to combat hereditary traits. Georges-Eugène Haussman's elaborate clearance of Paris to create the grand boulevards was motivated by a grandiose vision for the new French empire rather than the amelioration of the conditions of the poor, who were merely transported to ghettos on the outskirts of the city.[10] The late-nineteenth century saw the piecemeal construction of "model dwellings"; local case studies have shown these initiatives to have been more effective than any policing measures in razing brothels and common lodging houses.[11] Yet concerted state social

FIGURE 5.1: Overcrowding, and other sani-
tary derangements. *Builder,* June 14, 1862.
Slides 5958 and 5960. Wellcome Library,
London.

intervention—relating to the relief of poverty, the improvement of housing,
and welfare provision—remained controversial before the First World War.

Local urban authorities and corporations nevertheless attempted to play
a significant role in the design and delivery of urban governance through the
creation of local by-laws as well as the employment of police forces. The first
modern police forces of the early nineteenth century were concerned with
public order and the flow of traffic, including the clearing of city streets of all
obstructions to easy passage. Vagrants, as well as the drunk and disorderly,
required displacement and removal. Women known to be prostitutes became
targets of this form of street cleaning if, for example, they were behaving in
a "riotous or indecent manner" (1824 Vagrancy Act, England and Wales) or
were soliciting "to the annoyance of the inhabitants or passers-by" (1839 Metropolitan Police Act, London). Specific places such as parks, public squares,
and central thoroughfares were the focus of "clean-up" campaigns, while some
areas that were associated with prostitution—such as London's East End—saw

fewer arrests, as the poor were left to their own devices. Even if prostitution itself was not criminalized, women labeled "common prostitutes" were often made specific targets of public order legislation.[12]

Concerns about venereal disease (which were life threatening, given the lack of effective medical treatment) were also projected on to the figure of the female prostitute, who was viewed as the primary vector of disease. Debates centered on whether legal but state-regulated brothels might solve the disease problem. In Paris municipal regulations created a system of police registration and medical inspection that was, through the writings of Alexandre Jean Baptiste Parent-Duchâtelet, justified as a sanitary and medical response.[13] In England and Wales a form of regulation—through the Contagious Diseases (CD) Acts of the 1864, 1867, and 1869—was introduced in garrison towns partially in response to the Crimean War; these involved forced medical examinations of women assumed to be common prostitutes. Attempts to impose it upon other towns and cities were frustrated by the efforts of Josephine Butler and other campaigners who actively opposed the medical/scientific approach, which saw prostitution "as a necessary safety valve in a society in which men tended to marry late."[14] There were significant attempts to introduce CD Acts to a range of British colonies in the second half of the nineteenth century,[15] although they were "not simply or uniformly imposed" and were sometimes resisted or abandoned as unworkable.[16] Other forms of containment were adopted elsewhere. In the United States in the 1890s municipal authorities designated specific inner-city areas as red-light, restricted, or segregated districts, including New York's Tenderloin and New Orleans's Storyville.[17] While middle-class women were associated with the sanctity of the private sphere of home and family—which, in Britain and North America, was increasingly located in the secluded "safety" of the suburbs—prostitutes of the lower social classes tended to be viewed as "public" women or "wives" whose bodies and behaviors might be subjected to official scrutiny.[18]

In Britain the prominence of a liberal approach to governance (which emphasized minimal state intervention in both the market and family life) meant that a balancing act was constantly being attempted between individual freedoms and public surveillance in the name of a broader national interest. Individual autonomy was fiercely protected by the professional classes. In the spring of 1830, officers of London's newly formed Metropolitan Police made controversial use of covert surveillance tactics to clamp down on sexual activity between men in Hyde Park. When three defendants were tried for "assault with unnatural intent" (a phrase that was used to describe sexual acts between men that were not covered by the criminalization of sodomy),

FIGURE 5.2: The Lock Hospital, Hyde Park Corner, Westminster. Engraving c. mid-nineteenth century. Thomas Hosmer Shepherd after William Wallis. Wellcome Library, London.

the *Times* reported that lawyers in court "expressed the utmost indignation against the demoralizing system of policemen disguising themselves to ensnare the crime" (April 26, 1830). This was despite claims expressed by the chairman of the Bench in relation to a similar case heard a week previously that such offenses required punishment "to check the growth of evil and save the national character" (April 20, 1830). Demands were made for the introduction of distinctive police uniforms on the grounds that policing should be an open matter rather than the tool of a secret state apparatus (agents provocateurs). In a different context of the campaigns against the CD Acts and their implementation by the police, Josephine Butler made direct reference to "government tyranny" that flew in the face of a woman's "absolute sovereignty over her own person."[19] In subsequent decades, concerns that "respectable" women might be incorrectly arrested for soliciting led to further criticism of police methods. In a high-profile case of 1887, Miss Elizabeth Cass was incorrectly arrested on Regent Street, London, by Constable Endacott, leading to complaints that the police should not be acting as moral censors. As a result, arrests for prostitution-related offenses in London dropped by more than a half over the

following year.[20] The policing of street soliciting and importuning, as in the
case of other public order offenses, involved the exercise of considerable discretion. It never involved simply arresting all "offenders." Police forces might
issue informal instructions to officers to operate what might now be termed a
zero-tolerance policy targeted at certain areas of the city. Furthermore, decisions to arrest were often made on the spot by ordinary street constables, who
themselves wielded considerable levels of autonomy in deciding whether to
invoke judicial procedure or to dismiss with a warning. The policing of public
order offenses relating to immorality remained an issue of contentious debate,
as Stefan Slater's work on the policing of prostitution in London in the 1920s
has recently demonstrated.[21]

The context of the First World War led to a stepping up of the tactics
of sexual surveillance and regulation in Europe in a bid to prevent illegiti-
macy and the spread of venereal disease among the armed forces, to promote
women's status as virtuous mothers of the nation, and to counteract concerns
about social breakdown and moral degeneration. For troops in France, the traditional system of inspected brothels, or *maisons tolérées,* operated until 1918.
In Britain, anxieties about the spread of "khaki fever" among young women
who flocked to army bases as well as towns and cities in which soldiers were
concentrated led to the introduction of curfews and the setting up of voluntary
female police patrols. Made up of women of respectable middle-class status,
they patrolled railway stations, towns centers, parks, and major thoroughfares, separating young working-class women and servicemen through advice
and persuasion rather than formal powers of arrest. The controversial 40D of
the Defence of the Realms Act forced any woman to be medically examined,
under threat of fine or imprisonment, if more than one serviceman alleged
he had contracted a venereal disease from her. The CD Acts of the 1860s
had effectively been revived and applied to the entire female population, the
sexual double standard once again leading to the demonization of women.[22]

RELIGION AND THE VOLUNTARY SECTOR

The tension between the promotion of the state as moral arbiter and the rights
of the individual to self-determination within the privacy of the family was
to some extent resolved through the expansion of a third sector: voluntary
philanthropic organizations with close religious affiliations. Rather than relying on the law to regulate prostitution, the voluntary sector saw its role
as one based on moral persuasion and spiritual influence. Where the austere
Magdalen hospitals of the late-eighteenth century had sought to make sinners

into "penitents" through discipline, the newer institution of the Victorian "rescue home" aimed to save vulnerable young women who were either once "fallen" or in danger of "falling" through no fault of their own. Moreover, moral welfare work was seen in terms of "woman's mission to woman": it was assumed that the nobility and virtue of true womanhood would shine a spiritual light into troubled lives. A controlled environment of Bible study, needlework, and training in general domestic duties was designed to equip those "saved" for employment as domestic servants. Rescue homes were run along denominational lines by Catholic and Anglican sisterhoods and also by Jewish rescue organizations.[23] The Salvation Army emphasized its willingness to take young women from a range of denominational backgrounds; conversion was supported and encouraged but not assumed.

Increasingly, too, the voluntary sector worked closely with the state to deliver welfare provision to adolescent girls perceived to be in moral or sexual danger. As a number of recent studies have shown, from the 1880s onward

FIGURE 5.3: Midnight mission for fallen women, New York. Colored wood engraving. Wellcome Library, London.

legislation relating to the protection of children and young people also included provisions permitting young women under the age of consent to be
removed from their families and committed to institutional care.[24] In some
cases this involved rescue from abusive and violent family surroundings.
In other cases, mature young women of the urban poor (and in the United
States of immigrant families) were targeted for staying out late at night or
for exuberant behavior that was out of keeping with bourgeois notions of
feminine respectability. The rhetoric of "moral danger" reflected assumptions
about gender difference and the sexual double standard, since it was less commonly applied to boys. There has been considerable debate as to whether those
women who were involved in "rescue" work might be identified as feminist
and to what extent their interventions reinforced rather than challenged the
gender order. In depicting the women they worked with as "poor creatures"
requiring pity, they offered kindness and sympathy that also objectified. The
recasting of "deviant" women as "victims" to be saved—rather than social
"threats" to be locked up—still constructed them as "other" and disregarded
their own agency. From a realist position, however, it has been argued that
these women missionaries effected actual changes in women's lives, leading to
substantial material and physical improvement as well as exposing the realities
of sexual exploitation and violence.[25]

Effectively the nineteenth century saw a reconfiguration of religion and the
state through the growth of the voluntary sector of associations and societies.
The church had played an important structural role in the regulation of sexual
behaviors and reputations in the medieval and early modern period. Dealing
with "spiritual justice," ecclesiastical courts had heard cases involving matrimonial disputes (including accusations of adultery and fornication), incest,
and sexual slander (women were often prominent litigants defending their
reputations). Use of the church courts substantially declined in areas in which
they had been prominent in the nineteenth century (they were formerly dis-
solved in England in 1855) as secular courts took over their business (for example, through the development of divorce law in Protestant states).[26] There
were some anomalies: incest stood outside legal prohibition in England from
1855 until it was made a statutory offense in 1908. This general trend was not
a simple issue of the declining authority of the church, although their formal
regulatory function was clearly lost. Rather, evangelical groups emerged with
two important but related roles. First, as we have seen, they increasingly offered an important role as welfare providers, performing a social work function (both residential and "outdoor" work) where the state itself provided
minimal social services. Second, they went on to develop significant capacity

as campaigning and lobby groups in relation to state legislation relating to sexuality. The high point of this activity occurred between 1880 and 1914 as a coalition of social purity organizations (often with feminist support) put increasing pressure on governments to raise the age of consent. Their impact was significant as debates spread to colonial and imperial settings, as the next section of this chapter will demonstrate. Finally, in addition to lobbying, social purity organizations were also involved in the policing of the law, either by encouraging or instituting prosecutions (for sexual assault of minors or obscene publications, in the case of the National Vigilance Association) or through their own systems of surveillance of brothels (which were not always welcomed by police forces).

SEX CRIME AND THE RULE OF LAW

The nineteenth century saw significant changes in the criminal law relating to rape and sexual assault that arose from debates about the age of consent. The romantic ideal of childhood, which grew in influence from the late-eighteenth century onward, viewed children as innocents in need of protection from sexual knowledge and contamination. The first Societies for the Prevention of Cruelty to Children were founded in the 1860s (France and the United States) to protect child victims, to prosecute cases of abuse and neglect, and to campaign on issues relating to child welfare. In France the Code Pénal was revised in 1832 to make any attempt at sex with a child under the age of eleven punishable by five- to twenty-year prison sentence; this was raised to the age of twelve in 1863 (and twenty if the offender was a parent or guardian).[27] French forensic specialists Adolphe Toulmouche and Ambroise Tardieu were investigating the signs of sexual abuse on the bodies of both male and female children in the 1860s. Elsewhere, however, debates tended to focus on girl children only, a result of the preoccupation with virtuous femininity. In England and Wales the age of consent for girls was raised from twelve to thirteen in 1875, while the 1880s saw the emergence of orchestrated campaigns in Britain, its colonies, and North America to raise it further to sixteen.

Late-nineteenth-century campaigns to raise the age of consent brought together coalitions of social purity and feminist and child welfare activists. Social purity as an evangelical movement was concerned with the creation of a new moral order in the wake of fears about degeneration.[28] Purity involved the restriction of sexual impulses to the sanctity of holy (heterosexual) marriage and reproduction; in particular it emphasized the adoption of the same high moral standard by both men and women through the adoption of chivalrous models of masculinity. Sex itself was presented by social purity rhetoric in terms of the "sin" of "lust." The feminist movement of the mid-nineteenth century had already drawn attention to women's inferior position under the law, including their lack of protection from marital violence and the law's failure to recognize rape within marriage. The shift in the characterization of female prostitutes—from threat to victims—also drew attention to the plight of young women in general. Thus debates converged on the issue of consent to sex and on the complex issue of the age at which a female was sufficiently developed: physically, mentally, socially, and morally. Given their global significance, the debates surrounding age of consent and marriage provide an extremely useful lens through which ideas about age, gender, sexuality, race, and empire can be analyzed.

In 1885 the British newspaper editor William Thomas Stead published a sensationalist series of articles in the *Pall Mall Gazette* ("The Maiden Tribute of Modern Babylon") in which he alleged that girl children were being sold, purchased, and violated on the streets of London despite assumptions that it was the capital of a "civilized" nation.[29] The aim of the exposé was to ensure successful passage of the Criminal Law Amendment Bill, which included provisions to raise the age of consent for girls to sixteen, through the British parliament. Stead himself was accused of using underhanded investigative techniques and he found himself on trial at the Old Bailey accused, with his collaborators, of abduction and indecent assault. The publicity he generated ensured not only that the bill was passed but also that the debate spread across the globe; legislation in North America and the British colonies pursued similar trajectories. In New York, for example, the age of consent was raised from ten to sixteen in 1886 and further to eighteen in 1916. Recent research has shown, however, that debates in the British colonies were complex and varied. It was never the case that British rulers imposed age of consent legislation upon a colonized "other."[30]

For example, in Bengal, debates about age of consent merged with anxieties about the practice of Hindu child marriage, viewed by the British as a relic of a barbarous past. Discussion in both Britain and India in the 1880s was dominated by the divorce case of Rukhmabai, a Western-educated Hindu woman who refused to live with her uneducated, consumptive husband. She argued that the marriage, contracted when she was eleven, could be repudiated by her decision as an adult. Rukhmabai was threatened with imprisonment for not permitting conjugal rights; details of the case soon spread across Bengal and to Britain, where feminist campaigners such as Millicent Garrett Fawcett supported her cause. Rukhmabai's case was finally settled in 1888; she then moved to Britain to publicize the situation of women and children in India, appealing to the British government to intervene. The issue in her case was the contracting of marriage in childhood; in focusing attention on the family and sexuality, however, it also promoted debate about age of consent itself.[31]

The British government was, however, reluctant to interfere. British rule was deliberately based on a policy of non-intervention in matters relating to religion, the family, and the private sphere. The comments made by a former judge who had tried similar cases of annulment in British India for a period of thirty years before his retirement are revealing of both entrenched opinion regarding racial difference and a laissez-faire attitude:

> For a few cases where the rule [child marriage] works terrible wrong there are a thousand cases where it provides the girl with the home required. In an Eastern climate girls are precocious, and, unless early settled in her future home, the girl is almost certain to disgrace her family, and the result of such an event is either her murder or such loss of honour to the family that they will never be able to hold up their heads again. It is this feeling which makes the Indian opinion so decided against any change, and until this is got over, I fear we must elect to maintain their customs, however much they are opposed to ours. ... We shall not be acting justly to India if we too roughly set aside customs and rules which the experience of several thousand years has shown to be best for the general comfort.[32]

In India itself a range of viewpoints were articulated across the political and religious spectrum as attempts were made to raise the age of consent from ten to twelve. Hindu revivalist nationalists defended what they saw as a central component of religious practice; they argued that first intercourse was required at the onset of menarche (between the ages of ten and twelve) to prevent ancestral curses from falling on future offspring. Legislative change was supported, however, by a combination of Hindu reformists (seeking to modernize the religion from within), Liberal nationalists (seeking modernization to win the argument for independence), and Liberal Anglophones (who supported British rule). As the historian Tanika Sardar has convincingly demonstrated, the raising of the age of consent to twelve in 1891 was a result of political compromise among Bengalis rather than British regulatory intervention.[33] As the case of Rukhmabai illustrates, Indian women, far from being silenced, were active participants and campaigners.[34]

Ideas about racial difference—including white Western perceptions of Indian men as effeminate and degenerate and of Indian women and girls as prematurely sexualized—were exposed in debates relating to child marriage and were also manifest in the increasingly internationally focused campaigns against the "white slave trade" of the 1890s. These campaigns grew out of the coalitions and links that had been formed to raise the age of consent in Britain and North America; they often made use of the melodramatic language deployed by Stead in the Maiden Tribute articles, in which innocent femininity was cast against malevolent predatory masculinity. In pamphlets publicizing the prevalence of white slave trafficking in Britain and the United States, sexual danger was associated with men of Latin descent, both European and South American. Ice-cream parlors set up by immigrant Italians were typecast as recruitment grounds, while Buenos Aires was represented as the center of an international trade in young women.[35] The meaning of the "white slavery" metaphor was also contingent on the local. As Mara Keire has argued, it might be deployed to articulate progressive political agendas as well as racialist conservatism.[36] Thus U.S. urban reformers were using the language of white slavery in the years before the First World War to criticize the commercial interests that sought to maintain red-light districts; the metaphor of sexual exploitation was thus used to talk about economic exploitation.

What is notable, however, is that public debate about sexual assault focused on the vulnerability of youth, according its archetypical victim status. There has been considerable debate as to how adult women were positioned in terms of the criminal justice system. As the historian Martin Wiener has demonstrated in relation to England and Wales, male violence against women (including sexual violence) was increasingly problematized and condemned in nineteenth-century public debate. Within case law, notions of consent to sex were shifting as women's autonomy, self-determination, and status as individuals (rather than as the property of fathers and husbands) were recognized.[37] According to eighteenth-century medical jurisprudence it was impossible to rape an adult woman unless she was incapacitated by drink or drugs; active resistance was difficult to prove even when it could be demonstrated through torn clothing or severe physical injury.[38] Increasingly, however, verbal resistance and more minor forms of physical injury were viewed as evidence of sexual assault; there are even very rare examples of cases where women known to be prostitutes were able to bring successful prosecutions for rape.[39] These changes in women's legal status are important but they should not be overstated. Although Wiener's work suggests that more adult women were likely to use the courts to prosecute cases of rape in the nineteenth century than in the eighteenth, the vast majority of cases and, indeed, those most likely to secure conviction, were still those involving minors. In France, for example, during the late 1870s the victims in approximately 13 percent of sexual assault cases were adult women (the majority were minors).[40] In both France and England and Wales conviction rates were significantly higher in cases involving minors than those involving adult women. Moreover, the volume of prosecutions for sexual assault cases involving minors increased numerically as age-of-consent campaigns were publicized.[41] The sexual abuse of children tended to be associated with the poor, and successful prosecutions were most likely to be made against men of lower social class. Sigmund Freud linked neurosis among the Viennese bourgeoisie to childhood sexual trauma in published work of 1896 but later abandoned this theory; his reasons for doing so remain the subject of controversy.[42] The activities of the Societies for the Prevention of Cruelty to Children tended to focus on the slum areas of towns and cities; thus the families of the poor were more likely to be the object of surveillance than those of the bourgeoisie.

BEYOND THE STATE?

Because of the focus on cities that has driven research on the Western history of modern sexuality, we know surprisingly little about rural communities; continuities in rural areas tend to be assumed rather than tested. Historians also face the problem of bias in their sources. The official bureaucracy of the law was extremely efficient at recording legal process, which is why historians often turn to these types of records for their evidence.[43] The informal, the unofficial, and the ordinary are much harder to trace. The growth of the modern bureaucratic (and urbanized) state can certainly be associated with attempts by the authorities to persuade individuals and communities to make use of the formal mechanism of legal process to resolve disputes (and thus to police sexual boundaries). This came, to some extent, to replace older informal modes of community censure. Historians of early modern popular culture have analyzed the shaming rituals of "rough music" and *charivari*, which involved the beating of drums and pans as well as the theater of ritual inversion to mock and humiliate those who transgressed the gender and sexual order. Targets included "cuckolded" husbands who had failed to "tame" adulterous wives and, less frequently, wife beaters and those suspected of sexual offenses.[44] Certainly the symbolic ritual associated with the shaming ceremony was eroded in the nineteenth century. However, informal regulatory mechanisms as well

as the bonds of community action did not necessarily disappear, as those who
contrast the "modern" with the "traditional" sometimes suggest.

Within cities, individual neighborhoods were bound together by social proximity, the experience of poverty, and often powerful ethnic identities among
migrant groups. The notion of being part of a moral community with shared
values was expressed through informal regulatory mechanisms that included
gossip, ostracization, and verbal insult.[45] Oral history interviews relating to
early-twentieth-century Birmingham suggest that in "blatant" cases of incest,
"neighbours would give the man 'a bloody good hiding' and hold his head
under the communal stand-pipe while he was doused in cold water."[46] While
social commentators accused the poor of immorality as a result of overcrowding, evidence suggests that even families who shared one room often
partitioned it with a curtain to preserve a sense of personal modesty.[47] Moral
boundaries were policed even by those who had no choice other than to make
use of common lodging houses. In 1865 the *Times* reported on the case of a
male laborer who abducted a nine-year-old girl and took her to a notorious
lodging house on Flower and Dean Street in London's East End. The Irish
woman in charge asked "him if he was not ashamed of himself." Residents
took the law into their own hands: "some of the lodgers, indignant at the
prisoner bringing the child there, set upon him and struck him, upon which
he ran out of the house leaving the child behind."[48] The law was sometimes
invoked as a final resort after other tactics had been deployed. Moreover,
mob rule sometimes held sway when the courts acquitted individuals whom
the community wanted to see punished. In May 1880 a female mob gathered
outside Thames police court, threatening to lynch a German man alleged to
have forced a young woman into prostitution (the case had been discharged
by the magistrate).[49] Disturbing accounts of the use of mob violence can be
found in relation to the lynching of black men in the southern states of the
United States as a tactic to preserve racial purity and prevent miscegenation.
As Vron Ware has demonstrated, the language of "rape" was used to condemn what were in fact interracial relationships between consenting adults,
to justify murder, and to reinforce white supremacy in the decades after the
abolition of slavery.[50]

As the work of Michel Foucault has shown, an understanding of the ways
in which citizens learn to govern or regulate themselves is crucial and fundamental to any study of the mechanisms of rule in the modern state. Religious
discourse continued to have huge importance as a system of moral and ethical
knowledge about the relationship between self and the world, which was articulated through the language of sin, sanctity, and redemption. Increasingly, too,

FIGURE 5.4: Three London scenes titled "Love," "Law," and "Physic": a man being cajoled by two prostitutes, a young man being accosted by two debt-collectors, and a physician attending a patient. Colored etching by John Sheringham after George Cruikshank, 1821. G. Humphrey, London (28 St. James's St.). August 28, 1821. Wellcome Library, London.

scientific, medical, and (from the 1880s onward) psychiatric and sexological classifications demarcated behaviors in terms of normality and deviancy. These languages were to some extent absorbed, often gradually, into a broader popular culture, thus affecting an individual's assessment of self and others. Historians tend to agree that the late-nineteenth and early-twentieth centuries saw an increased delineation of specific sexual identities—including the construction of "the homosexual" and "the pedophile" as categories of perversion—which were suggestive of particular types of persona, interiority, or selfhood.[51] It is important, however, not to overstate the influence of these new scientific categories, and also to recognize continuities with the early modern period. As Anna Clark has recently argued, the dangers and pleasures associated with some forms of transgression were not clearly articulated but continued to be veiled by rumor, silence, and secrecy. She suggests the concept of "the twilight moment" to refer to behaviors that were neither condoned nor condemned as dangerous; examples include the passing on of folk remedies for abortion, the collection of erotica by wealthy "gentlemen," sexual relationships between white masters and their black female servants, and sexual acts between women that were "barely visible and only half understood."[52] Similar forms of behavior—although crucially differently constituted in terms of the dynamics of gender, race, and class—emerged as focal points of "moral panic" when the wider social order was perceived to be threatened; examples include interracial sex between white women and black men, the sale of "obscene" publications to lower social classes, and the criminalization of male homosexuality amid discussions about national and social purity.

Foucault's frameworks of analysis have, importantly, drawn attention to the "positive" (rather than repressive or prohibitive) effects of sexual knowledge/regulation in actively constructing "deviant" subcultures, practices, and identities. Studies of gay or queer communities in London and New York have depicted interactions between the police and the policed as mutually constitutive, particularly in relation to the use of urban space. As the Hyde Park episode cited earlier demonstrates, the police targeted particular areas or "hunting grounds" associated with particular groups; their activities led to displacement, reconfiguration, and the appropriation of other areas of the city. Moreover, queer identities were shaped by and in opposition to external social pressures and discourses. The law as regulatory framework generated tactics of resistance that aimed to circumvent its purview. The use of "polari" (cryptic slang widely used by London's queer community by 1920) and the often-subtle coding of identity through dress, grooming, cosmetics, and deportment were responses to surveillance aiming at secrecy and concealment, but they also created a sense of shared culture among an illicit group.[53]

Finally, it is also necessary to recognize the limitations of modern systems of surveillance. The sociologist Jeff Hearn has argued that "private patriarchy," the early modern assumption that a man's home was his "castle," was gradually replaced beginning in the mid-nineteenth century by a system of "public patriarchy" whereby a male-dominated state bureaucracy assumed control of the formerly private realm of the family.[54] Yet, as the discovery of the prevalence of child sexual abuse in the United States and Europe in the 1980s demonstrated, the majority of private homes continued to escape surveillance. While the principle of state intervention was to some extent won by the late-nineteenth century its delivery has only ever been piecemeal and has been subject to considerable volatility.[55]

CONCLUSION

As Foucault has argued so convincingly, the Victorians, far from being repressed about sex, were involved in extensive debate about its control, regulation, and channeling. During the course of the nineteenth century the criminal law was increasingly deployed with the aim of restricting sexual intercourse to heterosexual encounters between consenting adults. One of the most significant and lasting effects of the Victorian period was the protection of children and young people through the further development of age-of-consent legislation. While it is often suggested that child sexual abuse was discovered in the late-twentieth century, significant steps were taken to legislate for its prevention in the late-nineteenth century. Yet the desire to protect was bound up with a will to control, which involved the maintenance of a social order structured by assumptions about gender, class, and race. Strategies of prevention were typically used to control the activities of young women. During wartime in particular, the idea that a nation's strength was founded on the sexual continence of its mothers and daughters was pushed to the fore. The period 1820–1920 saw the expansion of the evangelical voluntary sector as a moral welfare provider and lobbyist for state legislation relating to sexuality, most specifically to protection of the young. The laissez-faire approach of the first half of the nineteenth century was gradually replaced with a more interventionist strategy, although this was not without negotiation and challenge. The state's determination to contain and manage sexual behaviors—and the underlying assumption that intimate behaviors were a matter of public concern—was, arguably, not overhauled until the turn toward more "permissive" legislation from the 1960s onward; in this sense, then, the Victorian legacy lasted well into the twentieth century.[56] As this chapter has also demonstrated, however, older informal community modes of regulation survived as striking continuities with a preindustrial past and, indeed, acted on occasion to criticize or oppose the intentions of statute law.

CHAPTER SIX

Sex, Medicine and Disease: From Reproduction to Sexuality

CHIARA BECCALOSSI

Medicine has an established tradition of addressing problematic desires: for a long time "sexual aberrations" were associated with mental illness; seduction, rape, sodomy, and hermaphroditism were conventional concerns of forensic medicine. The spread of venereal contagion has constantly compelled physicians to look at the consequences of various sexual behaviors. However, since Michel Foucault argued that the modern notions of sexuality emerged when nineteenth-century medical science delimited sexual deviance, historians, following Foucault's insight, have drawn extensive attention to the role of medicine in shaping ideas about sexuality in Western thought.[1] Much of this research has been devoted to the appearance of various "perversions," especially homosexuality, as disease categories.[2]

While there is no definitive and *longue durée* history devoted to the different aspects of the medicalization of sexuality, historians agree that in the nineteen century there was a growing medical interest in sexual behaviors. This phenomenon was connected to the increasing professionalization of medicine and the new key role that doctors came to play in the government. Nineteenth-century Western politicians, in part reacting to economic and military factors, became preoccupied with the health of the population and called for some forms of medical policing in industrial cities and barrack towns. Thus, governments took responsibility for the administration of public health and regulated medical practices and institutions. In turn, preoccupations with the size of the population meant that doctors had to pay attention to patterns of reproduction, and sexual activity in general became an area of concern. Anxiety over public health issues, in particular those related to sexually transmitted diseases, problematized sex in a new way by linking it to economic and social issues. It is worth noticing that despite the fact that nineteenth-century medicine was increasingly an international enterprise, it nevertheless developed in well-defined national contexts in response to local concerns. In the same way, medical sexual knowledge, despite being characterized by an increasingly international cosmopolitanism, also displayed national overtones.

Although what should be considered healthy sexual behavior had long occupied Western medical thought, in the nineteenth century physicians grouped together a series of sexual issues and made them the object of intense specialized analysis unparalleled in previous medical study. The aim of this chapter is not to explore the interplay of sexual medical knowledge with politics, morality, religion, philosophy, gender, and the broad culture of sexual identity. Instead, this chapter will provide an overview of how different branches of medicine contributed to the emergence of sexuality as a critical problem for science—which is not to say that medical knowledge about sexuality is monolithic. To address this topic, this chapter will focus on European medicine and the most relevant medical debates on sexual issues.

RATIONALIZATION OF REPRODUCTION

Thomas Robert Malthus and Charles Darwin provided important intellectual frameworks for nineteenth-century physicians, who increasingly classed the sexual instinct as a subject for scientific inquiry. In 1798, Malthus rationalized procreative sexuality, linking it to economic issues in his influential work *Essay on the Principle of Population*. As is well known, Malthus argued that populations tend to multiply faster than the means of subsistence. Famine, disease, wars, and sexual restraint limited an excessive population growth that would lead to the ruin of countries. To avoid misery, Malthus advocated sexual moderation and postponement of marriage (with strict celibacy) until one could support a family, but he deplored as a "vice" the use of artificial methods to limit reproduction.[3] Snowed under by the threat of overpopulation, moralists, persuaded by Malthusian arguments, no longer saw any reason for promoting sexual pleasures within certain conventional framework, as they had in the eighteenth century. Instead, they emphasized the irresponsibility and immorality of sexual gratification, and hence of sex, except within the sanctity of marriage and financial security.[4]

While Malthus set the tone of the nineteenth-century economic and political interest in the size and health of the population, some medical reformers (the so-called neo-Malthusians) departed from Malthus's recommendations and suggested that if the risk of excessive births was a social problem, the solution rested not in sexual restraint but in birth control.[5] Birth control advocates separated issues concerning reproduction from those of sexual behavior. In 1854, George Drysdale, an Edinburgh-trained neo-Malthusian doctor, published the radical text *Elements of Social Science, or Physical, Sexual, and Natural Region: An Exposition of the True Cause and Only Cure of the Three Primary Social Evils: Poverty, Prostitution and Celibacy.* Drysdale deplored ignorance surrounding sexual subjects and promoted the idea that procreation should be limited by contraceptive methods, not abstinence.[6] Drysdale believed that sexual activities with members of the opposite sex were healthy and necessary to both men's and women's bodies, arguing that chastity was unhealthy and non-procreative sex was normal.[7] This did not mean that Drysdale encouraged debauchery, as he thought that excessive sexual activity was dangerous, and as a result he prescribed that sexual intercourse twice a week was a normal and healthy average for men and women.[8]

The centrality of sexual instinct to men's and women's lives was also reinforced by Darwin's *The Descent of Man and Selection in Relation to Sex* (1871). Darwin was fully aware of the importance of mating to the evolutionary process and he was conscious of the methodological need to clarify evolution's relation to reproduction in his research.[9] In the second part of *The Descent of Man*, Darwin explained the theory of sexual selection, arguing that man has two main instincts: self-preservation and gratification of the sexual instinct. According to Darwin, in some instances competition between the members of species is for mates, rather than for food or living space.[10] Darwin also claimed that no aspect of animal physiology is as prone to variation as the reproductive system. The importance of the reproductive instinct in Darwin's explanation of evolution offered a significant theoretical foundation for late-nineteenth-century medical writers. Eight years after the first publication of *The Descent of Man*, the Austrian psychiatrist and sexologist Richard von Krafft-Ebing endorsed self-preservation and sexual gratification as the only two instinctual aims known to human physiology. In his celebrated *Lehrbuch der Psychiatrie* (1879; *Textbook of Psychiatry*), and later in *Psychopatia Sexualis* (1886), Krafft-Ebing traced the most basic features of human psychopathology in terms of the vicissitudes and perversions of just these two fundamental drives of life.[11]

UNHEALTHY SEX

Within this context of the scientific scrutiny of the sexual instinct, nineteenth-century medical literature overtly focused on the perceived pathological aspects of non-procreative sexual activity.[12] The following three sections address a number of issues relating to unhealthy sex: masturbation, venereal diseases and their relation to prostitution, and perversions of the sexual instinct.

Masturbation

Nineteenth-century medical debates about the grave dangers of "self-abuse" owed their catastrophic tones to the Swiss physician Samuel-Auguste-André-David Tissot, who, in his work *L'onanisme* (1760), following the anonymous British work *Onania* (ca. 1712), linked masturbation to a host of nervous and organic diseases.[13] Although throughout the nineteenth century, medical literature about the perils of masturbation proliferated, displaying a profound anxiety about the subject, two main concerns emerge in the analysis of onanism: a fear that the body could prematurely deteriorate by excessive loss of fluid, and that the fantasies that masturbatory sexual excitement raised could trigger a permanent morbid imagination.

The first concern was related to the principle of European physiology that various functions of the organism (nutritive, reproductive, etc.) were dependent on the maintenance of an equilibrium of vital forces. As a result, the overall "animal economy" could be depleted by an excessive expenditure, and sexual activity could exhaust the organism. In men abuse and waste of sperm could lead to a plethora of diseases, sexual dysfunction such as impotence, and nervous disorders. One of the most common disorders allegedly caused by masturbation was spermatorrhea, which was characterized by excessive and involuntary leaking of the seminal fluids. This illness, in its most severe form, was supposed to drive the organism to a fatal interruption of mental activities.

Nineteenth-century accounts of spermatorrhea were indebted to Claude-François Lallemand, professor of medicine at Montpellier. His study *Les pertes seminales involontaires* (*Involuntary Seminal Losses*), published in three volumes between 1836 and 1852, systematized medical knowledge on the topic and fostered the typical eighteenth-century onanism phobia.[14] Lallemand thought that it was not the loss of semen in itself that caused debility but "the nervous excitement and convulsive motion which usually accompany the discharge."[15] Lallemand's favorite therapies for the prevention of self-pollution and therefore masturbation were surgical treatments such as driving long needles through the perineum and into the prostate; catheterism, which involved the introduction of a catheter through the urethra and into the bladder, a procedure intended to arrest sexual excitement; cauterization of the prostatic section of the urethra with a solution of silver nitrate; and circumcision.[16]

The second issue that masturbation raised was its relationship to sexual fantasies. In the nineteenth century onanism was increasingly understood to be a symptom of mental disorders involving a perverted imagination, evidenced by the appearance of "insanity of masturbation" or "masturbatory insanity" in psychiatric treatises.[17] One the most influential French alienists,

FIGURE 6.1: In the late-nineteenth century it was a widely held belief that masturbation caused insanity and devices such as this were designed to prevent the wearer from touching or stimulating himself. They were often used in mental institutions and sometimes in the home. 1880–1920. Wellcome Library, London.

Jean-Étienne-Dominique Esquirol, linked masturbation and its effects on the imagination to a specific disease, "erotomania":

> Although this disease appears even in advanced age, nevertheless, it most frequently affects young people, especially of a nervous temperament, a lively and ardent imagination, and who are led away by the allurements of pleasures. It affects those also, who lead a life of indolence, and exalt the imagination by reading romances, and have received a voluptuous and effeminate education. Masturbation, by increasing the susceptibility of the nervous system ... also predisposes to erotic delirium.[18]

Young boys and girls with strong imaginations were especially endangered. Physicians believed that once thoughts were fixed on sexual themes, they tended to occupy the whole mind and to render the individual unfit for many everyday activities. Moreover, the onanist was inclined to achieve "deceitful" pleasures over and over again, causing the sexual imagination to interfere with other domains such as intellectual activities and feelings, and finally polluting the individual's free will. Throughout the nineteenth century masturbation was believed to corrupt individuals' minds and therefore predispose them to sexual perversions. In other words, masturbation represented the first step to disease and debauchery because it eroded self-discipline and self-control.[19]

Venereal Diseases and Prostitution

Among the many sexual health issues that doctors had to tackle was the problem of venereal diseases, such as syphilis and gonorrhea. Doctors did not know the exact cause of infection, but they were confident that venereal diseases were the result of promiscuous intercourse.[20] Thus, in the spirit of environmental medicine that prevailed at the beginning of the nineteenth century, it became crucial to control prostitutes, as they appeared to be the source of the contagion. The attempt to prevent the spread of venereal infection through the medical policing of prostitutes originated in France in 1810, when the law required a prostitute to be registered and to submit regularly to medical examinations for venereal diseases. At the same time the government promoted the establishment of special hospitals for prostitutes affected by syphilis and authorized the creation of brothels.[21] While not all European countries legalized brothels, between the 1860s and 1870s, a number of countries, such as Britain, Italy, France, Belgium, and the German states, made at least regular

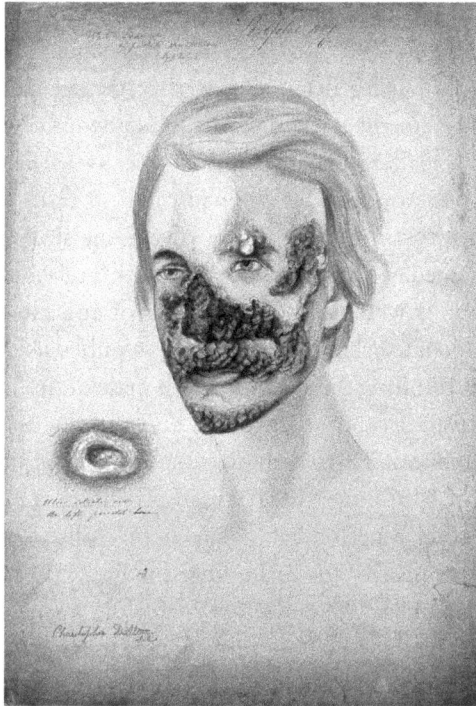

FIGURE 6.2: Pencil, white chalk, and watercolor
drawing illustrating severe pustule crustaceous
lesions on the head of a man suffering from
syphilis, 1855. The drawing at left shows a
detail of the ulcerated lesion above his left
eye. Christopher D'Alton. Wellcome Library,
London.

medical inspections of prostitutes compulsory.[22] On the one hand, the attempt
to control women selling their bodies plainly displays how sexuality became
increasingly regulated by the medical and legal professions. On the other hand,
the debate about prostitution and venereal diseases shows the extent to which
medicine was at the heart of state interventions on sexual practices.

As prostitutes came to be seen as the main source of venereal contagion,
a number of nineteenth-century doctors paid detailed attention to the forms
of prostitution evident in various cities. This medical investigation gave
rise to sociological analyses of sexuality, which eventually provided ample
opportunities for more explicit observations of wide-ranging sexual practices.
Alexandre Jean Baptiste Parent-Duchâtelet's *De la prostitution de la ville de*

Paris (1836; *Prostitution in the City of Paris*) is an influential instance of this kind of study of sexuality and illustrates how physicians tried to regulate sexual behaviors. Parent-Duchâtelet was a well-respected member of the Paris Heath Council and a member of the Royal Academy of Medicine; he also was recognized as a leading urban hygienist because of his study of sewers, dumps, and dissection rooms.[23] At the end of the 1820s, he began studying the phenomenon of prostitution by means of various strategies, ranging from analysis of current medical literature to firsthand interviews with prostitutes working in brothels, as well as superintendents of and physicians at venereal hospitals. Parent-Duchâtelet saw prostitution as a public health problem; it was an unavoidable evil resulting from an excess of male desire, and the task of the public hygienist was to promote cleanliness and security and contain venereal contagion. According to Parent-Duchâtelet, social factors such as poverty and the poor example of family members caused prostitution.[24] Yet a girl became a sex worker only after a period of "debauchery" following a disorderly life. It was their initial propensity toward a libertine lifestyle and laziness that led women to sell their bodies. The underlying principle was that a predisposition to debauchery was a matter of family provenance: to have "an ignoble origin," to be witness to "disorder in the home," led to vice and thus to prostitution.[25]

By the mid-nineteenth century, the prostitute's sexuality was defined as deviant and unnatural, and doctors expanded on the idea that prostitutes were the source of venereal diseases. Among the physicians who were strongly informed by Parent-Duchâtelet was the Briton William Acton, who specialized in venereology as a medical consultant at the London Lock Hospital and as an externe at the Female Venereal Hospital in Paris.[26] His first book, *A Complete and Practical Treatise on the Venereal Diseases and Their Immediate and Remote Consequences* (1841), was rooted in the conviction that women's vaginal discharges were the main source of venereal diseases.[27] In 1857, Acton published *Prostitution Considered in Its Moral, Social and Sanitary Aspects*.[28] The magnitude of the problem of venereal diseases in nineteenth-century society is well illustrated by Acton's remark that half of the outpatients of the London St. Bartholomew Hospital, where he worked, came to see a doctor because they had venereal diseases.[29] Drawing heavily on French physiology, which he learned when studying in Paris in the late 1830s, Acton also believed that male and female sexualities were fundamentally different. The absence of sexual desire characterized the normal women, while a strong sexual urge characterized men. Motherhood, marriage, and domesticity were basic female instincts. In these terms, the prostitute was a deviation from the normal woman because she was defined by her sexual drive.[30]

These kinds of medical assumptions about prostitution continued until the end of the nineteenth century. In 1893, the Italian psychiatrist Cesare Lombroso, considered the founder of criminal anthropology, published *La donna delinquente, la prostituta e la donna normale* (*The Female Offender, the Prostitute and the Normal Woman*) with his son-in-law Guglielmo Ferrero. In this work they systematized widely held notions within medical science. They portrayed the normal woman as the quintessentially good bourgeois mother, sexually passive, without any autonomy, dependent on the father of her children, naturally and organically monogamous and frigid.[31] Lombroso thought female deviancy was rooted in a woman's sexuality, and indeed the most common female deviation was prostitution. Prostitution, "a moral degeneration" and throwback on the evolutionary scale, was the most characteristic female "crime," and a woman became a prostitute more because of a special tendency of her organism than because of her poverty. Lombroso and Ferrero gave detailed descriptions of supposed bodily characteristics of prostitutes, and their physical anomalies were outward manifestations of an underlying condition of psychological abnormality.[32] Repeatedly quoting Parent-Duchâtelet,

FIGURE 6.3: Eight women representing the conditions of dementia, megalomania, acute mania, melancholia, idiocy, hallucination, erotic mania, and paralysis, in the gardens of the Salpêtrière Hospital, Paris. Lithograph by A. Gautier, 1857. Paris: Imp. Bertauts, 1857. R. Cadet, 11. Wellcome Library, London.

Lombroso and Ferrero continued to stigmatize the prostitute but stressed the prostitute's link to abnormal sexuality more than her link to venereal disease.

Perversions of Feeling

To fully appreciate medical developments concerning the knowledge of unhealthy sexualities, one must examine how psychiatrists came to understand insanity and its relationship to perverted feelings. Throughout the nineteenth century a critical problem for psychiatrists was how to differentiate people who displayed uncontrollable passions but were otherwise able to reason and judge coherently. Psychiatrists became increasingly concerned with those forms of insanity in which derangement was limited to a small number of ideas, emotions, and patterns of behavior. This kind of insanity was first identified in 1798 by the French physician Philippe Pinel, in the form of *manie sans délire* (mania without delirium). In his *Traité medico-philosophique sur l'aliénation mentale* (*Medico-philosophical Treatise on Mental Alienation*), he stressed that *manie sans délire* primarily involved the emotions. Pinel believed that the maniac's behavior was caused by a perverse, unrestrained constitution or inadequate education.[33] Subsequently, in order to deal with the problem of this form of insanity, Jean-Étienne-Dominique Esquirol introduced the term "monomania" around 1810. According to Esquirol, monomania indicated an *idée fixe*, a single pathological preoccupation in an otherwise sound mind. In the attempt to define precisely this form of mental derangement, Esquirol specified that the intelligence and the will could be diseased independently of one another.[34] In 1828, another French psychiatrist, Etienne-Jean Georget, went further and proposed that monomania could diminish the perpetrator's responsibility in criminal cases. In this way, Georget destabilized two fundamental principles in the diagnosis of insanity: the presence of delirium and the loss of reason.[35]

In Britain, psychiatrists were developing similar ideas. In 1833, the physician James Cowles Prichard developed the notion of "moral insanity" as a disorder of the emotions, instincts, and will:

> This form of mental disease has been said … to consist of morbid perversion of the feelings, affections, habits, without any hallucination or erroneous conviction impressed upon the understanding: it sometimes co-exists with an apparently unimpaired state of the intellectual faculties.[36]

Like Pinel, Prichard believed that passions could cause insanity. It was this broadening of the concept of insanity that eventually facilitated the systematic

FIGURE 6.4: Maniac in a straitjacket, in a
French asylum. Ambroise Tardieu, in Jean-
Etienne-Dominique Esquirol, *Des maladies
mentales* (Paris: Baillière, 1838), plate 13.
Rare Books Collection. Wellcome Library,
London.

inclusion of problematic sexual longings, such as same-sex desires, in the
psychiatric domain.[37]

During the last decades of the nineteenth century, psychiatrists referred
less to monomania and moral insanity and more often to degeneration to
explain mental disorders characterized by loss of willpower and perversions
of feelings.[38] In psychiatry, the idea of degeneration came from the physician
Bénédict Augustin Morel's *Traité des dégénérescences physiques, intellectuelles
et morales de l'espèce humaine* (1857; *Treatise on Physical, Intellectual and
Moral Degeneration of the Human Species*).[39] Degeneration was understood
to be a progressive decline: physical and mental capabilities deteriorated from
one generation to the next, with sterility as the last stage. Mental pathologies were often hereditary predispositions that, in combination with certain
determining factors such as alcoholism and syphilis, caused the degenerative

process to manifest itself more severely with each successive generation. A tendency toward insanity or perversions could be congenitally inherited from a "tainted" family whose history was characterized by mental illness, syphilis, or debauchery—in a word, by degeneration. The influence of environment was not dispelled, however, because acquired characteristics could be transmitted to future generations. Indeed, the demands of modern civilization on the nervous system were also responsible for the rise of mental disorders.

From the second half of the nineteenth century on, no other aspect of human experience was as closely tied to the concept of degeneration as sexuality.[40] On the one hand, degeneration was associated with a lack of inhibitory control of the higher faculties. Thus, degenerates were prey to their passions and unable to exercise their free will. On the other hand, nonreproductive sexual practices were believed to contribute to the moral, physiological, and mental deterioration that were thought to be afflicting European populations. Physical and moral corruption and an uncontrolled emotional state were often tied to perceived social problems, especially those of the urban areas. Sexual perversions came to be regarded as part of a wider spectrum of hereditary pathologies, which also included criminality, insanity, and abnormal gender behavior.

SEXOLOGY: FROM PHYSIOLOGY
TO PSYCHOLOGY

While earlier medical interest in sexual behavior had focused on masturbation, prostitution, and venereal diseases, in the 1860s psychiatrists and forensic doctors became preoccupied with the connection between mental illness and deviant sexual behaviors. Grounding their arguments in deterministic theories of hereditarian degeneration, Continental psychiatrists increasingly subscribed to the new view that in many cases sexual deviance was not the result of immoral choices but was symptomatic of innate characteristics. Psychiatrists in particular began focusing on sexual perversions, above all on homosexuality. The rise of sexology was indeed initially linked to the attempt to understand same-sex desires.

In 1849, the French physician Claude François Michéa and in 1852 the German forensic doctor Johann Ludwig Casper, in their analysis of sodomy, noticed that the sexual preference for members of the same sex was often innate and in men was accompanied by feminine attributes. Historians have interpreted these analyses as a decisive shift in the medical thinking about same-sex sexual behavior, from an emphasis on physiological characteristics entailed in the sodomitical act to an emphasis on same-sex sexual behaviors as a manifestation of a biological and psychological predisposition.[41] A more comprehensive psychiatric formulation of such a development occurred almost twenty years after these first insights. In 1868, Wilhelm Griesinger, a leading German psychiatrist who strongly supported the view that madness was caused by brain lesions, associated sexual desire for one's own sex with congenital "neuropathic" conditions. Griesinger underlined that often such diseased states expressed themselves only in the psychological realm and did not deeply alter the logical processes of the individual. A practitioner, Griesinger noticed, could easily underestimate the anomalous nature of these forms of neuropathy, with their "abnormal vagaries, instincts, drives, desires."[42] Griesinger's call for direction did not pass unnoticed, and in the following year his student Carl Westphal published the first psychiatric article on what he coined *conträre Sexualempfindung* (contrary sexual feeling). Westphal's article focused on the case history of a woman who, from an early age, had desired other

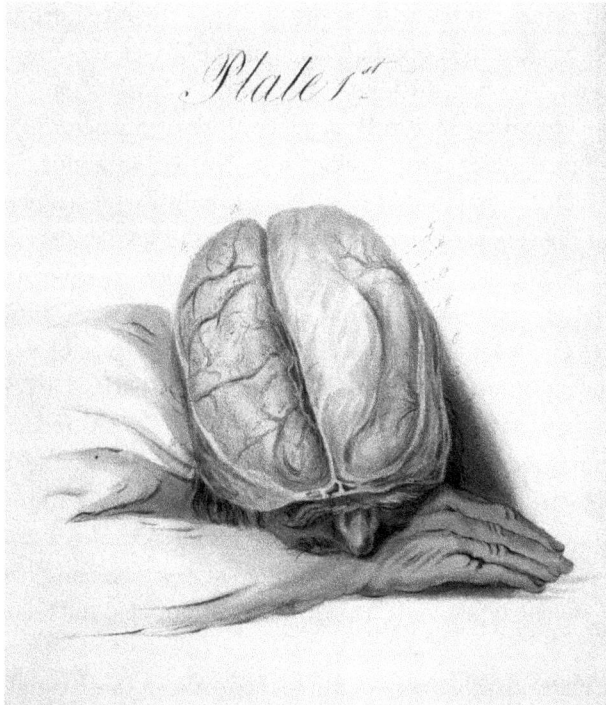

FIGURE 6.5: Sir Charles Bell (1774–1842): *The anatomy of the brain explained in a series of plates*, 1823. Plate 1: Watercolor drawing of the brain. Wellcome Library, London.

women, showed an aversion to men, and possessed the "feeling of having a man's nature." According to Westphal, this case revealed a psychopathic condition, but in the absence of other signs of pathology, he could not prove that the contrary sexual feeling existed as "a completely isolated phenomenon."[43] Westphal's text was pivotal in the debate around same-sex desires because it raised the question of the pathology of these feelings and sketched the main features of sexual inverts. Subsequently, the term *conträre Sexualempfindung* was taken up by Krafft-Ebing in 1877,[44] by the Italian forensic doctor Arrigo Tamassia in 1878, and finally by the French neurologist Jean-Martin Charcot and the French psychologist Valentin Magnan in 1882.[45] Following Westphal's text, European doctors began collecting case studies of sexual inverts whose main psychological characteristic was the gender discordance (the feeling of having the nature and characteristics of the opposite sex), but whose bodies were not marked by same-sex sexual practices. Sexological research on sexual inversion was initially mainly a Continental enterprise; indeed Britain at first displayed a certain reluctance to accept this new field of research.[46] In America it was not until the early 1880s that Westphal's work first made an impact, although this new research was taken up very quickly once introduced.[47]

An article by Krafft-Ebing published in 1877 set the tone for further sexological studies on various sexual deviations. Krafft-Ebing considered perversions of the sexual instinct to be degenerations of the nervous system.[48] He divided the abnormalities into a lack of sexual drive, an abnormal increase in sexual drive (such as nymphomania), the abnormally early (i.e., before puberty) appearance of the sexual instinct or presence of the sexual instinct in old age, and finally perversions not directed toward the preservation of the species (such as sexual inversion, necrophilia, lust-murders, etc.).[49] Following Krafft-Ebing's work, European sexologists fostered the analysis of sexual instinct and the classification of sexual pathologies. Ernest-Charles Lasègue, a French physician, introduced the term "exhibitionism" in 1877; Alfred Binet, another French psychologist, coined the term "fetishism" in 1887; and Krafft-Ebing introduced the terms "sadism" and "masochism" in 1890 and "pedophilia" in 1896.[50] Krafft-Ebing's oft-quoted *Psychopathia Sexualis* is an example of how sexology developed: each edition contained new cases and new categories of abnormal sexual types, which soon became popular outside the medical domain.[51]

Although many psychiatrists continued to believe that sexual perversions were sometimes acquired through a bad environment or the habit of masturbation, they stressed that all perversions were grounded in degenerate heredity. In his influential work on fetishism, Binet stressed the environmental causes of sexual perversions, arguing that the major forms of sexual pathologies were psychologically acquired through exposure to certain accidental events. He explained the development of sexual perversions in an individual by way of the association between ideas and certain pleasurable feelings experienced in childhood, without completely ruling out an organic link. Indeed, Binet insisted that heredity itself could not explain the particular attachment each fetishist displayed, but a hereditary degenerative substratum was necessary for the sexual perversion to appear. Furthermore, Binet admitted that all forms of love, even normal manifestations of love, were to some extent fetishistic, therefore problematizing the so-called normal forms of love.[52]

One of the first medical writers to break away from the idea that abnormal sexual behaviors were a sign or symptom of degeneration was the well-known British sexologist Havelock Ellis. His encyclopedic seven-volume *Studies in the Psychology of Sex* (1896–1928) illustrated different aspects of "normal" human sexuality. The first volume published was the controversial *Sexual Inversion*, initially coauthored with the literary critic John Addington Symonds. While earlier works on homosexuality, such as Krafft-Ebing's *Psychopatia Sexualis*, dealt solely with the pathological aspect of sexual inverts, Ellis, probably for the first time, did not portray sexual inverts as degenerates. As his case studies show, Ellis believed that homosexuality could be inborn, but he did not consider it a sickness. Homosexuality was simply an expression of the sexual instinct, a variation that could be found across history and across culture.[53]

COMPETING FIELDS

The Sexual Body

Despite an increasing emphasis on sexual types and psychologies within sexology, some medical branches continued to look at sexual matters from a more physiological point of view. Proctology, gynecology, and endocrinology competed with sexology in striving toward an understanding of sexual behaviors but fostered a physico-anatomical view of sexuality. Forensic doctors traditionally examined male genitals, looking for signs that could be used in court as evidence of sodomy. While some countries such as France and Italy adopted the Napoleonic Code, which did not punish same-sex sexual acts between men except in cases of violence, other countries, such as Britain or Germany, continued to prosecute pederasty throughout the nineteenth century.[54] In court, psychological arguments were useless; forensic evidence was important and treatises continued to instruct practitioners on how to interpret different bodily signs, mainly those found on the genitals and anus.[55] According to Auguste Ambroise Tardieu, professor of legal medicine at the University of Paris, there existed two types of sodomites: active (penetrating) and passive (penetrated). The former had pointed penises, the latter "infundibuliform" anuses.[56] Sexual crimes were considered the product of an offender's vices, rather than the result of a specific illness.

Proctology, the medical specialization in anal and rectal surgery, was a highly specialized medical branch, the practice of which St. Mark's Hospital in London was devoted. One of the common diseases that proctologists cured was the syphilitic infection of the rectum, which could be contracted by same-sex anal sexual practices. Proctologists occasionally engaged with the topic of same-sex sexual behavior, but they described it in terms of anatomical consequences, without concern for any psychological explanation of the phenomenon.[57]

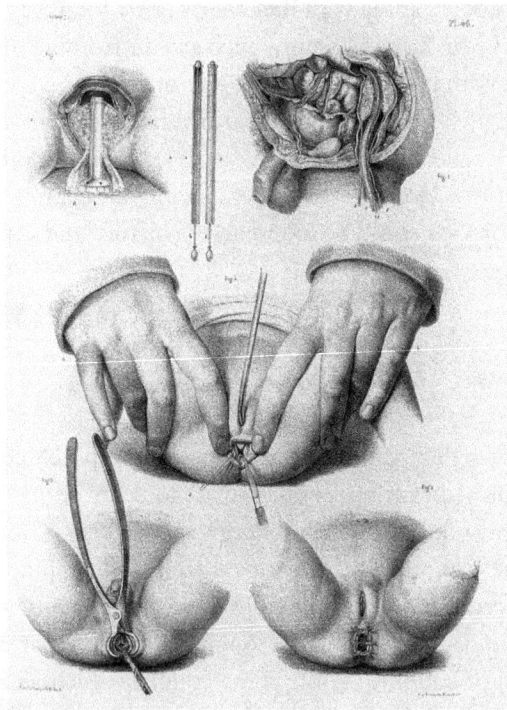

FIGURE 6.6: Various operations on the rectum. Lithograph by Nicolas Henri Jacob. In Jean Baptiste Marc Bourgery, *Traite complet de l'anatomie de l'homme,* vol. 7 (Paris: Delaunay, 1840), plate 46 General Collections. Wellcome Library, London.

During the nineteenth century, within the process of medical specialization, gynecology, the medical science devoted to women's sexual apparatus, was a growing discipline. Gynecologists reversed the focus of psychiatrists from the brain to the genitals. In 1844, the French physician Achille Chéreau dismissed Jan Baptist van Helmont's dictum that a woman was a woman because of her uterus.[58] According to Chéreau, the ovaries determined women's nature, and ovarian dysfunctions typically caused female disorders such as hysteria.[59] Nineteenth-century gynecologists argued that ovaries were the woman's link with nature: they were the seat of the sexual instinct and automatic behavior. Ovaries, gynecologists believed, regulated women's nervous systems; therefore diseased ovaries, or disordered menstruation, could lead to brain injury and thus to mental illness. These gynecological principles underpinned the belief that women were dominated by their sexual functions.

Moreover, a woman's body would yield evidence of her sexual practices to the trained eye of a gynecologist. Red, sore, or itching genitals were often noted as proof of masturbation, and an enlarged clitoris and labia were believed to be a prominent indicator of female diseases. Isaac Baker Brown, member of the Obstetrical Society of London, believed that surgical removal of the clitoris could cure madness, which was caused by masturbation. He performed clitoridectomies in his private clinic in London between 1859 and 1866.[60] Gynecologists also paid special attention to the size of the clitoris, as they believed that hypertrophy of the clitoris was evidence of nymphomania and lesbianism.[61] By the end of the century, medical practitioners were advocating the appointment of gynecologists to the staff of insane asylums and recommending routine gynecological examination in the diagnosis of women's mental disorders.[62]

Another medical branch that proposed a physical explanation for sexual behaviors was endocrinology. By the end of the nineteenth century, the existence of the endocrine function of the gonads and other glands such as the thyroid and the adrenals had been established. In 1905, the secretions of glands—the chemical nature of which nobody knew anything about—were named hormones (from the Greek for "excite" or "arouse") by the English physiologist Ernest Starling.[63] At the same time, in 1896 and 1900 respectively, two Viennese gynecologists, Emil Knauer and Josef Halban, described the chemical substances the ovaries secreted.[64] In 1916, William Blair-Bell, a prominent British gynecologist and pioneer in the study of endocrinology revealed that a normal woman's mental processes depended upon her metabolism, which in turn was controlled by her internal secretions. Sexual and maternal capacity depended upon the "proportion of femininity" in the individual woman's

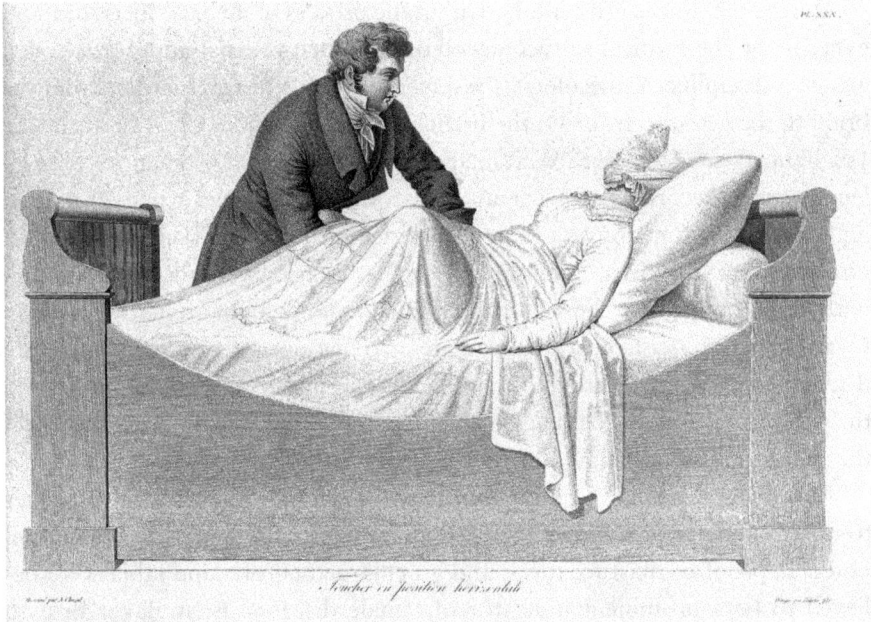

FIGURE 6.7: Vaginal examination in the horizontal position with the patient covered with a sheet. In Jacques Pierre Maygrier, *Nouvelles démonstrations d'accouchemens* (Paris: Bechet, 1822–1825), plate 30. Wellcome Library, London.

makeup.[65] Excessive ovarian secretion, however, produced "excessive sexuality, amounting perhaps to sexual insanity," and leading to masturbation or even sexual inversion.[66]

Psychoanalysis and Freud

In the early-twentieth century the main field competing with sexology was psychoanalysis. Sigmund Freud believed that sexuality played a key role in psychological development, since every neurosis had a specific sexual cause. One must be careful when analyzing Freud's sexual theory, as it changed over time, but he elaborated his most important ideas on sexual perversions in an early work, *Die Abhandlungen zur Sexualtheorie (Three Essays on the Theory of Sexuality* 1905). As Freud himself acknowledged, he was indebted to sexologists such as Havelock Ellis and Krafft-Ebing for his ideas on human sexuality.[67] However, while Freud took up a number of suggestions from nineteenth-century sexologists, one of the main differences between psychoanalysis and sexology was that the former was conceived mainly as a treatment for neurosis, while sexology emerged as a study of sexual pathologies but generally did not provide a medical cure.[68]

The first part of *Three Essays on the Theory of Sexuality* is devoted to "Sexual Aberrations." Here Freud covered extensively the subject of "inversion," and he was careful to separate "sexual aberrations" from inherited degeneration.[69] The concept of degeneracy had already appeared in Freud's earliest work on neurological diseases in childhood. Initially he believed that neurosis had its roots in a prenatal period and that neurotic individuals had some type of pathological disposition. Subsequently, in 1898, Freud published "Sexuality in the Aetiology of the Neuroses," in which he sought to discredit the notion that neurosis arose from degenerative or constitutional disorders or from functional exhaustion, such as that resulting from overwork. Most cases of neurasthenia or anxiety neurosis, he wrote, were the consequence of digression from the "normal vita sexualis," for example, masturbation.[70] Freud also emphasized the role of childhood experiences to explain the appearance of neuroses.[71] In *Three Essays on the Theory of Sexuality,* repeating Ellis's arguments, Freud made clear that sexual inverts could not be regarded as degenerates because there existed homosexuals who showed high intellectual faculties, and in some cultures same-sex sexual behavior was almost an institution and was charged with important social functions.[72] Freud believed that exclusive homosexual orientation was a complex blend of biological (bisexual potential) and psychological factors. He strongly opposed the distinction between inborn and acquired characteristics because he found that an individual's development depended on both. Finally, Freud established that an essential bisexuality was present in human beings and argued that it was not possible to draw a sharp delineation between perversion and a normal variety of sexuality.[73]

In the second essay Freud described the successive phases of the development of infantile sexuality. According to Freud, there is an autoerotic phase, during which any part of the body can be an erogenous zone, but its usual site is the mouth, with gratification achieved through sucking. After this "oral phase," the anus becomes the main erogenous zone, and the retention or expulsion of feces provides gratification. This zone is replaced in the third phase by the genitals, hence the frequency of infantile masturbation. During these phases the child is "polymorphously perverse," which means that the potential for all perversions is present, and under specific circumstances these may develop in many adults. Therefore, childhood experiences become pivotal for the understanding of sexual development.[74]

In the third essay Freud focused on puberty. Following biological development during puberty, the individual moves from autoeroticism to a focus on other sexual objects under the primacy of the genitals. Freud believed that libido, whether in men or women, is fundamentally "masculine" in nature, which meant that the libido was active. Freud described the development of a girl's sexuality as more complicated than that of a boy, as she moves from a phase in which the erogenous zone is the clitoris to one in which the erogenous zone is the vagina. This implied that a woman normally goes through a period of repression during puberty, which in turn explained women's greater propensity to neurosis, and especially to hysteria. A boy maintains his leading zone from childhood.[75] In the last part of this third essay, Freud explained the process of finding a sexual object, the first of which is the mother's breast. When the child is able to form an idea of the person to whom the organ that is giving him satisfaction belongs, the sexual instinct then becomes autoerotic. In opposition to an infantile sexuality (essentially autoerotic), Freud suggested an object-directed sexuality developed during puberty. The primal object, the mother, has by then long been denied, but the libidinal investment in a sexual partner after puberty is in fact a "rediscovery" of the mother.[76]

To summarize, Freud's sexual theory revolved around a number of themes: first, the inquiry into early events of sexual life, sexual fantasies, and their role in the subsequent emotional life of an individual; second, the concept of libido, or sexual instinct, which evolves through phases; and third, the vicissitudes of the love object choice, particularly the Oedipus complex. Finally, on the assumption of the preceding points, people develop a sexual libido that, depending on the experiences of childhood, could become fixed on different sexual objects and could lead to the development of different sexual perversions.[77] In establishing this theory, Freud essentially reorganized a number of themes that sexologists and allied psychologists had been developing since the 1870s.[78]

CONCLUSION

While proper sexual conduct had always been a concern, and sometimes even regulated in civil and penal legal codes, institutionalized religion, and philosophical and moral treatises, in nineteenth-century medicine sexuality became the crucial object of an ongoing scientific debate. Throughout the nineteenth and at the beginning of the twentieth centuries, medical discourses on sexual disorders were not monolithic and competing medical branches offered different views. In this period, sexuality was not radically embedded in a notion of identity, as it appears today. Yet sexuality became increasingly disconnected from reproduction when physicians first began policing sexual behavior in an attempt to contain the spread of venereal diseases and the deterioration of the body though sexual practices. The separation of sexuality from reproduction was intensified as psychiatrists addressed different psychological aspects of human sexual experiences in a systematic fashion. Sexual desires and behaviors appeared increasingly in disease nosologies, and sexuality eventually became an important subject for various medical branches and the main concern of sexologists. With the rise of psychoanalysis, sexual experiences and fantasies were believed to affect all people's psychological development and, as such, were a central part of being human.

CHAPTER SEVEN

Sex, Popular Beliefs and Culture: Discourses on the Sexual Child

GAIL HAWKES AND R. DANIELLE EGAN

Childhood is the time of innocence and happiness, the paradise of life, the lost Eden on which we look longingly back through the whole remaining course of our life.[1]

INTRODUCTION: THE PROBLEM OF CHILDHOOD

We cannot discuss childhood sexuality without beginning with a discussion of childhood: the child and the sexual child became the focus of examination and discussion at roughly the same historical moment.[2] As in accounts of adult sexuality, and especially adult female sexuality, embedded characterizations of one infuse assumptions of the other.[3] Thus, what the child is assumed to be (for example, innocent, corruptible) reflects qualities inherent in perceptions of childhood. Until relatively recently, childhood was inhabited by a passive entity, an ontological space constructed with reference to the adult world. This point has been critically explored by the second generation of social constructionists of childhood.[4] For these later theorists, childhood must be understood as more contextual and reflexive, the child within it less passive and more agentic. Of late, scholars have developed this notion of agency in the context of some more uncomfortable aspects of the adult-child distinction—the fascination and erotic attraction enveloped in this relationship, and the witting or unwitting complicity of the adult world with this.[5] The sensuous, the sexual (as opposed to sexualized), and the knowing child are illuminated in these studies—the genie had been let out of the bottle.[6]

The theoretical frameworks offered by nearly fifty years of scholarship confirm our choice to discuss childhood sexuality as a series of interlocking and historically contingent discourses. The terms under which the child was distinguished as a specific entity set boundaries around and a foundation for characterizations of childhood sexuality from the beginning. A key feature of this distinctiveness was its status of being in transition, of essential incompleteness. Seeing the child as the unformed but "to-be-adult" ensured that its sexuality would be in some way derived from, and referential to, that of the adult. Yet in what follows it will become evident that since the development of the concept of childhood, the child was never just an incomplete adult. Across the range of discourses that make up this chapter it will be apparent that behind the child seen as the "developing adult" were characteristics and potentialities that offered grounds for anxiety. Specifically (and this was evident first in the more benign articulations of the eighteenth-century exponents of pedagogy),[7] the child was understood as closer to nature. While this was seen as a positive, even romantic, association, this connection also rendered both the mind and body of the child a fertile terrain for observation, classification, and concern. As Nikolas Rose highlights, "the modern child has become the focus of innumerable projects that purport to safeguard it from physical, sexual and moral danger; to ensure its 'normal' development, you actively promote certain capacities or attributes such as intelligence, educability and emotional stability."[8]

In the eighteenth century, the dangers that threatened the child were from external sources, not from the inherently sexual body. Since "nature's instruction is slow and leisurely, [and] those of man are always premature,"[9] careful instruction was necessary to avoid these social influences that would sexualize the child's imagination, and through this its body.[10] The body of the child was susceptible, but only if prematurely stimulated by precocious experience. But the question of which was more at risk was not settled in this emerging commentary. In his 1760 treatise on masturbation, the Swiss physician Samuel Tissot identified the possibility of untimely sexual awakening in children by servants and warned of the importance of adult vigilance in the prevention of this outcome. He expressed the hope that parents and the educators of children would "discover in time this detestable practice and ... prevent the consequences."[11]

FIGURE 7.1: "Ex libris Frank Payne," a child standing, encircled by two snakes. Wellcome Library, London.

Tissot's advice identified more clearly the sexual *body* as the primary source of compulsive masturbation and in doing so complicated the Enlightenment pedagogic optimism about the acquisition of *reason* in the education of the child.

THE MASTURBATING CHILD IN THE NINETEENTH CENTURY

This primary problematization of the body foreshadowed the emergence of the view of masturbation as a sexual practice that was dangerous to individual and social health, a movement that has been well-documented by historians of sexuality.[12] More than this, it was within the discourse of "masturbation phobia" that the campaign against *childhood* masturbation, which had been conducted on a limited and individual basis in the eighteenth century, transformed into a public crusade, as "educators and doctors combated onanism like an epidemic that needed to be eradicated."[13] In the context of the nineteenth-century view of "the body as metaphorical for society," the focus of anxieties widened and intensified.[14] Masturbation now represented a threat not only to the individual body but also to society itself.[15] This ideological extension was reflected in the displacement of educational intervention by less benign physical intervention, itself given greater urgency by the search for both cause and treatment.

The English physician and surgeon William Acton identified multiple causes for the premature excitation of what he terms the sexual instinct of children, among them hereditary predisposition. In 1865, Acton wrote that he "firmly believes that moral as well as physical tendencies and irregularities can be transmitted to progeny."[16] Nevertheless, he attached more significance to external stimulation from benign and less benign sources, for example, accidental or deliberate bodily stimulus by fellow children or servants. Contemporaneously, the French physician Claude-François Lallemand, whose work widely circulated throughout nineteenth-century Europe, offered vivid examples taken from clinical case studies that underlined the intractability of the stimulated body, and thus the logical impossibility of self-control.[17] Acton later contributed to this escalating consensus, adding another layer of anxiety when he warned that "preventative treatment would itself excite sexual desires."[18] He nevertheless conceded that leaving the child in ignorance to scratch at irritated genitals would do more to encourage masturbation than washing it with cold water.[19]

Within the medical profession there were other developments that were to shape clinical responses to the problem of childhood masturbation and to further legitimate its authority. As Robert Darby argues in his work on William Acton, accidental or deliberate overstimulation of the body, especially of the genitals, was believed to lead inevitably to systemic "nervous irritation" and physical debilitation.[20] Excessive stimulation, especially of the sexual organs, set up a stimulus-response reaction, which, once established, was believed to be uncontrollable. Since this whole process operated at a somatic rather than conscious level, the only cure for the compulsion was to either remove the source or render the irritated area so painful to touch that the habit would be broken. In 1897, Dr. Emmett Holt, a world-renowned American pediatrician, wrote:

The kind of restraint which is necessary will depend upon the manner of masturbating. If by the hands, these must be tied during sleep, so that the child cannot reach the genitals; if by thigh friction, the thighs must be separated by tying one to each side of the crib. In inveterate cases a double-side splint, such as is used in fracture of the femur, may be applied. Corporal punishment is often useful in very small children.[21]

The American psychiatrist René Spitz found that between 1850 and 1879, treatments employed to "cure" masturbation extended beyond physical constraint to direct surgical intervention. These methods included chemical cautery, clitoridectomy, blistering of the thighs and genitals, infibulation of the labia majora, urethral cautery, and circumcision without anesthetic.[22] The degree to which the physical consequences of masturbation were irreversible was reflected in the range of preventative strategies, from the application of leeches and neck constraints to cautery with hot iron and amputation of the clitoris.[23]

Like eighteenth-century information on masturbation, the warnings were in popular circulation.[24] In 1845, a German doctor, Heinrich Hoffmann, wrote a book for his four-year-old son.[25] The text, *Der Struwwelpeter*, comprised a series of cautionary tales on the terrible consequences of disobedience to adult and especially parental authority, all illustrated in gruesome detail. This popular book for children dealt with misuses of the body: gluttony and laziness, including what in 1879 was to be identified by the German pediatrician S. Lindner as "pleasure sucking."[26] "The Story of Little Suck-a-Thumb," which vividly described the horrible consequences of persistent thumb-sucking, exemplified the blending of professional and popular discourses, where the body was seen as potentially both uncontrollable and "to be controlled." Conrad, the persistent (and secretive) thumb-sucker, was punished brutally by a giant scissor-wielding tailor.[27]

In the nineteenth century the child's body was seen as undeveloped physically and morally—yet at the same time burdened with the potential for sexual precocity. This understanding was articulated most clearly in relation to childhood autoeroticism in general but masturbation in particular, which was seen as especially compulsive and addictive. While there was shared with the eighteenth century a view that the child was an "adult in development," the distinctive feature of the nineteenth century was that the management of the body could no longer depend on the capacity of individual self-control. The emerging consensus that the body was a machine, sui generis, rendered it simultaneously accessible, analyzable, and passive.[28] This broader ideological development ensured the problematization of the childish body while at the same time offering compelling justification for its surveillance and training. "This pedagogisation was especially evident in the war against onanism, which in the West lasted nearly two centuries."[29]

In both medical and popular discourses, something new was being said about the child's body: it was simultaneously a machine beyond the bidding of conscious will and an entity that, once stimulated, was capable of compulsive behavior. As empirical medical knowledge of the body increased, accompanied

FIGURE 7.2: *Paul et Virginie*, 1851. Baldwin Historical Children literature digital collection, George A. Smathers Libraries, University of Florida.

by a parallel growth in professional prestige and legitimacy, so also did anxiety about the nature of the sexual child, lacking in will and reason, on the one hand, and alive with sexual sensibility on the other.

PRODUCING THE PRURIENT THROUGH THE PEDAGOGY OF PURITY: CHILDHOOD SEXUALITY AND THE SOCIAL PURITY MOVEMENT

In the late-nineteenth and early-twentieth centuries, cultural understandings of the child's place in the social order began to adjust to the wider impacts of modernity. Social and economic transitions such as rapid industrialization, urbanization, and immigration helped shape a recognizably different construction of adulthood and childhood.[30] In these shifts, the focus moved away from the problematic body and toward a more reformist and moralist discourse. This entailed framing the child as an idealized creature deserving of recreation and freedom, a construction that transformed children from utilitarian and productive members in the familial economy into affective symbols for society.[31] Children were reconceptualized as special in their own right, in need of affection and attention from parents. Yet the conditions that enabled this transition also intensified fears of their vulnerability to corruption from external influences. Social transformation occupied a double role within purity narratives; it was conceptualized as posing a threat at the same time as it contained the potential for sweeping moral transformation. Urbanization, perhaps the most radical of all the dynamics of modern society, epitomized this contradiction and duality, and the body of the child was increasingly seen as the means for its resolution. Accordingly, the child became a signifier for the complex and contradictory aspects of the modern condition, simultaneously full of potential vice and purity: a site of transformation and hope for the future.[32]

Between 1860 and 1915 social purity alliances flourished in Boston, New York City, London, Manchester, Sydney, Melbourne, Chicago, and Washington, D.C., growing "far beyond the immediate comprehension of even its leaders."[33] Purity campaigners also joined forces with progressive feminist organizations to lobby for the age of consent to be raised in Britain, Australia, and the United States.[34] As public support for the abolition of prostitution began to wane, the movement's attention turned toward the child as the means by which to curb sexual vice and moral turpitude. Purity activists increasingly insisted that a virtuous future would be ensured if the moral protection of children could be guaranteed. Accordingly, by the early 1870s, pedagogic instruction publications for bourgeois mothers and children proliferated in the United States, England, and Australia.[35]

Campaigners hoped that "sex, put under rational guidance, might well save the world."[36] Fusing the ideas of public health with morality, social purity advocates thus sought to create healthy and vice-free sons and daughters. Child-rearing manuals offered mothers techniques for promoting the social and moral well-being of their children, which would ensure the social and cultural health of a Christian nation.[37] But there were unavoidable obstacles that were integral to the process of urbanization: city life was thought to be particularly perilous for its child population.[38] The omnipresent danger of a corrupt social order and the overabundance of "licentious" individuals produced an atmosphere that intensified the need for parental vigilance. In particular it was believed that, lacking the traditional social norms that governed rural living, urban social settings imparted "no fixed standard of right or wrong, in relation to sex."[39] Similarly, the American physician and purity reformer Samuel Gregory lamented that the sexual instinct "appears two or three years earlier in the city than in the country; and four years younger, there, than nature ever designed."[40]

More than any other aspect of the life of the child, pedagogical training in the domain of sex was essential because "more care [was] needed to secure healthy, strengthening influences, for the early life of sex."[41] In their calls for corrective sexual training, social purity activists highlighted the need to protect children against the debasement of the "pure feelings of uncorrupted childhood."[42] Promoting purity suppressed the sexuality of the child in the service of a higher power—moral will. In this, women were seen as the central "enablers." Elizabeth Blackwell, the first female doctor in the United States, noted that an intelligent and civilized mother recognized the importance of her moral responsibility by "educating the sentiment of sex in girls into a controlling force," thereby helping to rid society of a future class of "outcast" women.[43] Maternal instruction ensured "the gradual growth of intelligent self control in the young life of sex."[44] The mother must train the unruly instinct to protect her child from the damaging effects of self-pollution in the present as well as in the future. The commitment to moral education within the social purity movement was founded on the belief that parents could produce "enlightened innocence" and vice-free children. Welsh postulated that

> In many minds innocence is confused with ignorance, when in reality the two conditions are opposed. Innocence is an asset to be treasured; ignorance is a liability to be discharged. It is always possible to enlighten innocence without destroying it. Indeed the innocence of ignorance is a fragile structure, whereas enlightened innocence is a tower of strength.[45]

But there was an inherent contradiction in the literature: campaigners promoted purity training in order to curb autoeroticism and future deviance.[46] The suggestion that children were always already on the verge of masturbation rendered purity a conceptual impossibility.[47] A distinctive feature of the purity discourse was the recognition that the mind as well as the body could be corrupted. For many reformers in the nineteenth century, freeing the imagination was emblematic of the new attitude of "letting a child be a child." But the potential autonomy of a child's imagination also created a new form of anxiety—imagination gone awry.[48]

Thus the influence of the mind over the body was a central epistemological tenet of purity reform. Imagination was dangerous and could easily morph from innocent concerns to sexual fantasy and thus interest—particularly when a child's sexual ideas were stimulated through the persuasion of others.[49]

The danger of the knowing child was his or her ability to *channel the imagination* of other children into the realm of the sexual. Sexual thoughts could break the ties that repressed instinct, and to this end, knowingness in children promoted the "undue prominence of instinct."[50] Thoughts could be translated into "filthy" and "indecent play," with disreputable companions providing instruction on sexual vice in the "dark recesses of the school yard."[51] Here it was the mind, rather than the unconscious body, that posed a threat to childish innocence and purity. Through the deployment of this complex dynamic, purity campaigners produced a highly ambivalent narrative on the sexuality of children. On the one hand, children could be educated away from sexual deviance and thus sexuality was seen as highly mutable. On the other hand, sexual prurience, if left to its own devices, could create degeneracy. This would, in turn, create more corruption.

We suggest that purity activists attempted to resolve this contradiction by creating a binary that allowed the child's sexuality to be understood as simultaneously present but normatively absent. The mobilization of the idea of the dangerously knowing child was an attempt to disentangle this ambivalent construction juxtaposing innocence with corruptibility. The English evangelist Henry Varley, in his *Address to Young Boys*, illuminated this strategy: all boys, he claimed, "as early as seven years of age" would masturbate, and the only way to avoid a moral crisis was to keep them away from the "corrupting influence of follow classmates."[52] Once the seeds of sexual corruption were "sown in the child's mind," the effects would persist throughout life.[53] Social purity movements needed the knowing child (just as they needed the prostitute and the degenerate male before it) to legitimate their existence. By equating erroneously acquired sexual knowledge with pathological sexual practice in the present and future, the discourse of purity became credible through its oppositional nature. Concomitantly, the existence of the knowing child legitimated the recognition of, and argument for, the management of childhood sexuality. The viability of the argument for the training in purity depended on the perpetuation of the sexual-nonsexual child contradiction. Social purity produced prurience in order to protect innocence.

"RATIONAL PROPHYLAXIS" AND "VICARIOUS PARENTHOOD": SEXUAL HYGIENE, EUGENICS, AND THE SEXUAL CHILD

It is not enough even to make a sound environment and then turn our children loose in it, inexperienced and driven by all sorts of natural and acquired desires and urges, all of which must be guided and some of which must be restrained, and trust to their own impulses and observations to enable them to hit upon the wise course of life.[54]

The first two decades of the twentieth century marked a shift of focus in the classification of adult sexuality from the abnormal to the normal.[55] As a result, a more nuanced management of the body, or what Foucault termed "biopower," took shape within discourses on sexuality.[56] Additionally, Frank Mort draws attention to the connection made between physical and racial health in the early part of the twentieth century.[57] This ideological transition was reflected in new attitudes to the sexual child as a conduit for the health of future generations,[58] a discursive transition that resonated with larger anxieties on racial fitness within the broader eugenics movement in the Anglophone West.[59] Under these conditions, sex and reproduction became "large human factors in giving rise to vigour, zest, love, marriage, home, happiness, aesthetic satisfactions, to higher ethical and moral standards, and to sympathetic and social evolution."[60] The objectives of eugenics articulated within the hygiene discourse replaced unreliable and indeed unsuccessful earlier attempts to improve health either through manipulation of the environment or with the predictability of natural selection and the "iron laws of heredity."[61] In this guise eugenics arguments had a strong influence on the hygiene movement through its elevation of the role of the child in the attainment of racial "health."[62]

Drawing on evolutionary anthropology, hygienists identified the significance of the child through the theory of recapitulation. Rooted in evolutionary anthropology, neo-Lamarckianism, and Spencerian sociology, the argument was that the individual moves through the same phases of evolution as the species, and thus the child mirrors an earlier stage of adult evolution—the savage.[63] Decrying earlier mistaken tactics that enshrouded sex within a conspiracy of silence, sexual hygienists highlighted the need for sexual instruction and the potential of pedagogical involvement.[64] In its transmission of accurate information, sex training promised to eradicate any morbid preoccupation with sex stemming from "the wrong knowledge" in both children and youths. The hygienist and physician Winfield Scott Hall, whose work was disseminated widely throughout the Anglophone West, warned that "little children fall into error because they have not had the benefit of wise counsel and guidance" that an education in sexual and social hygiene provided.[65] Children, as the parents of the future,[66] must understand that the real significance of sex education was related to sexual selection: that "which makes for individual happiness and racial well-being shall be exercised under the protection of a trained capacity for judgment of sexual charms."[67]

THE VICARIOUS PARENT
AND THE CHILD-AS-FUTURE

Sexual hygiene was about more than learning about reproduction from books; it was about a reformation of ideas, a reversal of fear and ignorance, and especially the child's role as a future spouse and future parent. Central to this was sowing the seeds of a new world of sexuality "as naturally as the rose in the garden blooms in June."[68] But this was to be a planned garden in which the dynamic was "vicarious parenthood."[69] The British reformer M. E. Robinson contended that science as a dispassionate and rational system of knowledge avoided the "gross sensuality" of less informed types of instruction.[70] The foregrounding of professional direction in the field of social hygiene rendered suspicious the abilities of "uneducated" parents.[71] "Most parents lack the skill and knowledge to impart adequate and accurate information on sex subjects to their children."[72] Parents would do more harm than good in the delicate task of providing knowledge if they ignored expert advice. By locating the site of expertise in scientific training, as opposed to enlightened moral instruction, the hygiene discourse demoted the parent from his or her former place of supremacy within purity and other sexual reform movements. Nevertheless, experts should "never lose sight of the fact that [they] are doing this work in [their] relation to vicarious parenthood."[73] In their role as vicarious parents, hygiene instructors had to be both parent and scientist, frank and sympathetic. In this way they could

> guide human evolution into whatever direction we wish, ... (1) improve the blood of the stock by selection and breeding (eugenics); (2) improve the general surrounding and condition of life of all the members of the species ... and (3) we may still more specifically educate and train each individual in early life.[74]

Sexual hygiene was not primarily directed toward the sensuality of the body but rather at "character-training" involving the "divine right to an honest, decent and constructive presentation of the meaning of sex in life, and to early *continuous sex character training*."[75] Character instruction laid the groundwork for acceptable behavior, mate preference, and the stability of the family in the future.[76] If correctly equipped before puberty with the principles of good breeding, young people would make the right "sexual selection" in the future.

The door flew open, in he ran,
The great, long, red-legged scissor-
man.
Oh! children, see! the tailor's come
And caught our little Suck-a-Thumb.
Snip! Snap! Snip! the scissors go;
And Conrad cries out—Oh! Oh! Oh!
Snip! Snap! Snip! They go so fast;
That both his thumbs are off at last.

Mamma comes home; there Conrad stands,
And looks quite sad, and shows his hands;—
"Ah!" said Mamma, "I knew he'd come
To naughty little Suck-a-Thumb."

FIGURE 7.3: Boy sucking thumb. Gutenberg ebook. Courtesy of the University of Florida Digital Collections. http://www.uflib.ufl.edu/ufdc/?b= UF00087058&v=00001.

Simultaneously possessing potentialities in need of instruction yet seemingly dormant until adulthood, the child in sexual hygiene narratives occupies an ambivalent position as a predictor of a future superior adulthood and the reproducer of the race and nation. This discourse both normalized and anodized the experience of sex. If sexual reproduction was "dealt with in a scientific spirit, the facts arouse no more emotion than *other facts in nature*."[77] Newell Edison on behalf of the American Social Hygiene Association argued that the task of sex education was both informational and directive. It should instruct children and youths in the government of their "sex impulse" so as to give them "the satisfaction of a rich expression of [their] own personality and at the same time to furnish outlets that do not bring [them] into serious conflicts with social standards."[78] Through these means, the sexual child in hygiene discourse was de-individualized and rendered passive, its potential as the future progenitor only realizable in its reproductive future.[79] This same process made possible an open, even a positive, attitude toward sex instruction of young children. Yet, simultaneously, this legitimating framework contributed to the desexualization of the child itself.

SEXOLOGY, PSYCHOANALYSIS, AND THE SEXUAL CHILD

> It is so easy to convince oneself of the regular sexual activities of children that one cannot help asking in astonishment how the human race can have succeeded in overlooking the facts and in maintaining for so long the wishful legend of the asexuality of childhood.[80]

One feature of the various discourses of the sexual child is the extent to which they overlap historically yet differ markedly in their motivations, premises, and arguments.[81] Sexology, the study of human sexuality in its physical, emotional, psychological, and cultural forms, was established, but not necessarily accepted by the scientific community, by the last two decades of the nineteenth century. Psychoanalysis—the analysis of the subconscious—began with Freud's application of this dimension of human life to the diagnosis and treatment of hysteria and neurosis in the very last years of the nineteenth century. Key writers of both sexology and psychoanalysis were notable for offering a distinctive approach to the sexual child: dispassionate, objective, and normalizing. Havelock Ellis (1859–1939), Sigmund Freud (1856–1939), and Albert Moll (1862–1939) all demonstrated through case studies that the normal child possessed the capacity for sexual responses and directed erotic experiences from a very early age.[82] They shared the view that the sexuality of the child had been hitherto ignored or misrepresented and, in their efforts to rectify this gap,[83] made references (often not entirely uncritical) to each other's work.[84]

Throughout his writing on infantile eroticism, Freud's concept of its constitution reflected his wider theory on the sexual drive, which "traced the play of influences which govern the evolution of infantile sexuality till its outcome in perversion, neurosis or normal sexual life."[85] Reversing his earlier claims for sexual manifestation in childhood being the result of adult seduction, he now challenged "the popular view that the sexual instinct is absent in childhood," in order to claim the essential nature of the "infantile sexual impulse."[86] However, given that his original and ongoing motivation were to understand the role played by childhood sexual experiences in adult neuroses, we argue that Freud's theory was not concerned to primarily normalize the idea of the *sexually agentic* child. Albert Moll's book, published seven years later, was rather differently motivated and offered a more normative framework for the independently sexual child: to gain scientific knowledge that would provide information about the sexual life of the child.[87] Moll's work, like Freud's, was empirically based, but he avoided dependence on "pathological considerations," relying instead on the childhood recollections of healthy individuals.[88]

Both writers recognize the specific phenomenon of childhood sexuality but they differ in their conceptions of its manifestation and, to a lesser extent, its potentialities. For Freud it resides in the notion of the instinct, "the psychical representative of an endosomatic, continuously flowing source of stimulation."[89] Freud's instinct involves somatic stimulation (erotic zones) that is not, initially, associated with genital excitation or reproductive function. He distinguishes the "continuously flowing source of stimulation" from a single event external in origin[90] and the *constant state* of the instinct—independent of external stimulus.[91] The instinct to pleasure has a number of primary somatic sources in infancy, some driven by survival and others instigated by the intimate physical relationship between the child and its carer. The key element is that these manifestations follow the urge to assuage a somatic "irritation" and to re-create the pleasurable sensation that follows. "The quest to re-experience the sensual pleasure from an external source constitutes the sexual aim of the infant and small child."[92] Similarly, under the age of four, any part of the child's body that can engage in such stimulus-response represents similar autoerotic potential. Freud says that once we understand the mechanism of instinct and aim, and the satisfaction that follows, "we have little more to learn about children's sexuality."[93] Moll's terminology, and to a lesser extent his argument, differs. The sexual *life* of the child, manifested in "the sexual impulse," takes two observable forms: detumescence and contrectation. The former he describes as "physical processes that take place in the sexual organs" where the impulse is directed toward "decreasing in size."[94] Moll addresses in detail the issue of "voluptuous sensations" experienced by young children as a consequence of detumescence.[95] Contrectation expressing itself in physical intimacy and deep emotional attachment can occur with, but more commonly without, any physical sexual excitation (and resolution through orgasm). The two components in children are often, but not always, experienced quite separately; the child may even masturbate to ease the tumescence without making any connection, necessarily, with the object of its intimate attraction.[96] Freud also acknowledges but accords less significance to the "psychical manifestations of love" in the pre-pubertal child, which can be "associated with the physical sensations of sexual excitation, so that the child cannot remain in doubt about the connection between the two."[97]

For both, a risk of dangerous perversion exists in the premature sexualization of children. Freud identifies sexual activities "for which they have no need."[98] "Needlessness" is defined here by the fact that they bear no relationship to normal sexual instinct, or its aim. For Moll, premature sexual development can occur as a result of hereditary or social influences. In the latter sense, he identifies inculcation by fellow children or adults prone to "paedophilia erotica."[99] This "premature sexual development" predisposes the child to prostitution or sexual abuse as well as to seducing other children.[100] Thus both theorize a capacity for active (and often problematic) sexual sensibility in the child, though there is often mutual disagreement and dismissal of the other's work.[101]

In addition to the normalization of sexual sentience, both make another equally radical claim. Freud's polymorphously perverse child lies at the heart of his theory of infantile sexuality[102] and is addressed more clearly in the 1915 footnote of *The Sexual Aberrations*, in which he acknowledges that in childhood the object of the sexual instinct may be of either sex, and that the "final sexual attitude" is not resolved until after puberty.[103] In addressing this point, Moll challenges Freud's argument that childhood sexual experiences are the source of adult neuroses—he says there is no evidence for this; indeed his case studies point to the contrary.[104] This is especially the case in the transition from undifferentiated to differentiated sexual attraction. The feelings and actions associated with contrectation[105] can be expressed between individuals of the same age and the same sex or the opposite, between children and animals, between the child (male or female) and adults or older children, even between the child and its parents.[106]

Freud argues that following the age of four to six years, the sexual instinct is suppressed and sublimated until puberty. But latency does not mean asexuality.[107] The extent to which sexual activity persists depends in part upon the individual, and in part upon the setting that may offer alternative outlets for the drive of the instinct (sublimation). Moll's "sexual lives of children" comprise two stages: birth to seven years, and eight to fourteen years, the latter roughly corresponding to Freud's latency period. Unlike Freud, Moll identifies this second stage as one in which the sexual life of the child blooms, with manifestations of both components of the sexual instinct evident.

Both acknowledge the need for "sexual enlightenment": talking about sex to the child is important. Their acknowledgement lacks the urgency and moral significance given it by the hygienists. For Freud "the sexual researches of children" are driven by instinctive curiosity, sadism, and instincts for cruelty and scopophilia.[108] Sexual enlightenment by an adult prevents the development of fears and prurient erroneous knowledge and should occur before the age of ten.[109]

Moll agrees that the child can be offered objective facts in the first stage of childhood, but information about the "subjective" elements should wait until well into the second stage, for "the child is quite unable to understand the dangers of sexual life, as long as it has no actual experience of sexual feelings."[110] However, he is clear that "we will not turn children into little angels," nor can masturbation be fully prevented by sexual enlightenment. Example, he says, is a better teacher than words.[111]

Freud's key contribution was to identify the erotically sensible child from birth. His theory disengaged the topic from the moral discourses that justified control and surveillance. Yet his identification of obstacles to satisfactory progression from infancy to puberty ensured that the discourses about the sexual child would continue to problematize its sexual autonomy and agency.[112] Moll's twin concepts of detumescence and contrectation recognize emotion, sensibility, and fantasy and in doing so normalize a spiritual as well as physical level of eroticism. Yet it would be inaccurate to characterize him as an advocate of full sexual recognition of the child. Arguably, he gets closer than Freud, but he still advises vigilance and protection. For both, the sexual propensities of the child, both male and female, are self-evident, are complex in their expression, and have the possibility of both positive and negative outcomes for both the individual and society.

TRAINING THE SEXUAL CHILD: THE DISCOURSE OF PROFESSIONAL CHILD-REARING

By the end of the first decade of the twentieth century, another discourse was emerging in concert with those already discussed—one whose primary feature was the insistence on specialized expertise in the scientific methods to train the parent to train the child.[113] Though more usually associated with industrial production and the rational management of the labor force, faith in the scientific direction of human activity was evident beyond the factory gate, and especially in the "reproductive" home.[114] In the interwar years, child welfare and development was being "institutionalized,"[115] while Stearns also argues that a new approach to children that dealt with more than simply health issues began to be used in the 1920s.[116] The target of professional child-rearing was not the child but the parents, as they were "rendered ... more helpless than ever, more abject in their dependence on expert opinion."[117] The parent (and here what was meant was the mother) could not be trusted to such a skilled task, equipped as she was with only maternal instincts, nor could the child be trusted to traverse the risks of its environment or of its internal drives without proper instruction. In the gap between nature and culture, "the expert emerged as the missing link, the modern parent's modern parent."[118]

There were two different theories that underpinned the approaches to "developing the sexual child." The planned and inflexible regimes inspired by Taylorism were reflected in the theories of behaviorist child-rearing professionals.[119] Nature offered no guiding blueprint, since "there are no instincts."[120] Especially dangerous for the "father of behaviorism," John Watson, was the prevailing popular view that "all infant and childish activities, whether 'good' or 'bad,' are due to the unfolding of the inborn equipment of the child."[121] The danger comes not from within but from (again) outside influences. Children are programmed by their experiences, and hence those who directed these were all important, for "modern methods of child guidance and mental hygiene point out the difference between a bad habit corrected and a habit corrected badly."[122]

When it comes to sexual habits, Watson seems less confident on the issue of instincts. He blurs the distinction between the possession of instincts and

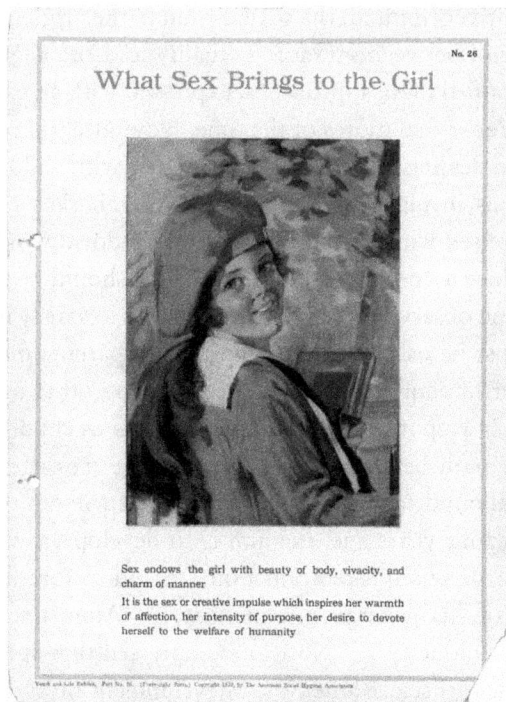

FIGURE 7.4: What sex brings to the girl (1922). Social Welfare History Archive, Andersen Library, University of Minnesota, Minneapolis.

the acquisition of bad habits through external influences. Two positions are evident, the first related to avoiding distracting influences: "The child must never be bathed in the same tub whether they are the same or different sexes although there should be no inhibitions about their seeing each other naked in or out of the bath."[123] Group childhood nudity is to be encouraged overall, but "after it sleeps, keep the hands below the sheets. However, as the child grows older, the same hands should be outside the sheets when it is put to bed."[124] The child may have no instincts, but the body and mind remain susceptible to diversion. But the absence of instinct does not equate to sexual inexperience: "Parents think that their children are innocent and want to keep them that way. But ... their innocent lambs have been learning about sex (using the term broadly) from the time their wavering footsteps at two years, took them into groups of 4–6 year old children."[125] It is not clear what prompted the "wavering footsteps" in the first place, though the implication is inherent sexual curiosity. Nor is this comment consistent with his advice to parents to leave their children unattended while playing naked with older children.[126]

Post-Freudian child-rearing literature arguably further "normalized" (and in doing so normatively limited) the sexual child in the original.[127] The original link made by Freud between infantile sexuality and the acquisition of adult heterosexuality framed these approaches, expressed with an explicitness that is striking given wider sexual mores of the time. Now, attention turned to avoiding repression and dealing positively and tolerantly with childish curiosity and sexual explorations in play. In responding to the childish curiosity, parents must not associate sex with shame and secrecy. To do so would distort development and produce a "perverted adult."[128] There should be no restriction on very young children observing peer and adult nudity to satisfy natural curiosity. Correct terms must be used for bodily parts, and parents must "treat naked bodies as a matter of course in bathing, dressing and other natural intimacies of family life."[129] In response to questioning by curious children, parents must tread the narrow path between conveying negative messages about sex and attaching a special importance and significance that will fan the wrong sort of curiosity.[130] After four years age, the aim is to develop "a wholesome objective attitude towards sex and reproduction, ... and to forestall the unwholesome influences of his general environment."[131] After six, more emphasis can be placed on "modesty."[132] No fear is expressed that speaking about sex will lead to precocious sex. Rather, the "development of an unhealthy sexual appetite" will result from *not* speaking frankly about sex.[133]

The homogeneity of this approach is challenged, however, by the phenomenon of childish "sex-play." Childhood and play are synonymous notions, evidence of curiosity and an autonomous child world. But child development books acknowledge a dimension of childish activity that requires particular attention, evidence that childish sexual curiosity is being directed into action.

> In some instances the play goes on quite openly, as in the case of two boys who one summer ran a popcorn and cool drink stand on a side street of their town. Every afternoon at about 4 o'clock a little girl sauntered down the street, disappeared beneath the bunting of the "pop" stand with one of the boys while the other unconcernedly continued to serve the trade.[134]

Sex-play demands parental response to precariously balance suppression (good) and repression (bad), and training the sexual child will circumvent any possible dangers. Parents are advised not to ignore but to defuse its "seriousness," since "ridicule is one of the surest methods of hurrying a thing to oblivion."[135] Negotiating the suppression-repression pitfall is delicate and its success depends upon efficacious training.

> The boy who has had a "full sex training from birth" sees the fun in sex, just as he sees it in everything else, if he has a sense of humour, without experiencing physical excitement in response to the mental action. HIS TRAINING RENDERS HIS OUTLOOK ON THE WHOLE QUESTION OBJECTIVE, NOT SUBJECTIVE.[136]

Proper training ensures that the child will filter these plays through the terms of adult surveillance and through this nullify its sensual experience. Sex-play becomes play sex and, through these mechanisms, is "desexualised."[137]

The message of both the behaviorist and post-Freudian discourses is that by nature parents are gardeners, not educators, and must learn the skills to become parent-experts. "One omission, one neglected occasion or one unconscious act by the parents is sufficient to encourage a 'weed' to grow in the child, which can then be uprooted only by unremitting effort."[138] For behaviorists, the problem is the right information: sexual knowledge gained from other children is unacceptable, and parents are incompetent to speak about sex. The information must come via the experts to the parents.[139] For post-Freudians the real danger is repression. Unlike suppression, which is the process by which the instinct is effectively socialized, repression means that the unaddressed sexual instinct is contained within the realm of the subconscious, is therefore not subject to active direction or control, and will foster neuroses and emotional pathologies.

Despite being less moralistic than previous characterizations of the sexual child, the discourse of development nevertheless continued the process by which sexual agency in the child was muted. Adult supervision continued, and curiosity and even sex-play were rewritten as something more anodyne and palatable. The primary role of the parent/gardener was to tread the line between repression and suppression (the former bad, the latter good) so that the child-as-adult would achieve psychologically and physically sound heterosexuality. This distinction must be carefully balanced. Avoiding repression did not mean free license: "everything connected with sex has for so long been under a ban that we must be careful now not to fly to the other extreme and preach sexual indulgence as a cure for repression."[140] For both, giving children sexual knowledge *before* adolescence is crucial: "we cannot leave the building of the road until it is time to embark upon the journey and then expect to find it safe and easy going."[141] Despite the acceptance of a sexual sensibility, and notwithstanding the presence or absence of instinct, the sexual child in development remained a hostage to the future. Neutralized by science and rational purpose, this was a discourse not about the sexual child, but about taking a reliable pathway to normative sexual adulthood.

CONCLUSION

Parents, families, educators, doctors and eventually psychologists would
have to take charge, in a continuous way, of this precious and perilous,
dangerous and endangered sexual potential.[142]

It would appear that the sexuality of the child came under scrutiny with the emergence of the child in modernity. Indeed, we feel justified in claiming that the modern child was "sexualized" from its very inception. Yet this claim invites more questions, and it is these that we have tried to address in this review of the key discourses of modernity. What, first, does the process of sexualization entail? What reference points are used in the isolation of this process? Where, if at all, does the child figure in this? How, if at all, do these discourses relate to wider issues of social order? In responding to these summary questions we can demonstrate both continuities and contradictions: first, the issue of sexualization, a term that attracts much current attention, especially in relation to young girls.[143] But sexualization does not entail the positive recognition of sexual agency. Additionally, it is an emotive and indistinct term that conveys few insights into either the problem or the solution. Instead, it further complicates by the range of assumptions behind the term. What is meant by "sexualization"? Has this to do with

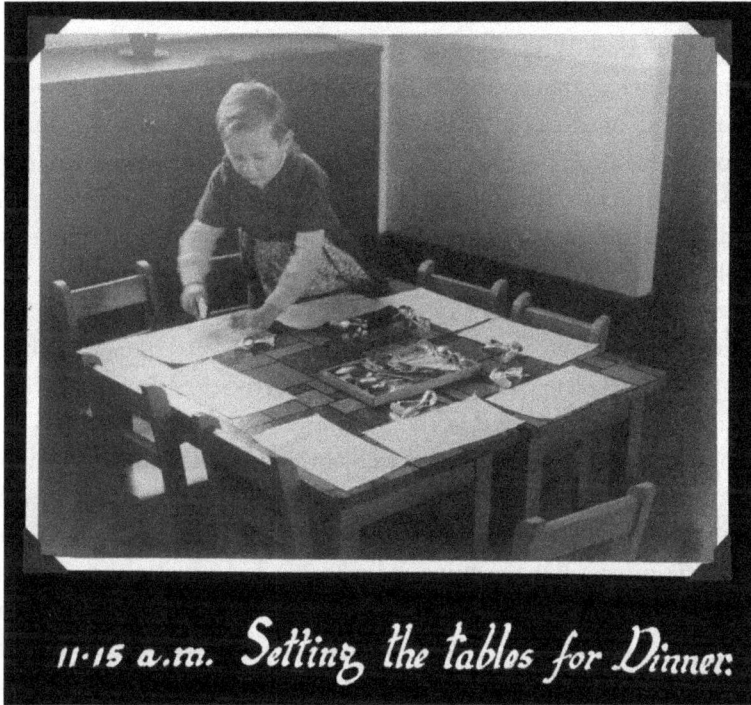

11·15 a.m. *Setting the tables for Dinner.*

FIGURE 7.5: Setting the table for dinner. Papers of Alexandre Gowie, manuscript, 1835–1987. National Library of Australia.

education or with firsthand experience? Is it implied and therefore normalized in biological development? Exactly what manifestations of sex is this referring to? Coitus? Fantasy? Homoerotic or autoerotic pleasures? Voyeuristic consumption? In popular usage, at least, the term remains indistinct yet always prejudicial.

Across our range of discourses and, still, to sexualize the child is to erode something inherently good, to render the child less of a child—at best to precociously age it, at worst to exploit and endanger it. In the discourses we have examine there has been evident continuity in the default condition of "the child"—not an adult, unformed, an adult-in-training to be educated, unknowing, innocent, and pure. All these adjectives code for another condition: the lack of sexual sensibility. Yet, and here is the first contradiction, without this sensibility, this consciousness, how is it that environment, instinct, or unconscious stimulation is so perilous? What exactly is the source of that peril? And what will be imperiled? The circular argument of innocence (the child is asexual and the danger is its sexualization, i.e., the end of innocence) does not enlighten. Another theme has been the problem of the body. The adult-child distinction was grounded in an assumption that the child was a to-be-adult in both body and mind. While the discourses we have summarized acknowledged both components of the distinction, the connection between the two was always the source of anxiety. As the sexual child became more the domain of professionals, medical, psychological, and educational, strategies to direct the mind-body connection became more complex and sophisticated. But as this occurred, the anxieties were intensified, not defused, and the possibility of the agentically sexual child remained a shadowy presence in the wings, always there but never placed at center stage.

The imputed characteristics of adult sexuality in Western culture that consistently posed a challenge to social order[144] rendered the sexuality of the child of special significance, given that the child itself was, throughout this period, understood as active and passive; driven by instincts or a tabula rasa; innocent, corruptible, and corrupting. This endemic instability that could not be ignored was given greater poignancy in the context of the final theme: the child as the carrier of the future. But the future of what? A hidden element across these discourses—"the dog that didn't bark"—is heteronormativity and its maintenance.[145] Heteronormativity entails the naturalization of male-female coitus; yet in what is said about the sexual child in these discourses there is little evidence of a "natural" predilection for heterosexuality.

The phenomenon of sexual pleasure is woven throughout the discourses on childhood sexuality, but without any obvious connection with heterosexual behavior, actual or incipient. In the nineteenth century childish erotic pleasures were the vector for pathological and destructive masturbation. Even with the relaxation of masturbation phobia and the inclusion of self-stimulation in a normal range of developing sexuality, there was anxiety about the threat posed to heterosexuality by overreliance on autoerotic activity, especially among women. The disciplines of sexology and, to a lesser extent, psychoanalysis (which relied more on clinical cases) widened the lens of normality, at least temporarily, through their firsthand accounts of a rich polymorphous and conscious sexual life of the child, but no conclusions were directly drawn about the implications for the "normality" of heterosexuality in child or adult. We are left with a final and unresolved contradiction: the terms under which the sexual child was constructed in Anglophone modernity ensured that the twinned topics, children and sex, would be perceived as simultaneously unstable, critical, and irresolvable and, for all this, never to be fully acknowledged or fully forgotten.

CHAPTER EIGHT

Prostitution: The Age of Empires

RAELENE FRANCES

In 1877 the newly installed governor of Hong Kong, Sir John Pope-Hennessy, learned to his dismay that two Chinese women, A-Sau and Tai-Yau, had fallen to their deaths while being chased across rooftops of the brothel district by officers of the British government. The commission of inquiry that Pope-Hennessy appointed to investigate this scandal exposed the system of imperial regulation of prostitution that had become a feature of the British Empire in the nineteenth century.[1] This chapter examines the relationship between the expansion of European empires in the nineteenth and early-twentieth centuries and prostitution. It is concerned with three major themes: the impact that empires had on sexual economies, the ways in which imperial governments intervened to regulate commercial sex, and finally how discourses around sexuality and prostitution contributed to imperial projects. The relationship between prostitution and empire sheds light on both sexual practices and understandings in the age of imperialism, as well as on the workings and meanings of empire.

SEXUAL ECONOMIES

While some form of sexual trade existed in many areas later colonized by Europeans, the process of colonization changed both the nature and scale of commercial sex. New forms of commercial sex arose in the context of new material circumstances created by colonialism. Most importantly, sex workers were increasingly drawn into the huge migration of labor, both free and unfree, around the world in the late-nineteenth and early-twentieth centuries. Millions of Indian, African, Chinese, and Pacific Islander laborers traveled to work in the cities and rural estates mushrooming in European colonies. They came to build railways, ports, and other infrastructure; to work in the mines and the rubber, sugar, and tea plantations; to fetch and carry and care for the colonists. The overwhelming majority of these laborers were single men, creating huge imbalances in the ratios of men to women among these ethnic groups and in the receiving colonies in general. In some cases, up to 98 percent of the migrant communities were male.[2] These male enclaves created a huge demand for sexual services, and women and children were brought in to meet the demand. Large-scale prostitution thus arguably emerged as "the feminised auxiliary service industry" in response "to changing male work patterns" that accompanied imperial expansion.[3]

The colonizers also fueled this demand for commercial sex, as government officials, entrepreneurs, workers, and soldiers accompanying the spread of empires were also overwhelmingly male. For some of these, at least, the prospect of exotic sexual experiences was part of the attractions of empire.[4] European colonial economies therefore increased the total demand for commercial sexual services and required much greater mobility of sex workers. At the same time, the infrastructure that supported modern empires—communications systems such as steamship and telegraph services and the opening of the Panama and Suez canals—facilitated this movement of both sex workers and clients from one part of the world to another.

The individuals who met this burgeoning demand for commercial sex came from many parts of the world, augmenting the local supply of sex workers drawn from both rural and urban areas, both male and female. In colonial Malaya, for instance, "they came from everywhere—Japan, China, Java, India, Thailand, eastern Europe—most recruited by pimps and procurers but others travelling independently to work in brothels in Penang, Ipoh, Singapore, Kuala Lumpur, and the small towns and settlements that grew up as trading posts around the plantations and the mines."[5] Japan and China supplied the majority of women operating in foreign locations in the Asia-Pacific region, while eastern European Jews (principally from Poland and later Russia), the French, and Italians were involved in an international movement of procurers, pimps, and workers who followed the trade routes west to South America, especially Brazil, Argentina, and Uruguay, and on to South Africa and Australia. Another route ran to the east, through North Africa, Egypt, and Constantinople, and the opening of the Suez Canal in 1869 provided easy access to Bombay, Colombo, Singapore, Saigon, Hong Kong, Shanghai, and Manila. A further traffic existed between Russia and Manchuria and north China, especially through the railhead at Harbin.[6] This highly mobile itinerant workforce moved not just within empires but also across imperial and national borders, seeking out new opportunities wherever they existed. In its reliance on the telegraph and the steamship to ensure fast communication of changing demands and fast delivery of workers to meet this demand, the organization of this traffic was essentially very modern.[7]

While colonialism created the demand and conditions whereby this international traffic in sex workers could flourish, it also altered existing local patterns of commercial sex or, in some cases, introduced prostitution where it had been previously unknown. China, for instance, had a well-established system of prostitution graduated according to the social class of clients, among other factors. "Shanghai's hierarchy of prostitution was structured by the class background of the customers, the native place of both customers and prostitutes, and the appearance and age of the prostitutes."[8] At the upper levels of courtesan establishments, sexual services formed a small part of what clients paid for, the courtesan filling a role more akin to that of mistress than prostitute. Lower down the scale, poorer, less educated women sold unceremonious intercourse in circumstances that often resembled slavery, their entire earnings being confiscated by brothel keepers who provided in return only minimal food and clothing. "Pawned" prostitutes at least in theory had some prospect of eventual freedom, being able to use half their earnings to pay off the debt incurred to the original traffickers and transferred to brothel keepers. In practice, it seems that few achieved such freedom.[9]

The arrival of Europeans brought an explosion in the demand for prostitution, drawing women into Shanghai not just to service the new residents and sojourners but also to go abroad, where increasing numbers of Chinese laborers were working in European enterprises in the Asia-Pacific region. Some were taken as far afield as the United States and Canada.[10] The supply of women and girls to service this burgeoning overseas demand was met principally by the daughters of the rural poor in southeast China, most sold by their parents to traffickers as the combined effects of social turmoil and natural disasters pushed many families to the verge of starvation.[11] The demand for sexual labor in Asia was such that women from neighboring French Indo-China (now Vietnam) were also drawn into the traffic, with kidnapped children of relatively prosperous parents smuggled aboard China-bound steamers along with the daughters of the destitute.[12]

At the higher end of the trade, the modernization of Chinese society in the late-nineteenth and early-twentieth centuries changed the class of clients patronizing courtesans. The more numerous and varied categories of merchants who supplanted the scholar elites placed less value on the "spiritual" qualities of courtesans. Their occupation in consequence became both more sexualized and more commercialized.[13]

Japan's famous and much-misunderstood geishas bore many similarities to China's courtesans, being both more and less than prostitutes. Brothel prostitution was also a well-established institution in Japan before the ascendancy of European powers in the Asia-Pacific region. However, economic developments in association with colonialism changed the ways in which prostitution was practiced.[14] When Japan opened its doors to the West in 1868, some of the first to embrace foreigners were women who left Japan's shores to work as *karayuki-san*, literally translated as "gone to China." Drawn principally from the overpopulated and economically depressed Kumamoto and Nagasaki

FIGURE 8.1: Portrait of a Japanese woman, 1890. Gretchen Liu. Courtesy of the National Archives of Singapore.

prefectures of the island of Kyushu, girls as young as seven were sold by their families to *zegen*, or procurers, who shipped them to Hong Kong, Kuala Lumpur, and Singapore, where they were trained in the arts of the brothel. From these staging posts they were re-shipped throughout Southeast Asia and the Pacific and as far west as Cape Town, where they worked off the debts accrued by their parents in their original purchase as well as additional debts accumulated during training. The trade in karayuki was the result of "a convergence of rural impoverishment, the traditional devaluation of female children, government suppression of practices used to limit family size and energetic [Japanese] overseas military and economic expansion."[15]

While in some senses the traffic in Japanese prostitutes overseas can be seen as a consequence of European colonial activities in the Asia-Pacific and Africa, it was also partly driven by Japanese imperial ambitions. Some men who organized this traffic—the zegen—defended their activities as being in the interests of national glory. Overseas prostitution certainly facilitated Japanese economic expansion throughout Asia as the presence of brothels encouraged a range of other associated businesses: hairdressers, kimono shops, pharmacies, florists, haberdasheries, laundries, restaurants, photographers, doctors, dentists, and cabinetmakers. The profits from brothels were also used in some cases to finance other Japanese industries, such as pearling vessels in northern Australia.[16] As James Warren argues, in effect, "the Japanese, who were still too weak to advance politically and militarily into Southeast Asia, progressed first economically by tacitly encouraging overseas migration and prostitution to develop their economic base." By the end of the Russo-Japanese war in 1905 there were nearly 700 karayuki-san in Singapore alone, a city they called *shinkinzan*, or the new gold mine, because of the profits to be made from the custom of coolies, soldiers, and sailors.[17]

Prostitution also had a long history in India before the arrival of the British. Records from the fourth century B.C.E. detail instructions as to the correct ways in which prostitutes should deal with their customers, and prostitutes played important and respected roles in Hindu mythology and religious ritual. In medieval India they were respected for their social, intellectual, and artistic skills as well as their sexual prowess in much the same way as other skilled artisans. Under the Moguls, courtesans were an important and public part of high court culture and society, while common prostitutes were also accepted as playing an important role in purifying towns, maintaining social order, and providing outlets for men's sexual drives.[18]

When the British East India Company arrived in India in the seventeenth century, there existed a range of forms of sexual exchange distinguished from

FIGURE 8.2: Klinghalese coolies, probably on a plantation in Deli (Sumatra). Courtesy of KITLV/Royal Netherlands Institute of Southeast Asian and Caribbean Studies.

each other by gradations of caste and class, regional variations, and degrees of the sacred and secular, the cultural and the coital.[19] Under the Raj, commercial sex drew in women from a wider variety of socioeconomic strata and also attracted a new clientele, especially in cities like Calcutta and Bombay that expanded rapidly as centers of British trade, industry, and governance. As well as the custom provided by the colonizers, colonial enterprises created a new class of prosperous Indians who assisted British commerce and administration and who were enthusiastic patrons of the sex industry.[20] For many women, prostitution was a means to survival when the new urban economies offered few other alternatives to women.[21] At the same time that colonial capitalism increasingly commercialized and commodified human relations, the breakdown of traditional social norms under colonialism propelled more women into prostitution. The grim fate that befell Hindu widows and single daughters of *kulin* Brahmans provided strong motivation for these women to seek an independent life as prostitutes. Both groups of women had long been well represented in the higher ranks of India's prostitutes; as social restraints weakened from the mid-nineteenth century onward, the numbers of women opting for this life increased significantly. One estimate for Calcutta in the middle of the nineteenth century calculated that 10,000 of the approximately 12,000 prostitutes in Calcutta were Hindu widows and daughters of *kulin* Brahmins.[22] The total number of prostitutes in Calcutta increased dramatically in the 1850s and 1860s, with the figure increasing to around 30,000 in 1867, despite no significant increase in the total population of the city.[23]

The circumstances under which prostitutes plied their trade also changed considerably under colonialism, as they were subjected to control and surveillance by colonial authorities and affected by new social norms introduced by colonialism in the eighteenth and nineteenth centuries. While we will look more closely at the impact of colonial regulations in relation to prostitution, it is possible to chart a broader transformation in the way that prostitutes were treated in India over this period, from sinners to criminals. As M. Satish Kumar explains, "the caste-based, hierarchical pre-colonial India accommodated the 'sinning' prostitutes as it did other socially functional occupational groups, such as sweepers, without identifying them as 'criminal.' However, in the colonial period prostitution was branded as a crime to be codified, regulated and controlled."[24] As well, although common prostitutes never enjoyed a very high social status in the Indian caste system, being placed only slightly above sweepers,[25] those who associated with "unclean foreigners" suffered a distinct decline in social standing, reviled as *gora-kamana* ("to earn one's living from the British soldier").[26]

Colonialism in India also redefined new groups of women, such as temple dancers, or *devadasi*, as prostitutes. Prior to British colonization, temple dancing girls were a distinct group of unmarried temple servants who had been dedicated to temple deities as young girls through rites resembling Hindu marriage ceremonies: "they performed a range of ritual services, derived incomes from endowments associated with their offices and enjoyed considerable prestige within 'traditional' Hindu society as 'eternally auspicious' women 'married' to temple deities."[27] Although temple dancing girls "typically entered into highly stylized relations of concubinage with upper caste elite males," they did not participate in the urban commercial sex trade.[28] Their social and legal status underwent a major change from the late 1860s, as Anglo-Indian courts made a confused attempt to interpret temple dancing in terms of Hindu caste systems, and patriarchal Hindu legal norms in relation to marriage. By the early-twentieth century, temple dancing girls had been criminalized as prostitutes and strong legal foundations had been established for their complete suppression as a viable group within Hindu society.[29]

In contrast to the situation in Asia, prostitution was unknown in Australian Aboriginal societies before the advent of British colonial settlement. Prostitution arrived in New South Wales with the First Fleet of convicts in 1788 and

FIGURE 8.3: "A Nautch," Indian dance. Major J. Luard, 1820. Courtesy of KITLV/ Royal Netherlands Institute of Southeast Asian and Caribbean Studies.

continued to play an important part in the early colony as both a sexual outlet for male colonists, both convict and free, and a source of earnings, principally for women. With the dispossession of the indigenous inhabitants and the rapid destruction of their traditional economies, Aboriginal people in contact with Europeans were soon drawn into the colonial economy. While some worked as laborers and domestic servants, the exchange of women's sexual services, either for money or goods, formed a key part of the ways in which whole groups survived on the fringes of white society.[30]

The British occupation of Australia also fostered widespread prostitution among the earliest female colonists. Established as a convict settlement, the British colony in New South Wales was characterized from the outset by a huge disparity in the ratio of males to females, with men outnumbering women by up to six to one for the first four decades of settlement. Incentives for women to sell sex were high, as the early colonial period provided few other economic opportunities for women outside marriage and domestic service. While subsequent immigration redressed this demographic imbalance to some extent, the reliance of the colonial economy on primary industries dependent on male labor (pastoralism and mining) meant an ongoing high demand for women's commercial sexual services. On the other hand, limited openings for women's paid labor continued to provide a pool of women willing to supply this demand.[31]

While New Zealand never experienced the extremes in sex ratios characteristic of the Australian convict colonies, there are some similarities. Prostitution was unknown in Maori society, but the disruption to tribal economic and social systems wrought by colonial occupation led many women of Maori descent into commercial sex in the townships. And although the involvement of European women in prostitution was never on the scale of that in the Australian convict colonies, economic opportunities for women were even more restricted and many poor immigrant women found their way into the sex industry.[32]

The British colonization of Kenya coincided with a series of ecological disasters that seriously disrupted local tribal economies and marriage systems dependent on bride-wealth derived from rural production. Local women and children responded by selling sex to the recently imported Indian laborers engaged in building the Uganda Railway, lured or coerced away from their homes by the plentiful supplies of food in the construction camps.[33] In the expanding city of Nairobi, local women sold sex in a variety of contexts—on the streets and from rented rooms; full time and part time; in conjunction with other services such as cooking, cleaning, and companionship or separately; to African and Indian laborers as well as Europeans—and accumulated enough capital to acquire property, invest in other entrepreneurial ventures, and subsidize family farms. Luise White argues that women's profits from sexual commerce formed a critical part of the successful adaptation and resistance of indigenous Kenyans to the dual challenge of widespread famine and colonial intervention and was seen by women "as a reliable means of capital accumulation, not as a despicable fate or a temporary strategy."[34] For women, urban prostitution provided not just the means of survival for themselves and their families, but also the opportunity to prosper independently and to "violate the norms of their communities" by owning and selling huts and becoming household heads.[35]

Farther south, in what is now South Africa, colonial economies created both new imperatives for indigenous women to engage in the sale of sexual services and new opportunities for them to do so. For instance, the growth of urban centers in Cape Town, Kimberley, and Johannesburg drew in large numbers of African and immigrant male laborers. Before the mining booms of the 1890s, prostitution in Cape Town was characterized by small-scale individual operators working on the streets or from private houses. The commercial sex industry was largely a women's business, with women operating independently of pimps or bullies.[36] They included some black women but were predominantly "Cape colored" (of mixed ancestry) and white. The overwhelming majority were locally born and were, as Charles van Onselen notes, the daughters of South Africa's old proletariat.[37]

The gold rush on the Witwatersrand from the mid-1880s attracted not just these women from farther south but also a significant new group of sexual entrepreneurs, groups of men and women who worked the international circuit from Europe to America and included the notoriously tough "Bowery Boys" of New York. Driven out of the United States by anti-prostitution campaigns, they sought a more tolerant field of activity and promising earnings in the towns servicing the gold fields. The outbreak of the Anglo-Boer War in 1899 also increased demand for sexual services as imperial troops poured into the ports and inland cities of the colony.[38]

Nor was it only women who were drawn into commercial sexual exchange in the context of colonialism. Male brothels in Tientsin, China, employed around 800 sex workers in 1900, and Singapore also had a half-dozen male brothels.[39] When the gold mines of the Transvaal drew in large numbers of African male laborers from Mozambique in the early twentieth century, the all-male compounds gave rise to a system of "mine marriage" tied to financial rewards. These "marriages" usually involved an older man forming a relationship with a younger male worker who provided sexual gratification, cooking, and washing in exchange for payment of money used by the younger man to provide the *lobola*, or bride price, that would eventually allow him to marry in his homeland. These relationships were usually monogamous and reportedly affectionate and do not fit neatly into a definition of prostitution as promiscuous sexual commerce. Nonetheless, mine marriages represented a new element in both African sexual practices and labor relations arising as a response to the new circumstances of the colonial capitalist economy.[40]

Internal migration of African male laborers also had consequences for the women they left behind. In Lesotho, for instance, in the early years of the twentieth century, increasing numbers of women were forced to assume responsibility for their own and their children's economic survival because of the outflow of male migrant labor to South Africa. They turned to beer brewing and prostitution, and many moved to the urban centers of South Africa or the major towns of Lesotho in order to maximize their earnings.[41]

Likewise, the U.S. annexation of the Philippines introduced a new element to the local sexual economy, with relatively well-paid U.S. troops proving a magnet for women throughout the region keen to provide commercial sexual services. Somewhat to the dismay of the progressive public in the United States, brothels in Manila prominently displayed U.S. flags as an incitement to the patronage of U.S. troops. As in other parts of Southeast Asia, the colonial city of Manila attracted a diverse range of international prostitutes, principally from China and Japan but also from the United States, Europe, and Australia.[42]

Little is known about the existence of prostitution in the Dutch East Indies before the colonial period. We do know that colonial conditions created a new demand for sexual services by the local workforce of male itinerant or "circular" labor; Chinese and European immigrants; and the Dutch armed services, among whom part of this demand was met by Indonesian concubines, who lived with soldiers in the garrisons even after this practice began to be increasingly frowned upon toward the end of the nineteenth century. Commercial prostitution satisfied the remaining demand, which increased as the incidence of concubinage decreased in the 1890s. Regular troopers in any case could at

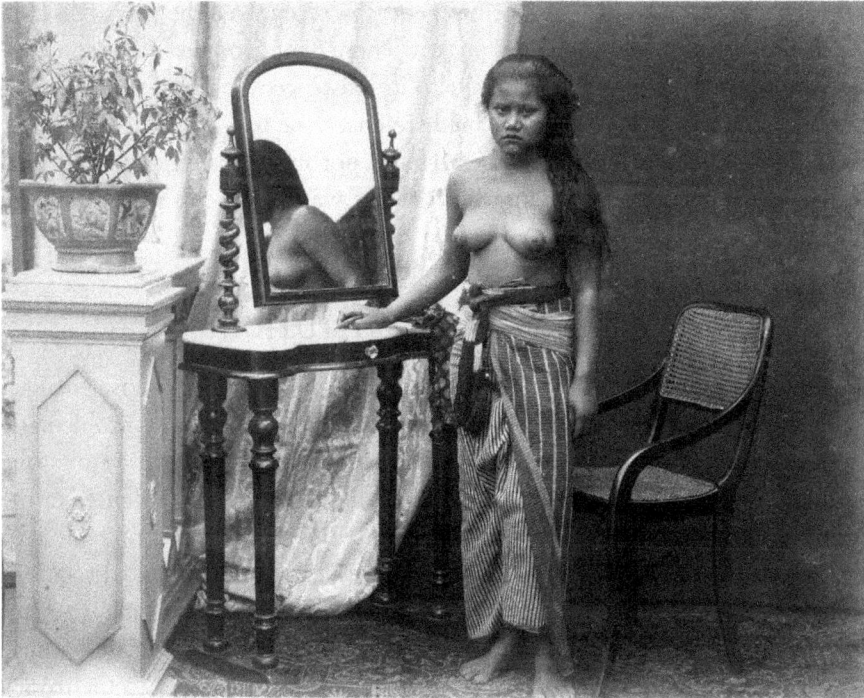

FIGURE 8.4: Prostitute in Java, Indonesia, 1897. Courtesy of KITLV/Royal Netherlands Institute of Southeast Asian and Caribbean Studies.

no stage afford to keep a concubine and thus provided a steady clientele for prostitutes.[43]

Prostitution thus played an integral role in the expansion of European empires in the nineteenth century. Prostitutes provided sex and companionship and sometimes also other domestic services such as cooking and cleaning that reproduced the military manpower and the predominantly male labor force of imperial economies. Although colonialism cannot be held entirely responsible for the conditions that drove so many colonized people into the sale of sex, colonial economies in many cases did contribute to this impoverishment by disrupting traditional economies and social systems. The earnings of prostitutes sustained not just individual sex workers but in many cases these earnings also supported extended communities in the context of acute economic and social dislocation, often exacerbated by environmental crisis. Colonial economies also created both the explosion in demand for sexual services and the infrastructure whereby it could be met by the transfer of sex workers from one part of the globe to another as the location of this demand shifted. Brothel prostitution also stimulated a range of related service industries, which in turn contributed to the growth of colonial cities and towns.

For their part, imperial authorities generally recognized the ways in which prostitution sustained the imperial project. They either connived at the commercial sex industry or turned a blind eye to its existence. Not until the twentieth century were any serious attempts made to check the traffic in persons. But as the following section demonstrates, this did not mean that imperial governments adopted a laissez-faire approach to the way in which the sex industry operated.

REGULATING PROSTITUTION

While colonization presented opportunities and challenges for those engaged in the sale of sex, the existence of wide-scale prostitution was problematic from the point of view of colonizers. On the one hand, prostitution was one solution to the potential social disorders arising from huge imbalances in the ratios of men to women: indeed, it was seen by most regimes as preferable to several alternative outlets for male sexual urges, that is, homosexual relationships or violence against "respectable" women (especially colonizing women). But prostitution challenged the imperial project on three grounds: first, because it was associated with the spread of venereal disease, especially to the troops who enforced the power of empire; second, because it provided opportunities for interracial sex, which had the potential to undermine the authority of colonizers and the virility of colonizing races; and third, because the presence of prostitutes from the colonizing race undermined the status of the colonizers in the eyes of the colonized. Given the variety of imperial contexts, however, there was neither one pattern of problematization nor one pattern of response by colonial authorities. Despite the variations, it is possible to point to the regulation of prostitution as "a critical prop of imperial rule" vital to the maintenance of racial and sexual privileges upon which colonial authority depended as well as to the attempt to control venereal disease.[44]

The issue of sexually transmitted disease had been of concern to European governments to varying degrees throughout the nineteenth century and assumed new prominence when it was declared the "new cholera" by the International Medical Congress at its meeting in Paris in 1867.[45] Many governments identified female prostitutes as the main sources of infection of such diseases and had already introduced measures to control prostitutes. The most notorious instances of imperial regulation of prostitution are the various incarnations of contagious diseases legislation within the British Empire. The British Contagious Diseases Acts of the 1860s are the best-known instances. They provided for the registration of all known female prostitutes within a ten-mile radius of garrison towns. These women were compulsorily examined for venereal disease and, if found to be diseased, were detained in a Lock Hospital until cured. The government hoped that such measures would ensure a disease-free pool of prostitutes for the use of its troops, thereby decreasing the alarming incidence of venereal disease in the army. The CD Acts were first and foremost imperial legislation designed to protect the health of the empire's fighting forces.[46]

It is generally assumed that this system was derived from Continental examples, especially that of France, which had, since the time of Napoleon, adopted a system of registering and inspecting known prostitutes and licensing brothels, or *maisons de tolérance*. But while the British CD Acts are the best-known imperial instances of this legislation, they are by no means the first examples of the biomedical regulation of prostitution within the British Empire. In Malta, police regulations dating to the time of the Knights Templar allowed for the inspection of prostitutes and continued under the British. Although these were found to be irregular when challenged in 1859, a new ordinance passed in 1861 confirmed these powers of inspection and prostitutes continued to be examined three times a month by a police physician and, if diseased, could be confined until cured. This experience was significant in influencing official opinion in favor of CD legislation in Britain.[47]

In the Crown colony of Hong Kong, official regulation of prostitution predated the English acts of the 1860s. In 1857 Governor Sir John Bowring was persuaded by naval officers on the China Station to introduce Ordinance 12. The British colonial secretary, Henry Labouchere, reluctantly endorsed this move, not just convinced by the high incidence of venereal disease in the navy but also hoping that increased control of brothels would have a beneficial effect on those he saw as the real victims of prostitution, that is, women and girls sold into brothel slavery.[48] The Venereal Disease and Contagious Diseases Ordinances were revised ten years later and formed part of an extensive network of official surveillance and control of the Chinese laboring population that was designed to tackle not just disease but also crime by regulating commercial sex. These measures provided for the registration of prostitutes and the licensing of brothels and the medical inspection of women who serviced non-Chinese clients. Women diagnosed as contagious were incarcerated until declared cured. Like the later metropolitan acts, the Hong Kong ordinances had a clear biopolitical rationale for the colonial state, designed as they were to ensure the security and efficiency of the empire. In this process, prostituted women were literally inscribed as colonial subjects.[49]

But while both the English and Hong Kong regulations were imperial legislation, there were important differences. The Hong Kong ordinances not only predated the English acts but were also farther reaching: they covered the entire colony (rather than just garrison towns) and provided for the licensing of brothels as well as the registration of prostitutes, a situation that clearly laid the state open to charges that it had legalized prostitution.[50] Another key difference between the English acts and the Hong Kong ordinances was the way in which sexual discipline was explicitly linked to questions of race: in Hong Kong, only those women who took non-Chinese clients were subject to medical examination and incarceration.[51] Under the 1867 ordinance, brothels were confined to designated localities catering separately to European and Chinese clients, in the eastern and western ends of the city, respectively. In fact the legislation was so sweeping that one concerned British official worried that it contained the statutory sanctions to "lock up the whole Chinese female population."[52] As well as licensing and inspecting brothels, the ordinances allowed police to break into and enter suspected houses and employed paid informers to track down "sly" brothels and prostitutes. Women convicted of infecting healthy men with disease were fined and imprisoned, while the costs of all these interventions were met by fees levied on brothel keepers and prostitutes. Such dramatic incursions on the liberty of the subject—even prostitute subjects—would have been unthinkable in Britain.[53]

The system of licensed prostitution in Hong Kong originally had two purposes: the control of the spread of venereal disease, particularly among the soldiers and sailors of the garrison, and the prevention of the exploitation of Chinese prostitutes. But throughout the system's period of operation, legally from 1857 to 1894 and then extralegally from 1900 to 1932, the first aim always took precedence.[54]

In India, British authorities had an even longer history of attempts to control infected prostitutes in the interests of the health of imperial soldiers. Government doctors there had been examining and detaining prostitutes in Lock Hospitals from at least the late-eighteenth century.[55] In some areas, expulsion was preferred to compulsory treatment. At Bangalore cantonment, infected women had their hair cut off and were then publicly expelled.[56] In India generally, the so-called bazaar system was common, whereby each regiment had a quota of prostitutes maintained by the regiment and inspected and treated by the subordinate medical establishment. These women often accompanied the regiment into the line, camping close by the barracks.[57] When more formal CD ordinances were enacted in India from the mid-1850s, there was already in existence an extensive system of surveillance and inspection of the sex trade, and every Indian presidency had Lock Hospitals. A cantonment act of 1864 extended CD control to all military areas of India, and Indian cities were authorized to pass similar legislation in 1868.[58]

Following the enactment of the British CD legislation, British military officials put pressure on colonial governments that had garrison towns or were ports of call for the army and navy to adopt similar measures. While some colonies ignored the request, a number did enact CD legislation, either to appease the British government and ensure the ongoing benefits such military visits brought to the local economy or for other local reasons.

In the Cape Colony, there was little local demand for legislation to control the spread of venereal disease before 1868. However, the War Office claimed that British troops at the Cape were being "more than decimated" by venereal disease and expected the colonial legislature to take appropriate action. But it was not until the War Office threatened to withdraw its troops from Cape Town that the colonial legislature passed the CD Act.[59] In Tasmania, pressure from the British navy was also crucial and coincided with a local desire to control prostitution in an attempt to transform the island from a convict dumping ground to a free colony.[60]

In New Zealand, imperial imperatives also coincided with local concerns: the main pressure for a CD Act came from colonists concerned to give authorities more power to suppress the perceived widespread prostitution of recently arrived single women immigrants.[61] Similarly, in Queensland, military considerations were irrelevant: the colonial parliament quickly seized upon the legislation as a way to control urban white female prostitutes, who were seen as spreading venereal infection to their white clients, thus undermining the virility of the new colony. It passed a CD Act in 1868, followed the next year by New Zealand. In Canada, Quebec and Ontario each introduced a CD Act in 1865, although in both cases the law was to be in effect for a trial period of five years only and was allowed to lapse in 1870.[62] In the case of Victoria, Australia, the legislation was promulgated but never brought into effect.[63]

In addition to these examples there were also CD ordinances in Ceylon and Jamaica (1867), Barbados (1868), Trinidad (1869), Singapore (1870), Penang (1872), Malacca (1873), Labuan (1877), and Fiji (1881). British-administered Lock Hospitals also opened in the Japanese treaty port of Yokohama and in Osaka, Tokyo, and Nagasaki.[64] Japan's implementation of the system appears to have stemmed at least in part from its desire to gain acceptance from other states, especially Britain, as "civilized" and "enlightened."[65]

Thus, a wide range of colonies adopted CD legislation. These included the plantation economies of the Caribbean and the white settler colonies of the southern hemisphere, the European and Europeanized colonies of the Mediterranean and North America, and the handful of Asian colonies scattered around the Indian and Pacific oceans. Mauritius, Seychelles, the Gambia, Sierra Leone, the Gold Coast, Natal, British Honduras, British Guiana, and Falkland Islands all escaped CD legislation.[66]

In all cases where colonies adopted CD legislation, the specific systems enshrined varied from colony to colony but in general were farther reaching than the system adopted in England. As we have seen, the English acts were restricted to a ten-mile radius of named military districts. No such geographical limitation was incorporated in any of the colonial legislation. Some systems went well beyond the English system in their intrusion into the working lives of prostitutes. Women in the Straits Settlements carried identity cards and, by the end of the century, were required to display their photographs and identifying details in the brothel at all times.[67] In Hong Kong, as we have seen, while the ordinances only applied to non-European women servicing foreign clients, police were provided with sweeping powers to search dwellings and detain women suspected of being noncompliant. The deaths of the two women mentioned at the beginning of this chapter, A-Sau and Tai-Yau, were the result of police exercising their powers under the CD ordinances.

In all these variations, we can discern certain patterns in the ways that legislation was formulated and applied, depending on the type and location of the colony concerned. In those colonies where the target population of prostitutes was predominantly white, the focus of the legislation was on the registration of individual women rather than on the licensing of brothels. In such cases, the onus was on the brothel keeper to register inmates. The licensing of brothels was regarded as more extreme, involving as it did state licensing of prostitution. Such a measure could only be justified where the prostitute population was seen as intrinsically more difficult to discipline than white prostitutes. And whereas the task in relation to white prostitutes was (as it was in the UK and Continental Europe) to demarcate the individual sex worker from the respectable woman by labeling the former deviant and abnormal, the task in those colonies with large nonwhite populations was to pathologize the sexuality of non-European races and cultures collectively as aberrant.[68]

The effects on the women who came within the scope of this legislation also varied with the precise provisions and their implementation. In general terms, the effect was to professionalize prostituted women by marking them out more clearly from the rest of the urban poor. In most cases, too, the legislation had the effect of concentrating brothels and prostitutes in more clearly defined, easily surveyed and disciplined urban spaces. In the case of Asian colonies such as Hong Kong, Singapore, and India, this demarcation was also a racial geography, marking out brothel territories according to the race and class of both inmates and clients. In all cases, the provisions fell more harshly on poorer prostitutes, who could not afford to bribe authorities or pay for lawyers.[69] Tai-Yau, one of the Chinese women who fell to her death in Hong Kong, is said to have sold her son into slavery in order to pay a $100 fine that she had previously received from the inspector of brothels.[70] Increasing sanctions against prostitutes also encouraged the involvement of men in the sex industry. These men helped women avoid the attentions of the authorities and assumed roles as procurers and pimps, in many cases displacing women.[71]

Some British colonies that did not enact CD legislation nonetheless had equally comprehensive systems of dealing with the perceived threat that professional prostitutes posed as purveyors of disease. In Gibraltar, colonial authorities utilized a long-standing law relating to "aliens" that allowed non-British subjects to reside or work in Gibraltar on temporary permits at the discretion of the governor. The British authorities used this discretion to regulate prostitutes, most of whom were Spanish. Women who refused or neglected to submit to the system of registration, regular medical examination, and hospitalization could be banished forthwith from the city and the garrison. Although this exercise of discretionary power was in theory only applicable to "alien" women, the authorities extended their control to locally born women by reserving the right to declare them "alien" and therefore subject to the regulation that applied to foreign-born women. The effects on the prostitute cohort were similar to those under other imperial CD legislation noted here: professionalization, geographical concentration, surveillance, and discipline.[72]

Legislation directed specifically at prostitutes was not, however, the only way in which colonial administrations sought to control prostitutes and the spread of venereal disease. In the British African colonies, control more usually meant segregation of whole populations rather than examining and quarantining prostitutes. In most colonial cities with European populations, disease was at the forefront of the colonizers' imagination and formed a potent metaphor for the threat posed by local Africans. Controlling disease provided a medical rationale for the removal and separation of African populations.[73] In Nairobi, the reduction of venereal disease was a key motivation for the enactment of legislation to control the location of African housing, and the Native Location Act was viewed as "the first measure towards the controlling of native prostitution."[74] Non-Africans (Europeans and elite Indians) were to be protected from "contamination" by the racial control of urban space.

So far, our discussion has focused primarily on the British Empire. However, it was by no means the only or first empire to attempt to control venereal disease in its colonies by controlling local prostitutes. The Dutch East Indies, for instance, adapted legislation introduced to the Netherlands by Napoleon during the French occupation under a 1852 "Regulation to counteract the damaging results of prostitution." The regulation provided that every public woman had to register with the police and be examined by a doctor, weekly if possible. If the woman was found to be infected, she was taken to hospital and detained until cured.[75]

It is not surprising, given France's domestic history of regulation, that her colonies also adopted methods to control prostitutes and subject them to medical inspection. Indeed, the French experience in Tahiti seems to have been just as important as the system in operation in France as a model influencing the British in drawing up the original CD Acts and their later extension to the colonies.[76] In China, the French ambassador had been urging some form of regulation of prostitution on the municipal authorities in the French Concession in Shanghai from at least 1868. Although the suggestion met with local support, the practical difficulties of policing all Chinese prostitutes led the French, like the British in Hong Kong, to restrict their ambitions to the control of those women serving foreigners. The British and French authorities in Shanghai combined forces in 1877 to keep a registry of brothels in both the International (formerly British) Settlement and the French Concession, and to license prostitutes and inspect Chinese brothels serving foreigners once a week.

European and Japanese prostitutes were exempt, being regarded as sufficiently self-regulating in relation to hygiene.[77]

In the Philippines, Spanish colonial authorities informally controlled expensive brothels that catered to wealthier clients, including colonial officials, although there was no official system of regulation in place until the last years of Spanish rule. With the influx of troops to quell the revolution in the Philippines, the question of venereal disease became of more general concern to the authorities. In 1898, brothels were officially brought under surveillance by the Board of Health, which licensed and inspected prostitutes on a weekly basis. Although the Spanish were replaced by U.S. forces soon after, the American military took over control of prostitution, setting up a red-light district in Manila, where weekly inspections of brothel inmates continued.[78]

By the time the Americans were regulating prostitution in their overseas empire, the tide had turned against CD legislation throughout the English-speaking world. Vigorous repeal campaigns waged in Britain by feminists, Christians, and civil libertarians from the late 1860s finally succeeded in the suspension of the acts in 1883 and their repeal in 1886. Spurred on by their success in domestic repeal, the Abolitionists, as they called themselves, also campaigned against the various colonial CD laws, forming impressive networks that crossed national and imperial borders to cooperate in the cause. Repeal in those colonies under direct British rule followed in 1888, precipitating ongoing tensions between the metropolitan government and colonial administrations, which resented what they regarded as ill-informed British interference in colonial policies.[79]

Despite the apparent success of the repeal campaign, regulation continued in practice in many jurisdictions, either legally or semi-officially. By the early 1900s, Hong Kong, the Straits Settlements, and India all had such systems in operation, which was famously exposed in India through a report by two American women missionaries, Elizabeth Andrew and Katharine Bushnell.[80] The white settler colonies of Queensland and New Zealand refused to repeal their CD Acts, as did the Cape Colony.

The First World War again brought military considerations to the fore as combatant armies sought to protect the virility of their troops against the debilitating effects of venereal disease. Again, prostituted women were targets of official control. In Egypt, as hundreds of thousands of Allied troops poured in to the northern cities in 1915, martial law brought non-Egyptian women under the same controls that had previously only applied to local women. Thereafter, all brothel inmates were required to register and undergo regular medical examination, and brothels were restricted to designated brothel districts.[81]

In Britain itself, mounting pressure on the government, especially from the colonies of white settlement concerned about the long-term effects of high rates of venereal infection among their troops serving in Europe, prompted the promulgation of Regulation 40D under the Defence of the Realm Act. This highly controversial regulation came into effect in March 1918 and made it an offense for any woman with communicable VD to solicit or to copulate with a member of the armed forces.[82]

Meanwhile, in Britain's colonies and dominions, authorities used the wartime crisis to extend their control over prostituted women. The Straits governor used the opportunity to rid Singapore of the embarrassing presence of twenty-six of the thirty-two European prostitutes who resided there, offering them free passage to leave the colony.[83] In Western Australia, police, magistrates, and the government medical officer colluded to bring about a de facto form of regulation in the capital, Perth, and in the goldfields town of Kalgoorlie. Once again, the threat that prostitutes allegedly posed to military recruits was the rationale, although some officials had been moving quietly in this direction since the early years of the century.[84]

Imperial forces fighting in France also had access to prostitutes registered under France's long-standing system of *maisons de tolérance*. However, as in the colonies, access by colored troops to European prostitutes was problematic from the point of view of the imperial authorities: restrictions on the movements of colored troops combined with their lower pay and their racial status prevented them from partaking of the solace afforded to white troops by the presence of tolerated French brothels.[85]

The ongoing existence of forms of regulation and the continued trafficking in women and children for the sex industry prompted a renewed campaign in the wake of the First World War. The newly formed League of Nations Traffic in Women and Children Committee was actively concerned with the colonial contexts of trafficking and exerted considerable pressure on governments to crack down on those engaged in facilitating the traffic. But while most parts of the British Empire succumbed to this pressure, the French resisted, and licensed prostitution remained legal in its various colonies throughout the 1920s and 1930s.[86]

DISCOURSES AND POLITICS

While imperial regulation of prostitution had important material consequences for the working lives of colonial peoples involved in selling sex, the issue of prostitution also played a critical part in the discourses and politics of empire.

As Philippa Levine and others have argued, British imperial attitudes to colonial prostitution were premised on the assumption that "prostitution offends no native sensibility," that it was a normal part of societies that brutalized women and were themselves intrinsically amoral or immoral.[87] British policy makers argued that the societies they colonized traditionally attached no shame—or certainly less shame—to the commercial sale of sexual services. This discourse validated the imperial project of bringing more civilized practices to "degenerate" colonial societies generally: "Like the crumbling civilizations or 'primitive' social structures to which she was compared, the prostitute was a throwback, a reminder of why imperial expansion was a 'civilizing mission.'"[88]

This discourse of indigenous degeneracy and widespread normalized prostitution also validated policies toward colonial subjects that would not have been contemplated in relation to the metropolis, such as the legalization of brothels and their classification according to race. Howell argues that the adoption of these more severe measures in the Crown colony of Hong Kong represented a crisis of government, where the colonial authorities found themselves, against their inclination, forced to adopt "Oriental" despotic power in order to deal with a problem perceived as essentially Chinese in nature. Colonial pragmatism required the adoption of methods that were otherwise seen as culturally alien and abhorrent to the supposedly freedom-loving British.[89] In this case, too, arguments about the nature of indigenous prostitution and indigenous societies also provided a convenient rationale for limiting the biomedical regulation of prostitution to those indigenous prostitutes in contact with European clients: British colonial authorities argued that inspection offended native sensibilities and should therefore not be imposed on those local prostitutes serving an exclusively Asian clientele.[90]

The British emphasis on indigenous prostitution also deflected attention from the impact of their own rule on local societies and assuaged any guilt they might feel at the sexual exploitation of indigenous women: since indigenous societies attached no shame to prostitution, colonizing men were not contributing to their social downfall by utilizing their services.

As we have seen in the case of the Indian *devadasi*, this "narrative of debasement" could lead to serious misrepresentation of indigenous practices, disregarding the art in favor of the sex and also ignoring the considerable independence and wealth of the *devadasi*. This failure to appreciate the religious dimensions of *devadasi* led to general condemnation of "temple harlotry" and penal sanctions against it.[91] Nor was this narrative of debasement confined to the British Empire. Whether we are considering the dancing girls of Java, the flower-boat singers of Vietnam, the courtesans of China, or the geisha in

FIGURE 8.5: Gentoo dancing girls from Madras, displaying jewelry, 1870. Nicholas and Curths. Archaeological Survey of India Collections. Copyright © The British Library Board. All rights reserved. Photo 1000/59(5438).

Japan, the discourses of colonialism reduced them all to the level of genital prostitution.[92]

An emphasis on naturalized precolonial forms of female prostitution thus masked the effects of colonialism in fueling sexual commerce and modifying its manifestations. So, too, imperial discourses in relation to boy prostitution often emphasized the essentially indigenous origins of pederasty (sex with boys) and downplayed the role of male colonizers as purchasers of indigenous boys' sexual services. Thus, Europeans generally claimed that boy prostitution was either indigenous to Vietnam or introduced by another Asian power: the Chinese.[93] Widespread resort to boy prostitutes by the French in Vietnam was a source of intense anxiety about the precariousness and fragility of French male heterosexual identity.[94] Connections were also drawn among opium smoking, pederasty or boy prostitution, and virulent forms of syphilis. Boy prostitution was thus seen as a threat to the moral fiber of soldiers as well as officers and administrators.[95] To lay the blame for pederasty on Oriental degeneracy was much easier than confronting the reality that European men were implicated in the spread of the sexual commerce in relation to boys.[96]

There were limits, however, to how far the recognition of European involvement in male prostitution translated into imperial policies in relation to the sex
industry. While regulation of female prostitutes was practiced in the French
colonies in Indo-China, the system was never extended to males, despite arguments by some observers that "the prostitution of *boys* is far more dangerous,
from the point of view of public health, than feminine prostitution."[97]

The presence of European prostitutes in the colonies also created serious
challenges for the colonizing powers, although European imperial powers
responded differently to these challenges. The French tended to take their
own prostitutes with them and seemed unconcerned with the impact that the
presence of French prostitutes had on the prestige of the colonizers. British
colonizers showed a much greater sensitivity on this issue, wherever possible deporting any British women as "a measure of far-reaching Imperial
necessity."[98] American colonial powers followed the British example, deporting American prostitutes from Manila.[99] Similar strategies were employed
in colonies such as Australia, which arguably practiced a form of "internal

ASIATIC AUSTRALIA—
A PHASE THAT IS
PASSING AWAY.
(Federal Parliament is now absolutely dominated
by the White Australia party.)

FIGURE 8.6: Japanese woman, cartoon. Benjamin
Minns, in *Bulletin,* January 7, 1904.

colonialism" in relation to the indigenous populations of the northern parts of the continent. Thus, prostitutes of European descent were not allowed in northern ports, and those who did attempt to set up business in the tropics were soon put aboard a southern-bound vessel.[100] In contrast, the prostitution of nonwhite women from certain ethnic groups was encouraged as necessary in light of the large number of nonwhite male laborers: Japanese prostitutes were considered particularly suitable in northern Australia, as they were in Johannesburg.[101] Similarly, in the Philippines, U.S. authorities encouraged the immigration of karayuki-san in part as a way of avoiding tensions with the local Moro population, who were very much opposed to their women consorting with American men.[102]

Despite semi-official intolerance of European prostitutes in the Eastern colonies, some women did escape policies of deportation. These women were variously constructed in contemporary discourse according to their social class and ethnic background. Sharp distinctions were drawn between women of English origin and the many eastern European and Russian Jews who, fleeing persecution and poverty in their homelands, found their way to the colonies in the late-nineteenth and early-twentieth centuries. The former, and their American counterparts, were constructed as rational, clean, businesslike, and successful women, in sharp contrast to their victimized Asian sisters. Lower-class prostitutes, especially Jews, were constructed as especially problematic, their presence in the colonies, like that of lower-class males, a distinct challenge to the status of the colonizers in the eyes of the colonized. The lowest rungs of the hierarchy were regarded as being on a par with the "natives." As Fischer-Tiné points out, "sometimes the hierarchies of class were even translated into the language of race, and the 'lower' segments of white colonial society were thus 'orientalized' much in the same manner as the colonial subjects."[103]

While the control of prostitution was central to the imperial project, it was also a key issue in the anti-imperial movement of the late-nineteenth and early-twentieth centuries: the regulation of prostitution in the British Empire in particular was held up as a powerful argument against American imperial adventures in Asia.[104] Much American social purity activism drew on republican anti-militarism in suggesting that regulated vice was an inevitable and tragic by-product of empire: colonies meant standing armies, standing armies meant prostitution, and prostitution meant that officers would attempt to regulate vice in the interests of disease control. This formula also drew on a "geography of moral restraint," which argued that the inevitable social and sexual demoralization of troops was compounded by the distance of colonies from the restraining home influences of the metropole.[105]

The opposition of metropolitan anti-imperialists to prostitution had its counterpart in the colonies themselves, where nationalists consistently linked colonial subjugation to imperial prostitution policies. In Java, for instance, in the 1910s, the women's sections of nationalist parties like Sarekat Islam launched vigorous campaigns against prostitution, seeing it as part of the degradation of women in colonial society.[106] In China, the existence of Chinese prostitutes, especially streetwalkers, became a symbol of national disaster, and the elimination of prostitution part of the nationalist project to become modern and shake off colonialism.[107]

So too in India, Hindu nationalists campaigned against prostitution, which was represented as both a product of colonialism and a remnant of a decadent Muslim regime. Muslim middle-class nationalists often stood alongside Hindus in their condemnation of prostitution, asserting their own claims to civilization and respectability. This campaign was so effective that by the end of this period many cities had banned prostitutes from their traditional haunts, forcing them into clearly demarcated spaces on the edges of the cites. Physically removed to the periphery, they were also effectively marginalized in terms of definitions of the modern Indian citizen. Indigenous nationalists were thus complicit in the British colonial project to control prostitutes as they challenged imperial power.[108]

Colonial nationalists were not the only ones who attached such importance to women and prostitution: gender definitions were critical to the nationalist movements that emerged in many parts of the world in the nineteenth century.[109] Women generally were seen as the bearers and reproducers of culture, and their behavior reflected on the group as a whole and its attempts to advance its cause. The visible presence of prostitutes was a cause for concern to nationalists, as it threatened to bring the group as a whole into disrepute. Thus, in 1891 Japanese pearl-shell masters on Thursday Island, off the northern coast of Australia, asked the government resident to evict the karayuki-san who did a thriving business with the pearlers and sailors of the region, fearing they would damage their past "goodly reputation." Similarly, the Turkish consul in Bombay in 1911 persuaded the government of India to repatriate prostitutes to Baghdad because they were bringing Arabs into disrepute.[110]

Robert Gregg has argued that in the late-nineteenth and early-twentieth centuries, U.S. Progressive opposition to prostitution as an institution coincided with the desire of nationalists to control the behavior of women in their own ethnic groups. Thus, "an imperial bond could be cemented, that might otherwise have been difficult to forge, between Progressive reformer and ethnic nationalist."[111] His argument can be extended: prostitution was critical to the European imperial project, providing not just a major rationale for "civilizing colonialism" but also, via regulation, the technology to control colonized populations. From the last quarter of the nineteenth century, prostitution also played a key part in the deconstruction of empires, providing for colonial nationalists and domestic reformers alike a powerful symbol of colonial oppression and imperial moral corruption. Importantly, the emotional and moral fervor attached to the figure of the victimized prostituted woman and child provided the energy to mobilize networks of opposition to prostitution that crossed national and imperial boundaries. These active and powerful networks achieved some success in the late 1880s and 1890s, shifting the balance of imperial policy temporarily away from regulation. In the early-twentieth century, international conventions prompted European and colonial governments to tighten sanctions against those who procured and exploited prostitutes, so that the traffic in persons became increasingly difficult. Although the First World War interrupted these campaigns, the Abolitionist activists were quick to take advantage of the new opportunities presented by the League of Nations. And as empires disintegrated and new nations emerged in the postwar era, prostitution once more became an important index of citizenship and a marker of national status.[112]

CONCLUSION

This brief overview of a vast literature on prostitution and empire has addressed three major themes: first, the relationship between empire and sexual economies; second, the ways in which colonialism provided new avenues for the exploration and expression of sexual desire; and third, the ways in which prostitution was related to issues of imperial security and efficiency. The case of A-Sau and Tai-Yau, whose deaths were described at the beginning of this chapter, reminds us in particular of the complexities of this third theme. On the one hand, their deaths suggest the far-reaching powers of the British Empire in its quest to regulate the colonial sex industry. On the other hand, their flight from the officials reminds us of the ongoing challenges that faced colonial authorities in their attempt to control colonized societies: control was only ever partial, and always contested.[113]

CHAPTER NINE

Erotica: Sexual Imagery, Empires, and Colonies

RUTH FORD

In 1907, Sir David Scott Mitchell's extensive private collection of Australiana was bequeathed to the public library of New South Wales following his death. When the collection was received by the library, it was found to contain "a number of erotica."[1] These "included a large number of illustrated nineteenth century French and English erotic texts—many notorious—and visual material comprising photographs of heterosexual and homosexual sex, hand coloured stereographs of semi-naked European women, and erotic engravings."[2] Mitchell—an eminent and wealthy New South Wales colonial—was no different from numerous gentlemen in Britain who had collections of erotica that were discovered by wives, family, or librarians on their death.[3] However, as well as British, French, and German nineteenth-century material, Mitchell's collection also included a substantial number of photographs of Japanese women and men having sex; a couple of images of naked women of color, including Polynesian women; and an album and scroll of Japanese drawings and prints of men and women engaged in acts of copulation and cunnilingus. This diverse collection of erotica—including images from Asia and the Pacific—in an Australian colony twelve thousand miles away from the hub of the production of erotic imagery in Europe raises questions about erotic imagery and sexuality in the Age of Empire.

This chapter considers the relationship among erotic imagery, empires, and colonies in the context of the circulation (and regulation) of pornography. First, it explores the ways in which colonialism provided new erotic material from Asian and Pacific colonies and the East, and new objects/subjects for erotic imagery. Such imagery entering imperial global markets provided arenas for the exploration and depiction of sexual desire for viewers' sexual pleasure and arousal. Second, I consider the ways in which the Age of Empire enabled global circulation of erotic imagery and expanded markets with colonies. Global trade in erotic imagery was part of global sexual economies, like prostitution.[4] This global traffic in turn generated new regulation and policing. Third, I examine how changes in photographic and printing technologies produced new genres of erotic imagery and increased circulation and audiences. Access by the middle and working classes resulted in increased regulation and policing of erotic imagery. These subjects are explored against the backdrop of a brief overview of the nature and circulation of erotic imagery and literature in the nineteenth-century West.

EROTICA IN THE NINETEENTH-CENTURY WEST

Historical studies of pornography in Europe and America highlight its emergence as a distinct concern of the state—and as a distinct category and as a literary and visual practice—by the early- to mid-nineteenth century and the increasing regulation and restriction of the obscene to exclude women and the lower classes from their consumption.[5] These studies have largely focused upon the rise of literary pornography—with vast attention paid to erotic classics, such as Walter's *My Secret Life*, and a myriad of other titles, including *The Way of a Man with a Maid; Lady Polkingham, or They Do It All;* and multiple volumes of *The Pearl*.[6] These works have been used to examine the limits of the Victorian erotic imagination, with their descriptions of sex acts, or bodies, and of practices such as flagellation, deflowering, and rape, as well as anal, oral, and penetrative sex and masturbation. Before the rise of literacy through the spread of education and changes in print culture, drawn and printed material had been restricted to the social elite.[7] Lynn Hunt points to the link between the new ideals of domesticity and the ideology of separate spheres, which were dependent on assertions of fundamental female and male sexual difference, and the regulation of pornography, which transgressed the boundaries establishing difference. "As new biological and moral standards for sexual difference evolved, pornography seemed to become more exotic and dangerous," argues Hunt, and "had to be stamped out."[8]

The form, content, and distribution of erotica during the nineteenth century in Britain and Europe underwent considerable change. Iain McCalman argues that early-nineteenth-century British erotica was linked to revolutionary activity and ideas but this changed by the late 1920s.[9] Similarly, Lynn Hunt argues that politically motivated pornography, associated with subversive politics, was replaced by a focus on bodies and sexual acts and a depiction of sexual pleasure as an end in itself by the 1830s. Hunt identifies a shift in the early-nineteenth century to "modern pornography, with its mass-produced text or images devoted to the explicit description of sexual organs or activities with the sole aim of producing sexual arousal in the reader or viewer."[10] Such political associations and their regulation created a specific context for the control of erotica and its associated sexual pleasures.

New technologies have always been exploited by pornographers. Printed books, lithographs, and etchings were all put to erotic use as soon as they were available, in much the same ways that home movies, then video, then the Internet readily adapted to pornographic use in the latter half of the twentieth century. The same kinds of networks for the production and distribution of erotica quickly adapted to the potential of these new technologies. A case in point is the way the invention of photography had a dramatic impact on erotic imagery—both its form and circulation. The photograph's depiction of a "real life" scene added to the vicarious pleasure of seeing real women engaged in sexual acts, while adapting the erotic possibilities that had been explored in hundreds of titles of pornographic novels and in the mass circulation of erotic material.

The early forms of photographs in the 1840s meant, first, that such images were taken by photographers in studios with attached darkrooms, and most commonly created daguerreotypes (a direct positive process). This resulted in the upper classes being the predominant purchasers of erotic photographs from the 1840s to the 1860s.[11] However, as both photographic technologies changed, with the dry plate process and negatives, production and reproduction became cheaper and photographs began to circulate more widely. With the invention of the Kodak camera in 1888 (and cellulose nitrate film), photography became accessible to the amateur and created new opportunities for the production of erotic photographs. In addition, the development of the mutoscope and magic lantern meant that erotic imagery entered the circulation of fairs and other public spectacles, augmenting the erotic pleasures already existent in the form of various titillating sideshows and *tableaux vivants*, in which thinly veiled nudity and other erotic possibilities were exploited for a mass market.

Homosexuality was extremely uncommon as a theme in Victorian erotica, notes Kearney.[12] However, while most erotica depicted women for the heterosexual male gaze, there was an emerging market in images of men for homosexual men. For example, Wilhelm von Gloeden (born in Germany in 1856) and his cousin Guglielmo Plüschow (born in 1852), who lived in Italy from the 1870s, became known for their photographs of nude local youths throughout Europe, Britain, and the United States.[13]

EROTICS OF EMPIRE: GLOBAL EXOTICISM AND EROTIC IMAGERY

Among Mitchell's erotica collection are a large number of Japanese erotic drawings, prints, scroll paintings, and sculptures.[14] *Shunga* ("images of spring"), the generic name given to the erotic paintings, prints, scrolls, illustrated books, and sculptures (netsuke) of Japan, emerged from a cultural tradition of openly sexual art in Japan—the origins of which predate by several centuries the sexually explicit wood-block prints (ukiyo-e) produced from the mid-seventeenth to the mid-nineteenth century.[15] Shunga's subjects commonly included male-female, male-male, and female-female sexual relations and female masturbation, and women were often shown as active participants in sex acts. Joshua Mostow points to the "complex web of reciprocal and interweaving relations between men, wives, prostitutes and young men" illustrated in shunga.[16] However, Julie Davis emphasizes that "such images were designed as part of a fantasy of sexual practise" and performed voyeuristic functions for their predominantly male audiences.[17]

When Japan opened its doors to the West in 1868, its sexually explicit art increasingly came to the attention of Westerners, who began collecting this genre. Shunga was clearly popular in fin-de-siècle Paris and artistic circles. From the late 1870s, the Paris art dealers Hayashi and Bing actively sought shunga and ukiyo-e to sell in the European market. In 1891, writer and art critic Edmond de Goncourt wrote enthusiastically about shunga within a broader work on ukiyo-e, and a book titled *Japanische Erotik* was published anonymously in Germany in 1907.[18] However, shunga was also collected more broadly. Evans notes that although the moral climate of Europe, particularly Victorian England, precluded the open display of Japanese erotic art, it was actively collected.[19] In the late-nineteenth century, some shunga were produced chiefly for export to the West, argues Evans.

Mitchell's collecting of shunga may have been an attempt to obtain evidence "of the cultural character of an otherwise little-known land" in order to satisfy "a broader curiosity about the world at large" or for salacious interest.[20] It is unclear whether colonial collectors such as Mitchell purchased their shunga directly from Japan or via dealers in Australia, France, England, and the United States.[21] Not only were original prints and scrolls collected by art collectors, artists, and the elite, but shunga prints were also copied and reproduced for underground circulation. Jack Lindsay recounts a Sydney brothel owner commissioning copies of "amorous Japanese woodcuts" in the early 1920s.[22]

In addition to the importing of shunga from Japan, erotic art from India, China, and Persia was collected and texts were translated. *The Kama Sutra of Vatsyayana* was translated by Sir Richard Burton and F. F. Arthurnot and first published in 1883. It was followed by the publication of *Ananga-Ranga or the Hindu Art of Love* in 1885 and *The Perfumed Garden of the Cheikh Nefzaoui: A Manual of Arabian Erotology* in 1886.[23] Such works were seen as "scientific"; they "detailed, categorised, observed, explained and analysed" different cultures' sexual practices, notes Sigel. However, in emphasizing that the described sexual practices should be distinguished from British ones,

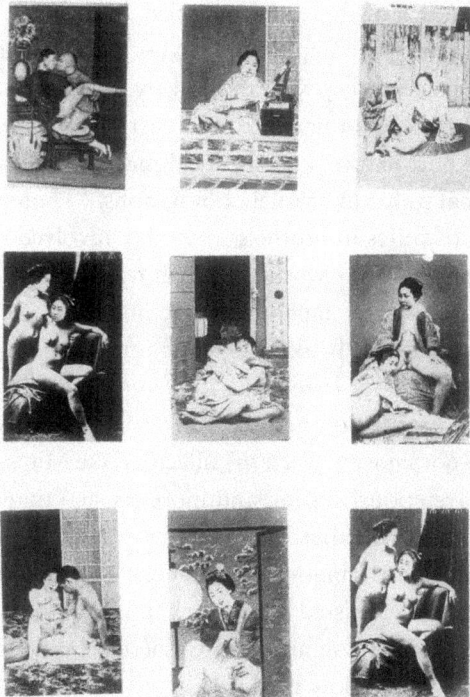

FIGURE 9.1: Japanese men and women, c. 1907.
Mitchell Library, State Library of NSW, Australia.

especially if they challenged European ideologies about nature, biology, masculinity, and sexual and gendered difference, they were part of a broader imperial agenda.[24]

Approximately half of the 117 albumen photographs in Mitchell's collection were of Japanese women and men. Within this series of Japanese photographs, the most common images were of Japanese women and men having sex together (65 percent) in couples (59 percent), threesomes (5 percent), and a foursome (1 percent). Women photographed solo either masturbating or with their genitals on display were also common (20 percent). There was also a small number of images that depicted, or hinted at, women being sexual with each other (7 percent) and men having anal sex with men (4 percent). The invention of photography allowed an existing art form to be adapted to photography, as some compositions and sexual poses similar to those in shunga were depicted in photographs. Elizabeth and Stanley Burns argue that Japanese photographic conventions were inspired by the aesthetics of the colored wood-block print medium of ukiyo-e.[25] However, these sexually explicit black-and-white photographs of various sexual acts are in stark contrast to the hand-colored photographs of geishas and courtesans that filled souvenir tourist albums.[26] Little is known of these photographs' provenance and whether they were produced primarily for export or for both local and export markets. However, evidence suggests they were most likely taken in brothels by Japanese photographers and formed an underground part of both the significant Japanese photograph export market and the local market.[27] They were part of the broader international traffic in brothel photographs.[28] Photographing Japanese female and male prostitutes in brothels inevitably involved the complex international traffic in Japanese sex workers, which was created by colonialism.[29]

The inclusion of so many Japanese erotic images in Mitchell's collection suggests his interest in sexually explicit erotic images from another culture—and perhaps his pleasure—or even arousal—from viewing them. Edward Said points to the strong association between the Orient and sex in the European imaginary.[30] We do not know if Western collectors like Mitchell had a romantic view of Japan as mysteriously erotic and more sensual than the West, reflecting Said's notion of the sexualized Orient.[31] The desiring colonial gaze upon the exotic other and the fascination and interest in Japan in upper-class and artistic circles (*Japonisme*) existed at the same time that the Australian colonies expressed intense anti-Japanese and anti-Chinese sentiment and fear of "the Asiatic hordes," and "the yellow peril."[32]

There are also other photographs of women of color in Mitchell's collection. These are mostly of individuals, and unlike the photographs of the European or Japanese women, many are frontal and side-on views. Some of these images appear to be of Pacific—or even Australian Aboriginal—women and have some similarities to images that circulated in the Australian colonies depicting natives. They also draw on image genres within racial science and anthropology, in which photographs were seen to provide and record "factual" knowledge about "racial types," "specimens," and "tribes."[33] The photographs highlight the links between visual representations in erotica and photographs taken for the purposes of sexology, racial science, and anthropology that were used in the elaborate construction of sexual and racial taxonomies.[34] They helped construct sex and race as biological categories. Sigel suggests that "pornographers" used a scientific model to justify representations of colonized sexuality, infusing a colonial hierarchy with meaning for the purpose of titillation.[35]

The blurring of the lines between nineteenth-century anthropological studies of the customs and marriage and sexual practices of other races and of erotica sexualizing, eroticizing, and fetishizing the exotic other is evident in a notorious book in Mitchell's collection, *Untrodden Fields of Anthropology: Observations on the Esoteric Manners and Customs of Semi-civilised Peoples; Being a Record of 30 Years' Experience in Asia, Africa, America and Oceania*.[36] The book is a pseudo-ethnographic text containing illustrations of naked women and was written anonymously—and distributed—by the famed Victorian English pornographer Charles Carrington.[37] *Untrodden Fields* highlights the racial discourses that informed pornography, anthropology, sexology, and notions of femininity and female sexuality.[38] The text described itself as a "remarkable study of the sixth sense [genital sense] and its strange and curious manifestations and aberrations among barbarous races." It reasserted the importance of studying sex organs "as comparative points of racial differences."[39] Among other sexual customs, *Untrodden Fields* told readers that "in Egypt, sapphism ... is almost the fashion" and "all the ladies of the harem have each an *amie*," while "amongst the coloured women of Martinique" and "among the negroes and mulattoes of French Creole countries," "fricatrices and lesbians" were very common. A footnote provided more explicit details regarding homosexuality among women in Bali: "the methods of gratification adopted are either digital or lingual, or else by bringing the parts together (tribadism)." It referred to the excessive (homo)sexuality of women of color, recounting the story of a white mother forced to stay at home because of the "excessive admiration of the mulatto women and negresses and the impudent invitations they dared to address to her," tantalizing readers with the possibilities not just of lesbian sex but of cross-racial lesbian sex. It outlined the "scandalous scenes ... in which the guilty parties were always of a different race" but asserted that "lesbian love or tribadism" was rare among Arab women, and that "a certain degree of civilisation was necessary to give birth to this vice."[40] Such descriptions drew on typical tropes in Victorian pornographic writing of cross-racial and cross-class sex, highlighting the colonialist, gendered, and classed power structures in such erotica.

The context of empire and colonial relations were central to the nature of erotica. Joanna de Groot emphasizes the economic and political context of the development of Orientalist art and literature, including semi-pornographic products.[41] Images of exotic and anthropological studies were constituted within the relations of imperialism, argue Nicholas Thomas and Elizabeth Edwards.[42] British, French, and Americans "viewed sexualised images ... of those they had conquered, as part of the right of conquest," argues Sigel. She highlights the links between individuals in anthropology clubs and collectors of erotica.[43] Exoticism increased, argues Sigel, as "imperialism provided new arenas for pornographic exploitation and as the world became a backdrop for sexual adventure."[44]

Three of the photographs in figure 9.2 depict women naked, but with their faces masked or veiled, except for their eyes. These images suggest a fascination with the forbidden, with "penetrating" the harem and gaining access to the

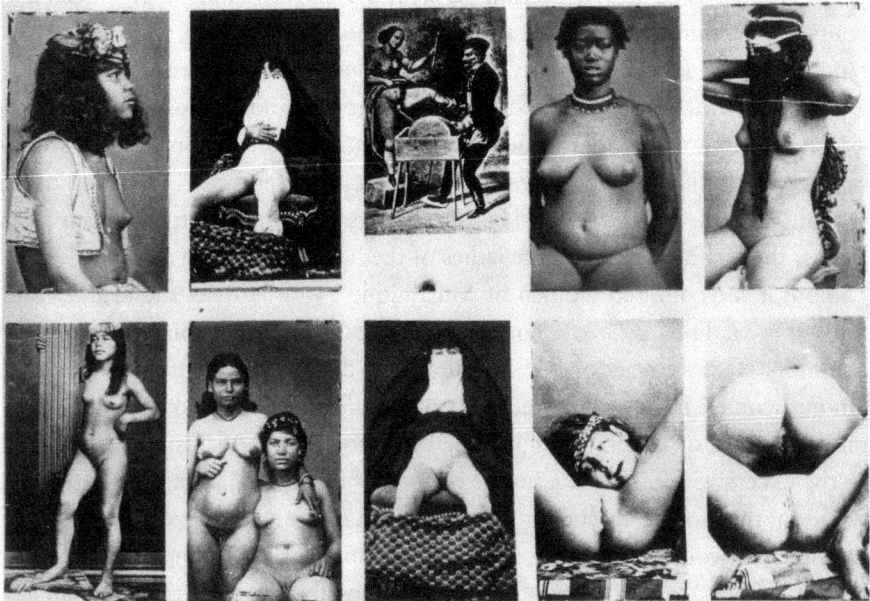

FIGURE 9.2: Pacific Australian Aboriginals, c. 1907. Mitchell Library, State Library of NSW, Australia.

women within.[45] Sigel suggests that the veiled but naked exotic deepened the imperial gaze, emphasizing the exoticism and hyper-sexuality of non-European women.[46] Anne McClintock notes that colonial photography, "framed by metaphors ... of scientific knowledge as penetration, promised to seek out the interiors of the feminised orient and there capture as surface, in the image of the harem woman's body, the truth of the world."[47]

Mitchell's acquisition of photographs of women of color underscores the sexual fascination with the racial other. Significantly, while Mitchell's collection of erotic images of non-European women illustrate the colonizing male gaze and sexual fascination with the racial other—suggesting perhaps the fantasy of transgressive cross-racial sex—they do not depict interracial sex.[48] The photographs afforded the voyeuristic illusion of penetrating the forbidden spaces of female sexual life across race, class, and sexual orientation without physically crossing over the dangerous lines.[49] McClintock points to the pleasure of voyeurism produced through mastering in fantasy a situation that is fundamentally dangerous and threatening. The fascination with the exotic racial other—romanticized and feared in the Western cultural imaginary as primal, sensual, and lustful—and the sexual other links imperialist discourses and sexual discourses in the nineteenth century.

At the same time that white upper-class men in North America, Europe, and its colonies were importing, viewing, and reading erotica featuring people of color from around the world, self-styled "white men's countries" in Australasia and North America worked to exclude those peoples they defined as not-white, including Japanese, Pacific Islanders, Chinese, and Indians—the very people who were the subjects of the erotica circulating within global sexual commerce.[50]

SEXUAL COMMERCE AND GLOBAL TRADE IN EROTIC IMAGERY

Alongside the emergence of new erotic material from empires' colonies and the East, and the changing nature of erotic imagery within the context of colonization, the latter half of the nineteenth century saw global trade in erotic imagery—and national regulation to try to restrict it—dramatically escalate. Mitchell's erotica collection included photographs from Britain, France, and Germany and highlights the global circulation of images from European empires to their colonies. His collection includes the kinds of photographs that are standard in late-nineteenth century erotica and similar to those in other Victorian erotica collections.

Among Mitchell's photographs are a set of fifty-three hand-colored ster-eographs, mostly of semi-clad women, probably from the 1880s and most likely from Britain. Looking at these through a stereoscope produced a three-dimensional effect, adding another element to the viewer's pleasure. Figure 9.3 depicts two partially dressed women in underwear, with their dresses beside them, sitting outside, leaning against each other's bodies with their breasts partially visible. The voyeurism is made more explicit through the addition of a male figure creeping up to watch them unobserved through the long grass. The women appear to be caught in a moment's languid reverie either before or after sexual activity. This photograph utilizes the genre of the male gaze—integral to fine art as well as to pornography—with the woman as an object of voyeurism structured through the averted female gaze. The images draw on the naturalist tradition in pornography: the women are seen as part of nature, indeed abandoning themselves to their "true" nature, while men observe. The photographs portray the forbidden sight of women's bodies but also hint at physical intimacy between the women. These images (and those in figure 9.4) are typical of two genres of erotic photography circulating in Europe at the time. Other images in Mitchell's collection are more sexually explicit (figures 9.5, 9.6, 9.7), showing sexual organs, pubic hair, and uro-lagnia, as well as a variety of sexual acts, including female-female oral sex, male-female penetrative sex, male-female oral sex, and various masturbatory and pair and trio sex acts. These photographs depict a range of behaviors and sexual acts similar to those described in erotic literature (and those classified by European sexologists such as Richard von Krafft-Ebing and Havelock Ellis).

Mitchell's collection highlights the links between eroticizing the racial other and the sexual other—including the whore and the lesbian.[51] One photograph in figure 9.5 (top third on right) portrays one woman performing cunnilingus on another. Both are naked except for their boots and knee-length stockings. Figure 9.8 (top right) depicts two women, one, semi-naked, standing, leaning against a chair, the other sitting naked on a cushion, except for boots and knee-length stockings, licking her vulva, her tongue clearly visible. The pose empha-sizes the oral sex, but the body stance and the averted eyes and sideways tilt of the head also enable the viewer to gaze unchallenged at the women's breasts, nipples, and thighs. The half-removed clothing and the backdrop of lush velvet curtains and a solid panel door add to the domestic fantasy of the scene. Poses clearly invite the viewer's sexual desire through the graphic depiction of female sexual organs and buttocks in the center point of the photograph. The pubic hair is also exaggerated, in what appears to be a wig.

FIGURE 9.3: Women in underwear, c. 1907. Mitchell Library, State Library of NSW, Australia.

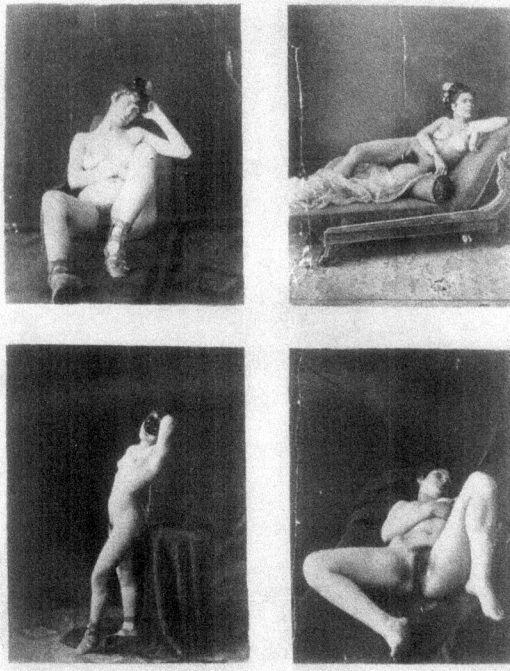

FIGURE 9.4: Four naked women, c. 1907. Mitchell Library, State Library of NSW, Australia.

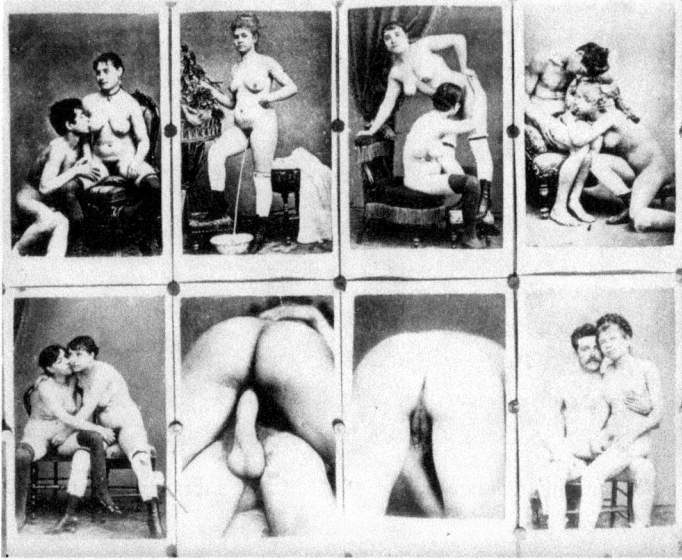

FIGURE 9.5: Eight pornographic images, c. 1907. Mitchell Library, State Library of NSW, Australia.

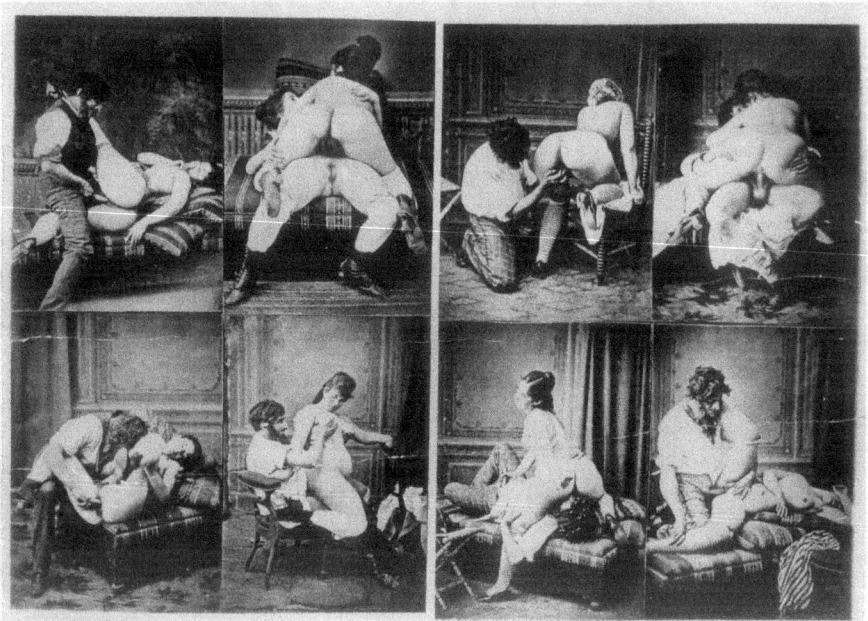

FIGURE 9.6: Eight pornographic images (man-woman), c. 1907. Mitchell Library, State Library of NSW, Australia.

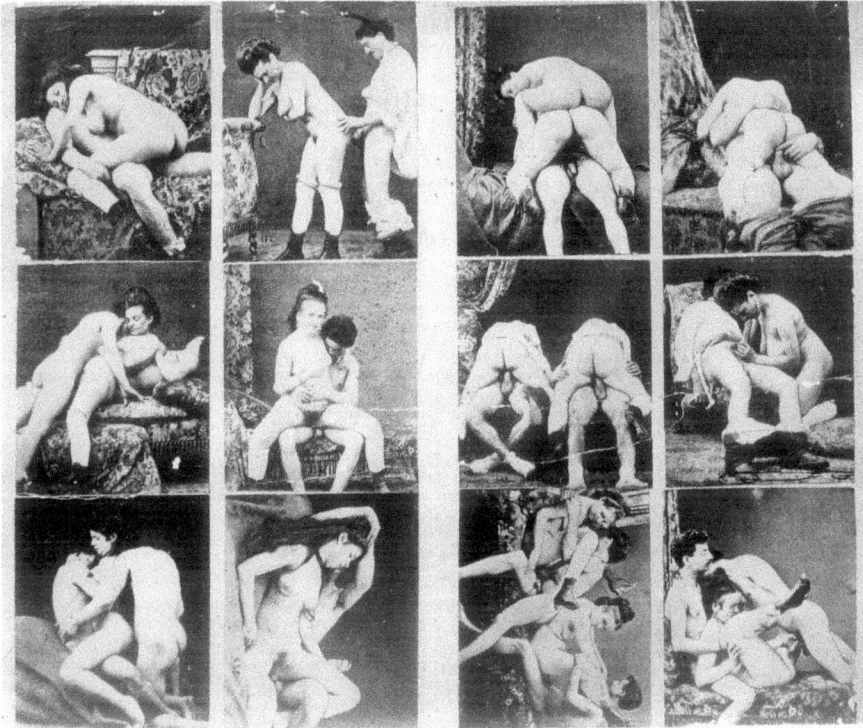

FIGURE 9.7: Twelve pornographic images (group sex), c. 1907. Mitchell Library, State Library of NSW, Australia.

The other element is the depiction, in both these photographs and novels of the time, of women's sexual appetite for each other, of women seducing other women, and of women having sex with each other. Unlike most medical and social discourses of the period, erotica—both imagery and literature— mythologized women as intensely physical, intensely lustful beings. In erotic literature, the traditional figure of the whore plays a crucial role—she is sexually promiscuous and the embodiment of lust. The whore existed to fulfill men's fantasies and provide sexual pleasure. Lesbians, like whores, were not seen as real women. Ironically, while the images of lesbian sex were produced for men's pleasure and sexual arousal, the women in the pictures were mythologized as performing sex for their own pleasure to fulfill their lust—without men. In the context of the late-nineteenth century, when even the sight of women's buttocks and loins and breasts was seen as highly lewd and ideals of womanhood emphasized feminine virtue, modesty, and motherhood, women seducing other women made for highly risqué and lascivious reading or viewing. Further, as

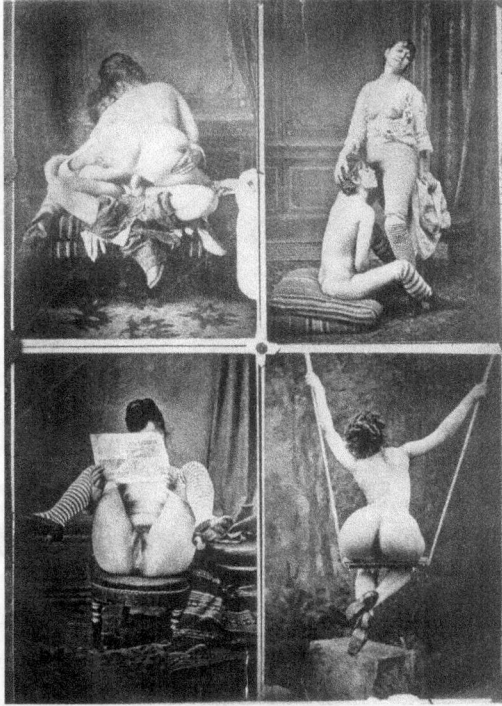

FIGURE 9.8: Four pornographic images, c. 1907.
Mitchell Library, State Library of NSW, Australia.

the lesbian was not named or visible in public discourse and was understood in
terms of highly deviant sexual practices, the forbidden and transgressive nature
of an encounter with a lesbian would have added to the vicarious pleasure and
excitement of a licentious fantasy.

Absent in Mitchell's collection were photographs depicting naked individual men or male homosexual desire, although such images circulated across
the globe. Jason Goldman notes that von Gloeden's nudes circulated in a clandestine market that extended from Sicily to Continental Europe, Britain, and
the United States. These were sold, like many of the photographs Mitchell
purchased from Europe, via catalogs and mail order. In addition, there was the
hand-to-hand traffic in risqué von Gloeden photographs. Goldman notes that
many of von Gloeden's special clients were elite men, including Oscar Wilde
and Friedrich Krupp—who had the means to travel to the baron's studio in
Italy, where they could acquire the photographs in person.[52] John Addington
Symonds, a classical scholar who also identified as an "invert" and "homosexual," collected nude photographs by von Gloeden and Plüschow—and also

sent photographs to friends. Goldman challenges gay communities' nostalgia for von Gloeden and points to the unequal distributions of power and money that complicated the models' consent to be photographed. Patricia Berman argues that "in photographing youths in the impoverished Sicilian town of Taormina, and in procuring their sexual favors for himself and his wealthy guests, von Gloeden colonized both the boys and their culture."[53] Such exploitation lies at the heart of many forms of transnational erotic imagery in the nineteenth century.

Mitchell's collection of British, French, and German erotic imagery—in addition to his Japanese material—indicates that upper-class colonial men purchased European material via mail order in a similar way that British gentlemen did. The imagery also highlights different genres of erotic photography, both domestic and from different nation-states. Alongside this collecting of erotic photographs by gentlemen in the colonies—with little apparent interference from the state—existed increasing regulation and policing that aimed to prevent the circulation of "obscene" imagery across the globe, as global trade in erotica increased with expanding markets from imperial expansion and changing photographic and printing technologies.

REGULATION

In July 1875, Louis Binds, a merchant importer of haberdashery and fancy goods in Melbourne, in the colony of Victoria, was charged with importing indecent photographs under the 1857 Customs Act, which prohibited the import of "indecent or obscene prints."[54] Customs officials had discovered the indecent photographs during a routine examination of goods to ascertain whether they were free of duty. The photographs, which had been placed in a small loop in the stems of meerschaum cigar holders and were looked at through a small magnifying glass, were in a case of goods consigned by Donat Dussing and Company of Austria.[55]

This case was one of several charges of importing indecent and obscene prints and photographs in the colony of Victoria in the 1860s and 1870s. Cases like this one highlight both the increasing circulation of "obscene" imagery across the globe and the ways nation-states and colonies introduced regulation and policing aimed to prevent trade in erotica—both within empires and across imperial and national borders. Changing photographic and printing technologies that enabled the cheap mass production of images were central to this expansion. However, integral to the development of global trade in erotica were the material conditions created by colonialism. Increasing trade in erotic imagery occurred within the context of a growth in commerce and international trade resulting from expanding markets with imperial expansion. The infrastructure that supported modern empires—including steamships and telegraph services and the opening of the Panama and Suez canals—facilitated increased global trade in erotic imagery, as part of the changing nature and scale of sexual commerce more broadly.[56]

New legislation focused particularly on regulating the importation of materials deemed obscene. Clauses specifying prints, paintings, photographs, postcards, and lithographic or other engravings in legislation indicate that visual erotica was increasingly viewed as a threat.[57] In the colony of Victoria, the 1857 and 1883 Customs Acts included in their lists of goods "absolutely prohibited" from import "blasphemous indecent or obscene prints paintings books cards lithographic or other engravings or other blasphemous indecent or obscene articles."[58] In Britain, the 1876 Customs Consolidation Act prohibited the import of "indecent or obscene prints, paintings, photographs, books, cards, lithographic or other engravings, or any other indecent or obscene articles." In the colony of Queensland, the 1880 Post Card and Postal Note Act rendered any person who sent "by post any obscene print, photograph, or any paper, packet, or post card containing any word, mark, or design of an indecent, obscene, libelous, or grossly offensive character" liable to a penalty of up to £100.[59] Britain's 1884 Post Office (Protection) Act and 1889 Indecent Advertisements Act also focused on preventing the circulation of obscene materials, particularly photographs and postcards. New Zealand passed its Post Office Act in 1893 and Post and Telegraph Act in 1901. Australia's Custom Act, passed after Federation in 1901, prohibited the import of "blasphemous indecent or obscene works or articles," with a £100 fine for offenses. Canada and India both passed Post Office Acts in 1908.

Outside the British Empire, there was also increased regulation against the importing of erotica. The U.S. 1873 Act for the Suppression of Trade in, and Circulation of, Obscene Literature and Articles of Immoral Use (known as the Comstock Law) increased penalties against the mailing of obscene materials.[60] France reinforced morality laws in 1898 and 1908. Colligan notes the "wave of international legislation against the global traffic in obscenity" in the late-nineteenth and early-twentieth centuries. In 1910, an International Conference for the Suppression of Obscene Publication was held in Paris.[61] This suggests that moral reformers wanted to share strategies and collaborate in combating international trafficking of erotica.

A significant proportion of the prosecution related to obscenity in the colony of Victoria was for importing photographs and other erotic imagery. It is likely the detected cases were only a small fraction of the import market of erotica; however, they provide insight into the global trade in erotic imagery. A series of cases shows the active policing and prosecutions for importing erotic material in Victoria from the 1860s to the 1880s. In 1862, Angus May was charged with having "unlawfully imported prohibited goods" in the form of five hundred packs of "obscene [French] playing cards" with "indecent engravings" and "pictures of a most disgusting character" on them via a London vessel.[62] In 1865, Woolf Davis, an importer—and a well-known figure in the Melbourne Jewish community—was charged with importing a number of indecent and obscene prints, paintings, books, and engravings. These had been found inside "a false bottom underneath the tin lining" of a case on a Liverpool ship.[63] In 1868, John Beauchamp, William Davies, and Thomas J. Ruddall, photographers in Melbourne, were charged with "being the possessor[s] of obscene photographic prints and negatives." The customs official alleged that "none of the pictures were of colonial production: the figures were German and French."[64] In 1870, customs authorities seized "indecent photographs, prints and engravings" consigned from London to a firm in Ballarat, a provincial town.[65] In 1875, Adolphus Oppenheimer, a merchant from Melbourne, was charged with importing seventy-nine indecent and obscene prints and photographs from François Dernaz, a Paris photographer.[66] In 1881, Charles H. Smith, the proprietor of a depot for American goods in Melbourne, was charged with selling "indecent and obscene photographs" of German and French origin.[67] In 1884, Julius Schrievogel, an elderly German man, faced charges at the Melbourne city court on two separate charges of "selling obscene photographs" that he had received from Hamburg via the steamer *Etna*.[68]

Photographs, prints, and engravings concealed in secret compartments and microscopic photographs concealed in the handles of penholders, paper knives, and cigar holders and detected by customs officials suggest that exporters were highly creative and skilled in hiding material. Although customs officials were alert to hiding practices, it is likely the prosecutions were only a fraction of the material imported. Importers—often well-off merchants—charged with importing indecent and obscene visual material tended to be represented by lawyers. They were often initially convicted; however, many successfully appealed. The fines were substantial; however, merchants paid them rather than serving time in prison.

Both the court cases in the colony of Victoria and Mitchell's private collection provide evidence of the global traffic in erotic imagery, as photographs were exported from London, Paris, Austria, and Germany to the Australian colonies. They highlight the entanglement of sexual commerce with general commerce as merchants imported erotic imagery in conjunction with other goods. The cases emphasize that traffic in erotica imagery not only occurred within nation-states or in close nation-states, as in the erotica trade within Europe, but was a far-reaching international trade both within empires and across imperial and national borders. This emerging global sexual commerce was dependent on steamships and telegraph services—the infrastructure of modern empires—as erotic imagery transversed the major imperial routes to and from India, South Africa, and Australia, as well as across the Atlantic.

Alongside this active policing of colonial merchants importing erotic imagery from Europe, upper-class individuals such as Mitchell who obtained material privately via mail order or perhaps via booksellers were rarely prosecuted. Mitchell's erotica collection shows similar origins to the those in the cases discussed here—Paris, Germany, Austria, and London—although he obtained it through a very different method of purchase than on the streets.

CHANGING TECHNOLOGY AND EXPANDING AUDIENCES

It is hard to know how common the circulation of pornography was among upper-class men in the Australian colonies in the nineteenth and early-twentieth centuries. Most of Mitchell's books and visual material originated from mid- and late-nineteenth-century Britain, France, and Germany, and from Japan.[69] It appears most of his collecting was done from the Australian colonies, via Australian and international booksellers and via mail order. Ronald Pearsall's work on Britain emphasizes the emergence of mail order erotica and mailed flier advertisements.[70] Similarly, Sigel's work on Britain illustrates the extensive international trade in erotica via catalogs and mail order.

Julie Peakman has shown the extent to which women had begun to read and view pornography in the British context by the end of the eighteenth century. While women may have viewed their husbands' or lovers' erotica, and while servants—both male and female—had opportunities to view employers' collections, and prostitutes could gaze at images in the brothels they worked in, they themselves were unlikely to purchase erotic imagery. In nineteenth-century Australian colonies, erotic books and images were predominantly available to the male social elite. The fact that photographs often cost £1–2 for twenty images meant working-class men earning six shillings a day were unlikely to purchase them. Further, the social context for the production and consumption of pornography was almost exclusively a masculine one. Pornography was almost always written by men, for men, and usually depicted women. Pornography, through its literary and visual representations, "offered women's bodies as a focus for male bonding," argues Lynn Hunt. "Men wrote about sex for other male readers" and "men read about women having sex with other women or with multiple partners" for their own sexual arousal.[71]

Increasing regulation, detection, and prosecution also point to the increasing concerns of the state and moral reformers regarding visual erotica from the 1860s as new photographic technologies enabled the production and reproduction of erotic imagery for new audiences. Image production and circulation was no longer limited to the upper classes. Further, concern about erotic imagery becoming available to women, rather than being the exclusive domain of men, was not just an Australian trend. Julie Peakman highlights the increasing crackdown on erotic material in Britain at the end of the eighteenth century.[72] Colette Colligan argues that obscenity did not emerge as a significant publishing enterprise and a print crime in Britain, Europe, and North America until the nineteenth century.[73]

Research on Britain highlights the anxiety regarding mass production of erotica and working-class readers, but more particularly of images in erotic literature tainting the minds of the lower classes, which were seen as having low morals or being most susceptible to demoralization. In an 1822 *Quarterly Review* article, the author argued that rumors about lack of copyright and the resulting piracies resulted in the Lord Byron's poem "Don Juan" being distributed to "a class of readers" of "ungovernable passions" susceptible to its "indecencies"; no sooner was it whispered that there was no property in "Don Juan" than ten presses were at work, some publishing it with obscene engravings, others in weekly numbers, and all in a shape that brought it within the reach of purchasers on whom its poison would operate without mitigation—who would search its pages for images to pamper a depraved imagination.[74]

There was a significant increase in legislation from the 1850s—the time when photographic technology enabled the production and reproduction of erotic imagery, making imagery available not just to the upper classes. In England, the Obscene Publications Act was passed in 1857, giving statutory authority to existing common law against obscenity, and authorizing police to search suspect premises and seize and destroy obscene materials.[75] When Lord Campbell spoke to the bill in parliamentary debates, he emphasized that the intention of the act was not to prosecute the fine arts or literature but to combat the cheap mass-produced publications resulting in increased circulation of obscenity to the masses:

> It was not alone indecent papers of a high price, which was a sort of check, that were sold, but periodical papers of the most licentious and disgusting description were coming out week by week, and sold to any person who asked for them, and in any numbers.[76]

By the 1870s there was a further increase in regulation combating both local production and the import and distribution of erotic imagery. This legislation specified photographs, in addition to prints, paintings, drawings, postcards, and lithographic and other engravings, indicating that photographic erotic imagery and the possibilities for mass production and circulation were increasingly viewed as a threat. In British colonies, legislation often drew on imperial acts. In the colony of Victoria, an Obscenity Act was passed in 1876.[77] In the colony of New South Wales, a similar act—the Obscene Publications Act—was passed in 1880.[78] This was followed by the Indecent Publications Act of 1900 (New South Wales).[79] After Federation in 1901, Australia passed the Obscene and Indecent Publications Act. "Obscene publication" included "any obscene book paper newspaper or printed matter of any kind whatsoever and any obscene writing print picture photograph lithograph drawing or representation."[80] In Western Australia, the 1902 Criminal Code included under "Offences against Morality" a section on "Obscene publications and Exhibitions."[81] Most of these acts also prohibited—and policed—"any article or thing designed or intended for the prevention of conception or procuring of abortion."[82]

In addition to the ongoing ordering from overseas catalogs by wealthy individuals, imported erotica—in the form of photographs, prints, and books—was being distributed extensively in the Australian colonies by booksellers, newsagents, and street hawkers from the 1860s on. Prosecutions provide evidence of distribution networks, consumers, and street costs of erotic imagery, as well as policing methods. In 1869, a young man named William Thompson was charged with offering "obscene photographs" for sale at the races. Thompson was sentenced to "three months' imprisonment with hard labour."[83] In 1870, William Price was charged at the Melbourne city court with "having obscene photographs and cards in his possession."[84] In 1865, Mrs. Mary Dixon, a bookshop keeper of Little Collin Street, Melbourne, was charged with—and later convicted and imprisoned for—having "a number of indecent pictures" and publications in her possession.[85] Despite often just fining importers, in this case, it appears they decided to proceed with prosecution at the police court partly because of the concerns regarding the corruption of youth—and partly because the distributor was a woman. Mary Dixon's shop was also a circulating library where school books were bought, sold, and exchanged. Sergeant Summerhayes stressed that he had seen "a number of boys in the shop" and that "there was a large number of school books on the premises" and that "she was visited by six or seven college boys" at her house. At the appeal, the magistrate upheld the conviction, concluding that he "considered it a melancholy case that the appellant was a woman and mother."[86]

Concern about young people and women gaining access to erotic imagery was similar in Britain and America.[87] Lynda Nead notes the attempt to legislate against the print shops, which displayed risqué material and sold erotica behind the counter on London's Holywell Street, in that "the presence of respectable women in Holywell St. alarmed contemporaries and became a central justification for supporters of legislation."[88] The cases also highlight the contrast between wealthy gentlemen purchasing erotic material without state intervention by mail order and the experience of young middle- and upper-class youths purchasing material on the streets. The cases indicate anxiety about women being involved in distribution of erotica and the consumers being middle- and upper-class school and college boys. The fact that modern women were becoming viewers and consumers of erotica is highlighted by Monte Punshon, another Australian colonial. Born in 1882, Punshon embraced the possibilities opening up to white middle-class women in the early-twentieth century. She drew on the language of passionate friendship to express her love for women, yet her scrapbooks included an erotic photograph of a female nude and a photograph depicting two female dancers, wearing partially see-through garments, gazing at and pursuing each other around a pillar, their hands and arms touching. The images she collected suggest Punshon's pleasure and desire in looking at women's bodies and indicate her active erotic gaze, a gaze of desire that reappropriated the male gaze. She created new meanings from a visual culture in which men looked at women. Her desiring gaze was enabled by the historical circumstances of modernity, including an emerging visual consumer culture.[89]

Reports of cases emphasized that material was imported, stressing that the "filth" came from overseas, rather than being locally produced. In 1868, John Beauchamp, William Davies, and Thomas J. Ruddall, photographers of Collins and Bourke Street, Melbourne, were charged with "being the possessor[s] of obscene photographic prints and negatives." The Melbourne *Age* reported: "The pictures were loathsome in the highest degree, and they were calculated to cause pain by the reflection that the human mind could become so far degraded as to prostitute the splendid achievements of science to such shameful purposes." The paper concluded, "It is satisfactory, however, to know that they were not manufactured in this colony."[90] In an 1881 case, photographs of German origin—from a calendar series that depicted women and men, with erect penises, in various coital positions and an act of fellatio—were described as "filthy and obscene in the highest degree."[91] Australian colonies' first anti-obscenity legislation, as in North America, "was directed at imports, as if domestic manufacture was inconceivable."[92] However, as well as widespread distribution of imported erotic imagery, there is evidence of the reproduction of imported material locally and the production of erotic imagery within the Australian colonies. Both practices evaded customs. Imported photographic negatives were easier to conceal and then hundreds of prints could be made and sold.

The emergence of mass-market postcards with changing printing technology created new markets and audiences for erotic imagery—as well as policing and new acts to regulate "indecent" postcards. Large numbers of erotic postcards were produced between the 1890s and 1920s in Germany, Austria, and France and exported.[93] Erotic postcards, like erotic photographs, were diverse, but they commonly included images of naked or stripping women. Images of couples having sex, flagellation, and eroticization of maids were also prevalent. Like circulating photographs, postcards often reproduced classical nudes from art, in an attempt to escape obscenity laws. By the 1880s, Postal Acts in Britain—and its colonies—prohibited the mailing and circulation of obscene postcards. However, most erotic postcards were not sent through the post despite their format, with a space for an address and brief message on one side. Rather they were purchased from mail order catalogs, street vendors, stalls, and newsagents for private or group viewing. Colonial anecdotal evidence also indicates that such postcards were obtained on Continental trips or from sailors. Australian artist Norman Lindsay tells of a friend of his older brother, Lionel, returning from the "Grand Tour of Europe" in 1894 with "some French postcards designed in a key of the skittish pornographic."[94] Norman, then fifteen years old, sketched copies of these postcards and circulated them in the Victorian country town he lived in.

Erik Norgaard comments that erotic postcards were "never intended to be sent through the post" but were meant to give visual pleasure.[95] Similarly, William Ouellette noted that "erotic postcards were rarely sent through the mails and remained unused preserved in the jacket pockets of male travellers."[96] However, anecdotal evidence suggests that such postcards also circulated among young people of both sexes. Norman Lindsay recounts passing around his facsimiles of French erotic postcards to female friends at the races, in the mid-1890s, which "produced the desired shocked giggles." One girl kept the cards in her purse, which was then stolen.[97]

An exception to the prohibition again erotic postcards being mailed openly was postcards of black women and other women of color. Racial otherness made erotica acceptable as ethnographic images. In his study of Algerian postcards, Malek Alloula points to the latent eroticism of colonial postcards, which frequently depicted exposed "alluring breasts" and half-naked dancers, suggesting the women that they "pin" were "akin to the butterflies and insects that museums of natural history and taxidermists exhibit[ed] in their glass display cases."[98] Ouellette notes that "both elaborately veiled and totally nude, ethnic women" were common postcard subjects and were "rendered more acceptable by their aura of 'foreignness.'"[99] Victorian erotic postcards both "hypersexualised and desexualised" colonial subjects and the foreign, argues Sigel.[100]

FIGURE 9.9: Two naked women, c. 1800. Public Records Office of Victoria, VPRS 30/ P0, Unit 574, 1881, Australia.

Ouellette notes that the medium of erotic postcards was "suggestion, calculated concealment and revelation, the ideal tease."[101] Postcards emphasized mystery and intrigue and the concealing and revealing of the female body through images containing masks and drapery, with nudity. Some postcards contained images of nude women covered by an actual piece of fabric, which involved the participant physically and provided the viewer with "a substitute version of real-life lifting and peeping."[102] Some erotic postcards, particularly those obtained from international catalogs or overseas travel, were predominantly accessible to upper-middle-class and upper-class audiences. Others were accessible to both young people and the working classes. It was those postcards circulating for sale on the streets and in public spaces that attracted the attention of morality campaigners, the police, and courts.

In 1920, Constable Patrick Hogan saw postcards "suggestive of indecency" exhibited in the window and on the counter of a shop in Melbourne and purchased them. The shopkeeper was charged by police with having "offered for sale postcards of an indecent nature." At the Court of Petty Sessions, the police magistrate, K. Notley Moore, said he could not see "anything indecent" in the cards, commenting that "some people could find indecency in the leg of a piano." The City Bench—comprising a police magistrate, a former commissioner of police, and a retired schoolmaster—dismissed the charges and awarded the shopkeeper two guineas' costs.[103] However, the press, the community, and the judiciary were not unanimous in their opinion of what was indecent. The *Argus* (April 16, 1920) challenged the magistrate's comments and the ruling, saying:

> Many vulgar and indecent postcards are exposed for sale in Melbourne. Many of them may be "within the law," though far out-side the bounds of propriety. There is always some difficulty in dealing with an evil of this kind, and it must be admitted that Australia is much better off in this respect than some older countries. Evidently there are a few persons who find it profitable ... to cater for those of prurient taste. ... The pernicious stuff falls into the hands of the youth of both sexes, and a great deal of mischief is done.

The *Argus* published two letters to the editor supporting their position. The first letter, by Thomas Strong, urged that steps be taken to "absolutely prohibit the sale (or exposure) of a certain class of postcard" currently displayed in shop windows. The writer described "the crowds of men and youths blocking the footpath in their eagerness to view these evils," writing: "I have blushed to

FIGURE 9.10: Man and woman, c. 1800.
Public Records Office of Victoria, VPRS 30/
P0, Unit 574, 1881, Australia.

think that anyone could so far lose their sense of decency or self respect as to stop to gaze at these disgusting pictures" (*Argus,* April 19, 1920).

The second letter, by the convener of the Public Questions Department of the Council of Churches, reminded readers that one of the picture cards inspected in the city court was considered by another magistrate as so vulgar and "morally filthy in its suggestiveness that it secured, some time ago, a conviction against its vendor." He challenged Police Magistrate Moore for treating the pictures "so lightly," commenting that "to commercialise pictures of licentious suggestiveness is a peril to society, and should be condemned and not joked about," and noting that "any pure-minded parent would be seriously concerned if he found such picture-cards in the possession of any member of his family."[104] The Crown appealed the decision, and at the court hearing, Mr. Justice Hood said, "Some of them were vulgar, and one of them was grossly indecent. ... In the interests of the community the sale of such cards should be stopped. They would have a demoralising influence on young people." Justice

Hood set aside the decision of the lower court and the shopkeeper was fined £15, with £2/2/ costs.[105] The case highlights debates over what imagery was "indecent" and illustrates the diversity of societal and legal reactions to erotic postcards, demonstrating that postcards with erotic imagery circulated widely and were available to young men and young women. It was the availability of the erotic postcard to young people, the working classes, and both genders that provoked alarm among moral campaigners, the police, and elements of the judiciary. Previously, erotic photographs had been restricted to the elite.[106]

New technologies of moving pictures from 1895 created new possibilities for erotic imagery—and new forms of censorship and regulation. Moving pictures "created new representations of the sexualised body and provided new opportunities for erotic viewing," argues Lynda Nead.[107] In 1896, Maxim Gorky, after having his first glance of cinema, commented, "I am convinced that these pictures will soon be replaced by others of a genre more suited to the Concert Parisien. ... They will show a picture entitled: As She Undresses, or Madam at Her Bath, or A Woman in Stockings."[108] By 1896, erotic films had been made in both Paris and London. In 1896, Frenchman Eugène Pirou produced the film Le coucher de la Marie, in which French cabaret star Louise Willy performed a striptease. The film was shown in at least three venues in Paris and caused a sensation.[109] It was followed by a number of films, mainly based around the striptease, produced by Georges Méliès and Charles Pathé. This genre of films, known as scènes grivoises d'un caractère piquant, was circulated in catalogs internationally.[110] Four other films, in 1897, drew comment in the photographic press for their salacious material and were "all deemed to be unsuitable for public exhibition." The films—The Temptation of Saint Anthony, The Artists's Model, A Bride Unrobing, and A French Lady's Bath—were distributed by the firm of Philipp Wolf, which was of the largest supplier of films in Europe, with offices in Berlin, Paris, and London, and specialized in French films, particularly Méliès titles.[111] In contrast to photographs and stereographs, film enabled group viewing of erotica. Simon Brown argues that in general British or foreign risqué films were not welcome in the general British marketplace of urban music halls and fairgrounds but were more targeted to a male "smoking concert" or "smoking room" audience. His research highlights both the distribution and exhibition of erotic or risqué film to smoking concerts—men-only gatherings, mostly of middle- and upper-class men.[112] Pathé's (French) erotic films were advertised in British catalogs, although the extent to which they were purchased or viewed in Britain is unknown.

Film created new forms of regulation and censorship in the West. The National Board of Censorship of Moving Pictures was established in America in

1909; the British Board of Censors was formed in 1913, and in Australia, the Commonwealth Censorship Office was established in 1917.[113] Such censorship boards, concerned with protecting public morals, meant erotic and sexually explicit moving pictures were viewed underground—in smoking concert, men's clubs, and brothels—rather than in music halls and cinemas.

Sexually explicit films—colloquially known as "stag films" in America and "blue movies" in Britain—generally catered to private audiences and existed underground, escaping both the censorship of censor bodies and prosecution. These films were shown in private homes, men's clubs, and brothels. They were predominantly advertised in catalogs and knowledge about their existence—and screenings—spread by word of mouth and through networks. Di Lauro and Rabkin suggest that viewing stag films became a rite of passage among American young men.[114] The cost of purchasing stag films meant that they generally circulated only within middle- and upper-class networks.

Erotic films, like earlier visual material, also circulated internationally. For example, a stag film found in the Australian National Film and Sound Archives Last Film Search and initially thought to be an Australian film from 1917 was found to be an edited version of the 1917–1919 American film *A Free Ride*.[115] The content and style of erotic films varied in national contexts. For example, the British *A Victorian Lady in Her Boudoir* (1896) situates the viewer as an invisible interloper who watches a woman undress. Similarly, *Bride's First Night* (1898) enables erotic voyeurism of "penetration of a private space." Brown argues that British risqué films presented "tantalising suggestive narratives" with sexual overtones, whereas films coming out of France—including films produced by Pathé—Austria, and Germany had more explicit sexual imagery, including nudity and explicit sexual scenarios.[116] "British risqué films were about looking and seeing, as opposed to that which was seen," suggests Brown, in contrast to Pathé's French films, which represented "the frenzy of the visible."[117]

CONCLUSION

Erotic collections emerged in the context of a developing global economy and imperialism. Erotic imagery in the Age of Empire was different from earlier textual descriptions and images because of the sexualized and feminized realm of empire. An erotica collection in the Australian colonies collected from Europe and Asia by an upper-class white male colonist points to erotic imagery as imperial spectacle.

The development of photographic technology in the nineteenth century enabled erotica to expand in new directions and gave it the capacity to produce explicit visual images of sex and women's bodies, in a medium distinct from earlier texts, engravings, and sketches. Photography enabled the explicit portrayal of sexual intercourse and other sex acts and the graphic depiction of women's bodies and sexual organs in ways that were not previously possible. The "truth effects" of photography and film—that the camera captured real women and men really doing "it"—added to the viewer's pleasure of looking at erotica, intensifying excitement.

Erotic material received from France, Austria, Germany, and England demonstrates the transnational traffic in erotic imagery in the mid- to late-nineteenth century—and the creativity of exporters in concealing erotica. Such cases also provide insight into the importing practices, distribution networks, and buyers and audiences of erotic imagery in the colonies, and the regulation and policing of material deemed obscene. The development of photographic and printing technologies increased circulation and availability, making erotic imagery no longer predominantly limited to the upper classes but now available to the middle and working classes. This development led to increased regulation and policing of erotic imagery in attempts to exclude women and the lower classes from their consumption. The tens of thousands of "obscene photographs" repeatedly obtained in raids across the globe during the 1870s through the 1890s emphasizes the extensive sexual commerce of erotic imagery and the failure of policing to deter consumers keen to purchase and view such images. By the early-twentieth century, the collection of erotic imagery had changed substantially from being a gentleman's pursuit to one also available to the middle and working classes and to both (white) women and men.

NOTES

Chapter 1

1. See Lytton Strachey, *Eminent Victorians* (London: Chatto and Windus, 1918); Lytton Strachey, *Queen Victoria* (London: Chatto and Windus, 1921).
2. We side with Michel Foucault on the incompatibility of phenomenology and history. See his introduction to Georges Canguilhem, *The Normal and Pathological*, trans. Caroline R. Fawcett (New York: Zone Books, 1989).
3. Michel Foucault, *The Will to Knowledge,* vol. 1 of *The History of Sexuality*, trans. Robert Hurley (Harmondsworth, UK: Penguin, 1998), chap. 1.
4. An important example here is the 1877 trial of Anne Besant and Charles Bradlaugh for the publication of Charles Knowlton's *Fruits of Philosophy*, which detailed cheap contraceptive techniques. For more details, see Roger Manvell, *The Trial of Annie Besant and Charles Bradlaugh* (London: Elek, 1976).
5. See http://www.oldbaileyonline.org for a glimpse into the richness of legal source materials. The basis of this Web site—the *Old Bailey Sessions Papers*—has been exploited already by historians such as Joel P. Eigen and Rictor Norton. See Joel P. Eigen, *Witnessing Insanity* (New Haven, CT: Yale University Press, 1995); Joel P. Eigen, *Unconscious Crime* (Baltimore: Johns Hopkins University Press, 2003); Rictor Norton, "Recovering Gay History from the Old Bailey," *London Journal* 30, no. 1 (2005): 39–54.
6. See Ivan Crozier, "'All the Appearances Were Perfectly Natural': The Anus of the Sodomite in Nineteenth-Century Medical Discourse," in *Body Parts: Critical Explorations in Corporeality*, ed. Christopher E. Forth and Ivan Crozier (Lanham, MD: Lexington Books, 2005); Ivan Crozier and Gethin Rees, "Making a Space for Medical Expertise: Forensic Discussions of Sexuality Assault in Nineteenth-Century Medicine," *Law, Culture and Humanities* (forthcoming).
7. Angus McLaren, *Birth Control in Nineteenth-Century England* (London: Croom Helm, 1978); Miriam Benn, *Predicaments of Love* (London: Pluto Press, 1992); Lesley A. Hall, *Hidden Anxieties: Male Sexuality, 1900–1950* (Cambridge: Polity Press, 1991).

8. Ivan Crozier, "Havelock Ellis, Eonism, and the Patient's Discourse," *History of Psychiatry* 11 (2000): 125–54; Ivan Crozier, "Pillow Talk: Credibility, Trust and the Sexological Case History," *History of Science* 46 (2008): 375–404.

9. See Michael Mason, *The Making of Victorian Sexuality* (Oxford: Oxford University Press, 1994), and *The Making of Victorian Sexual Attitudes* (Oxford: Oxford University Press, 1994).

10. See, for example, Bruce Haley, *The Healthy Body and Victorian Culture* (Cambridge, MA: Harvard University Press, 1978); J. A. Mangan and James Walvin, eds., *Manliness and Morality: Middle-Class Masculinity in Britain and America, 1800–1940* (New York: St. Martin's Press, 1987).

11. See Roy Porter and Marijke Geswijt-Hofstra, eds., *Cultures of Neurasthenia* (Amsterdam: Rodopi, 2000).

12. Lynda Nead, *Myths of Sexuality: Representations of Women in Victorian Britain* (Oxford: Blackwell, 1988).

13. Ana Carden-Coyne, *Reconstructing the Body: Classicism, Modernism, and the First World War* (Oxford: Oxford University Press, 2009).

14. See, for example, Franklin S. Klaf, trans., *Psychopathia Sexualis with Especial Reference to the Antipathic Sexual Instinct: A Medico-forensic Study*, by Richard von Krafft-Ebing (London: Arcade, 1965), 3–4.

15. John Addington Symonds, *A Problem in Greek Ethics Being an Inquiry into the Phenomenon of Sexual Inversion Addressed Especially to Medical Psychologists and Jurists* (London: Privately printed, 1901), in particular 1, 13–14. See also "Appendix A: A Problem in Greek Ethics by John Addington Symonds," in Havelock Ellis and John Addington Symonds, *Sexual Inversion: A Critical Edition*, ed. Ivan Crozier (Basingstoke, UK: Palgrave Macmillan, 2008), 227–95.

16. John Addington Symonds, *A Problem in Modern Ethics Being an Inquiry into the Phenomenon of Sexual Inversion. Addressed Especially to Medical Psychologist and Jurists* (London: Charles R. Dawes ex Libris, 1896), 5.

17. For more on Burton's work in this area, and more generally, see Dane Kennedy's excellent *The Highly Civilized Man: Richard Burton and the Victorian World* (Cambridge, MA: Harvard University Press, 2005).

18. Richard F. Burton, "Terminal Essay. Section D: Pederasty," in *A Plain and Literal Translation of the Arabian Nights Entertainments, Now Intituled the Book of the Thousand Nights and a Night with Introduction Explanatory Notes on the Manners and Customs of Moslem Men and Terminal Essay upon the History of the Nights* (London: Burton Club, 1886), 10:205–54. The essay on pederasty appeared only in 1885 and 1886 editions.

19. Ellis and Symonds, *Sexual Inversion*, 96–114.

20. Iwan Bloch, *Sex Life in England* (New York: Gargoyle Press, 1934). Bloch especially considers the English fascination with bondage and discipline.

21. Steven Marcus, *The Other Victorians: A Study of Sexuality and Pornography in Mid-Nineteenth-Century England* (London: Corgi Books, 1970); Alex Comfort, *The Anxiety Makers: Some Curious Preoccupations of the Medical Profession* (London: Nelson, 1967); Ronald Pearsall, *The Worm in the Bud: The World of Victorian Sexuality* (London: Weidenfeld and Nicolson, 1969).

22. Foucault's early ideas about sexuality are found in the lectures in *Abnormal*, given in 1974–1975. See Michel Foucault, *Abnormal: Lectures at the Collège de France, 1974–1975,* ed. Valerio Marchetti and Antonella Salomoni, trans. Graham Burchell (London: Verso, 2003).

23. Foucault, *The Will to Knowledge*, 18.

24. Ibid., 58–70, 115–22.

25. Ibid., 42–44, 53–73.

26. We use "sexology" here anachronistically, but following standard use in the history of sexology. The word, a translation of the German word *Sexualwissensschaft*, was coined in 1906, although its use can be traced at least to the 1860s, when the American feminist Elizabeth Willard entitled a book *Sexology*. However, Willard's understanding of the term referred more to the relationship between sexes rather than to the *scientia sexualis*. See Chris Waters, "Sexology," in *Palgrave Advances in the Modern History of Sexuality*, ed. Matt Houlbrook and Harry G. Cocks (Basingstoke, UK: Palgrave Macmillan, 2006), 42–43.

27. Foucault, *The Will to Knowledge*, 42–44, 53–73.

28. Ibid., 104–5.

29. Rachel P. Maines, *The Technology of Orgasm: "Hysteria," the Vibrator, and Women's Sexual Satisfaction* (Baltimore: Johns Hopkins University Press, 1998).

30. Foucault, *The Will to Knowledge*, 104–5.

31. See Ian Hacking, "Making up People," in *Reconstructing Individualism: Autonomy, Individuality, and the Self in Western Thought*, ed. Thomas C. Heller et al. (Stanford, CA: Stanford University Press, 1986); Hacking, "Kinds of People: Moving Targets," http://www.britac.ac.uk:80/pubs/src/britacad06/index.cfm; Arnold I. Davidson, *The Emergence of Sexuality: Historical Epistemology and the Formation of Concepts* (Cambridge, MA: Harvard University Press, 2001).

32. For a handful of such interpretations, see Theo van der Meer, "Sodomy and Its Discontents: Discourse, Desire and the Rise of a Same-Sex and Proto-Something in the Early Modern Dutch Republic," *Historical Reflections* 33 (2007): 41–67; Harry Oosterhuis, *Stepchildren of Nature: Krafft-Ebing, Psychiatry, and the Making of Sexual Identity* (Chicago: University of Chicago Press, 2000). It is hardly worth mentioning the myriad of Anglophone historians who have whole-heartedly adopted Foucault's date for the birth of sexology—Carl Westphal's paper, which was neither from 1870 nor published in the *Archiv für Neurologie*—and have constantly cited it despite having clearly never read this piece. See Carl Westphal, "Die conträre Sexualempfindung: Symptom eines neuropathischen (psychopathischen) Zustandes," *Archiv für Psychiatrie und Nervenkrankheiten* 2 (1869): 73–108, translated in Michael A. Lombardi-Nash, ed., *Sodomites and Urnings: Homosexual Representations in Classic German Journals* (Binghamton, NY: Harrington Park Press, 2006), 87–120.

33. Mason, *The Making of Victorian Sexuality* and *The Making of Victorian Sexual Attitudes*.

34. Owsei Temkin, *The Double Face of Janus and Other Essays in the History of Medicine* (Baltimore: Johns Hopkins University Press 1977), 432.

35. George L. Mosse, *Nationalism and Sexuality: Respectability and Abnormal Sexuality in Modern Europe* (New York: H. Fertig, 1985).

36. Elisabeth Ladenson, *Dirt for Art's Sake: Books on Trial from "Madame Bovary" to "Lolita"* (Ithaca, NY: Cornell University Press, 2006), 17–77.

37. Paul. E. Stepansky, "A Footnote to the History of Homosexuality in Britain: Havelock Ellis and the Bedborough Trial of 1898," in *Essays in the History of Psychiatry,* ed. Edwin R. Wallace and Lucius C. Pressley (Columbia, SC: Wm. S. Hall Psychiatric Institute, 1980), 96–97. Incidentally, Havelock Ellis translated *La terre* from the French.

38. Molly McGarry, "Spectral Sexualities: Nineteenth-Century Spiritualism, Moral Panics, and the Making of U.S. Obscenity Law," *Journal of Women's History* 12 (2000): 8–29.

39. Important here is Peter Gay's premier volume of the *Education of the Senses,* titled *The Bourgeois Experience: Victoria to Freud* (Oxford: Oxford University Press, 1984).

40. See Lesley A. Hall, "Hauling down the Double Standard: Feminism, Social Purity and Sexual Science in Late Nineteenth-Century Britain," *Gender and History* 16, no. 1 (2004): 36–56, which argues that feminist criticisms of the double standard in the nineteenth century were the first sources of the problematization of sexuality, before sexology. Such a view misses the importance of early sexological writings in addition to embodying some naive historiographical conceptions, but nevertheless, the fact remains that there was significant Victorian criticism of the fact that men could have sex outside marriage in ways that women were unable to do if they were to maintain their hard-won air of respectability.

41. Marcus, *The Other Victorians*; Ronald Pearsall, *Public Purity, Private Shame: Victorian Sexual Hypocrisy Exposed* (London: Weidenfeld and Nicolson, 1976); Fraser Harrison, *The Dark Angel: Aspects of Victorian Sexuality* (London: Sheldon Press, 1977); Gay, *The Bourgeois Experience;* Mason, *The Making of Victorian Sexual Attitudes;* Patricia Anderson, *When Passion Reigned: Sex and the Victorians* (New York: Basic Books, 1995).

42. Londa Schiebinger, "Skeletons in the Closet: The First Illustrations of the Female Skeleton in Eighteenth-Century Anatomy," *Representations* 14 (1986): 42–82; Ludmilla Jordanova, *Sexual Visions: Images of Gender in Science and Medicine between the Eighteenth and Twentieth Centuries* (Madison: University of Wisconsin Press, 1989).

43. See, for example, Cesare Lombroso and Guglielmo Ferrero, *La donna delinquente, la prostituta e la donna normale* (Turin: Roux 1893); Cesare Lombroso and Guglielmo Ferrero, *Criminal Woman, the Prostitute, and the Normal Woman,* trans. Nicole Hahn Rafter and Mary Gibson (Durham, NC: Duke University Press, 2004).

44. Patrick Geddes and J. Arthur Thomson, *The Evolution of Sex* (London: Walter Scott, 1889). This biological idea underpinned the discourses on sadomasochism. For more, see Ivan Crozier, "Philosophy in the English Boudoir: Havelock Ellis, Love and Pain, and Sexological Discourses on Algophilia," *Journal of the History of Sexuality* 13 (2004): 275–305.

45. Theresa McBride, "Public Authority and Private Lives: Divorce after the French Revolution," *French Historical Studies* 17 (1992): 747–60, especially 749–50.

46. Lesley A. Hall, *Sex, Gender and Social Change in Britain since 1880* (Basingstoke, UK: Macmillan, 2000), 10.

47. George Drysdale, *The Elements of Social Science or Physical, Sexual and Natural Religion: An Exposition of the True Cause and Only Cure of the Three Primary Social Evils: Poverty, Prostitution, and* Celibacy (London: Privately printed, 1854).

48. Anne Summers, "'The Constitution Violate': The Female Body and the Female Subject in the Campaigns of Josephine Butler," *History Workshop Journal* 48 (1999): 1–15.

49. Barbara Caine, *English Feminism, 1780–1920* (Oxford: Oxford University Press, 1997), 123.

50. McLaren, *Birth Control in Nineteenth-Century England*, 206; Lesley A. Hall, "'I Have Never Met the Normal Woman': Stella Browne and the Politics of Womanhood," *Women's History Review* 6 (1997): 157–82.

51. Roy Porter and Lesley A. Hall, *The Facts of Life: The Creation of Sexual Knowledge in Britain, 1650–1950* (New Haven, CT: Yale University Press, 1995), 208–9, 216–18.

52. Martha Vicinus, ed., *Suffer and Be Still: Women in the Victorian Age* (Bloomington: Indiana University Press, 1972).

53. Frank Mort, *Dangerous Sexualities: Medico-moral Politics in England since 1830*, 2nd ed. (London: Routledge, 2000); Judith R. Walkowitz, *Prostitution and Victorian Society: Women, Class and the State* (Cambridge: Cambridge University Press, 1980).

54. Sheila Jeffreys, *The Spinster and Her Enemies: Feminism and Sexuality, 1880–1930* (London: Pandora Press, 1985); Margaret Jackson, *The Real Facts of Life: Feminism and the Politics of Sexuality c. 1850–1940* (London: Taylor and Francis, 1994).

55. Susan K. Kent, *Sex and Suffrage in Britain, 1860–1914* (Princeton, NJ: Princeton University Press, 1987); Lucy Bland, *Banishing the Beast: English Feminism and Sexual Morality, 1885–1914* (London: Penguin, 1995).

56. Lesley A. Hall, "Suffrage, Sex and Science," in *The Women's Suffrage Movement: New Feminist Perspectives,* ed. Maroula Joannou and June Purvis (Manchester: Manchester University Press, 1998), 188–200; Hall, *Sex, Gender and Social Change;* Hall, "Hauling down the Double Standard."

57. Helena Whitbread, ed., *I Know My Own Heart: The Diaries of Anne Lister (1791–1840)* (London: Virago Press, 1988); Martha Vicinus, *Intimate Friends: Women Who Loved Women, 1778–1928* (Chicago: University of Chicago Press, 2004).

58. Chiara Beccalossi, "Havelock Ellis: Sexual Inverts as Independent Women," in *Tribades, Tommies and Transgressives: History of Sexualities,* ed. Mary McAuliffe and Sonja Tiernan, vol. 1 (Newcastle, UK: Cambridge Scholars Press, 2008), 218–23.

59. Edward Carpenter, *The Intermediate Sex: A Study of Some Transitional Types of Men and Women* (London: Swan Sonnenschein, 1908), 16. This work is a collection of essays written between 1894 and 1908. Jeffrey Weeks, *Sex, Politics and*

Society: The Regulation of Sexuality since 1800, 2nd ed. (London: Longman, 1989), 172.

60. Alison Oram, "Cross-Dressing and Transgender," in *The Modern History of Sexuality*, ed. Harry G. Cocks and Matt Houldbrook (Basingstoke, UK: Palgrave Macmillan, 2006), 263–66. See also Geertje Mak, "Sandor/Sarolta Vay, from Passing Woman to Sexual Invert," *Journal of Women's History* 16 (2004): 54–77; Lisa Duggan, *Sapphic Slashers: Sex, Violence, and American Modernity* (Durham, NC: Duke University Press, 2000).
61. Vicinus, *Intimate Friends*, 31–55.
62. Leila J. Rupp, "Loving Women in the Modern World," in *Gay Life and Culture: A World History*, ed. Robert Aldrich (London: Thames and Hudson, 2006), 241.
63. Suzanne Rodriguez, *Wild Heart. A Life: Natalie Clifford Barney's Journey from Victorian America to Belle Epoque Paris* (New York: Ecco, 2002).
64. Carroll Smith-Rosenberg, "The Female World of Love and Ritual," *Signs* 1 (1975): 1–29. This article was reprinted in her *Disorderly Conduct: Vision of Gender in Victorian America* (New York: Knopf, 1985). Lillian Faderman, *Surpassing the Love of Men: Friendships between Women from the Renaissance to the Present* (London: Women's Press, 1991). For more recent literature adopting this view, see Jennifer Terry, *An American Obsession: Science, Medicine, and Homosexuality in Modern Society* (Chicago: University of Chicago Press, 1999); Duggan, *Sapphic Slashers*.
65. Esther Newton, "The Mythic Mannish Lesbian: Radclyffe Hall and the New Woman," *Signs* 9 (1984): 557–75; Carrol Smith-Rosenberg, "Discourses of Sexuality and Subjectivity: The New Woman, 1870–1936," in *Hidden from History: Reclaiming the Gay and Lesbian Past*, ed. Martin Duberman, Martha Vicinus, and George Chauncey (New York: New American Library, 1989), 264–80; Lisa Duggan, "The Trials of Alice Mitchell: Sensationalism, Sexology and the Lesbian Subject in Turn-of-the-Century America," *Signs* 18 (1993): 791–814.
66. Martha Vicinus, "They Wonder to Which Sex I Belong: The Historical Roots of the Modern Lesbian Identity," in *Homosexuality. Which Homosexuality?* ed. Dennis Altman, Carole Vance, Martha Vicinus, and Jeffrey Weeks (London: GMP, 1989), 485.
67. Vicinus, *Intimate Friends*. See also Sharon Marcus, *Between Women: Friendship, Desire, and Marriage in Victorian England* (Princeton, NJ: Princeton University Press, 2007).
68. Laura Doan, *Fashioning Sapphism: The Origin of the Modern Lesbian Culture* (New York: Columbia University Press, 2001).
69. Claude François Michéa, "Des deviations de l'appétit vénérien," *Union Medicale*, July 1849, 338–39; Johann Ludwig Casper, "Ueber Nothzucht und Päderastie und deren Ermittelung Seitens des Gerichtesarztes," *Vierteljahrschrift für gerichtliche öffentliche Medizin* 1 (1852): 21–78. On the importance of these texts, see, for example, Gert Hekma, "A History of Sexology: Social and Historical Aspects of Sexuality," in *From Sappho to De Sade: Moments in the History of Sexuality*, ed. Jan Bremmer (Longon: Routledge, 1989), 173–93; Gert Hekma, "A Female Soul in a Male Body: Sexual Inversion as Gender Inversion in Nineteenth Century Sexology," in *Third Sex, Third Gender: Beyond Dimorphism in Culture and*

History, ed. Gilbert Herdt (New York: Zone Books, 1994), 213–39; Oosterhuis *Stepchildren of Nature,* 39; Ellis and Symonds, *Sexual Inversion,* 18–19.

70. Wilhelm Griesinger, "Vortrag zur Eröffnung der psychiatrischen Clink," *Archiv für Psychiatrie und Nervenkrankheiten* 1 (1868): 636–54.
71. Westphal's article is discussed in more depth in Crozier, "Pillow Talk."
72. Hekma, "A Female Soul in a Male Body," 218–22.
73. Richard von Krafft-Ebbing, "Über gewisse Anomalies des Geschlechtstriebs und die klinisch-forensich Verwertung derselben als eines wahrscheinlich funktionellen Degenerationszeichens des centralen Nervensystems," *Archiv für Psychiatrie und Nervenkrankheiten* 7 (1877): 291–312.
74. Chiara Beccalossi, "The Origin of Italian Sexological Studies: Female Sexual Inversion ca. 1870–1900," *Journal of the History of Sexuality* 18 (2009): 109–11; Vernon A. Rosario, *The Erotic Imagination: French Histories of Perversity* (New York: Oxford University Press, 1997), 69, 83–89.
75. Oosterhuis, *Stephchildren of Nature,* 131–258.
76. For an interesting analysis of this trial, see Gary Edmond, "The Law Set: The Legal-Scientific Production of Medical Propriety," *Science, Technology & Human Values* 26 (2001): 191–226.
77. Harry G. Cocks, *Nameless Offences: Homosexual Desire in the Nineteenth-Century England* (London: I. B. Tauris, 2003), 105–14; William A. Cohen, *Sex Scandal: The Private Parts of Victorian Fiction* (Durham, NC: Duke University Press, 1996), 73–129.
78. See H. Montgomery Hyde, *The Cleveland Street Scandal* (London: W. H. Allen, 1976).
79. Bland, *Banishing the Beast,* 289.
80. Michael S. Foldy, *The Trials of Oscar Wilde: Deviance, Morality, and Late-Victorian Society* (New Haven, CT: Yale University Press, 1997), 89–90; David Pritchard, *Oscar Wilde* (New Lanark, UK: Geddes & Grosset, 2001), 149.
81. Isabelle Hull, *The Entourage of Kaiser Wilhelm II, 1888–1918* (New York: Cambridge University Press, 1982).
82. Mary McIntosh, "The Homosexual Role," *Social Problems* 16 (1968): 182–92.
83. Jeffrey Weeks, *Coming Out: Homosexual Politics in Britain, from the Nineteenth Century to the Present* (London: Quartet Books, 1977).
84. Weeks, *Sex, Politics and Society;* Jeffrey Weeks, *Sexuality and Its Discontents: Meanings, Myths and Modern Sexualities* (London: Routledge and Kegan Paul, 1985); George Chauncey, "From Sexual Inversion to Homosexuality: Medicine and the Changing Conceptualization of Female Deviance," *Salmagundi* 58–59 (1982–83): 114–46: David M. Halperin, *One Hundred Years of Homosexuality: And Other Essays on Greek Love* (London: Routledge, 1990).
85. George Chauncey, *Gay New York: Gender, Urban Culture, and the Making of the Gay Male World, 1890–1940* (New York: Basic Books, 1994).
86. Continental ideas did creep into British psychiatric discourses on homosexuality, however. See Ivan Crozier, "Nineteenth-Century British Psychiatric Writing about Homosexuality before Havelock Ellis: The Missing Story," *Journal of the History of Medicine and Allied Sciences* 63 (2008): 65–102.

87. See Crozier and Rees, "Making a Space for Medical Expertise."

88. For more on the history of rape, see Roy Porter and Sylvana Tomeselli, eds., *Rape* (Oxford: Blackwell, 1986).

89. Summers, "The Constitution Violate."

90. For a sample of some of this material, see Laura J. Engelstein, "Gender and the Juridical Subject: Prostitution and Rape in Nineteenth-Century Russian Criminal Codes," *Journal of Modern History* 60 (1988): 458–95; Jean Louis Guereña, "Prostitution and the Origins of the Governmental Regulatory System in Nineteenth-Century Spain: The Plans of the Trienio Liberal, 1820–1823," *Journal of the History of Sexuality* 17 (2008): 216–34; Philippa Levine, "Consistent Contradictions: Prostitution and Protective Labour Legislation in Nineteenth-Century England," *Social History* 19 (1994): 17–35; Mary Gibson, *Prostitution and the State in Italy, 1860–1915* (New Brunswick, NJ: Rutgers University Press, 1986).

91. Frances B. Smith, "Labouchere's Amendment to the Criminal Law Amendment Act," *Historical Studies* 17 (1976): 165–73.

92. See Ivan Crozier, "The Medical Construction of Homosexuality and Its Relation to the Law in Nineteenth-Century England," *Medical History* 45, no. 1 (2001): 61–82.

93. See James Steakley, *The Homosexual Emancipation Movement in Germany* (New York: Arno Press, 1975).

94. Antony Copley, *Sexual Moralities in France, 1780–1980: New Ideas on the Family, Divorce, and Homosexuality: An Essay on Moral Change* (London: Routledge, 1989).

95. See Crozier, "'Philosophy in the English Boudoir." For more on Jack the Ripper, see Judith R. Walkowitz, *City of Dreadful Delight: Narratives of Sexual Danger in Late-Victorian London* (Chicago: University of Chicago Press, 1992).

96. For example, Patrizia Guarnieri, *A Case of Child Murder: Law and Science in Nineteenth-Century Tuscany* (Cambridge: Polity Press, 1996); Maria Tatar, *Lustmord: Sexual Murder in Weimar Germany* (Princeton, NJ: Princeton University Press, 1995).

97. Scholars who have relied heavily on medical texts while wishing to make cultural arguments include Mak, "Sandor/Sarolta Vay"; Matt Cook, *London and the Culture of Homosexuality, 1885–1914* (Cambridge: Cambridge University Press, 2003); Sean Brady, *Masculinity and Male Homosexuality in Britain, 1861–1913* (Basingstoke, UK: Palgrave Macmillan, 2005). For a word of caution about reading sexological case histories for such information, see Crozier, "Havelock Ellis, Eonism, and the Patient's Discourse" and "Pillow Talk."

98. John Noyes, *The Mastery of Submission: Inventions of Masochism* (Ithaca, NY: Cornell University Press, 1997). Literary studies offer a broader reading of this material. Marianne Noble, *The Masochistic Pleasures of Sentimental Literature* (Princeton, NJ: Princeton University Press, 2000); Jay Prosser, *Second Skins: The Body Narratives of Transsexuality* (New York: Columbia University Press, 1998); Lisa Downing, *Desiring the Dead: Necrophilia and Nineteenth-Century French Literature* (Oxford: Legenda, 2003); Lisa Downing, "Death and the Maidens:

A Century of Necrophilia in Female-Authored Textual Production," *French Cultural Studies* 14 (2003): 157–68; Midas Dekkers, *Dearest Pet: On Bestiality*, trans. Paul Vincent (New York: Verso, 2000); Lisa Downing and Dany Nobus, "The Iconography of Asphyxiophilia: From Fantasmatic Fetish to Forensic Fact," *Paragraph: A Journal of Modern Critical Theory* 27 (2004): 1–15.

99. See, for an early example, H. Montgomery Hyde, *A History of Pornography* (London: Heinemann, 1964). More recently, see Lisa Z. Sigel, *Governing Pleasures: Pornography and Social Change in England, 1815–1914* (New Brunswick, NJ: Rutgers University Press, 2002).

100. This material is examined in Ivan Crozier, "The Sexual Body, 1920–Present," in *Cultural History of the Human Body*, ed. Ivan Crozier, vol. 5 (Oxford: Berg, 2010).

101. For Foucault's views of space, see among other places, "Questions on Geography," in Michel Foucault, *Power/Knowledge: Selected Interviews and Other Writings, 1972–1977*, ed. Colin Gordon (Sussex, UK: Harvester Press, 1980).

102. Matt Houlbrook, *Queer London: Perils and Pleasures in the Sexual Metropolis, 1918–57* (Chicago: University of Chicago Press, 2005). See also Cook, *London and the Culture of Homosexuality*; Morris B. Kaplan, "Who's Afraid of John Saul? Urban Culture and the Politics of Desire in Late Victorian London," *GLQ: A Journal of Lesbian and Gay Studies* 5 (1999): 267–314.

103. Alain Corbin, *Women for Hire: Prostitution and Sexuality in France after 1850*, trans. Alan Sheridan (Cambridge, MA: Harvard University Press, 1990); Walkowitz, *Prostitution and Victorian Society* and *City of Dreadful Delight*; Frances Finnegan, *Poverty and Prostitution: A Study of Victorian Prostitutes in York* (Cambridge: Cambridge University Press, 1979).

104. Françoise Barret-Ducrocq, *Love in the Tome of Victoria: Sexuality, Class, and Gender in Nineteenth-Century London*, trans. John Howe (London: Verso, 1991).

Chapter 2

We would like to thank Hubert Kennedy for providing us with the Ulrichs image.

1. For an account of this process of categorization, see, for instance, Michel Foucault, *The Will to Knowledge*, vol. 1 of *The History of Sexuality*, trans. Robert Hurley (Harmondsworth, UK: Penguin, 1998); Alan Sekula, "The Body and the Archive," *October* 39 (1986): 3–64; Dana Seitler, "Queer Physiognomies; or, How Many Ways Can We Do the History of Sexuality?" *Criticism* 46 (2004): 71–102.

2. A full account of this invention is given in Jean-Claude Féray and Manfred Herzer, "Homosexual Studies and Politics in the 19th Century: Karl Maria Kertbeny," *Journal of Homosexuality* 19 (1990): 23–48. See also Jonathan Ned Katz, *The Invention of Heterosexuality* (New York: Plume, 1996), 51–55.

3. Foucault, *The Will to Knowledge*, 38–39.

4. Kertbeny quoted in Féray and Herzer, "Homosexual Studies," 36.

5. Kertbeny quoted in ibid., 35. "Pygist" is after the Greek πυγξξειν, "to engage in anal intercourse."
6. Kertbeny quoted in ibid., 39.
7. Ibid., 36.
8. Kertbeny quoted in ibid., 36–37.
9. Ibid., 40–46.
10. In the context of nineteenth-century medical and legal writing, "pederasty" signified both the age-structured relationships of classical Athens and, through an etymological confusion with the Latin *paedicatio*, what we would now call homosexual anal sex. See Hubert Kennedy, "Karl Heinrich Ulrichs: First Theorist of Homosexuality," in *Science and Homosexualities*, ed. Vernon A. Rosario (New York: Routledge, 1997), 30.
11. See ibid., 26. See also Nikki Sullivan, *A Critical Introduction to Queer Theory* (Edinburgh: Edinburgh University Press, 2003), 4–5.
12. Hubert Kennedy, *Karl Heinrich Ulrichs: Pioneer of the Modern Gay Movement* (San Francisco: Peremptory, 2002), 185.
13. Harry Oosterhuis, *Stepchildren of Nature: Krafft-Ebing, Psychiatry, and the Making of Sexual Identity* (Chicago: University of Chicago Press, 2000), 38; Arnold I. Davidson, *The Emergence of Sexuality: Historical Epistemology and the Formation of Concepts* (Cambridge, MA: Harvard University Press, 2001), 120.
14. Kennedy, "Karl Heinrich Ulrichs: First Theorist," 27.
15. Ibid., 30. Ulrichs's use of the term *Keim* is not connected to the then-emergent field of what is now known as germ theory in the history of medicine. The German term itself predates germ theory, appearing, for example, in Immanuel Kant's *Critique of Pure Reason*. For more on Kant's use of the term, see Phillip R. Sloan, "Performing the Categories: Eighteenth-Century Generation Theory and the Biological Roots of Kant's A Priori," *Journal of the History of Philosophy* 40 (2002): 229–53.
16. Ulrichs quoted in Kennedy, "Karl Heinrich Ulrichs: First Theorist," 31.
17. Ibid., 27.
18. Blumenstok quoted in ibid., 36.
19. Féray and Herzer, "Homosexual Studies," 29.
20. Kertbeny quoted in Kennedy, *Karl Heinrich Ulrichs: Pioneer*, 188.
21. Ulrichs quoted in Féray and Herzer, "Homosexual Studies," 29.
22. Ulrichs quoted in Kennedy, *Karl Heinrich Ulrichs: Pioneer*, 192.
23. Westphal quoted in Manfred Herzer, "Kertbeny and the Nameless Love," *Journal of Homosexuality* 12 (1985): 18.
24. Féray and Herzer, "Homosexual Studies," 34.
25. Ibid., 34.
26. Eve Kosofsky Sedgwick, *Epistemology of the Closet* (Berkeley: University of California Press, 1990), 1–2.
27. Herzer, "Kertbeny and the Nameless Love," 18.
28. Féray and Herzer, "Homosexual Studies," 29.
29. Ibid., 37–38.
30. Herzer, "Kertbeny and the Nameless Love," 7.
31. Katz, *The Invention of Heterosexuality*, 19–20, 207.

32. On the use of the term "heterosexual" in Krafft-Ebing, see Oosterhuis, *Stepchildren of Nature*, 50–51, esp. 51: "In Krafft-Ebing's work heterosexuality (as well as homosexuality) began to vacillate between normalcy and perversion."
33. Katz, *The Invention of Heterosexuality*, 20.
34. Ibid., 82.
35. Foucault, *The Will to Knowledge*, 43.
36. See David M. Halperin, *How to Do the History of Homosexuality* (Chicago: University of Chicago Press, 2002), 10–13.
37. Ibid., 14.
38. Chrys Ingraham, *White Weddings: Romancing Heterosexuality in Popular Culture*, 2nd ed. (New York: Routledge, 2008), 7 (emphasis removed).
39. Ibid., 16.
40. Thomas Laqueur, *Making Sex: Body and Gender from the Greeks to Freud* (Cambridge, MA: Harvard University Press, 1990), 50, 52, 123–24, 126, 229.
41. Foucault, *The Will to Knowledge*, 38. The original French can be found in Foucault, *La volonté de savoir* (Paris: Gallimard, 1976), 53.
42. Monique Wittig, *The Straight Mind and Other Essays* (Boston: Beacon Press, 1992), 40–41.
43. Ibid., 42.
44. Sedgwick, *Epistemology of the Closet*, 1.
45. Ibid., 2.
46. For a forceful analysis of the connections between media constructs of homosexual men as promiscuous and the AIDS crisis, see Leo Bersani, "Is the Rectum a Grave?" *October* 43 (1987): 197–222.
47. Sedgwick, *Epistemology of the Closet*, 3; David M. Halperin, *Saint Foucault: Towards a Gay Hagiography* (Oxford: Oxford University Press, 1995), 45.
48. The supplement, Derrida explains, is a necessary addition to a system that represents itself as already complete and, in its exposure of the limits of that system, it problematizes the dominant term's self-representation as autonomous and all-encompassing in a way that endangers it: while the supplement "is exterior to [and] ... supervenes upon" the dominant term, it does so "always by way of compensation for [*sous l'espèce de la suppléance*] what *ought* to lack nothing at all in itself." Jacques Derrida, *Of Grammatology*, trans. Gayatri Chakravorty Spivak (Baltimore: Johns Hopkins University Press, 1976), 145.
49. Halperin, *Saint Foucault*, 44 (emphasis in original).
50. Halperin, *How to Do the History of Homosexuality*, 10.
51. Leo Bersani, *Homos* (Cambridge, MA: Harvard University Press, 1995), 5.
52. Katz, *The Invention of Heterosexuality*, 181.
53. Ibid., 21.
54. Ibid., 16–17.
55. Ibid., 182.
56. Ibid., 19.
57. Ibid., 52.
58. Davidson, *The Emergence of Sexuality*, 23.

59. Sedgwick, *Epistemology of the Closet*, 46–47.
60. Kertbeny quoted in Féray and Herzer, "Homosexual Studies," 35.
61. Kertbeny quoted in ibid, 36.

Chapter 3

1. Jeffrey Weeks, *Making Sexual History* (Cambridge: Polity Press, 2000), 1.
2. Michel Foucault, *The Will to Knowledge,* vol. 1 of *The History of Sexuality,* trans. Robert Hurley (Harmondsworth, UK: Penguin, 1998), esp. 17–35, 51–74.
3. Homosexuality as a specifically categorized mental disorder was removed from the *Diagnostic and Statistical Manual* in 1973. The *International Classification of Diseases (ICD)* had retained homosexuality as a category of mental disorder in the 1978 edition, *ICD-9*, but this was removed by the next edition, published in 1992. George Mendelson, "Homosexuality and Psychiatric Nosology," *Australian and New Zealand Journal of Psychiatry* 37 (2003): 678–83.
4. Herb Kutchins and Stuart Kirk, *Making Us Crazy: DSM—the Psychiatric Bible and the Creation of Mental Disorders* (London: Constable, 1999), 59.
5. Harry Oosterhuis, *Stepchildren of Nature: Krafft-Ebing, Psychiatry, and the Making of Sexual Identity* (Chicago: University of Chicago Press, 2000), esp. 209–71.
6. Ibid., 215.
7. Chris Waters, "Sexology," in *Palgrave Advances in the Modern History of Sexuality*, ed. Matt Houlbrook and Harry G. Cocks (Basingstoke, UK: Palgrave Macmillan, 2006), 41–63.
8. Joseph Bristow, *Sexuality* (London: Routledge, 1997), 19.
9. Carolyn J. Dean, *Sexuality and Modern Western Culture* (New York: Twayne, 1996), 19.
10. Julie Peakman, ed., *Sexual Perversions, 1670–1890* (Basingstoke, UK: Palgrave Macmillan, 2009), 1–49.
11. Dean, *Sexuality and Modern Western Culture*, 19. For an analysis of same-sex desires and medical categories such as moral insanity, see Chiara Beccalossi, "Nineteenth-Century European Psychiatry on Same-Sex Desires: Pathology, Abnormality, Normality and the Blurring of Boundaries," *Psychology & Sexuality* (forthcoming).
12. Havelock Ellis and John Addington Symonds, *Sexual Inversion: A Critical Edition,* ed. Ivan Crozier (Basingstoke, UK: Palgrave Macmillan, 2008), 18.
13. Arnold I. Davidson, "Sex and the Emergence of Sexuality," *Critical Inquiry* 14, no. 1 (1987): 47.
14. Ivan Crozier, "The Medical Construction of Homosexuality and Its Relation to the Law in Nineteenth-Century England," *Medical History* 45, no. 1 (2001): 79. See also Ivan Crozier, "'All the Appearances Were Perfectly Natural': The Anus of the Sodomite in Nineteenth-Century Medical Discourse," in *Body Parts: Critical Explorations in Corporeality,* ed. Christopher E. Forth and Ivan Crozier (Lanham, MD: Lexington Books, 2005), 70.

15. Antony Copley, *Sexual Moralities in France, 1780–1980: New Ideas on the Family, Divorce, and Homosexuality: An Essay on Moral Change* (London: Routledge, 1989), 104.
16. Oosterhuis, *Stepchildren of Nature*, 66–67.
17. Dean, *Sexuality and Modern Western Culture*, 20.
18. Oosterhuis, *Stepchildren of Nature*, 66–67. See also Hubert Kennedy, "Karl Heinrich Ulrichs: First Theorist of Homosexuality," in *Science and Homosexualities*, ed. Vernon A. Rosario (New York: Routledge, 1997).
19. Dean, *Sexuality and Modern Western Culture*, 20, citing Davidson, "Sex and the Emergence of Sexuality."
20. Dean, *Sexuality and Modern Western Culture*, 20.
21. Ibid. (emphasis mine).
22. Oosterhuis, *Stepchildren of Nature*, 64.
23. Ibid.
24. Dean, *Sexuality and Modern Western Culture*, 20–21.
25. Siobhan Somerville, "Scientific Racism and the Invention of the Homosexual Body," in *Sexology in Culture: Labelling Bodies and Desires*, ed. Lucy Bland and Laura Doan (Cambridge: Polity Press, 1998), 60–76.
26. Ibid.
27. John Addington Symonds, *A Problem in Modern Ethics* (London: Privately printed, 1896), 51. Although highly critical of the explorer Sir Richard Burton's theories on theories on homosexuality, Symonds had adapted Burton's hypothesis that there existed a "sodatic zone" around the world encompassing southern Europe, Africa, parts of Asia, and Central and South America, where male homosexuality was particularly prevalent and tolerated. See Sean Brady, *Masculinity and Male Homosexuality in Britain, 1861–1913* (Basingstoke, UK: Palgrave Macmillan, 2005), for a fuller discussion of *A Problem in Modern Ethics*. See Colette Colligan, "A Race Born of Pederasts: Sir Richard Burton, Homosexuality, and the Arabs," *Nineteenth-Century Contexts* 25, no. 1 (2003): 1–20, for a full discussion of Burton's theorizing of the sodatic zone. See also James Nelson, *Publisher to the Decadents: Leonard Smithers in the Careers of Beardsley, Wilde, Dowson* (University Park: Pennsylvania State University Press, 2000).
28. John Addington Symonds, *A Problem in Modern Ethics*.
29. See Brady, *Masculinity and Male Homosexuality*, 157–210; Ellis and Symonds, *Sexual Inversion*, 34–53, for a fuller examination of Symonds and Ellis's collaboration on the project of *Sexual Inversion*. See also Sean Brady, ed., *John Addington Symonds (1840–1893) and Homosexuality: A Critical Edition of Sources* (Basingstoke, UK: Palgrave Macmillan, forthcoming).
30. Somerville, "Scientific Racism," 70.
31. Brady, *Masculinity and Male Homosexuality*, 140–41.
32. Ibid., quoting Nancy Leys Stepan and Sander Gilman, "Approaching the Idioms of Science: The Rejection of Scientific Racism," in *The Bounds of Race: Perspectives on Hegemony and Resistance*, ed. Dominic LaCapra (Ithaca, NY: Cornell University Press, 1991).

33. Brady, *Masculinity and Male Homosexuality*, 4–24. See also George Chauncey, *Gay New York: Gender, Urban Culture, and the Making of the Gay Male World, 1890–1940* (New York: Basic Books, 1994).

34. John Marshall, "Pansies, Perverts and Macho Men: Changing Conceptions of Male Homosexuality," in *The Making of the Modern Homosexual,* ed. Kenneth Plummer (London: Hutchinson, 1981), 148.

35. See Rictor Norton, *Mother Clap's Molly House: The Gay Subculture in England, 1700–1830* (London: Gay Men's Press, 1992); Randolph Trumbach, "Sex, Gender, and Sexual Identity in Modern Culture: Male Sodomy and Female Prostitution in Enlightenment London," in "The State, Society, and the Regulation of Sexuality in Modern Europe," special issue, part 1, *Journal of the History of Sexuality* 2, no. 2 (1991): 186–203.

36. See Jeffrey Weeks, *Sex, Politics and Society: The Regulation of Sexuality since 1800,* 2nd ed. (London: Longman, 1989); David M. Halperin, *One Hundred Years of Homosexuality: And Other Essays on Greek Love* (London: Routledge, 1990).

37. Chauncey, *Gay New York*, 12.

38. See Franz Eder, Lesley A. Hall, and Gert Hekma, eds., *National Histories,* vol. 1 of *Sexual Cultures in Europe* (Manchester: Manchester University Press, 1999); Chiara Beccalossi, *Female Sexual Inversion: Same-Sex Desires in Italian and British Sexology, ca. 1870–1920* (Basingstoke, UK: Palgrave Macmillan, forthcoming).

39. The notable recent exception being Beccalossi's *Female Sexual Inversion.*

40. For recent discussion on sexuality between women and sexology, see Chiara Beccalossi, "Havelock Ellis: Sexual Inverts as Independent Women," in *Tribades, Tommies and Transgressives,* ed. Mary McAuliffe and Sonja Tiernan, vol. 1 of *History of Sexualities* (Newcastle, UK: Cambridge Scholars Press, 2008), 211–28.

41. Copley, *Sexual Moralities in France, 1780–1980*, 135.

42. Robert Nye, "Sex and Sexuality in France since 1800," in Eder, Hall, and Hekma, *National Histories,* 93.

43. Copley, *Sexual Moralities in France, 1780–1980*, 135.

44. Nye, "Sex and Sexuality in France since 1800," 94.

45. Ibid., 93.

46. Ibid., 95. See also Simon Szretzer, Robert Nye, and Frans van Poppel, "Fertility and Contraception during the Demographic Transition: Qualitative and Quantitative Approaches," *Journal of Interdisciplinary History* 34, no. 2 (2003): 141–54.

47. Nye, "Sex and Sexuality in France since 1800," 95.

48. See Robert Nye, "The History of Sexuality in Context: National Sexological Tradition," *Science in Context* 4, no. 2 (1991): 387–406. See also Daniel Pick, *Faces of Degeneration: A European Disorder, c. 1848–1918* (Cambridge: Cambridge University Press, 1989), for a fuller discussion of degeneration theorists.

49. Nye, "Sex and Sexuality in France since 1800," 96.

50. Ibid., 99–100.

51. Leslie Choquette, "Homosexuals in the City: Representations of Lesbian and Gay Space in Nineteenth-Century Paris," in *Homosexuality in French History and Culture,* ed. Jeffrey Merrick and Michael Sibalis (London: Harrington Park Press, 2001), 149–67.

52. Robert Aldrich, *Colonialism and Homosexuality* (London: Routledge, 2003), 331. See also Robert Aldrich, "Homosexuality in the French Colonies," in Merrick and Sibalis, *Homosexuality in French History and Culture*, 201–18.

53. Quoted in Aldrich, *Colonialism and Homosexuality*, 329–30, and in Jarrod Hayes, *Queer Nations: Marginal Sexualities in the Maghreb* (Chicago: University of Chicago Press, 2000), 30.

54. Aldrich, *Colonialism and Homosexuality*, 58, quoting Dr. Tranchant and Lieutenant Desvignes, in *Les condamnés militaries du pénitencier de Bousset* (1911).

55. Aldrich, *Colonialism and Homosexuality*, 59.

56. Ibid., 60, citing Dr. R. Jude, *Les dégénérés dans les bataillons d'Afrique* (Vannes, 1907), 30–33.

57. Ibid., 61.

58. Ibid., 63.

59. Oosterhuis, *Stepchildren of Nature*, 33.

60. Ibid.

61. Christopher E. Forth, *Masculinity and the Modern West: Gender, Civilization and the Body* (Basingstoke, UK: Palgrave Macmillan, 2008), 151–52.

62. Oosterhuis, *Stepchildren of Nature*, 54. See also Matt Cook, *London and the Culture of Homosexuality, 1885–1914* (Cambridge: Cambridge University Press, 2003), for discussion of urban life and the categorizations of sexologists.

63. Anne O'Brien, "Missionary Masculinities, the Homoerotic Gaze and the Politics of Race: Gilbert White in Northern Australia, 1885–1915," *Gender and History* 20, no. 1 (2008): 76.

64. Ibid., 71, citing H. Carey, "Companions in the Wilderness? Missionary Wives in Colonial Australia," *Journal of Religious History* 19 (1995): 227–48.

65. Ibid., 73, citing Carey, "Companions in the Wilderness?"

66. Ibid., quoting Gilbert White, *Thirty Years in Tropical Australia* (S.P.C.K., 1918).

67. Ibid., quoting White, *Thirty Years*.

68. Ibid., 74, quoting White, *Thirty Years*.

69. Ibid., quoting Gilbert White, *Answer Australia* (Sydney: Australian Board of Missions, 1927), 26.

70. Ibid., 81, citing White, *Answer Australia*.

71. Ibid, quoting White, *Answer Australia*.

72. Ibid.

73. See Brady, *Masculinity and Male Homosexuality*, 194–209, for a full discussion of analysis of Carpenter's sexuality by historians.

74. Ellis and Symonds, *Sexual Inversion*, 54.

75. See Brady, *Masculinity and Male Homosexuality*, and Harry G. Cocks, *Nameless Offences: Homosexual Desire in the Nineteenth Century* (London: I. B. Taurus, 2003).

76. Edward Carpenter, *My Days and Dreams: Being Autobiographical Notes* (London: Allen & Unwin, 1916), 28.

77. Brady, *Masculinity and Male Homosexuality*, 196–98.

78. Parminder Bakshi, "Homosexuality and Orientalism: Edward Carpenter's Journey to the East," *Prose Studies* 13, no. 1 (1990): 157.
79. Brady, *Masculinity and Male Homosexuality*, 196–98.
80. Bakshi, "Homosexuality and Orientalism," 155–77.
81. Ronald Hyam, *Empire and Sexuality: The British Experience* (Manchester: Manchester University Press, 1990), 88.
82. Sheila Rowbotham, *Edward Carpenter: A Life of Love and Liberty* (London: Verso, 2008), 153, quoting Edward Carpenter, *From Adam's Peak to Elephanta: Sketches in Ceylon and India* (London: Swan Sonnenschein, 1892), 58.
83. Rowbotham, *Edward Carpenter*, 153.
84. Brady, *Masculinity and Male Homosexuality*, 198.
85. Ibid., 159.
86. Hyam, *Empire and Sexuality*, 91.
87. Ibid., 91.
88. Brady, *Masculinity and Male Homosexuality*, 38–40.
89. Hyam, *Empire and Sexuality*, 71.
90. In July 2009, a Delhi high court ruled the Indian penal code, in respect to consenting acts of sex between men in private, to be incompatible with human rights and the Indian constitution. Nonetheless, the statute remains intact as a Victorian legacy to modern India.
91. Dennis Judd, *Empire: The British Imperial Experience from 1765 to the Present* (London: Harper Collins, 1996), 171.
92. Hyam, *Empire and Sexuality*, 34.

Chapter 4

1. Michel Foucault, *The Will to Knowledge,* vol. 1 of *The History of Sexuality,* trans. Robert Hurley (Harmondsworth, UK: Penguin, 1998), 36.
2. Mario Praz, *The Romantic Agony,* 2nd ed., trans. A. Davis, ed. F. Kermode (Oxford: Oxford University Press, 1970), xvi.
3. See, for example, Daniel Pick, *Faces of Degeneration: A European Disorder, c. 1848–1918* (Cambridge: Cambridge University Press, 1989), 167–75, for a discussion of Bram Stoker's *Dracula* (1897) as a text exemplifying the ideas of racial and sexual otherness found in degeneration theory; Rachel Mesch, *The Hysteric's Revenge: French Women Writers at the Fin de Siècle* (Nashville, TN: Vanderbilt University Press, 2006), on French naturalist women writers of the nineteenth century and their responses to sexological models of female desire; and, for discussions of the influence of nineteenth-century sexological ideas about lesbianism in Radclyffe Hall's *The Well of Loneliness* (1928), see Heike Bauer, *English Literary Sexology: Translations of Inversion, 1860–1930* (London: Palgrave Macmillan, 2009), and Clare L. Taylor, *Women, Writing and Fetishism, 1890–1950: Female Cross-Gendering* (Oxford: Oxford University Press, 2003).
4. See Joseph Bristow, *Sexuality* (London: Routledge, 1997), 21–22.
5. Ibid., 20–25.

6. Arnold I. Davidson, *The Emergence of Sexuality: Historical Epistemology and the Formation of Concepts* (Cambridge, MA: Harvard University Press, 2001), chap. 3.

7. See Dany Nobus, "Locating Perversion, Dislocating Psychoanalysis," in *Perversion: Psychoanalytic Perspectives/Perspectives on Psychoanalysis,* ed. Dany Nobus and Lisa Downing (London: Karnac, 2006), 6.

8. See Harry Oosterhuis, *Stepchildren of Nature: Krafft-Ebing, Psychiatry, and the Making of Sexual Identity* (Chicago: University of Chicago Press, 2000).

9. Georges Canguilhem, *Le normal et le pathologique* (Paris: Presses Universitaires de France, 1966).

10. Vernon A. Rosario, "On Sexual Perversion and Transsensualism," in Nobus and Downing, *Perversion,* 328.

11. Krafft-Ebing revised the manual several times over a number of years, adding to the later editions increasing numbers of case studies and new subcategories of sexual variation. I shall cite in English from Chaddock's translation of the seventh edition or Rebman's translation of the tenth edition when more detail or greater accuracy of translation is afforded by one version or the other.

12. C. G. Chaddock, trans., *Psychopathia Sexualis with Special Reference to Contrary Sexual Instinct: A Medico-legal Study,* by Richard von Krafft-Ebing (Philadelphia: F. A. Davis, 1920), 1.

13. Ibid.

14. Oosterhuis, *Stepchildren of Nature,* 13.

15. F. J. Rebman, trans., *Psychopathia Sexualis with Especial Reference to Antipathic Sexual Instinct: A Medico-legal Study,* by Richard von Krafft-Ebing (London: Rebman, 1901), 203.

16. Chaddock, *Psychopathia Sexualis,* 19.

17. Ibid., 18.

18. Rebman, *Psychopathia Sexualis,* 91.

19. See Michel Dansel, *Le sergent Bertrand: Portrait d'un nécrophile heureux* (Paris: Albin Michel, 1991); Lisa Downing, *Desiring the Dead: Necrophilia and Nineteenth-Century French Literature* (Oxford: Legenda, 2003); Vernon A. Rosario, *The Erotic Imagination: French Histories of Perversity* (New York: Oxford University Press, 1997), 58–62.

20. Rebman, *Psychopathia Sexualis,* 91.

21. "L'instinct pousse le sujet au coït, même avec les cadavres." Alexis Epaulard, *Vampirisme: Nécrophilie, nécrosadisme, nécrophagie* (Lyon: Stock, 1901), 87. All translations from this text are mine.

22. "Le vampirisme d'origine génitale." Ibid.

23. Alfred Moll, *Handbuch der Sexualwissenschaften mit besonderer Berücksichtigung der Kulturgeschichtlichen Beziehungen* (Leipzig: F.C.W. Vogel, 1912).

24. Chaddock, *Psychopathia Sexualis,* 13.

25. Ibid.

26. See Pick, *Faces of Degeneration.*

27. Chaddock, *Psychopathia Sexualis,* 14.

28. Ibid., 13.

29. Rebman, *Psychopathia Sexualis*, 203.

30. Ibid.

31. Ibid., 191.

32. Ibid., 95.

33. Foucault, *The Order of Things*, trans. Alan Sheridan (London: Routledge, 1989), 229.

34. Work by a range of scholars has demonstrated various filiations between Zola's novel and the ideas of doctors including Bernard, Krafft-Ebing, Lombroso, Morel, and Nordau. See Lisa Downing, "The Birth of the Beast: Death-Driven Masculinity in Monneret, Zola and Freud," *Dix-Neuf* 5 (2005): 28–46; Geoff Woollen, ed., *Zola: "La bête humaine": Colloque du centenaire à Glasgow* (Glasgow: Glasgow University Press, 1995); and Pick, *Faces of Degeneration* 84–85.

35. See Geoff Woollen, "Une nouvelle de Camille Lemonnier: De 'Jacques l'Eventreur' à *La bête humaine*," *Les Cahiers naturalistes* 69 (1995): 167–77.

36. "Beau garçon au visage rond et régulier, mais que gâtaient des mâchoires trop fortes." Emile Zola, *La bête humaine*, vol. 6 of *Œuvres completes* (Paris: Cercle du livre précieux, 1967), 48. All translations from this text are mine.

37. "Le Jacques Lantier a bien quelques caractéristiques anatomiques du criminel né." Cesare Lombroso, "*La bête humaine* et l'anthropologie criminelle," *La Revue des revues* 4, no. 23 (1892): 261.

38. Max Nordau, *Degeneration*, trans. George L. Mosse (Lincoln: University of Nebraska Press, 1993), 451.

39. Rebman, *Psychopathia Sexualis*, 86.

40. "Tuer une femme, tuer une femme! Cela sonnait à ses oreilles, du fond de sa jeunesse, avec la fièvre grandissante, affolante du désir. Comme les autres, sous l'éveil de la puberté, rêvent d'en posséder une, lui s'était enragé à l'idée d'en tuer une." Zola, *La bête humaine*, 61. All translations from this text are mine.

41. "Vierge et guerrière; dédaigneuse du mâle." Ibid., 58.

42. "Elle avait la curiosité des accidents." Ibid., 68.

43. "L'homme efféminé, délicat, lâche; la femme masculine, violente, sans tendresse." Zola, "Préface au roman d'un inverti-né," in *Nos ancêtres les pervers: La vie des homosexuels au dix-neuvième siècle,* ed. Pierre Hahn (Paris: Olivier Orban, 1979), 234.

44. For a more detailed consideration of this feature of *La bête humaine*, see my article "The Birth of the Beast."

45. "L'illustration littéraire de manuels de psycho-pathologie sexuelle." Claude Dauphiné, *Rachilde* (Paris: Mercure de France, 1991), 53.

46. "Louis, je suis décidée à ne pas vous donner d'héritier. ... Je ne veux ni enlaidir ni souffrir. De plus, *je suis assez*, en étant, et si je pouvais finir le monde avec moi, je le finirais." Rachilde, *La marquise de Sade* (Paris: Gallimard, 1996), 214. All translations from this text are mine.

47. "[Elle] n'eut avec lui ni les pudeurs des jeunes filles, ni les goûts des prostituées, mais une nonchalance indifférente." Ibid., 219.

48. Ibid., 285.

49. Ibid.
50. Chaddock, *Psychopathia Sexualis*, 3.

Chapter 5

1. William A. Coote, "The Suppression of the White Slave Traffic," in *Fighting the Traffic in Young Girls,* ed. Ernest A. Bell (Chicago: G. S. Ball, 1910), 30. Coote was the secretary of the London-based National Vigilance Association. American activists included the Chicago-based lawyers Edwin W. Simms, Clifford G. Roe, and James R. Mann, whose campaigns for federal anti-trafficking legislation led to the 1910 Mann Act, which aimed to stop the transportation of women and girls between states.
2. It is not the intention of this chapter to identify and review all criminalized or prohibited forms of sexual behavior or communication; rather my focus is on the strategies and tactics associated with regulation and the ways in which they have been evaluated by historians. The behaviors discussed here are presented as examples. Similarly this chapter aims to offer a general survey of trends and issues. Like any overview, it should not be assumed to apply uniformly. To a large extent the dynamics of regulation can only be explored through the micro-historical, which reveals patterns that are uneven, variable, and contingent upon local particularities.
3. For more in-depth discussion of this, see Philip Hubbard, *Sex and the City: Geographies of Prostitution in the Urban West* (Aldershot, UK: Ashgate, 1999), and Matt Houlbrook, "Towards a Historical Geography of Sexuality," *Journal of Urban History* 27 (2001): 497–504.
4. Eric Lampard, "The Urbanizing World," in *The Victorian City: Images and Realities,* ed. Harold J. Dyos and Michael Woolff, 2 vols. (London: Routledge, 1973), 1:3–57; Andrew Lees and Lynn Hollen Lees, *Cities and the Making of Modern Europe* (Cambridge: Cambridge University Press, 2007).
5. Frank Mort, *Dangerous Sexualities: Medico-moral Politics in England since 1830,* 2nd ed. (London: Routledge, 2000); Elizabeth Wilson, *The Sphinx in the City: Urban Life, the Control of Disorder, and Woman* (Berkeley: University of California Press, 1991).
6. Eugène Buret, *De la misère des classes laborieuses en Angleterre et en France* (Paris, 1840), cited in Anne-Louise Shapiro, "Paris," in *Housing the Workers,* ed. M. Daunton (Leicester: Leicester University Press, 1990), 33.
7. Ibid.
8. Friedrich F. Engels, *The Condition of the Working Class in England in 1844,* trans. Florence K. Wischnewetzky (London: Sonnenschein, 1892), 65.
9. Gertrude Himmelfarb, *The Idea of Poverty* (New York: Knopf, 1984).
10. John Merriman, "Urban Space and the Power of Language: The Stigmatization of the Faubourg in Nineteenth-Century France," *Social Science Information* 38 (1999): 329–51. Baron Georges-Eugène Haussmann was commissioned by Napoleon III to undertake a program of planning reform in central Paris.
11. Jerry White, *Rothschild Buildings: Life in an East End Tenement Block, 1887–1920* (London: Routledge, 1980).

12. See, for example, Robert D. Storch, "Police Control of Street Prostitution in Victorian London: A Case Study of Police Action," in *Police and Society,* ed. David H. Bayled (Beverly Hills, CA: Sage, 1976), 49–73.

13. For example, Alexandre Jean Baptiste Parent-Duchâtelet, *De la prostitution dans la ville de Paris, considéréré sous le rapport de l'hygiène publique, de la morale et de l'administration* (Paris: Ballière, 1836). On France, see Alain Corbin, *Les filles de noce* (Paris: Aubier, 1978). For an excellent comparative discussion, see Bertrand Taithe, "Consuming Desires: Female Prostitutes and 'Customers' at the Margins of Crime and Perversion in France and Britain, c. 1836–85," in *Gender and Crime in Modern Europe,* ed. Margaret L. Arnot and Cornelie Usborne (London: UCL Press, 1999), 150–72.

14. Taithe, "Consuming Desires," 157. On the CD Acts, see Judith R. Walkowitz, *Prostitution and Victorian Society: Women, Class and the State* (Cambridge: Cambridge University Press, 1980).

15. Philippa Levine, *Prostitution, Race and Politics: Policing Venereal Disease in the British Empire* (New York: Routledge, 2003); Elizabeth B. Van Heyningen, "The Social Evil in the Cape Colony, 1868–1902: Prostitution and the Contagious Diseases Acts," *Journal of South African Studies* 10, no. 2 (1984): 170–97.

16. Richard Phillips, "Heterogeneous Imperialism and the Regulation of Sexuality in British West Africa," *Journal of the History of Sexuality* 14 (2005): 291–315; Richard Phillips, "Imperialism and the Regulation of Sexuality: Colonial Legislation on Contagious Diseases and Ages of Consent," *Historical Geography* 28 (2002): 339–62.

17. Thomas C. Mackey, *Red Lights Out: A Legal History of Prostitution, Disorderly Houses and Vice Districts, 1780–1917* (London: Taylor and Francis, 1987); Neil L. Shumsky, "Tacit Acceptance: Respectable Americans and Segregated Prostitution, 1870–1910," *Journal of Social History* 19 (1986): 665–79; Alecia P. Long, *The Great Southern Babylon: Sex, Race and Respectability in New Orleans, 1865–1920* (Baton Rouge: Louisiana State University Press, 2004).

18. Wilson, *Sphinx and the City.*

19. Josephine Butler, "An Appeal to the People of England (1870)," in *The Sexuality Debates,* ed. Sheila Jeffreys (London: Routledge, 1987), 126.

20. Stefan Petrow, *Policing Morals: The Metropolitan Police and the Home Office, 1870–1914* (Oxford: Clarendon Press, 1994).

21. Stefan Slater, "Pimps, Police and Filles de Joie: Foreign Prostitution in Interwar London," *London Journal* 32 (2007): 53–74.

22. Susan R. Grayzel, *Women's Identities at War: Gender, Motherhood, and Politics in Britain and France during the First World War* (Chapel Hill: University of Carolina Press, 1999); Angela M. Woollacott, "'Khaki Fever' and Its Control: Gender, Class, Age and Sexual Morality on the British Homefront in the First World War," *Journal of Contemporary History* 29 (1994): 25–47.

23. Susan Mumm, "'Not Worse than Other Girls': The Convent-Based Rehabilitation of Fallen Women in Victorian Britain," *Journal of Social History* 29 (1996): 527–46; Maria Luddy, *Women and Philanthropy in Nineteenth-Century Ireland* (Cambridge: Cambridge University Press, 1995); Leanne McCormick, "Sinister Sisters?

The Portrayal of Ireland's Magdalene Asylums in Popular Culture," *Cultural and Social History* 2 (2005): 374–79.

24. Tamara Myers, *Caught: Montreal's Modern Girls and the Law, 1869–1945* (Toronto: University of Toronto Press, 2006); Pamela Cox, *Gender, Justice and Welfare: Bad Girls in Britain, 1900–1950* (Basingstoke, UK: Palgrave, 2003); Linda Mahood, *Policing Gender, Class and Family: Britain, 1850–1940* (London: UCL Press, 1995); Linda Gordon, *The Politics and History of Family Violence* (London: Virago, 1989); Sylvia Schafer, *Children in Moral Danger and the Problem of Government in Third Republic France* (Princeton, NJ: Princeton University Press, 1997).

25. Catherine Euler, "'The Iron Fetters of Our Souls': Nineteenth-Century Feminist Strategies to Get Our Bodies into the Political Agenda," in *Everyday Violence in Britain, 1850–1950,* ed. S. D'Cruze (Harlow, UK: Pearson, 2000), 198–212.

26. Laura Gowing, *Domestic Dangers: Women, Words and Sex in Early Modern London* (Oxford: Oxford University Press, 1996); Rosemary Mitchison and Leah Leneman, *Sexuality and Social Control: Scotland, 1660–1780* (Oxford: Blackwell, 1989); Stephen M. Waddams, *Sexual Slander in Nineteenth-Century England: Defamation in the Ecclesiastical Courts, 1815–55* (Toronto: University of Toronto Press, 2000).

27. James M. Donovan, "Combating the Sexual Abuse of Children in France, 1825–1913," *Criminal Justice History* 15 (1994): 59–95.

28. Edward J. Bristow, *Vice and Vigilance: Purity Movements in Britain since 1700* (Dublin: Gill and Macmillan, 1977).

29. For a detailed discussion, see Judith R. Walkowitz, *City of Dreadful Delight: Narratives of Sexual Danger in Late-Victorian London* (Chicago: University of Chicago Press, 1992).

30. Phillips, "Imperialism and the Regulation of Sexuality."

31. Himani Bannerji, "Age of Consent and Hegemonic Social Reform," in *Gender and Imperialism,* ed. Clare Midgeley (Manchester: Manchester University Press, 1998), 21–43; Antoinette Burton, "From Child Bride to Hindoo Lady: Rukmabai and the Debate on Sexual Respectability in Imperial Britain," *American Historical Review* 103 (1998): 1119–46; Geraldine Forbes, "Women and Modernity: The Issue of Child Marriage in India," *Women's Studies International Quarterly* 2 (1979): 407–19; Tanika Sardar, "Rhetoric against the Age of Consent: Resisting Colonial Reason and the Death of a Child-Wife," *Economic and Political Weekly,* September 4, 1993, 1869–78.

32. Letter to the *Times,* March 18, 1887.

33. Sardar, "Rhetoric against the Age of Consent."

34. Padma Anagol, *The Emergence of Feminism in India, 1850–1920* (Aldershot, UK: Ashgate, 2006).

35. See, for example, Anon., *Startling Truths on the White Slave Traffic* (London: Success Publishing, c. 1912); Bell, *Fighting the Traffic in Young Girls.*

36. Mara L. Keire, "The Vice Trust: A Reinterpretation of the White Slavery Scare in the United States, 1907–1917," *Journal of Social History* 35 (2001): 5–41.

37. Martin Wiener, *Men of Blood: Violence, Manliness and Criminal Justice in Victorian England* (Cambridge: Cambridge University Press, 2004). For a similar argument

that both French and English rhetoric surrounding prostitution increasingly problematized male behavior from 1870 onward, see Taithe, "Consuming Desires."

38. Anna Clark, *Women's Silence, Men's Violence: Sexual Assault in England, 1770–
    1845* (London: Pandora, 1987).

39. Wiener, *Men of Blood*, 108.

40. Donovan, "Combating the Sexual Abuse of Children in France," 60.

41. Ibid.; Louise A. Jackson, *Child Sexual Abuse in Victorian England* (London: Rout-
    ledge, 2000); Stephen Robertson, *Crimes against Children: Sexual Violence and
    Legal Culture in New York City, 1880–1960* (Chapel Hill: University of North
    Carolina Press, 2005).

42. Jeffrey Masson, *The Assault on Truth: Freud's Suppression of the Seduction Theory*
    (Harmondsworth, UK: Penguin, 1985).

43. For a useful discussion of ways in which historians work with these types of
    sources, see Stephen Robertson, "What's Law Got to Do with It? Legal Records
    and Sexual Histories," *Journal of the History of Sexuality* 14 (2005): 161–85.

44. Edward P. Thompson, *Customs in Common* (London: Merlin, 1991); Natalie Zemon
    Davis, *Society and Culture in Early Modern France* (London: Duckworth, 1975).

45. On Irish and Jewish communities in the East End of London, see, for example,
    Ellen Ross, *Love and Toil: Motherhood in Outcast London* (Oxford: Oxford Uni-
    versity Press, 1993).

46. Carl Chinn, *They Worked All Their Lives: Women of the Urban Poor in England,
    1880–1939* (Manchester: Manchester University Press, 1988), 152.

47. Evidence of the Reverend Alfred Fryer, Questions 5872–75, in *British Parlia-
    mentary Papers*, 1884–1885, XXX.1, Royal Commission on the Housing of the
    Working Classes.

48. *Times*, November 30, 1865, and December 7, 1865.

49. *East London Observer*, May 15, 1880.

50. Vron Ware, *Beyond the Pale* (London: Verso, 1992).

51. For an overview, see Jeffrey Weeks, *Sex, Politics and Society: The Regulation of
    Sexuality since 1800,* 2nd ed. (London: Longman, 1989).

52. Anna Clark, "Twilight Moments," *Journal of the History of Sexuality* 14 (2005): 156.

53. Matt Houlbrook, *Queer London: Perils and Pleasures on the Sexual Metropolis,
    1918–1957* (Chicago: University of Chicago Press, 2005); George Chauncey, *Gay
    New York: Gender, Urban Culture, and the Making of the Gay Male World, 1890–
    1940* (New York: Basic Books, 1994).

54. Jeff Hearn, *Men in the Public Eye* (London: Routledge, 1992).

55. Edward Ross Dickinson, "Policing Sex in Germany, 1882–1982: A Preliminary
    Statistical Analysis," *Journal of the History of Sexuality* 16 (2007): 204–50.

56. Weeks, *Sex, Politics and Society.*

Chapter 6

1. Michel Foucault, *The Will to Knowledge,* vol. 1 of *The History of Sexuality,* trans.
   Robert Hurley (Harmondsworth, UK: Penguin, 1998), 36–73.

2. See, for example, Jeffrey Weeks, *Sexuality and Its Discontents: Meaning, Myths
   and Modern Sexualities* (London: Routledge and Kegan Paul, 1985), 64–95;

Gert Hekma, "A Female Soul in a Male Body: Sexual Inversion as Gender Inversion in Nineteenth Century Sexology," in *Third Sex, Third Gender: Beyond Dimorphism in Culture and History,* ed. Gilbert Herdt (New York: Zone Books, 1994), 213–39; Vernon A. Rosario, ed., *Science and Homosexualities* (New York: Routledge, 1997); Arnold I. Davidson, *The Emergence of Sexuality: Historical Epistemology and the Formation of Concepts* (Cambridge, MA: Harvard University Press, 2001).

3. Lesley A. Hall, "Malthusian Mutations: The Changing Politics and Moral Meaning of Birth Control in Britain," in *Malthus, Medicine, and Morality: "Malthusianism" after 1798,* ed. Brian Dolan (Amsterdam: Rodopi, 2000), 142.

4. Roy Porter and Lesley A. Hall, *The Facts of Life: The Creation of Sexual Knowledge in Britain, 1650–1950* (New Haven, CT: Yale University Press, 1995), 127.

5. Ibid., 127–28.

6. George Drysdale, *The Elements of Social Science or Physical, Sexual and Natural Religion: An Exposition of the True Cause and Only Cure of the Three Primary Social Evils: Poverty, Prostitution, and Celibacy* (London: E. Truelove, 1882), 77. This book was quite successful as it went through many editions in the nineteenth century.

7. Ibid., 78, 80–83.

8. Ibid., 84.

9. David Kohn, "Theories to Work By: Rejected Theories, Reproduction, and Darwin's Path to Natural Selection," *Studies in the History of Biology* 4 (1980): 80–87.

10. Charles Darwin, *The Descent of Man, and Selection in Relation to Sex* (Princeton, NJ: Princeton University Press, 1981), part 2.

11. Frank J. Sulloway, *Freud, Biologist of the Mind: Beyond the Psychoanalytic Legend* (Cambridge, MA: Harvard University Press, 1992), 253–54.

12. Sander L. Gilman, *Sexuality: An Illustrated History* (New York: Wiley, 1989), 231.

13. Tissot published a shorter version of *L'onanisme* in Latin in 1859. Masturbation in the eighteenth century has an extensive historiography. See, for example, Jean Stengers and Anne Van Neck, *Masturbation: The History of a Great Terror* (New York: Palgrave Macmillan, 2001); Michael Stolberg, "An Unmanly Vice: Self-Pollution, Anxiety and the Body in the Eighteenth Century," *Social History of Medicine* 13, no. 1 (2000): 1–22; Thomas Laqueur, *Solitary Sex: A Cultural History of Masturbation* (New York: Zone Books, 2004), 25–183.

14. Claude-François Lallemand, *A Practical Treatise on the Causes, Symptoms and Treatment of Spermatorrhoea,* trans. Henry J. McDougall (Philadelphia: Blanchard and Lea, 1858).

15. Robert Darby, "Pathologizing Male Sexuality: Lallemand, Spermatorrhea, and the Rise of Circumcision," *Journal of the History of Medicine and Allied Sciences* 60, no. 3 (2005): 293.

16. Ibid., 293–94.

17. E. H. Hare, "Masturbatory Insanity: The History of an Idea," *Journal of Mental Science* 108 (1962): 2–25.

18. Jean-Etienne Dominique Esquirol, *Mental Maladies: A Treatise on Insanity,* trans. E. K. Hunt (New York: Hafner, 1965), 342.

19. Philipp Gutmann, "Hermann Joseph Löwenstein's Dissertation: De Mentis Aberrationibus Ex Partium Sexualium Conditione Abnormi Oriundis (1823)," *History of Psychiatry* 15 (2004): 458–59.
20. Mary Spongberg, *Feminizing Venereal Disease: The Body of the Prostitute in Nineteenth-Century Medical Discourse* (London: Palgrave Macmillan, 1997), 36.
21. Ibid., 36–37.
22. Roger Davidson and Lesley A. Hall, *Sex, Sin and Suffering: Venereal Disease and European Society since 1870* (London: Routledge, 2001).
23. A. F. La Berge, "A.J.B. Parent-Duchâtelet: Hygienist of Paris, 1821–1936," *Clio Medica* 12 (1977): 278–301.
24. Alexandre Jean Baptiste Parent-Duchâtelet, *De la prostitution dans la ville de Paris, considérée sous le rapport de l'hygiène publique, de la morale et de l'administration* (Paris: Baillière, 1837).
25. Ibid., chap. 1.
26. Frank Mort, *Dangerous Sexualities: Medico-moral Politics in England since 1830*, 2nd ed. (London: Routledge, 2000), 60–63.
27. Spongberg, *Feminizing Venereal Disease*, 46–50.
28. Ivan Crozier, "William Acton and the History of Sexuality: The Professional and Medical Contexts," *Journal of Victorian Culture* 5 (2000): 13–16.
29. William Acton, *Prostitution Considered in Its Moral, Social, and Sanitary Aspects* (London: John Churchill and Sons, 1870), 52.
30. Mort, *Dangerous Sexualities*, 60–61.
31. Cesare Lombroso and Guglielmo Ferrero, *La donna delinquente, la prostituta e la donna normale* (Turin: Roux, 1893), 57.
32. Ibid. For an overview in English of Lombroso and Ferrero's work, see Cesare Lombroso and Guglielmo Ferrero, *Criminal Woman, the Prostitute, and the Normal Woman*, trans. Nicole Hahn Rafter and Mary Gibson (Durham, NC: Duke University Press, 2004).
33. H. Sass and S. Herpertz, "Personality Disorders," in *A History of Clinical Psychiatry: The Origin and History of Psychiatric Disorders,* ed. German E. Berrios and Roy Porter (London: Athlone Press, 1999), 633.
34. Jan Goldstein, *Console and Classify: The French Psychiatric Profession in the Nineteenth Century* (Cambridge: Cambridge University Press, 1990), 152–96. This distinction was crucial for psychiatrists who had to appear in the courtroom to defend insane people.
35. Ibid.
36. Cited in Vieda Skultans, *Madness and Morals: Ideas on Insanity in the Nineteenth Century* (London: Routledge, 1975), 6.
37. See Chiara Beccalossi, "Nineteenth-Century European Psychiatry on Same-Sex Desires: Pathology, Abnormality, Normality and the Blurring of Boundaries," *Psychology & Sexuality* (forthcoming).
38. On degeneration, see Daniel Pick, *Faces of Degeneration: A European Disorder, c. 1848–1918* (Cambridge: Cambridge University Press, 1989).
39. Morel was born in Vienna, but he was educated as a physician in France and then practiced as a psychiatrist in France.

40. Sander L. Gilman, *Difference and Pathology: Stereotypes of Sexuality, Race, and Madness* (Ithaca, NY: Cornell University Press, 1985), 191–92.

41. Claude François Michéa, "Des déviations de l'appétit vénérien," *Union Medicale*, July 1849, 338–39; Johann Ludwig Casper, "Ueber Nothzucht und Päderastie und deren Ermittelung Seitens des Gerichtesarztes," *Vierteljahrschrift für gerichtliche öffentliche Medizin* 1 (1852): 21–78. On the importance of these texts, see, for example, Gert Hekma, "A History of Sexology: Social and Historical Aspects of Sexuality," in *From Sappho to De Sade: Moments in the History of Sexuality,* ed. Jan Bremmer (London: Routledge, 1989), 173–93; Hekma, "A Female Soul in a Male Body"; Harry Oosterhuis, *Stepchildren of Nature: Krafft-Ebing, Psychiatry, and the Making of Sexual Identity* (Chicago: University of Chicago Press, 2000), 39; Ivan Crozier, introduction to Havelock Ellis and John Addington Symonds, *Sexual Inversion: A Critical Edition,* ed. Ivan Crozier (Basingstoke, UK: Palgrave Macmillan, 2008), 18–19. Phrenologists linked sexual function to the cerebellum and occasionally observed same-sex desires; see, for example, Philipp Gutmann, "On the Way to Scientia Sexualis: 'On the Relation of the Sexual System to the Psyche in General and to Cretinism in Particular' (1826) by Joseph Häussler," *History of Psychiatry* 17 (2006): 45–53; Michael Lynch "'Here Is Adhesiveness': From Friendship to Homosexuality," *Victorian Studies* 29 (1985): 67–96; Michael Shortland, "Courting the Cerebellum: Early Organological and Phrenological Views on Sexuality," *British Journal of the History of Science* 20 (1987): 173–99. Recently early modern historians have shown how much earlier than the nineteenth century science attributed same-sex desires to inborn temperament and dispositions; see Kenneth Borris and George Rousseau, eds., *The Sciences of Homosexualities in Early Modern Europe* (London: Routledge, 2008).

42. Wilhelm Griesinger, "Vortrag zur Eröffnung der psychiatrischen Clink," *Archiv für Psychiatrie und Nervenkrankheiten* 1 (1868): 636–54.

43. Carl Westphal, "Die conträre Sexualempfindung: Symptom eines neuropathischen (psychopathischen) Zustandes," *Archiv für Psychiatrie und Nervenkrankheiten* 2 (1869): 73–108, translation in Michael A. Lombardi-Nash, ed., *Sodomites and Urnings: Homosexual Representations in Classic German Journals* (Binghamton, NY: Harrington Park Press, 2006), 87–120. The importance of this case and its effects on psychiatric writing about homosexuality is discussed in Ivan Crozier, "Pillow Talk: Credibility, Trust and the Sexological Case History," *History of Science* 46 (2008): 375–404.

44. Richard von Krafft-Ebbing, "Über gewisse Anomalies des Geschlechtstriebs und die klinisch-forensich Verwertung derselben als eines wahrscheinlich funktionellen Degenerationszeichens des centralen Nervensystems," *Archiv für Psychiatrie und Nervenkrankheiten* 7 (1877): 291–312.

45. Chiara Beccalossi, "The Origin of Italian Sexological Studies: Female Sexual Inversion, ca. 1870–1900," *Journal of the History of Sexuality* 18 (2009): 109–11; Vernon A. Rosario, *The Erotic Imagination: French Histories of Perversity* (New York: Oxford University Press, 1997), 69, 83–89.

46. Sean Brady, *Masculinity and Male Homosexuality in Britain, 1861–1913* (Basingstoke, UK: Palgrave Macmillan, 2005), 119–56; Ivan Crozier, "Nineteenth-Century

British Psychiatric Writing about Homosexuality before Havelock Ellis: The Missing History," *Journal of the History of Medicine and Allied Sciences* 63 (2008): 65–102.

47. See Jennifer Terry, *An American Obsession: Science, Medicine, and Homosexuality in Modern Society* (Chicago: University of Chicago Press, 1999).

48. The importance of this article is discussed in Oosterhuis, *Stepchildren of Nature*, esp. 43–55. Eventually Krafft-Ebing dissociated homosexuality from a state of psycho-neuropathic degeneration in 1901; see Sulloway, *Freud, Biologist of the Mind*, 311.

49. Krafft-Ebbing, "Über gewisse Anomalies."

50. Oosterhuis, *Stepchildren of Nature*, 44–45.

51. The first edition of *Psychopathia Sexualis* was published in 1886, followed by twelve expanded versions; the last edited by Krafft-Ebing was published in 1903.

52. Robert Nye, "The Medical Origins of Sexual Fetishism," in *Fetishism as Cultural Discourse*, ed. Emily Apter and William Pietz (Ithaca, NY: Cornell University Press, 1993), 13–30.

53. Ellis and Symonds, *Sexual Inversion*.

54. The Prussian code, which included a law prohibiting sexual contact between members of the same sex, was adopted in 1871 with the unification of Germany.

55. Ivan Crozier, "'All the Appearances Were Perfectly Natural': The Anus of the Sodomite in Nineteenth-Century Medical Discourse," in *Body Parts: Critical Explorations in Corporeality*, ed. Christopher E. Forth and Ivan Crozier (Lanham, MD: Lexington Books, 2005), 79.

56. Rosario, *The Erotic Imagination*, 72–78.

57. Crozier, "All the Appearances Were Perfectly Natural."

58. Jan Baptist van Helmont was an influential seventeenth-century Belgium physician.

59. Ornella Moscucci, *The Science of Woman: Gynaecology and Gender in England, 1800–1929* (Cambridge: Cambridge University Press, 1990), 34; Chandak Sengoopta, "The Modern Ovary: Constructions, Meanings, Uses," *History of Science* 38 (2000): 428.

60. Moscucci, *The Science of Woman*, 105.

61. Carol Groneman, "Nymphomania: The Historical Construction of Female Sexuality," *Signs* 19 (1994): 337–67.

62. Ibid.

63. Chandak Sengoopta, *The Most Secret Quintessence of Life: Sex, Glands, and Hormones, 1850–1950* (Chicago: University of Chicago Press, 2006), 3–4.

64. Moscucci, *The Science of Woman*, 34.

65. William Blair-Bell, *The Sex Complex: A Study of the Relationships of the Internal Secretions to the Female Characteristics and Function in Health and Disease* (London: Baillière, Tindall and Cox, 1916).

66. Porter and Hall, *The Facts of Life*, 172–73.

67. Sigmund Freud, *On Sexuality: Three Essays on the Theory of Sexuality and Other Works*, trans. James Strachey (New York: Penguin, 1977), 45.

68. Even if some sexologists used hypnotism to treat sexual inversion, most of the sexological works were not interested in treating sexual pathologies.
69. Freud, *On Sexuality*, 49–50.
70. Nye, "The Medical Origins of Sexual Fetishism," 28.
71. Gilman, *Difference and Pathology*, 204–13.
72. Freud, *Three Essays*, 45–52.
73. Ibid., 45–87.
74. Ibid., 88–126.
75. Ibid., 127–54.
76. Ibid. Freud established here what later he would call the Oedipus complex.
77. For a general overview, see Sulloway, *Freud, Biologist of the Mind;* Henry F. Ellenberger, *The Discovery of the Unconscious: The History and Evolution of Dynamic Psychiatry* (New York: Basic Books, 1970), 418–570; Vern L. Bullough, *Science in the Bedroom: The History of Sex Research* (New York: Basic Books, 1994), 61–91.
78. Sulloway, *Freud, Biologist of the Mind.*

Chapter 7

1. Arthur Schopenhauer quoted in George Boas, *The Cult of Childhood* (London: Warburg Institute, 1966), 69.
2. Philippe Aries, *Centuries of Childhood: A Social History of Family Life* (New York: Knopf, 1962); John Cleverley and Denis Charles Phillips, *Visions of Childhood: Influential Models from Locke to Spock* (New York: Teachers College, 1986); Lloyd deMause, ed., *The History of Childhood* (London: Souvenir Press, 1976); Laurence Stone, *The Family, Sex and Marriage in England, 1500–1800* (London: Harper and Row, 1979); Ivy Pinchbeck and Margaret Hewitt, *Children in English Society,* 2 vols. (London: Routledge, 1969); Linda Pollock, *Forgotten Children: Parent-Child Relations from 1500 to 1900* (Cambridge: Cambridge University Press, 1983); C. John Sommerville, *The Rise and Fall of Childhood* (Beverly Hills, CA: Sage, 1982); Karin Calvert, *Children in the House: The Material Culture of Early Childhood, 1600–1900* (Boston: Northeastern University Press, 1992); Neil Postman, *The Disappearance of Childhood* (London: Vintage, 1994); Hugh Cunningham, *Children and Childhood in Western Society since 1500* (London: Longman, 1995); Colin Heywood, *A History of Childhood: Children and Childhood in the West from Medieval to Modern Times* (Cambridge: Polity Press, 2001); Joseph Zornado, *Inventing the Child: Culture, Ideology, and the Story of Childhood* (New York: Garland, Brown, 2001); Marilyn Brown, ed., *Picturing Children: Constructions of Childhood between Rousseau and Freud* (New York: Ashgate, 2002).
3. Since the biblical story of the Fall, the sexuality of women has been present/absent, healthy/pathological, active/passive, and a metaphor for social instability. There is a parallel between the constructions of the sexual child and the sexual woman that we will not elaborate here. We wish merely to indicate the degree to which there is an embedded level of acceptance of some expressions of sexuality and of anxiety about others.

4. Allison James, Christopher Jenks, and Alan Prout, *Theorising Childhood* (Cambridge: Polity Press, 1998); Allison James and Alan Prout, *Constructing and Reconstructing Childhood* (London: Falmer Press, 1997); Berry Mayall, *Towards a Sociology for Childhood: Thinking from Children's Lives* (Buckingham, UK: Open University Press, 2002); Jens Qvortrup, ed., *Studies in Modern Childhood: Society, Agency, Culture* (London: Palgrave Macmillan, 2005); Andrew O'Malley, *The Making of the Modern Child* (London: Routledge, 2003).

5. David Buckingham and Sarah Bragg, *Young People, Sex and the Media: The Facts of Life* (London: Palgrave, 2004); R. Danielle Egan and Gail Hawkes, *Theorizing the Sexual Child in Modernity* (New York: Palgrave Macmillan, 2010); R. Danielle Egan and Gail Hawkes, "The Problem with Protection: Or, Why We Need to Move towards Recognition and the Sexual Agency of Children," *Continuum Journal of Media and Cultural Studies* 23, no. 3 (2009): 389–400; James R. Kincaid, *Child-Loving: The Erotic Child and Victorian Culture* (New York: Routledge, 1992); Anne Higonnet, *Pictures of Innocence: The History and Crisis of Ideal Childhood* (London: Thomas and Hudson, 1998); Judith Levine, *Harmful to Minors: The Perils of Protecting Children from Sex* (Minneapolis: University of Minnesota Press, 2002); Philip Jenkins, *Moral Panic: Changing Concepts of the Child Molester in Modern America* (New Haven, CT: Yale University Press, 1998).

6. As James Kincaid comments, "But what if, in our culture, 'the child' and 'the sexual' are not independent terms to begin with? What if we can hardly think of one without the other, if they grew up together and are, in our discourse and in our minds, inseparable? I think the modern child and modern ideas of what constitute sexual allure and even sexual activity were developed only yesterday—in the last two centuries." James R. Kincaid, "Four Questions and Answers," http://www.ipce.info/ipceweb/Library/four_questions.htm (accessed January 6, 2008).

7. See, for example, Cotton Mather's *The Education of Children* (1708), Jean-Jacques Rousseau's *Emile* (1755), and James Nelson's *An Essay on the Government of Children* (1756).

8. Nikolas Rose, *Governing the Soul* (London: Routledge, 1989), 45.

9. Jean-Jacques Rousseau, *The Emile of Jean Jacques Rousseau* (London: Heinemann, 1963), 98–99.

10. Vern A. Rosario, *The Erotic Imagination: French Histories of Perversity* (New York: Oxford University Press, 1997), 108ff.; Roy Porter and Lesley A. Hall, *The Facts of Life: The Creation of Sexual Knowledge in Britain, 1650–1950* (New Haven, CT: Yale University Press, 1995), 18–19.

11. Tissot (1781), quoted in Richard P. Neuman, "Masturbation, Madness, and the Modern Concepts of Childhood and Adolescence," *Journal of Social History* 8, no. 3 (1975): 4.

12. R. Hamowy, "Medicine and Crimination of Sin: 'Self-Abuse' in Nineteenth Century America," *Journal of Libertarian Studies* 1, no. 3 (1977): 229–70; Jean Stengers and Ann Van Neck, *Masturbation: The History of a Great Terror* (New York: Palgrave Macmillan, 2001); Michael Stolberg, "An Unmanly Vice: Self-Pollution, Anxiety and the Body in the Eighteenth Century," *Social History of Medicine* 13, no. 1 (2000): 1–22; Ivan Crozier, "'Rough Winds Do Shake the Darling Buds of

May': A Note on William Acton's Conception of Childhood Sexuality," *Journal of Family History* 26 (2001): 411–20; Robert Darby, "The Masturbation Taboo and the Rise of Routine Male Circumcision: A Review of the Historiography," *Journal of Social History* 27 (2003): 737–57; Robert Darby, *A Surgical Temptation: The Demonization of the Foreskin and the Rise of Circumcision in Britain* (Chicago: University of Chicago Press, 2005); Thomas Laqueur, *Solitary Sex: A Cultural History of Masturbation* (New York: Zone Books, 2004); Peter Singy, "The History of Masturbation: An Essay Review," *Journal of the History of Medicine and Allied Sciences* 59, no. 1 (2004): 112–21.

13. Michel Foucault, *The History of Sexuality: An Introduction* (New York: Vintage, 1990), 42.

14. Catherine Gallagher and Thomas Laqueur, *The Making of the Modern Body: Sexuality and Society in the Nineteenth Century* (Berkeley: University of California Press, 1987), vii; Bryan Turner, *The Body and Society: Explorations in Social Theory*, 2nd ed. (London: Sage, 1996), 175.

15. Sterling Fishman, "The History of Childhood Sexuality," *Journal of Contemporary History* 17, no. 2 (1982): 277.

16. William Acton, *The Functions and Disorders of the Reproductive Organs in Childhood, Adult Age and Advanced Life Considered in Their Physiological, Social and Moral Relations* (London: John Churchill and Sons, 1865), 4.

17. Claude-François Lallemand, *A Practical Treatise on the Causes, Symptoms and Treatment of Spermatorrhoea*, trans. Henry J. McDougall (Philadelphia: Blanchard and Lea, 1858). Though the original was in French, this text was translated and published in German and in English both before and after Lallemand's death in 1853. Darby, *A Surgical Temptation*.

18. William Acton, *The Functions and Disorders*, 6.

19. Ibid.

20. Robert Darby, "William Acton's Antipodean Disciples: A Colonial Perspective on His Theories of Male Sexual (Dys)function," *Journal of the History of Sexuality* 13 (2004): 157–82.

21. Emmett Holt, *The Diseases of Infancy and Childhood* (New York: Appleton, 1897), 698.

22. René A. Spitz, "Authority and Masturbation: Some Remarks on a Bibliographical Investigation," *Psychoanalytical Study of the Child* 7 (1952): 502.

23. Stengers and Van Neck, *Masturbation*, 114; Darby, *A Surgical Temptation*, 146, 156ff.

24. See Porter and Hall, *The Facts of Life*; Laqueur, *Solitary Sex*.

25. This text was translated into thirty-five languages and entering its twenty-fifth edition in 1859. See David Blamires, "Some German and English Travesties of Struwwelpeter," in *Connections: Essays in Honour of Eda Sagarra on the Occasion of Her 60th Birthday*, ed. Peter Skrine, Rosemary Wallbank-Turner, and Jonathon West (Stuttgart: Hans-Dieter Heinz Akademischer Verlag, 1993).

26. Jonathan Gillis, "Bad Habits and Pernicious Results: Thumb Sucking and the Discipline of Late-Nineteenth-Century Paediatrics," *Medical History* 40, no. 1 (1996): 57.

27. Snip! Snap! Snip! the scissors go;
    And Conrad cries out—Oh! Oh! Oh!
    Snip! Snap! Snip! They go so fast;
    That both his thumbs are off at last.

    Mamma comes home; there Conrad stands,
    And looks quite sad, and shows his hands;
    "Ah!" said Mamma[.] "I knew he'd come
    To naughty little Suck-a-Thumb."

    (H. Hoffman, "The Story of Little Suck-a-Thumb," http://www.fln.vcu.edu/struw
    wel/daumen_e.html).
28. David Armstrong, *Political Anatomy of the Body: Medical Knowledge in Britain in the Twentieth Century* (Cambridge: Cambridge University Press, 1983), 6.
29. Foucault, *The History of Sexuality*, 104.
30. Vivienne Zelizer, *Pricing the Priceless Child: The Changing Social Value of Children* (Princeton, NJ: Princeton University Press, 1985); Karen Sanchez-Eppler, *Dependent States: The Child's Part in Nineteenth-Century American Culture* (Chicago: University of Chicago Press, 2005); Peter Stearns, *Anxious Parents: A History of Modern Childrearing in America* (New York: New York University Press, 2003).
31. Zelizer, *Pricing the Priceless Child.*
32. R. Danielle Egan and Gail Hawkes, "Producing the Prurient through the Pedagogy of Purity: Childhood Sexuality and the Social Purity Movement," *Journal of Historical Sociology* 20, no. 4 (2007): 443–61.
33. David J. Pivar, *Purity Crusade: Sexual Morality and Social Control, 1868–1900* (Westport, CT: Greenwood Press, 1973), 85. For more on social purity activists and prostitution or venereal disease in the Anglophone West, see Robert Darby, "Pathologizing Male Sexuality: Lallemand, Spermatorrhea, and the Rise of Circumcision," *Journal of the History of Medicine and Allied Sciences* 60, no. 3 (2005): 283–319; Alyson Brown and David Barrett, *Knowledge of Evil: Child Prostitution and Child Sexual Abuse in Twentieth Century England* (London: Willian, 2002); Lesley A. Hall, "Hauling down the Double Standard: Feminism, Social Purity and Sexual Science in Late Nineteenth-Century Britain," *Gender and History* 16, no. 1 (2004): 36–56; Michael Mason, *The Making of Victorian Sexuality* (Oxford: Oxford University Press, 1994); Jeffery P. Moran, "Modernism Gone Mad: Sex Education Comes to Chicago, 1913," *Journal of American History* 83, no. 2 (1996): 481–513; Paula Bartley, *Prostitution: Prevention and Reform in England, 1860–1914* (London: Routledge, 1999); Jill Matus, *Unstable Bodies: Victorian Representations of Sexuality and Maternity* (Manchester: University of Manchester Press, 1995).
34. J. C. Burnham, "The Progressive Era Revolution in American Attitudes toward Sex," *Journal of American History* 59, no. 4 (1973): 885–908. Although several purity activists wrote pieces prior to 1870, the majority of the literature occurred after 1870.
35. Pivar, *Purity Crusade.*
36. Roger G. Walters, *Primers for Prudery: Sexual Advice for Victorian America* (Baltimore: Johns Hopkins University Press, 2000), 16.
37. Frank Mort, *Dangerous Sexualities: Medico-moral Politics in England since 1830*, 2nd ed. (London: Routledge, 2000); Alan Hunt, *Governing Morals: A Social History*

of Moral Regulation (Cambridge: Cambridge University Press, 1991); David Wagner, *The New Temperance: The American Obsession with Sin and Vice* (Boulder, CO: Westview Press, 1997).

38. Henry Varley cautioned that society was "honey-combed" with immoral and prurient influences that were particularly dangerous to children. Henry Varley, *Private Address to Boys and Youths: On an Important Subject Containing Invaluable Information* (London: Office of the Christian Commonwealth, 1884), 1.

39. Elizabeth Blackwell, *Counsel to Parents on the Moral Education of Their Children in Relation to Sex*, 7th ed. (London: Hatchards Piccadilly, 1884), 32.

40. Samuel Gregory, *Facts and Important Information for Young Women on the Subject of Masturbation; with Its Causes, Prevention and Cure* (New York: Arno Press, 1974), 56. This conceptualization of the rural social setting as conforming and governable, and that of the cities as the opposite, was a commonplace in this period.

41. Blackwell, *Counsel to Parents*, 18.

42. Ibid.

43. Elizabeth Blackwell, *Essays in Medical Sociology* (London: Ernest Bell, 1902), 282.

44. Blackwell, *Counsel to Parents*, 13.

45. D. A. Welsh, *The Massacre of the Innocents* (Sydney: Workers' Educational Association of New South Wales, 1917), 9.

46. Constructed as a skill to be taught rather than an innate form of knowledge, motherhood during the mid- to late Victorian period began to involve experts in domestic management and child rearing. Stearns, *Anxious Parents*.

47. Egan and Hawkes, "Producing the Prurient."

48. Sanchez-Eppler, *Dependent States*. In her research on the place of the child in nineteenth-century America, Sanchez-Eppler argues that the fragility and corruptibility of the child's imagination catalyzed panics on the influence of literature and the call to ban fictional accounts from the child's library. We are employing her theory of the excitable imagination in arguing that the panic surrounding corrupt companions drew on similar conceptions of the imagination and its potential dangers.

49. Egan and Hawkes, *Theorizing the Sexual Child*.

50. Blackwell, *Counsel to Parents*, 16.

51. Varley, *Private Address to Boys*, 5.

52. Ibid.

53. Richard Arthur, *The Needed Change in the Age of Consent: An Appeal for the Better Protection of Our Girls* (Sydney: Christian World Press, 1896), 7.

54. Thomas W. Galloway, *Sex and Social Health* (New York: American Hygiene Association, 1924), 127.

55. Mort, *Dangerous Sexualities;* Jeffrey Weeks, *Sex, Politics and Society: The Regulation of Sexuality since 1800*, 2nd ed. (London: Longman, 1989); Foucault, *The History of Sexuality*.

56. Foucault, *The History of Sexuality*.

57. Mort, *Dangerous Sexualities*, 169.

58. This transition clearly extended beyond the body of the child and had a particularly powerful influence on the bodies of women as well. We see this view in responses of

the medical profession to the class differential in fertility rates in the first decades of the twentieth century and to the calls for wide provision of birth control.

59. The term "race" had pliancy in the nineteenth and early-twentieth centuries. As Nancy Ordover notes, the word "race" was used "during the late nineteenth and early twentieth centuries to refer, at any given time, to religion, color, class and/or national origins." Nancy Ordover, *American Eugenics: Race, Queer Anatomy, and the Science of Nationalism* (Minneapolis: University of Minnesota Press, 2003), 4.

60. Galloway, *Sex and Social Health*, 126.

61. Ibid., 170. The social hygiene movement is situated within a much broader public concern with the hygienic and the preoccupation with prevention. For example, Wohl argues that the end of the nineteenth century saw an increasing focus on the advantage of cleanliness and prevention. Anthony S. Wohl, *Endangered Lives: Public Health in Victorian Britain* (Cambridge, MA: Harvard University Press, 1983). Moreover, various institutions produced scientific studies on subjects ranging from the benefits of various forms of hygiene such as clean water, food, and clothing to rational potential of mental hygiene and even the hygienic potential of arithmetic. P. W. Musgrave, "Morality and the Medical Department: 1907–1974," *British Journal of Educational Studies* 25, no. 2 (1977): 136–54.

62. Mort, *Dangerous Sexualities;* Porter and Hall, *The Facts of Life;* Burnham, "The Progressive Era Revolution."

63. Christopher Jenks, *Childhood* (London: Routledge, 1996); Hugh Cunningham, *Children of the Poor: Representing Childhood since the Seventeenth Century* (Oxford: Blackwell, 1991).

64. Michael Imber, "Toward a Theory of Curriculum Reform: An Analysis of the First Campaign for Sex Education," *Curriculum Inquiry* 12, no. 4 (1982): 339–62; B. Strong, "Ideas of the Early Sex Education Movement in America, 1890–1920," *History of Education Quarterly* 12 (1972): 129–61; Burnham, "The Progressive Era Revolution."

65. Winfield Scott Hall, *Sexual Education for Sex Problems: Sex Hygiene by the Highest Authority* (Philadelphia: International Bible Houses, 1916), 19.

66. R. Danielle Egan and Gail Hawkes, "Childhood Sexuality, Normalization and the Social Hygiene Movement in the Anglophone West, 1900–1935," *Social History of Medicine* (forthcoming).

67. Wren J. Grinstead, "Reading for Teachers of Sex Hygiene," *School Review* 22, no. 4 (1914): 250; William M. Gallichan, *A Textbook of Sex Education for Parents and Teachers* (Boston: Small, Maynard, 1921); Marie Stopes, *Sex and the Young* (London: G. P. Putnam's Sons, 1926); Margaret Sanger, *What Every Boy and Girl Should Know* (New York: Brentano's, 1927).

68. Hall, *Sexual Education*, 30.

69. Ibid.

70. M. E. Robinson, "The Sex Problem," *Journal of International Ethics* 21, no. 3 (1911): 332.

71. Newell Edison, "Sex Education as a Community Problem," *Journal of Educational Sociology* 8, no. 6 (1935): 361–70; Valerie Parker, "Social Hygiene and the Child," *Annals of the American Academy of Political and Social Science* 121 (1925): 46–52; Walter Robie, *Sex and Life: What the Experienced Should Teach and What*

the *Inexperienced Should Learn* (Boston: Gorham Press, 1920); Maurice Bigelow, *Sex-Education: A Series of Lectures Concerning Knowledge of Sex in Its Relation to Human Life* (New York: Macmillan, 1916); Galloway, *Sex and Social Health.*
72. Bigelow, *Sex Education,* 22.
73. Hall, *Sexual Education,* 19–20.
74. Galloway, *Sex and Social Health,* 127.
75. Parker, "Social Hygiene," 46.
76. Ibid.; Ray H. Everett, "Social Hygiene and Public Health," *Social Forces* 2, no. 1 (1923): 61–64; Hall, *Sexual Education;* Grinstead, "Reading for Teachers."
77. Parker, "Social Hygiene," 46.
78. Edison, "Sex Education," 362.
79. "By introducing sexual hygiene we are breaking with the tradition of the past which professed to leave the process by which the race is carried on to Nature, to God, especially to the devil. We are claiming that it is a matter for individual personal responsibility, deliberately exercised in the light of precise knowledge which every young man and woman has a right, or rather a duty, to possess." Havelock Ellis, *The Task of Social Hygiene,* Project Gutenberg, 2007, http://www.gutenberg.org/files/22090/22090-h/22090-h.htm.
80. Peter Gay, ed., *The Freud Reader* (London: Vintage, 1995), 24.
81. For reasons of limited space, we will limit the narrative to Sigmund Freud, *On Sexuality: Three Essays on the Theory of Sexuality and Other Works,* trans. James Strachey (New York: Penguin, 1977), and Albert Moll, *The Sexual Life of the Child,* Books Reborn, http://www.ipce.info/booksreborn/moll, interposed where necessary with references to Havelock Ellis's *Studies in the Psychology of Sex,* Psyplexus, http://www.psyplexus.com/ellis. As we argue elsewhere, other coterminous sexologists recognized the existence of active sexuality in prepubescent children. Egan and Hawkes, *Theorizing the Sexual Child.*
82. Similar recognition can be found in the work of Iwan Bloch (1872–1922); Magnus Hirschfeld (1868–1935); and, earlier than both, Max Dessoir. See, for more details on Hirschfeld and Bloch, Egan and Hawkes, *Theorizing the Sexual Child;* Frank J. Sulloway, *Freud, Biologist of the Mind: Beyond the Psychoanalytic Legend* (Cambridge, MA: Harvard University Press, 1992).
83. See, for example, Moll, *The Sexual Life,* 14.
84. See, for example, Ivan Crozier, "Taking Prisoners: Havelock Ellis, Sigmund Freud, and the Politics of Constructing the Homosexual, 1897–1951," *Social History of Medicine* 13 (2000): 447–66.
85. Freud, *On Sexuality,* 87. Freud's work on childhood sexuality has been claimed by Marcus to be the one most revised and revisited by its author. The reference volume in this chapter contains footnote additions from 1920 and beyond.
86. Freud, *Three Essays,* 88. Angela Richards comments that before 1897, "infantile sexuality was [by Freud] regarded as no more than a dormant factor, only liable to be brought into the open, with disastrous results, by an adult." Richards in Freud, *Three Essays,* 36. For a recent and more detailed critical analysis of Freud's complete writings on child sexuality, see Egan and Hawkes, *Theorizing the Sexual Child.*

87. "Other writers, such as Freud, Bell, and Kötscher, have contributed certain data towards the solution of these questions; no comprehensive study of the subject has hitherto been attempted." Moll, *The Sexual Life*, xii.

88. Ibid., 15.

89. Freud, *Three Essays*, 83.

90. These terms are important, as they identify the pioneering nature of this theory and its location within the early discipline of psychoanalysis, which, as he puts it, lies, "*on the frontier between the mental and the physical.*" Ibid.

91. Here Freud's theory confronts directly the preexisting characterizations of childhood sexuality as either the outcome of "degeneracy" or as pathological manifestations in response to external stimulus, either accidental from the environment or intentional stimulation from adults. See previous notes and Freud, *Three Essays*, 89 n. 1.

92. Freud, *Three Essays*, 101. Freud uses the example of thumb-sucking, citing the work of a Hungarian pediatrician named Lindner, who "clearly recognized the sexual nature of this activity and emphasized it without qualification. In the nursery, sucking is classed along with other kinds of 'sexual naughtiness' in children." Ibid., 96. See also our previous comments on *Struwellpeter*.

93. Freud, *Three Essays*, 102. Moll, on the other hand, argues that thumb-sucking "has as little to do with sexuality as have the functions of the stomach or any other non-genital organs." Moll, *The Sexual Life*, 14. He suggests that Freud is not really interested in identifying the sexual life of the child but is more interested in identifying "manifestations of the sexual instinct for therapeutic reasons." Ibid.

94. Ibid., 29.

95. Moll discusses, at length, evidence suggesting that children under reproductive age and of both sexes can secret fluid during sexual excitation. Ibid., 52–57.

96. Ibid., 60–61.

97. Freud, *Three Essays*, 176. See also Sanford Bell, "A Preliminary Study of the Emotion of Love between the Sexes," *American Journal of Psychology* 13, no. 3 (1902): 325–54.

98. Freud, *Three Essays*, 109.

99. Moll, *The Sexual Life*, 219.

100. Ibid., 196, 198–99.

101. This is especially the case with Moll, who, for example, claims Freud's connections between early sexual experiences and adult neuroses to be "arbitrary" and scientifically unfounded. Ibid., 190.

102. See also Jonathan Dollimore, *Sexual Dissidence: Augustine to Wilde, Freud to Foucault* (Oxford: Oxford University Press, 1991).

103. Freud, *Three Essays*, 57.

104. See also extended case studies offered by Ellis in appendices in vols. 3–4 of Ellis, *Studies in the Psychology of Sex*.

105. Vern L. Bullough, *Science in the Bedroom: A History of Sex Research* (New York: Basic Books, 1994).

106. See Bell, "A Preliminary Study," 325–54.

107. "From time to time a fragmentary manifestation of sexuality which has evaded sublimation may break through; or some sexual activity may persist through the whole duration of the latency period until the sexual instinct emerges with greater intensity at puberty." Freud, *Three Essays*, 95.
108. Freud, *Three Essays*, 112. See Egan and Hawkes, *Theorizing the Sexual Child*.
109. Freud, *Three Essays*, 180.
110. Moll, *The Sexual Life*, 290.
111. Ibid., 302–3.
112. When we use the word "autonomy," we are using the term to refer to the child's capacity to make and act upon decisions that involve the use of its body.
113. Here, as Hulbert reminds us, the success of Taylorism—scientific management of production—was the legitimating framework for child training. Anne Hulbert, *Raising America: Experts, Parents, and a Century of Advice about Children* (London: Vintage, 2004), 36. Following the work of Frederick Taylor in *The Principles of Scientific Management* (1911), this approach recommended the following of precise regimes laid down in steps that were detailed and timed in every aspect of their execution.
114. Indeed, the mechanistic dynamic of modernization is exemplified in the work of Emmett Holt, whose book remained a stalwart of infant care for decades. Reading his work a century later, one is struck by the lack of sentiment, indeed, any emotion, in a work intended as a direct support for mother and child. Holt's commitment was to technical training, efficacy, and outcome, and the child presented a vehicle for this. Holt, *The Diseases*, 6.
115. Kereen Reiger, *The Disenchantment of the Home: Modernizing the Australian Family* (Melbourne: Oxford University Press, 1985).
116. Stearns, *Anxious Parents;* M. Cable, *The Little Darlings: A History of Child Rearing in America* (New York: Charles Scribner's Sons, 1975); Hulbert, *Raising America*. Hulbert identifies the emergence of a "child-rearing science" as being involved with the moral and the social. Hulbert, *Raising America*, 106.
117. Christopher Lasch, *Haven in a Heartless World: The Family Besieged* (New York: Basic Books, 1977), 18; Joseph Hawes, *Children's Health in America: A History* (New York: Twayne, 1991), 32.
118. Hulbert, *Raising America*, 36.
119. A term referring to the school of psychology founded by John Watson based on the belief that behaviors can be measured, trained, and changed. Behaviorism was established with the publication of John Watson's classic paper "Psychology as the Behaviorist Views It" (1913), Classics in the History of Psychology, http://psychclassics.asu.edu/Watson/views.htm.
120. John Watson, *The Psychological Care of the Infant and Child* (New York: W. W. Norton, 1978), 38.
121. Ibid., 15.
122. Frances Strain, *New Patterns in Sex Teaching: The Normal Sex Interests of Children and Their Guidance from Infancy to Adolescence* (New York: D. Appleton-Century, 1934). For detailed critical analysis of this discourse, see Gail Hawkes and R. Danielle Egan, "Developing the Sexual Child," *Journal of Historical*

Sociology 21, no. 4 (2008): 443–65; Egan and Hawkes, *Theorizing the Sexual Child*.

123. Watson, *The Psychological Care*, 116.
124. Ibid., 137–38.
125. Ibid., 155.
126. Ibid., 125–26.
127. The child development texts we reviewed were pale imitations of the explicit claims made by Freud about the active sexuality of the child.
128. Frances Wickes, *The Inner World of Childhood: A Study in Analytic Psychology* (New York: D. Appleton, 1927), 15.
129. Thomas Wood, Marian Lerrigo, and Thurman Rice, *Sex Education: A Guide for Teachers and Parents* (New York: Thomas Nelson and Sons, 1937), 3.
130. M. Dennett, *The Sex Education of Children* (London: George Routledge and Sons, 1932), 3–4.
131. Wood, Lerrigo, and Rice, *Sex Education*, 12.
132. John Anderson, *Happy Childhood: The Development and Guidance of Children and Youth* (New York: D. Appleton-Century, 1933), 196.
133. August Forel, *The Sexual Question: A Scientific, Psychological, Hygienic and Sociological Study for the Cultured Classes* (London: Rebman, 1908), 475 (emphasis added).
134. Strain, *New Patterns in Sex Teaching*, 85. Strain goes on to recognize sexual activity between cousins. "The object was to obtain the 'lowdown' on anything pertaining to sexual knowledge or experience. When they finally discovered the phenomenon known as coitus, they realized they had reached the goal of their researches." The children in this example did not achieve the "grand finale" because "training or conscience" intervened. Ibid. There is no suggestion of judgment here, or anxieties about precocious sexuality: the only consideration in both examples was the frequency of the activity and the age of the participants. She concludes that if "the two children involved are fairly equal in age and in maturity and hardy in constitution" then it is not harmful. Ibid., 85–86.
135. Carl Renz and Mildred Renz, *Big Problems on Little Shoulders* (New York: Macmillan, 1935), 114. This attitude extends to dealing with a report of sexual abuse by an adult nurse. A four-year-old child was left with her nurse while her mother was out of the house. "Returning home … the little girl, shocked and frightened, told her mother about an offense that the nurse had committed. … The mother simply said 'well, dear, that was not a polite thing for Nurse to do. Nurse evidently does not know what is polite and what is not. I am sorry you were frightened (sympathy should not be denied, but it should not encourage self-pity). … Nurse doesn't always have nice manners.'" Ibid., 116.
136. Marion Piddington, *Tell Them! or The Second Stage of Mothercraft: A Handbook of Suggestions for the Sex Training of the Child* (Sydney: Moore's Book Shop, 1926), 51.
137. By the end of our period, some books were acknowledging the partial autonomy of the individual child, indicating a more laissez-faire approach, the precursor of "the permissive era" of child rearing, which in the U.S. context was "complete

by 1948." Jay Meschling, "Advice to Historians on the Advice to Mothers," *Journal of Social History* 9, no. 1 (1975): 44. See also William Graebner, "The Unstable World of Benjamin Spock: Social Engineering in a Democratic Culture, 1917–1950," *Journal of American History* 67, no. 3 (1980): 613. Graebner identifies the more democratic model of child-rearing evident in Spock but also draws attention to his characterization of the child as "unstable, a potential tyrant and incipient demagogue."

138. Ruth Metraux, "Parents and Children: An Analysis of Contemporary German Child-Care and Youth-Guidance Literature," in *Childhood in Contemporary Cultures,* ed. Margaret Mead and Martha Wolfenstein (Chicago: University of Chicago Press, 1955), 214.

139. Watson, *The Psychological Care,* 174.

140. Wickes, *The Inner World,* 281.

141. Ibid., 288.

142. Foucault, *The History of Sexuality,* 104.

143. R. Danielle Egan and Gail Hawkes, "Girls, Sexuality and the Strange Carnalities of Advertisements: Deconstructing the Discourse of Corporate Paedophilia," *Australian Feminist Studies* 23, no. 57 (2008): 307–22.

144. Gail Hawkes, *Sex and Pleasure in Western Culture* (Cambridge: Polity Press, 2004).

145. Across these discourses gender is silent—even in Freud, until puberty, the manifestations of a sexual life in the child are evident in both girls and boys.

Chapter 8

My thanks to Alicia Gray, Susanne Protschky, and Rachel Woodlock, who provided valuable research assistance and stimulating discussions on this subject.

1. Philip Howell, "Prostitution and Racialised Sexuality: The Regulation of Prostitution in Britain and the British Empire before the Contagious Diseases Acts," *Environment and Planning D: Society and Space* 18 (2000): 329.

2. Lenore Manderson, "Colonial Desires: Sexuality, Race, and Gender in British Malaya," *Journal of the History of Sexuality* 7, no. 3 (1997): 374; Lenore Manderson, *Sickness and the State: Health and Illness in Colonial Malaya, 1870–1940* (Cambridge: Cambridge University Press, 1996), 166. Of the 5,580 Chinese residents of Manila in 1855, only ten were female. Luis C. Dery, "Prostitution in Colonial Manila," *Philippine Studies* 39, no. 4 (1991): 447.

3. Philippa Levine, "'Rough Usage': Prostitution, Law, and the Social Historian," in *Rethinking Social History: English Society, 1570–1920,* ed. Adrian Wilson (Manchester: Manchester University Press, 1993), 276.

4. Kenneth Ballhatchet, *Race, Sex and Class under the Raj: Imperial Attitudes and Policies and Their Critics, 1793–1905* (London: Weidenfeld and Nicolson, 1980). For a lively debate about the coercive nature of this sexual adventuring, see Ronald Hyam, "Empire and Sexual Opportunity," *Journal of Imperial and Commonwealth History* 14, no. 2 (1986): 34–90; Mark T. Berger, "Imperialism

and Sexual Exploitation: A Response to Ronald Hyam's 'Empire and Sexual Opportunity,'" *Journal of Imperial Commonwealth History* 17, no. 1 (1988): 83–99; Ronald Hyam, "'Imperialism and Sexual Exploitation': A Reply," *Journal of Imperial and Commonwealth History* 17, no. 1 (1988): 90–99. See also Ronald Hyam, *Empire and Sexuality: The British Experience* (Manchester: Manchester University Press, 1990).

5. Manderson, *Sickness and the State*, 166. See also Lenore Manderson, "Migration, Prostitution and Medical Surveillance in Early Twentieth-Century Malaya," in *Migrants, Minorities and Health: Historical and Contemporary Studies*, ed. Lara Marks and Michael Worboys (London: Routledge, 1997).

6. Hyam, *Sexuality and Empire*, 142–45. For the Jewish traffic and campaigns against it, see Edward J. Bristow, *Vice and Vigilance: Purity Movements in Britain since 1700* (Dublin: Gill and Macmillan, 1977).

7. Harald Fischer-Tiné, "'White Women Degrading Themselves to the Lowest Depths': European Networks of Prostitution and Colonial Anxieties in British India and Ceylon, ca. 1880–1914," *Indian Economic and Social History Review* 40, no. 2 (2003): 172; Raelene Frances, *Selling Sex: A Hidden History of Prostitution* (Sydney: Allen & Unwin, 2007), chap. 11.

8. Gail Herschatter, *Dangerous Pleasures: Prostitution and Modernity in Twentieth-Century Shanghai* (Berkeley: University of California Press, 1997), 34. See also Gail Herschatter, "The Hierarchy of Shanghai Prostitution, 1870–1949," *Modern China* 15, no. 4 (1989): 463–98. The precise nature of this hierarchy is the subject of an exchange between Herschatter and Christian Henriot. See Christian Henriot, "'From a Throne of Glory to a Seat of Ignominy': Shanghai Prostitution Revisited (1849–1949)," *Modern China* 22, no. 2 (1996): 132–63, and Gail Herschatter, "'From a Throne of Glory to a Seat of Ignominy': Shanghai Prostitution Revisited (1849–1949): A Response," *Modern China* 22, no. 2 (1996): 164–69. See also Sue Gronewold, *Beautiful Merchandise: Prostitution in China, 1860–1936* (New York: Haworth, 1982).

9. Lai Ah Eng, *Peasants, Proletarians and Prostitutes: A Preliminary Investigation into the Work of Chinese Women in Colonial Malaya*, Research Notes and Discussion Paper No. 59 (Singapore: Institute of Southeast Asian Studies, 1986), 29–30.

10. Tamara Adilman, "A Preliminary Sketch of Chinese Women and Work in British Columbia, 1858–1950," in *Not Just Pin Money: Selected Essays on the History of Women's Work in British Columbia*, ed. Barbara K. Latham and Robert J. Pazdro (Victoria, BC: Camosun College, 1984), 59; Lucy Cheng Hirata, "Chinese Immigrant Women in Nineteenth-Century California," in *Women in America: A History*, ed. Carol Ruth Berkin and Mary Beth Norton (Boston: Houghton Mifflin, 1979), 223–24.

11. James Francis Warren, *Ah Ku and Karayuki-San: Prostitution in Singapore, 1870–1940* (Oxford: Oxford University Press, 1993), chap. 2; Lai, *Peasants, Proletarians and Prostitutes;* Elizabeth Sinn, "Chinese Patriarchy and the Protection of Women in 19th-Century Hong Kong," in *Women and Chinese Patriarchy: Submission, Servitude and Escape*, ed. Maria Jaschok and Suzanne Miers (Hong Kong: Hong Kong University Press, 1994).

12. Julia Martinez, "*La Traite des Jaunes*: Trafficking in Women and Children across the China Seas," in *Many Middle Passages: Forced Migration and the Making of the Modern World,* ed. Cassandra Pybus, Markus Rediker, and Emma Christopher (Berkeley: University of California Press, 2007); Julia Martinez, "The Chinese Trade in Women and Children from Northern Vietnam," in *The Trade in Human Beings for Sex,* ed. P. Legros, J. Le Roux, and G. Faure (Bangkok: IRASEC, forthcoming). See also Paul Monet, *Les jauniers, histoire vraie* (Paris: Gallimard, 1930); Legrand, directeur du port de commerce et chef de la police indigène à le Consul à Haiphong, April 25, 1880, Indochine FM SG, Anciens fonds, Carton 1 Dossier A00 (16), CAOM, Aix-en-Provence; Gilles Raffi, "Haiphong, origines, conditions et modalités du développement jusqu'à 1921" (doctoral thesis, Université de Provence, 1994).

13. Christian Henriot, *Prostitution and Sexuality in Shanghai: A Social History, 1849–1949,* trans. Noël Castelino (Cambridge: Cambridge University Press, 2001). See also Henriot, "From a Throne of Glory."

14. For a discussion of the integral role of prostitution in the development of modern Japan, see Sheldon Garon, "The World's Oldest Debate? Prostitution and the State in Imperial Japan, 1900–1945," *American Historical Review* 98, no. 3 (1993): 710–32.

15. Cynthia Enloe, *Does Khaki Become You? The Militarization of Women's Lives* (London: Pluto Press, 1983), 31. For other historical accounts of the karayuki-san, see Frances, *Selling Sex,* 46–60; Noreen Jones, *No. 2 Home: A Story of Japanese Pioneers in Australia* (Freemantle: Fremantle Arts Centre Press, 2002); Sone Sachiko, "Karayuki-San of Asia, 1868–1938: The Role of Prostitutes Overseas in Japanese Economic and Social Development" (MPhil thesis, Murdoch University, 1980); Hiroshi Shimizu, "Karayuki-San and the Japanese Economic Advance into British Malaya, 1870–1920," *Asian Studies Review* 20, no. 3 (1997): 107–32; C. Sissons, "Karayuki-San: Japanese Prostitutes in Australia, 1887–1916—I," *Historical Studies* 17, no. 68 (1977): 323–41; C. Sissons, "Karayuki-San: Japanese Prostitutes in Australia, 1887–1916—II," *Historical Studies* 17, no. 69 (1977): 474–88; Yamazaki Tomoko, *Sandakan Brothel No. 8,* trans. Karen Colligan-Taylor (New York: M. E. Sharpe, 1999); C. Moore, "'A Precious Few': Melanesian and Asian Women in Northern Australia," in *Gender Relations in Australia: Domination and Negotiation,* ed. Kay Saunders and Raymond Evans (Sydney: Harcourt Brace and Jovanovich, 1992), 67; Warren, *Ah Ku and Karayuki-San;* James F. Warren, "Prostitution and the Politics of Venereal Disease: Singapore, 1870–98," *Journal of Southeast Asian Studies* 21 (1990): 360–61; J. Mark Ramseyer, "Indentured Prostitution in Imperial Japan: Credible Commitments in the Commercial Sex Industry," *Journal of Law, Economics and Organisation* 7 (1991): 89–116; Bill Mihalopoulos, "The Making of the Prostitutes: The *Karayuki-San,*" *Bulletin of Concerned Asian Scholars* 25 (1993): 41–56; Motoe Terami-Wada, "Karayuki-San of Manila: 1880–1920," *Philippine Studies* 34 (1986): 287–316.

16. Frances, *Selling Sex,* 46–60.

17. Warren, *Ah Ku and Karayuki-San,* 35.

18. Charu Gupta, *Sexuality, Obscenity, Community: Women, Muslims and the Hindu Public in Colonial India* (New York: Palgrave, 2001), 109. See also Judy Whitehead, "Bodies Clean and Unclean: Prostitution, Sanitary Legislation, and Respectable Femininity in Colonial North India," *Gender and History* 7, no. 1 (1995): 41–63; Dagmar Engels, "The Changing Role of Women in Bengal, 1890–1930" (Ph.D. thesis, School of Oriental and Asian Studies, London, 1987); Dagmar Engels, "The Limits of Gender Ideology: Bengali Women, the Colonial State, and the Private Sphere, 1890–1930," *Women's Studies International Forum* 12 (1989): 425–37.

19. Satish M. Kumar, "'Oriental Sore' or 'Public Nuisance': The Regulation of Prostitution in Colonial India, 1895–1889," in *(Dis)placing Empire: Renegotiating British Colonial Geographies,* ed. Lindsay J. Proudfoot and Michael M. Roche (Burlington, VT: Ashgate, 2005), 158–59; Veena Talwar Oldenburg, *The Making of Colonial Lucknow, 1856–77* (Princeton, NJ: Princeton University Press, 1984), 132–36.

20. Sumanta Banerjee, *Under the Raj: Prostitution in Colonial Bengal* (New York: Monthly Review Press, 1998), 74.

21. Pauline Rule, "Prostitution in Calcutta, 1860–1940: The Pattern of Recruitment," in *Class, Ideology and Woman in Asian Societies,* ed. Gail Pearson and Lenore Manderson (Hong Kong: Asian Research Service, 1987), 66.

22. Banerjee, *Under the Raj*, 80–89.

23. Ibid., 77.

24. Kumar, "'Oriental Sore' or 'Public Nuisance,'" 159.

25. Ballhatchet, *Race, Sex and Class under the Raj*, 162–63. This contrasts with Ronald Hyam's claims that prostitution was an "old and honourably established business" before the raj. Hyam, "Empire and Sexual Opportunity," 65. It should be noted that the status of women selling sex varied considerably according to the original social group of the women and of the clientele, with a huge gulf between the higher-class women who served the Mogul courts and poor women who worked in the villages.

26. Banerjee, *Under the Raj*, 68.

27. Kunal M. Parker, "'A Corporation of Superior Prostitutes': Anglo-Indian Legal Conceptions of Temple Dancing Girls, 1900–1914," *Modern Asian Studies* 32, no. 3 (1998): 559–60; Veena Talwar Oldenburg, "Lifestyle as Resistance: The Case of the Courtesans of Lucknow, India," *Feminist Studies* 16 (1990): 259–88; Engels, "The Changing Role of Women," 90–92; Frédérique Apffel-Marglin, *Wives of the God King: The Rituals of the Devadasis of Puri* (Delhi: Oxford University Press, 1985).

28. Parker, "A Corporation of Superior Prostitutes," 562.

29. Ibid., 559–60. See also Philippa Levine, "'A Multitude of Unchaste Women': Prostitution in the British Empire," *Journal of Women's History* 15, no. 4 (2004): 161; Whitehead, "Bodies Clean and Unclean," 50–51.

30. Frances, *Selling Sex*, part 2; Dawn May, *Aboriginal Labour and the Cattle Industry: Queensland from White Settlement to the Present* (Cambridge: Cambridge University Press, 1994); Ann McGrath, *Born in the Cattle: Aborigines in Cattle Country* (Sydney: Allen & Unwin, 1987), chap. 4; Ann McGrath, "'Black Velvet': Aboriginal

Women and Their Relations with White Men in the Northern Territory, 1910–1940,"
in *So Much Hard Work: Women and Prostitution in Australian History*, ed. Kay
Daniels (Sydney: Fontana/Collins, 1984); Raymond Evans, "'Don't You Remember Black Alice, Sam Holt?' Aboriginal Women in Queensland History," *Hecate* 8,
no. 2 (1982): 15; Diane Bell, *Daughters of the Dreaming* (Sydney: Allen & Unwin,
1983), 98–100. For instances of indigenous Canadian women becoming involved in
prostitution under colonialism, see Jo-Anne Fiske, "Colonization and the Decline of
Women's Status: The Tsimshian Case," *Feminist Studies* 17, no. 3 (1991): 523.

31. Frances, *Selling Sex*. See also Raelene Frances, "A History of Female Prostitution in
    Australia," in *Sex Work and Sex Workers in Australia,* ed. Roberta Perkins, Gar-
    reth Prestage, and Frances Lovejoy (Kensington: University of New South Wales
    Press, 1994), 27–52.

32. Charlotte Macdonald, "The 'Social Evil': Prostitution and the Passage of the
    Contagious Diseases Act (1869)," in *Women in History: Essays on European
    Women in New Zealand,* ed. Barbara Brookes, Charlotte Macdonald, and
    Margaret Tennant (Wellington: Allen & Unwin/Port Nicholson Press, 1986),
    13–34; Charlotte Macdonald, *A Woman of Good Character: Single Women as
    Immigrant Settlers in Nineteenth-Century New Zealand* (Wellington: Allen &
    Unwin, 1990), 173–88.

33. Luise White, *The Comforts of Home: Prostitution in Colonial Nairobi* (Chicago:
    University of Chicago Press, 1990), 31–33.

34. Ibid., 2.

35. Ibid., 222. See also Anne McClintock, "Screwing the System: Sexwork, Race
    and the Law," *Boundary 2*, 19, no. 2 (1992): esp. 83–84, for a good summary of
    White's arguments regarding the subversive implications of women's prostitution
    accumulations.

36. Charles van Onselen, "Prostitutes and Proletarians, 1886–1914," in *New Baby-
    lon*, vol. 1 of *Studies in the Social and Economic History of the Witwatersrand,
    1886–1914* (New York: Longman, 1982), 108.

37. Ibid., 107.

38. Elizabeth B. Van Heyningen, "The Social Evil in the Cape Colony, 1868–1902:
    Prostitution and the Contagious Diseases Acts," *Journal of Southern African Stud-
    ies* 10, no. 2 (1984): 170–97; Van Onselen, "Prostitutes and Proletarians"; Ros
    Posel, "'Continental Women' and Durban's 'Social Evil,' 1899–1905," *Journal of
    Natal and Zulu History* 12 (1989): 1–13.

39. Hyam, *Empire and Sexuality*, 62.

40. Ross G. Forman, "Randy on the Rand: Portuguese African Labour and the Dis-
    course on 'Unnatural Vice' in the Transvaal in the Early Twentieth Century,"
    Journal of the History of Sexuality 11, no. 4 (2002): 570–609.

41. Tshidiso Maloka, "*Khomo Lia Oela*: Canteens, Brothels and Labour Migrancy in
    Colonial Lesotho, 1900–40," *Journal of African History* 38 (1997): 101.

42. Paul Kramer, "The Darkness that Enters the Home: The Politics of Prostitution
    during the Philippine-American War," in *Haunted by Empire: Geographies of In-
    timacy in North American History,* ed. Ann Laura Stoler (Durham, NC: Duke
    University Press, 2006), 366–404.

43. John Ingleson, "Prostitution in Colonial Java," in *Nineteenth and Twentieth Century Indonesia: Essays in Honour of Professor J. D. Legge*, ed. David P. Chandler and M. C. Ricklefs (Clayton, Vic.: Southeast Asian Studies, Monash University, 1986), 124; Hanneke Ming, "Barracks-Concubinage in the Indies, 1887–1920," *Indonesia* 35 (1983): 70–71; Lai, *Peasants, Proletarians and Prostitutes*, 29–30. For a recent reinterpretation of the role of concubinage, see Ann Laura Stoler, *Carnal Knowledge and Imperial Power: Race and the Intimate in Colonial Rule* (Berkeley: University of California Press, 2002), esp. chap. 3. See also Ann Laura Stoler, "Making Empire Respectable: The Politics of Race and Sexual Morality in Twentieth-Century Colonial Cultures," in *Imperial Monkey Business: Racial Supremacy in Social Darwinist Theory and Colonial Practice*, ed. Jan Breman (Amsterdam: VU University Press, 1990); and Elsbeth Locher-Scholten, "The Nyai in Colonial Deli: A Case of Supposed Mediation," in *Women and Mediation in Indonesia*, ed. Sita van Bemmelen, Madelon Djajadiningrat-Nieuwenhuis, Elsbeth Locher-Scholten, and Elly Touwen-Bouwsma (Leiden: KITLV Press, 1992), 265–79.

44. Philip Howell, "Prostitution and the Place of Empire: Regulation and Repeal in Hong Kong and the British Imperial Network," in Proudfoot and Roche, *(Dis)placing Empire*, 176. See also Anne McClintock, *Imperial Leather: Race, Gender and Sexuality in the Colonial Contest* (New York: Routledge, 1995); Ann Laura Stoler, *Race and the Education of Desire: Foucault's "History of Sexuality" and the Colonial Order of Things* (Durham, NC: Duke University Press, 1995); Philippa Levine, *Prostitution, Race and Politics: Policing Venereal Disease in the British Empire* (New York: Routledge, 2003); Linda Bryder, "Sex, Race and Colonialism: An Historiographical Overview," *International History Review* 20, no. 4 (1998): 806–22.

45. Alain Corbin, "Le péril vénérien au début du siècle: Prophylaxis sanitaire et prophylaxis morale." *Recherches* 11, no. 29 (1977): 245, cited in Maria Luisa Camagay, "Prostitution in Nineteenth Century Manila," *Philippine Studies* 36 (1988): 241–55.

46. Judith R. Walkowitz, "The Making of an Outcast Group: Prostitutes and Working Women in Nineteenth-Century Plymouth and Southampton," in *A Widening Sphere: Changing Roles of Victorian Women*, ed. Martha Vicinus (Bloomington: Indiana University Press, 1977), 72–94; Judith R. Walkowitz and Daniel J. Walkowitz, "'We Are Not Beasts of the Field': Prostitution and the Poor in Plymouth and Southampton under the Contagious Diseases Acts," *Feminist Studies* 1 (1973): 73–106; Judith R. Walkowitz, *Prostitution and Victorian Society: Women, Class and the State* (Cambridge: Cambridge University Press, 1980); Francis B. Smith, "Ethics and Disease in the Later Nineteenth Century: The Contagious Diseases Acts," *Historical Studies* 15, no. 57 (1971): 118–35.

47. Howell, "Prostitution and Racialised Sexuality."

48. Ibid., 328.

49. Philip Howell, "Race, Space and the Regulation of Prostitution in Colonial Hong Kong," *Urban History* 31, no. 2 (2004): 234–35.

50. Ibid., 234.

51. Ibid., 230. See also Levine, *Prostitution, Race and Politics*; Philippa Levine, "Modernity, Medicine, and Colonialism: The Contagious Diseases Ordinances in

Hong Kong and the Straits Settlements," *Positions* 6 (1998): 675–705; Kerrie L. MacPherson, "Caveat Emptor! Attempts to Control the Venereals in Nineteenth Century Hong Kong," in *New Countries and Old Medicine: Proceedings of an International Conference on the History of Medicine and Health,* ed. Linda Bryder and Derek A. Dow (Auckland: Pyramid Press, 1995), 72–78; Kerrie L. MacPherson, "Conspiracy of Silence: A History of Sexually Transmitted Diseases and HIV/AIDS in Hong Kong," in *Sex, Disease, and Society: A Comparative History of Sexually Transmitted Disease and HIV/AIDS in Asia and the Pacific,* ed. Milton Lewis, Scott Bamber, and Michael Waugh (Westport, CT: Greenwood Press, 1997), 85–112; Norman Miners, *Hong Kong under Imperial Rule, 1912–1941* (Hong Kong: Oxford University Press, 1987), 191–206.

52. Cited in Howell, "Prostitution and Racialised Sexuality," 329.
53. Ibid.
54. R. J. Miners, "State Regulation of Prostitution in Hong Kong, 1857 to 1941," *Journal of the Hong Kong Branch of the Royal Asiatic Society* 24 (1984): 143–61. This article provides a good description of the various regimes.
55. Douglas M. Peers, "Soldiers, Surgeons and the Campaigns to Combat Sexually Transmitted Diseases in Colonial India, 1805–1860," *Medical History* 42 (1998): 137–60; Whitehead, "Bodies Clean and Unclean," 41–63.
56. M. Sundra Raj, *Prostitution in Madras: A Study in Historical Perspective* (Delhi: Konark, 1993), 25; Levine, *Prostitution, Race and Politics*, 39.
57. Levine, *Prostitution, Race and Politics*, 39.
58. Ibid., 39–40.
59. Van Heyningen, "The Social Evil in the Cape Colony," 173.
60. Mary Murnane and Kay Daniels, "Prostitutes as 'Purveyors of Disease': Venereal Disease Legislation in Tasmania, 1868–1945," *Hecate* 5, no. 1 (1979): 5–21.
61. Macdonald, "The 'Social Evil,'" 13–34; Macdonald, *A Woman of Good Character*, 173–88.
62. Helen Boritch, *Fallen Women: Female Crime and Criminal Justice in Canada* (Toronto: ITP Nelson, 1997), 103. Boritch states that the legislation was both "unenforced and essentially unenforceable" because of the lack of suitable hospitals for treating infected prostitutes. She also notes that the controversy that erupted in the UK in the late 1860s may also have convinced politicians of the wisdom of allowing the law to lapse. See also Constance B. Backhouse, "Nineteenth-Century Canadian Prostitution Law: Reflections of a Discriminatory Society," *Histoire Sociale/Social History* 18, no. 36 (1985): 387–423.
63. Frances, *Selling Sex*, 157–62; Raymond Evans, "'Soiled Doves': Prostitution in Colonial Queensland," in Daniels, *So Much Hard Work*; Enid Barclay, "Queensland's Contagious Diseases Act, 1868—'The Act for the Encouragement of Vice' and Some Nineteenth Century Attempts to Repeal It, Part 1," *Queensland Heritage* 2, no. 10 (1974): 27–34; Enid Barclay, "Queensland's Contagious Diseases Act, 1868—'The Act for the Encouragement of Vice' and Some Nineteenth Century Attempts to Repeal It, Part 2," *Queensland Heritage* 3, no. 1 (1974): 21–29; Kay Daniels, "Prostitution in Tasmania during the Transition from Penal Settlement to 'Civilised' Society," in Daniels, *So Much Hard Work*.

64. Levine, *Prostitution, Race and Politics*, 40.

65. Jean Kehoe, "Medicine, Sexuality and Imperialism: British Medical Discourses Surrounding Venereal Disease in New Zealand and Japan: A Socio-historical Analysis" (Ph.D. thesis, Victoria University of Wellington, 1992), 266, cited in Bryder, "Sex, Race and Colonialism," 818. See also Garon, "The World's Oldest Debate?" 712, for discussion of the ways in which the modern Japanese system of regulation grafted European models onto various existing schemes for licensing and concentrating prostitution under the Tokugawa shogunate. See also D. Eleanor Westney, *Imitation and Innovation: The Transfer of Western Organizational Patterns to Meiji Japan* (Cambridge, MA: Harvard University Press, 1987), 50. Garon makes the point that the regulation of prostitution was a key part of Japan's modernization strategy: "It formed part of the national government's well-conceived program of managing society so that men would postpone the decision to marry, young women would employ their sexuality in a socially efficient and orderly manner, and wives would endure their husbands' infidelities in the interests of family stability." Garon, "The World's Oldest Debate?" 729–30.

66. Levine, *Prostitution, Race and Politics*, 40–14. The Natal government attempted to introduce CD legislation in 1886 and 1890. On the first occasion, the bill was defeated by a concerted local campaign; in 1890, the bill was passed with little opposition but was disallowed by the secretary of state for the colonies. See Jeremy C. Martens, "'Almost a Public Calamity': Prostitutes, 'Nurseboys,' and Attempts to Control Venereal Diseases in Colonial Natal, 1886–1890," *South African Historical Journal* 45 (2001): 27–52.

67. Levine, "A Multitude of Unchaste Women," 161.

68. Some of the more sophisticated accounts of these systems of regulation analyze them with reference to Michel Foucault's theories regarding power and sexuality. These accounts chart the extension of the power of the modern state into new social terrain through a bureaucratic apparatus of disciplinary surveillance. In Foucault's account, by the nineteenth century, sexuality was redefined as a force requiring control, attention, and regulation by the state: prostitution and venereal disease were especially singled out as twin threats to the security and efficiency of the state. "Abnormal" sexualities such as prostitution were therefore cast as dangerous, and the individuals involved invoked as internal enemies of the state. The regulation of prostitution both in Europe and in the colonies can be read as part of this project to police and discipline the prostitute population, drawing on biopolitical technologies of power that provided for the identification, inscription, and surveillance (both panoptic and medical) of prostitutes and the confinement of prostitution to particular spaces and places. For Foucault, see Michel Foucault, *Discipline and Punish: The Birth of the Prison*, trans. Alan Sheridan (London: Allen Lane, 1977), and *The History of Sexuality: An Introduction* (New York: Vintage, 1990). For a discussion of these approaches, see Howell, "Race, Space and the Regulation of Prostitution." See also K. Luker, "Sex, Social Hygiene and the State: The Double-Edged Sword of Social Reform," *Theory and Society* 27, no. 2 (1998): 601–34; Paul W. Werth, "Through the Prism of Prostitution: State, Society and Power," *Social History* 19 (1994): 1–15; Stoler, *Race and the Education of Desire*. The case of the regulation of prostitution

raises broader issues about the nature of power in colonial societies, and the extent to which Foucauldian notions of "governmentality" might be applicable in colonial contexts. Some commentators have suggested that the more repressive and coercive nature of such regimes in the colonies points to a premodern text of coercion rather than a "modern" text of discipline. Further, these colonial societies were more distinguished by the racial objectification of collectively understood "others" than the modern self-disciplining subjects of Western ambition. See Levine, "Modernity, Medicine, and Colonialism," 683. Alternatively, other historians have drawn on a concept of "imperial/colonial governmentality" in which colonial societies were governed by forms of power that, although admittedly "cruder, more coercive and authoritarian" than those linked with modern Western liberalism and neoliberalism, were nonetheless increasingly disposed to accommodate social "realities" constructed by colonial ethnocultural discourse. See Howell, "Race, Space and the Regulation of Prostitution," 248; Michel Foucault, "Governmentality," in *The Foucault Effect: Studies in Governmentality,* ed. Graham Burchell, Colin Gordon, and Peter Miller (London: Harvester Wheatsheaf, 1991).

69. See Banerjee, *Under the Raj,* 127, for Bengali examples.
70. Howell, "Prostitution and Racialised Sexuality," 330.
71. Banerjee, *Under the Raj,* 147–48.
72. Philip Howell, "Sexuality, Sovereignty and Space: Law, Government and the Geography of Prostitution in Colonial Gibraltar," *Social History* 29, no. 4 (2004): 445.
73. Maynard Swanson, "The Sanitation Syndrome: Bubonic Plague and Urban Native Policy in the Cape Colony, 1900–1909," *Journal of African History* 18 (1977): 408–10; Megan Vaughan, *Curing Their Ills: Colonial Power and African Illness* (Cambridge: Cambridge University Press, 1991); Alexander Butchart, *The Anatomy of Power: European Constructions of the African Body* (Books: Zed Books, 1998). Charles van Onselen also points out that the 1903 Immorality Act in Natal was in large part a response to concerns about the broader issue of sex across the color line in the case of African men visiting white prostitutes. Van Onselen, "Prostitutes and Proletarians," 137.
74. White, *The Comforts of Home,* 46.
75. Liesbeth Hesselink, "Prostitution: A Necessary Evil, Particularly in the Colonies. Views on Prostitution in the Netherlands Indies," in *Indonesian Women in Focus: Past and Present Notions,* ed. Elsbeth Locher-Scholten and Anke Niehof (Dordrecht: Foris, 1987), 206.
76. Philip Howell, "Prostitution and Racialised Sexuality," 325.
77. Henriot, *Prostitution and Sexuality in Shanghai,* 205, 275–78.
78. Dery, "Prostitution in Colonial Manila," 475–89; Kramer, "The Darkness that Enters the Home," 366–404. See also Ken de Bevoise, *Agents of Apocalypse: Epidemic Disease in the Colonial Philippines* (Princeton, NJ: Princeton University Press, 1995), chap. 3; Greg Bankoff, *Crime, Society and the State in the Nineteenth-Century Philippines* (Manila: Atenco de Manila University Press, 1996), chap. 2; Camagay, "Prostitution in Nineteenth Century Manila."
79. Levine, *Prostitution, Race and Politics,* chap. 4; Philippa Levine, "Rereading the 1890s: Venereal Disease as 'Constitutional Crisis' in Britain and British India,"

Journal of Asian Studies 55, no. 3 (1996): 585–612; Martens, "Almost a Public Calamity," 51.

80. Their report was released in 1893 and published in 1899 as *The Queen's Daughters in India*. For a discussion of this episode and the historiography surrounding it, see Levine, *Prostitution, Race and Politics*, 104–7.
81. Levine, *Prostitution, Race and Politics*, 157.
82. Ibid., 163.
83. Ibid., 158.
84. Roger Davidson, "Dealing with the 'Social Evil': Prostitutes and Police in Western Australia, 1895–1924," in Daniels, *So Much Hard Work*, 162–91; Frances, *Selling Sex*, chap. 12.
85. Levine, *Prostitution, Race and Politics*, 166–67.
86. For example, Herschatter, *Dangerous Pleasures*, 206.
87. Levine, "A Multitude of Unchaste Women," 159. See similar sentiments in the Dutch East Indies in Hesselink, "Prostitution: A Necessary Evil," 213.
88. Levine, "A Multitude of Unchaste Women," 160.
89. Howell, "Race, Space and the Regulation of Prostitution," 237.
90. Ibid. While Howell seems to accept these rationalizations, the prohibitive costs of applying the system of regulation to all Hong Kong prostitutes were possibly a more important reason for the limitation. Questions of cost and practicality (i.e., lack of a health department, inadequacy of the police force) were given as the reasons why the system in Shanghai was similarly limited to Chinese prostitutes serving Europeans. See Henriot, *Prostitution and Sexuality in Shanghai*, 276–78.
91. Levine, "A Multitude of Unchaste Women," 161.
92. Frank Proschan, "'Syphilis, Opiomania and Pederasty': Colonial Constructions of Vietnamese (and French) Social Diseases," *Journal of the History of Sexuality* 11, no. 4 (2002): 615.
93. Ibid., 618–19.
94. Ibid., 634.
95. Ibid., 612.
96. Although this view was not unanimously held by the French, see ibid., 626. For an excellent analysis of the meanings of same-sex nonpenetrative thigh sex in the context of immigrant African labor in the Transvaal, see Forman, "Randy on the Rand," 570–609. Forman shows how understandings of same-sex sexual behaviors among male immigrant mine workers (both Chinese and African) were linked to British discourses about the morality of their empire (in contrast to that of the Portuguese) and also to the politics of managing labor relations and racial policy in the Transvaal.
97. Proschan, "Syphilis, Opiomania and Pederasty," 612.
98. Fischer-Tiné, "White Women Degrading Themselves," 178. For the existence of European prostitutes as a serious threat to the status of colonizers, see, for example, Fischer-Tiné, who has detailed references to secondary sources in his footnote on 164. Also see John G. Butcher, *The British in Malaya, 1880–1941: The Social History of a European Community in Colonial Southeast Asia* (Kuala Lumpur: Oxford University Press, 1979), 197.

99. Eileen P. Scully, "Prostitution as Privilege: The 'American Girl' of Treaty-Port Shanghai, 1860–1937," *International History Review* 20 (1998): 874.

100. Frances, *Selling Sex*, 74–77.

101. Louis Franklin Freed, *The Problem of European Prostitution in Johannesburg* (Johannesburg: Juta, 1949), 9.

102. Kramer, "The Darkness that Enters the Home," 378.

103. Fischer-Tiné, "White Women Degrading Themselves," 181. See also Scully, "Prostitution as Privilege," 855–83.

104. David J. Pivar, "The Military, Prostitution, and Colonial Peoples: India and the Philippines, 1885–1917," *Journal of Sex Research* 17, no. 3 (1981): 256–69.

105. Kramer, "The Darkness that Enters the Home," 384.

106. Ingleson, "Prostitution in Colonial Java," 131. See also Hesselink, "Prostitution: A Necessary Evil," 211.

107. Herschatter, *Dangerous Pleasures*, 11, 171–75.

108. Gupta, *Sexuality, Obscenity, Community*, 108–22. See also Whitehead, "Bodies Clean and Unclean," 41–63.

109. Robert Gregg, "Apropos Exceptionalism: Imperial Location and Comparative Histories of South Africa and the United States," in *Inside Out, Outside In: Essays in Comparative History* (London: Macmillan, 2000), 17. See also Anne McClintock, "Family Feuds: Gender, Nationalism, and the Family," *Feminist Review* 44 (1993): 61; Donna J. Guy, "'White Slavery,' Citizenship and Nationality in Argentina," in *Nationalisms and Sexualities,* ed. Andrew Parker, Mary Russo, Doris Summer, and Patricia Yaeger (London: Routledge, 1992), 201–17; Donna J. Guy, *Sex and Danger in Buenos Aires: Prostitution, Family, and Nation in Argentina* (Lincoln: University of Nebraska Press, 1991).

110. For Thursday Island, see Frances, *Selling Sex*, 76; for the Turkish consul, see S. M. Edwardes, *Crime in India* (London: Oxford University Press, 1924), 87.

111. Gregg, "Apropos Exceptionalism," 17.

112. Raelene Frances, "White Australia and the White Slave Traffic: Gender, Race and Citizenship," *International Review of Social History* 44, Supplement (1999): 101–22.

113. For a discussion of this dialectic between imperial ambitions and the resistance of the colonized, see B.S.A. Yeoh, *Contesting Space: Power Relations and the Urban Built Environment in Colonial Singapore* (Kuala Lumpur: National University of Singapore, 1996).

Chapter 9

1. The terms "erotica," "pornography," and "pornographers" entered the English language in the mid-nineteenth century. The word "pornography" appeared for the first time in 1842, and "pornographers" in 1847, while the second edition of *The Oxford English Dictionary* dates the first English use of "erotica" to 1854. Class has been central to the label of "erotica," with connotations of high art and literature, as opposed to the label "pornography" as obscene, lewd, cheap smut. I use both

terms in this chapter. I tend to use "erotica" when publishers, readers, viewers, and distributors used this term themselves and use "pornography" when it was used by contemporaries—either by moral reformers, police, or others; however, moral reformers tended to use "obscene" or "indecent" much more extensively. Julie Peakman defines pornography as "material that contains graphic descriptions of sexual organs and/or action written with the prime intention of sexually exciting the reader." See Julie Peakman, *Mighty Lewd Books: The Development of Pornography in Eighteenth-Century England* (Hampshire, UK: Palgrave Macmillan, 2003), 5–7. On the origins of the word "pornography," see *The Oxford English Dictionary*. Walter Kendrick, *The Secret Museum* (Berkeley: University of California Press, 1996), 1–2, 17, 244.

2. For an outline of David Scott Mitchell's erotica collection and the library's handling of it, see Ruth Ford, "Contested Desires: Narratives of Passionate Friends, Married Masqueraders and Lesbian Love in Australia, 1918–1945" (Ph.D. thesis, La Trobe University, 2000), 31–48.

3. See Steven Marcus, *The Other Victorians: A Study of Sexuality and Pornography in Mid-Nineteenth-Century England* (London: Corgi Books, 1970); Ronald Pearsall, *The Worm in the Bud: The World of Victorian Sexuality* (London: Weidenfeld and Nicolson, 1969), 364–415; Ronald Pearsall, *Public Purity, Private Shame: Victorian Sexual Hypocrisy Exposed* (London: Weidenfeld and Nicolson, 1976); Patrick J. Kearney, *The Private Case: An Annotated Bibliography of the Private Case Erotica Collection in the British (Museum) Library* (London: J. Landesman, 1981); Kendrick, *The Secret Museum*; Lisa Z. Sigel, *Governing Pleasures: Pornography and Social Change in England, 1815–1914* (New Brunswick, NJ: Rutgers University Press, 2002).

4. See Raelene Frances, "Prostitution in the Age of Empires," in this volume.

5. On nineteenth-century Britain and Europe, see Lynn Hunt, "Obscenity and the Origins of Modernity, 1500–1800," in *The Invention of Pornography: Obscenity and the Origins of Modernity, 1500–1800,* ed. Lynn Hunt (New York: Zone Books, 1993), 10–3; Lynn Hunt, "Pornography and the French Revolution," in Hunt, *The Invention of Pornography*, 302–5; Kendrick, *The Secret Museum*, 31; Peter Gay, *The Bourgeois Experience: Victoria to Freud,* vol. 1 of *Education of the Senses* (Oxford: Oxford University Press, 1984), 358–79. On the United States, see Colette Colligan, *Traffic in Obscenity from Byron to Beardsley: Sexuality and Exoticism in Nineteenth-Century Print Culture* (New York: Palgrave Macmillan, 2006); Helen Lefkowitz Horowitz, *Rereading Sex: Battles over Sexual Knowledge and Suppression in Nineteenth-Century America* (New York: Vintage, 2003).

6. See Marcus, *The Other Victorians;* Kendrick, *The Secret Museum;* Patrick J. Kearney, *A History of Erotic Literature* (London: Macmillan, 1982); Pearsall, *Public Purity, Private Shame;* Sigel, *Governing Pleasures.*

7. "Porn as a regulatory category was invented in response to the perceived menace of the democratisation of culture," argues Lynn Hunt. "It was only when print culture opened the possibility of the masses gaining access to writing and pictures …, when it began to seem possible that anything at all might be shown to anybody," that new classifications, regulation, and censoring, via obscenity laws,

emerged. Hunt, "Obscenity and the Origins of Modernity," 10; Kendrick, *The Secret Museum*, 57.

8. Hunt argues that nineteenth-century English moral reformers were "determined to keep dangerous literature out of the hands of women and children." Hunt, "Obscenity and the Origins of Modernity," 45; Hunt, "Pornography and the French Revolution," 305.

9. Iain McCalman, "Unrespectable Radicalism: Infidels and Pornography in Early Nineteenth-Century London," *Past and Present* 104 (1984): 74–110.

10. Hunt, "Obscenity and the Origins of Modernity," 10–13; Hunt, "Pornography and the French Revolution," 302–5. See also Kendrick, *The Secret Museum*, 31.

11. In *Public Purity, Private Shame*, Pearsall notes the high costs of images in Britain in the 1840s through the 1860s.

12. Kearney, *A History of Erotic Literature*, 112.

13. Jason Goldman, "'The Golden Age of Gay Porn': Nostalgia and the Photography of Wilhelm von Gloeden," *GLQ: A Journal of Lesbian and Gay Studies* 12, no. 2 (2006): 237–58.

14. The shunga were usually produced in the form of scrolls, series of prints of twelve scenes, or illustrated books, not as images in isolation. Tom Evans and Mary Anne Evans, *Shunga: The Art of Love in Japan* (New York: Paddington Press, 1975), 8–9.

15. In its depiction of the sexual practices that formed part of Japanese culture, shunga ukiyo-e have been interpreted very differently by Western commentators. Tom Evans and Mary Anne Evans argue that shunga were regarded as everyday art, a joyous celebration of sexuality rather than forbidden erotica, and that "there was no equivalent to the Western concept of pornography, and no connection was made between moral corruption and the representation of sex." Evans and Evans, *Shunga*, However, David Bell argues that shunga "were considered at best vulgar, more usually as obscene," and were banned by the government throughout the period of their production in Tokugawa Japan. David Bell, review of *Japanese Erotic Fantasies: Sexual Imagery of the Edo Period*, *New Zealand Journal of Asian Studies* 10, no. 1 (2003): 150–58; David Bell, "Ukiyo-e in New Zealand," *New Zealand Journal of Asian Studies* 10, no. 1 (2008): 33.

16. Joshua Mostow, "The Gender of Wakashu and the Grammar of Desire," in *Gender and Power in the Japanese Visual Field*, ed. Joshua Mostow, Norman Bryson, and Maribeth Graybill (Honolulu: University of Hawaii Press, 2003); David Bell, review of *Gender and Power in the Japanese Visual Field*, *New Zealand Journal of Asian Studies* 5, no. 2 (2003): 197–201.

17. Julie Davis, *Utamaro and the Spectacle of Beauty* (Honolulu: University of Hawaii Press, 2005), 198; David Bell, "The Source and the Period Eye: New Perspectives on Japanese Visual Culture," *New Zealand Journal of Asian Studies* 10, no. 2 (2008): 138–40.

18. De Goncourt's works were on the Japanese artists Kitagawa Utamaro and Katsushika Hokusai. Shunga prints were also collected by many artists, including Aubrey Beardsley, Edgar Degas, Henri de Toulouse-Lautrec, Gustave Klimt, Auguste Rodin, Pablo Picasso, and Vincent van Gough. Edmond de Goncourt, *Utamaro: Le peintre*

des maisons vertes (Paris, 1891); Edmond de Goncourt, *Hokusai* (Paris, 1896); Anon., *Japanische Erotik: Sechsunddreisig Holzschnitts von Moronubu, Harunobu, Utamaro* (Munich, 1907); Evans and Evans, *Shunga*.

19. During the Meiji period (1868–1912) while Europeans were collecting shunga, it was banned in Japan, although it continued to be produced furtively. The Evanses argue that the rejection of ukiyo-e in the Meiji period enabled Western collections to be made. They suggest that a number of (unpublicized) donations of shunga to major museums in Europe occurred when heirs and executors found collections of ukiyo-e among their relatives' collections. Evans and Evans, *Shunga*, 268.

20. Bell notes that such collections reveal a facet of colonial processes, as "collecting activities were instrumental in establishing world views that rationalised and justified colonisation," and that the development of archives and libraries was closely linked to the role of knowledge in establishing power relations. Bell, "Ukiyo-e in New Zealand," 36.

21. Research on imports of Japanese material (general and shunga) to New Zealand, another colony in Australasia, indicates that material was exported directly from Japan as well as via a very circuitous route involving countries on the other side of the world. David Bell notes that one eminent New Zealander's collection of ukiyo-e was not obtained directly from Japan but was imported via the United States, while James Beattie identifies direct import of Japanese material artifacts and plants. Sigel notes that by the end of the nineteenth century, America began to focus on issues of the "other" located in the Far East in a manner similar to the ways British pornography focused on India. Bell, "Ukiyo-e in New Zealand," 36; Sigel, *Governing Pleasures*, 178; J. Beattie, J. Heinzen, and J. P. Adam, "Japanese Gardens in New Zealand, 1850–1950: Transculturation and Transmission," *Studies in the History of Gardens and Designed Landscapes* 28, no. 2 (2008): 219–36.

22. Jack Lindsay, *The Roaring Twenties: Literary Life in Sydney, New South Wales in the Years 1921–6* (London: Bodley Head, 1960), 48.

23. None of these works appeared in Mitchell's collection; however, the *Kama Sutra* appeared in the collection of Sir William Dixon, another upper-class gentleman from the colony of New South Wales who had a significant collection of both erotic literature and imagery. Ford, "Contested Desires"; Sigel, *Governing Pleasures*, 65–67, 176.

24. Sigel, *Governing Pleasures*. Richard Burton's Orientalist discussions of what happens in brothels and Charles de Montesquieu's fictious *Lettres persanes* (1721) are similar.

25. Stanley Burns and Elizabeth Burns, *Geisha: A Photographic History, 1872–1912* (Brooklyn, NY: Power House Books, 2006).

26. See Eleanor Hight, "The Many Lives of Beato's 'Beauties,'" in *Colonialist Photography: Imag(in)ing Race and Place*, ed. Eleanor Hight and Gary Sampson (London: Routledge, 2002); Burns and Burns, *Geisha*.

27. In 1862, two photographic studios were opened by Japanese men in Nagasaki and Yokoham and by 1870 there were over one hundred studios, which catered mainly to foreign residents and tourists. By 1886 most photographic studios were Japanese-operated ones. Western tourism to Japan increased during the 1880s and peaked

during the 1890s and tourist photographs and postcards were popular souvenirs. In 1897, 24,923 photographs were exported to America and 20,242 to Europe. Alongside souvenir photo albums produced for export with photographs of "traditional customs and scenes, Japanese beauties, and famous views," underground brothel photographs were evidently taken and exported. On the history of photography in Japan, see Philbert Ono, "Chronological History of Photography in Japan in 1868–1919 (Meiji 1–Taisho 8)," http://photoguide.jp/txt/PhotoHistory_1868-1919; Anne Tucker, ed., *The History of Japanese Photography* (New Haven, CT: Yale University Press in association with the Museum of Fine Arts, Houston, 2003). On the history of pornography in Japan, 1890–1910, see Keisho Ishiguro, *Meijiki No Porunogurafi [Pornography in the Meiji Era]* (Tokyo: Shinchosha, 1996).

28. While there are significant differences in composition, framing, and props, this material from Japan has some similarities with the genre of European brothel photography and with another genre of Orientalist photography: opium dens.

29. See Raeline Frances's discussion of Japan supplying a large number of women to brothels operating (outside Japan) throughout the Asia-Pacific region in "Prostitution: The Age of Empires."

30. Edward Said, *Orientalism: Western Conceptions of the Orient* (London: Penguin, 1995).

31. The view of the eminent painter Sir Arthur Streeton was that the Orient was "dangerously enervating, feminine, passive, a seductive place where masculinity might go limp." Quoted in Alison Broinowski, *The Yellow Lady: Australian Impressions of Asia* (Melbourne: Oxford University Press, 1992), vi, 5.

32. Racial prejudice and fears were evident in the 1901 Immigration Restriction Act, which restricted the entry of Chinese, Japanese, and Indians—and all peoples labeled "Asiatics"—to Australia; the 1902 Australian Franchise Act, which denied political rights to natives of Asia; and official reports describing the "degrading customs" and "vicious tendencies" of the Chinese, brutal violence and riots in which Europeans physically attacked Chinese (men) and burned their tents and stores. See Marilyn Lake and Henry Reynolds, *Drawing the Global Colour Line: White Men's Countries and the Question of Racial Equality* (Carlton, Vic.: Melbourne University Press, 2008).

33. On photography and anthropology, see Elizabeth Edwards, ed., *Anthropology and Photography, 1860–1920* (New Haven, CT: Yale University Press, 1992); Hight and Sampson, *Colonialist Photography;* Anne Maxwell, *Colonial Photography and Exhibitions: Representations of the "Native" and the Making of European Identities* (London: Leicester University Press, 1999); Raymond Corbey, "Ethnographic Showcases," *Cultural Anthropology* 8, no. 3 (1993): 338–69; Raymond Corbey, "Alterity: The Colonial Nude," *Critique of Anthropology* 8, no. 3 (1988): 75–92; Melissa Banta and Curtis Hinsley, eds., *From Site to Sight: Anthropology, Photography and the Power of Imagery* (Cambridge, MA: Peabody Museum Press, 1986), 58–65.

34. Mitchell owned a copy of Richard von Krafft-Ebing, *Psychopathia Sexualis: With Especial Reference to Contrary Sexual Instinct: A Medico-legal Study* (Philadelphia: F. A. Davis, 1893).

35. Sigel, *Governing Pleasures*.

36. Mitchell's collection included other anthropological works dealing with sexual practices in other cultures, including Hubert Howe Bancroft's *Native Races of the Pacific States* (vols. 1–5, 1874), which detailed the treatment of homosexuality and other sexual issues in Pacific Coast Native American tribes. The nineteenth century saw a trend toward "armchair anthropology" of an erotic nature, with works such as Hermann Ploss's very widely distributed *Das Weib, in der Natur-und Völkerkunde* [*Woman in Natural History and Folklore*], 2 vols. (Leipzig: Griebens, 1884), detailing sexual practices in many cultures (although Mitchell didn't own this). While relating to this genre of anthropology, *Untrodden Fields* was a known erotic text. Anon., *Untrodden Fields of Anthropology: Observations on the Esoteric Manners and Customs of Semi-civilised Peoples; Being a Record of 30 Years' Experience in Asia, Africa, America and Oceania* (Paris: Librairie des Bibliophiles, 1896).

37. The author, listed as an unnamed "French army surgeon," was Charles Carrington (Paul Ferdinando). Carrington had set up a shop in Paris in 1895 following crackdowns by police and conducted an expansive mail order trade via catalogs and intermediaries in London. Kearney, *A History of Erotic Literature*, 156; Sigel, *Governing Pleasures*, 84.

38. See Siobhan Somerville, "Scientific Racism and the Emergence of the Homosexual Body," *Journal of the History of Sexuality* 5, no. 2 (1994): 243–66.

39. Anon., *Untrodden Fields of Anthropology*, x, xiv.

40. Ibid., 323–24, 339–40.

41. Joanna de Groot, "'Sex' and 'Race': The Construction of Language and Image in the Ninetenth Century," in *Cultures of Empire: A Reader: Colonisers in Britain and the Empire in the Nineteenth and Twentieth Centuries*, ed. Catherine Hall (Manchester: Manchester University Press, 2000), 46–50.

42. Nicholas Thomas, "Colonial Conversions: Difference, Hierarchy, and History in Early Twentieth-Century Evangelical Propaganda," in Hall, *Cultures of Empire*, 298; Edwards, *Anthropology and Photography*.

43. Sigel also argues that "the combination of imperialism, sadism, and sexism signalled the emergence of a new relationship between sexuality and society; the word and the flesh became bound together quite literally and figuratively to form a new type of pornography." Sigel, *Governing Pleasures*, 50.

44. Ibid., 60.

45. Malek Alloula, *The Colonial Harem* (Minneapolis: University of Minnesota Press, 1986).

46. Sigel, *Governing Pleasures*.

47. Anne McClintock, *Imperial Leather: Race, Gender and Sexuality in the Colonial Contest* (New York: Routledge, 1995).

48. The first issue of the *Pearl*, an illustrated Victorian erotic periodical published in Britain from 1879 to 1880, included a color lithograph illustration of four women of color providing—or about to provide—sexual services to two white men. Sigel's study of nineteenth-century Britain identifies images of interracial sex in catalogs. Perhaps these were more threatening for a colonial to purchase. Kearney, *A History of Erotic Literature*, 104; Sigel, *Governing Pleasures*, 99.

49. As McClintock notes in relation to Arthur Mumby in *Imperial Leather*, 132–80.

50. See Lake and Reynolds, *Drawing the Global Colour Line*.

51. On exoticizing the class "other" and the racial "other," see McClintock's discussion of Hannah Cullick and Arthur Mumby. McClintock, *Imperial Leather*, 132–80.

52. Goldman, "The Golden Age of Gay Porn."

53. Ibid., 252; Patricia Berman, "F. Holland Day and His 'Classical' Models: Summer Camp," *History of Photography* 18 (1994): 353. Robert Aldrich argues that during von Gloeden's time, "the Mediterranean, especially Italy, provided a destination for many homosexual authors and artists who fled their home countries. The hospitality of Italy to their interests, sexual and cultural, was closely connected to the socioeconomic conditions there." Robert Aldrich, *The Seduction of the Mediterranean: Writing, Art and Homosexual Fantasy* (London: Routledge, 1993), x.

54. Customs Act 1857 [Victoria], sections 34, 165.

55. *Age*, July 6, 1875; August 3, 1875; August 6, 1875.

56. Frances makes this point in relation to prostitution and the international traffic in sex workers and the global mobility of clients. See Frances, "Prostitution in the Age of Empires."

57. Colligan argues that it was post-1870s international legislation that specified prints, paintings, photographs, postcards, and lithographic or other engravings, but in the Australian colonies it was earlier, although photographs were not included until the 1880s. Colligan, *Traffic in Obscenity*, 12.

58. Persons importing, shipping, or having custody of such goods were to be fined £100 at the election of the customs commissioner. The colony of Victoria's 1883 Customs Act included the prohibited list and fines of the earlier 1857 act, as well as incorporating a clause regarding the destruction of prohibited goods. Customs Act 1857 [Victoria], sections 34, 165.

59. *Brisbane Courier*, November 2, 1880.

60. On the American 1873 Comstock Act, see Kendrick, *The Secret Museum*, 125–57; Horowitz, *Rereading Sex;* John D'Emilio and Estelle Freedman, *Intimate Matters: A History of Sexuality in America* (New York: Perennial Library, 1989), 159–60.

61. Colligan, *Traffic in Obscenity*, 12.

62. *Age*, November 23, 1862.

63. *Age*, March 3, 1870.

64. *Age*, October 30, 1868.

65. *Age*, March 3, 1870.

66. *Age*, February 5, 1875; February 6, 1875.

67. *Age*, April 5, 1881; May 7, 1881.

68. *Age*, May 7, 1884.

69. The circulation of Japanese erotic material in a period of intense anti-Japanese sentiment awaits investigation by scholars.

70. Pearsall, *The Worm in the Bud*.

71. Hunt is referring to the sixteenth to eighteenth centuries here. Hunt, "Obscenity and the Origins of Modernity," 44.

72. Peakman, *Mighty Lewd Books*.

73. Colligan acknowledges the rich body of erotic writing and imagery in Britain in the eighteenth century, some of which faced legal prosecution, but notes that before the nineteenth century, obscenity in Britain was dealt with by common law. Colligan, *Traffic in Obscenity*, 10.

74. Ibid., 28.

75. Ibid., 11.

76. Quoted in ibid.

77. The preamble to the act emphasized the expediency of granting additional powers "for the suppression of the trade in books prints drawings and other obscene articles." The act granted power to any police magistrate or justices of the peace to issue a search warrant where a complainant had reason to believe that "any obscene books papers newspapers pamphlets magazines periodicals letter-press writings prints pictures photographs lithographs drawings or other representations are kept in any house shop room or other place" for the purpose of sale, distribution, exhibition, lending, or "being otherwise published" for "purpose of gain." Obscenity Act 1876 (Act 40 Vic. No. 544), sections 1, 2.

78. It was similar to the 1876 Victorian Act in granting power to seize and destroy obscene material and prosecute the individuals who possessed such material, and for fines but had lesser imprisonment periods of three months' imprisonment for a first offense and six months' imprisonment for a second or subsequent offense. Obscene Publications Act (NSW), 1880 (Act 43 Vic. No. 24), "An Act for more effectually preventing the Sale of Obscene Books Pictures Prints and other Articles."

79. Ibid.

80. Penalties were £20 or three months' imprisonment for a first offense, and £50 or six months' imprisonment for a second or subsequent offense. After the Federal Act, following Federation of Australian colonies in 1901, states also passed new legislation.

81. Chapter 22—Offences against Morality Section 204—Obscene publications and Exhibitions. 1902 Criminal Code (Western Australia), Act No. 14 of 1902.

82. Kendrick, *The Secret Museum*, 134.

83. *Age*, November 16, 1869.

84. *Age*, July 28, 1870; July 29, 1870.

85. The senior customs officer stated that "during the last fourteen or fifteen months, he had seized indecent slides, prints, and c., to the value of between £6000 and £7000; but in the majority of these cases a fine of £100 was levied by consent, and the parties were not proceeded against at the police." *Age*, October 7, 1865.

86. *Age*, November 4, 1865.

87. See Sigel, *Governing Pleasures*.

88. Lynda Nead, *Victorian Babylon: People, Streets and Images in Nineteenth-Century London* (New Haven, CT: Yale University Press, 2000), 182.

89. The provenance of the photograph is unknown, but the other images in the scrapbook are newspaper cuttings, predominantly from the 1920s and 1930s. The clippings are mostly about adventurous and independent career women—both single and married—who rejected conventional feminine roles and dress and expectations of motherhood and domesticity. The scrapbooks emphasize women

undertaking activities traditionally seen as masculine; women claiming masculine privileges in work, dress, sports, and recreation; and women eschewing the traditional feminine domestic sphere. There are also articles about theatrical cross-dressing and male impersonators and women who claimed the masculine privileges of male wages, social circles, and sexual access to women by passing as men and marrying others of their sex. Ruth Ford, "Speculating on Scrapbooks, Sex and Desire: Issues in Lesbian History," *Australian Historical Studies* 106 (1996): 111–26; Ford, "Contested Desires."

90. *Age*, October 30, 1868.

91. *Age*, April 5, 1881; May 7, 1881.

92. Kendrick makes this point. Kendrick, *The Secret Museum*, 119–26.

93. Erik Norgaard, *With Love: The Erotic Postcard* (London: MacGibbon and Kee, 1969), 6; Paul Hammond, *French Undressing: Naughty Postcards from 1900 to 1920* (London: Bloomsbury Books, 1988).

94. Norman Lindsay, *My Mask: For What Little I Know of the Man behind It* (Sydney: Angus and Robertson, 1970); James Cockington, *Banned: Tales from the Bizarre History of Australian Obscenity* (Sydney: ABC Books for the Australian Broadcasting Corporation, 2005), 5.

95. Norgaard, *With Love*, 6–10.

96. William Ouellette, *Fantasy Postcards* (London: Sphere, 1976), 56.

97. Lindsay, *My Mask;* Cockington, *Banned*, 5–6.

98. Alloula, *The Colonial Harem*, 78–94.

99. Ouellette, *Fantasy Postcards*, 64.

100. Sigel, *Governing Pleasures*, 123.

101. Ouellette, *Fantasy Postcards*, 56.

102. Ibid.

103. *Age*, April 16, 1920.

104. *Argus.*

105. *Age*, May 11, 1920; June 10, 1920; June 11, 1920.

106. On 1890s "cartomania," see Sigel, *Governing Pleasures*, 119.

107. Lynda Nead, "Strip: Moving Bodies in the 1890s," *Early Popular Visual Culture* 3, no. 2 (2005): 135–50. See also Jill Julius Matthews, "Blue Movies in Australia: A Preliminary Study," *National Film and Sound Archive Journal* 2, no. 3 (2007): 1–12.

108. Gorky (1896), quoted in Simon Brown, "Early Cinema in Britain and the Smoking Concert Film," *Early Popular Visual Culture* 3, no. 2 (2005): 166.

109. The film was directed by Albert Kirchner, who traded in risqué postcards. Brown, "Early Cinema in Britain."

110. Stephen Bottomore notes that one such film (probably Pirou's) had to be withdrawn from a London music hall in 1897 "after protests from the more respectable clientele." Stephen Bottomore, "Eugène Pirou," in *Who's Who of Victorian Cinema: A Worldwide Survey,* ed. Stephen Herbert and Luke McKernan (London: British Film Institute, 1996), 112.

111. Brown, "Early Cinema in Britain," 167.

112. Ibid.

113. Stephen Bottomore, "Archives Section: Morals and Moving Pictures (1910),"
     Early Popular Visual Culture 3, no. 2 (2005): 197; Ina Bertrand, "Government
     Regulation of Film Exhibition in Australia to 1960" (Ph.D. thesis, La Trobe
     University, 1973); Ina Bertrand, *Government and Film in Australia* (Sydney:
     Currency Press, 1981).
114. A. Di Lauro and G. Rabkin, *Dirty Movies: An Illustrated History of the Stag
     Film, 1915–1970* (New York: Chelsea House, 1976).
115. Thanks to Craig Brittain and Jill Matthews for sharing their ideas about this film.
     See Matthews, "Blue Movies in Australia."
116. Brown, "Early Cinema in Britain."
117. "Frenzy of the visible" is Williams's phrase. Linda Williams, *Hard Core: Power,
     Pleasure, and the "Frenzy of the Visible"* (Berkeley: University of California Press,
     1989), 36.

BIBLIOGRAPHY

Acton, William. *The Functions and Disorders of the Reproductive Organs in Child- hood, Adult Age and Advanced Life Considered in Their Physiological, Social and Moral Relations*. London: John Churchill and Sons, 1865.

Acton, William. *Prostitution Considered in Its Moral, Social, and Sanitary Aspects*. London: John Churchill and Sons, 1870.

Adilman, Tamara. "A Preliminary Sketch of Chinese Women and Work in British Columbia, 1858–1950." In *Not Just Pin Money: Selected Essays on the History of Women's Work in British Columbia*, edited by Barbara K. Latham and Robert J. Pazdro. Victoria, BC: Camosun College, 1984.

Aldrich, Robert. *Colonialism and Homosexuality*. London: Routledge, 2003.

Aldrich, Robert. "Homosexuality in the French Colonies." In *Homosexuality in French History and Culture*, edited by Jeffrey Merrick and Michael Sibalis. London: Harrington Park Press, 2001.

Aldrich, Robert. *The Seduction of the Mediterranean: Writing, Art and Homosexual Fantasy*. London: Routledge, 1993.

Alloula, Malek. *The Colonial Harem*. Minneapolis: University of Minnesota Press, 1986.

Anagol, Padma. *The Emergence of Feminism in India, 1850–1920*. Aldershot, UK: Ashgate, 2006.

Anderson, John. *Happy Childhood: The Development and Guidance of Children and Youth*. New York: D. Appleton-Century, 1933.

Anderson, Patricia. *When Passion Reigned: Sex and the Victorians*. New York: Basic Books, 1995.

Anon. *Japanische Erotik: Sechsunddreisig Holzschnitts von Moronubu, Harunobu, Utamaro*. Munich, 1907.

Anon. *Startling Truths on the White Slave Traffic*. London: Success Publishing, c. 1912.

Anon. *Untrodden Fields of Anthropology: Observations on the Esoteric Manners and Customs of Semi-civilised Peoples; Being a Record of 30 Years' Experience in Asia, Africa, America and Oceania*. Paris: Librairie des Bibliophiles, 1896.

Apffel-Marglin, Frédérique. *Wives of the God King: The Rituals of the Devadasis of Puri*. Delhi: Oxford University Press, 1985.

Aries, Philippe. *Centuries of Childhood: A Social History of Family Life*. New York: Knopf, 1962.

Armstrong, David. *Political Anatomy of the Body: Medical Knowledge in Britain in the Twentieth Century*. Cambridge: Cambridge University Press, 1983.

Arthur, Richard. *The Choice: A Purity Booklet for Young Men*. Sydney: William Brooks, 1903.

Arthur, Richard. *The Needed Change in the Age of Consent: An Appeal for the Better Protection of Our Girls*. Sydney: Christian World Press, 1896.

Arthur, R. *The Training of Children in Purity: A Booklet for Parents*. Melbourne: George Robertson, n.d.

Backhouse, Constance B. "Nineteenth-Century Canadian Prostitution Law: Reflections of a Discriminatory Society." *Histoire Sociale/Social History* 18, no. 36 (1985): 387–423.

Bakshi, Parminder. "Homosexuality and Orientalism: Edward Carpenter's Journey to the East." *Prose Studies* 13, no. 1 (1990): 155–77.

Ballhatchet, Kenneth. *Race, Sex and Class under the Raj: Imperial Attitudes and Policies and Their Critics, 1793–1905*. London: Weidenfeld and Nicolson, 1980.

Banerjee, Sumanta. *Under the Raj: Prostitution in Colonial Bengal*. New York: Monthly Review Press, 1998.

Bankoff, Greg. *Crime, Society and the State in the Nineteenth-Century Philippines*. Manila: Atenco de Manila University Press, 1996.

Bannerji, Himani. "Age of Consent and Hegemonic Social Reform." In *Gender and Imperialism*, edited by Clare Midgeley. Manchester: Manchester University Press, 1998.

Banta, Melissa, and Curtis Hinsley, eds. *From Site to Sight: Anthropology, Photography and the Power of Imagery*. Cambridge, MA: Peabody Museum Press, 1986.

Barclay, Enid. "Queensland's Contagious Diseases Act, 1868—'The Act for the Encouragement of Vice' and Some Nineteenth Century Attempts to Repeal It, Part 1." *Queensland Heritage* 2, 10 (1974): 27–34.

Barclay, Enid. "Queensland's Contagious Diseases Act, 1868—'The Act for the Encouragement of Vice' and Some Nineteenth Century Attempts to Repeal It, Part 2." *Queensland Heritage* 3, no. 1 (1974): 21–29.

Barker-Benfield, G. J. *The Culture of Sensibility: Sex and Society in Eighteenth-Century Britain*. Chicago: University of Chicago Press, 1996.

Barret-Ducrocq, Françoise. *Love in the Tome of Victoria: Sexuality, Class, and Gender in Nineteenth-Century London*. Translated by John Howe. London: Verso, 1991.

Bartley, Paula. *Prostitution: Prevention and Reform in England, 1860–1914*. London: Routledge, 1999.

Bashford, A., and C. Strange. "Public Pedagogy: Sex Education and Mass Communication in the Mid-Twentieth Century." *Journal of the History of Sexuality* 13, no. 1
(2004): 71–99.

Bauer, Heike. *English Literary Sexology: Translations of Inversion, 1860–1930.* London: Palgrave Macmillan, 2009.

Beattie, J., J. Heinzen, and J. P. Adam. "Japanese Gardens in New Zealand, 1850–1950:
Transculturation and Transmission." *Studies in the History of Gardens and Designed Landscapes* 28, no. 2 (2008): 219–36.

Beccalossi, Chiara. *Female Sexual Inversion: Same-Sex Desires in Italian and British
Sexology, ca. 1870–1920.* Basingstoke, UK: Palgrave Macmillan, forthcoming.

Beccalossi, Chiara. "Havelock Ellis: Sexual Inverts as Independent Women." In *Tribades, Tommies and Transgressives*, edited by Mary McAuliffe and Sonja Tiernan.
Vol. 1 of *History of Sexualities*. Newcastle, UK: Cambridge Scholars Press,
2008.

Beccalossi, Chiara. "Nineteenth-Century European Psychiatry on Same-Sex Desires: Pathology, Abnormality, Normality and the Blurring of Boundaries." *Psychology &
Sexuality* (forthcoming).

Beccalossi, Chiara. "The Origin of Italian Sexological Studies: Female Sexual Inversion,
ca. 1870–1900." *Journal of the History of Sexuality* 18 (2009): 103–20.

Beecher, C., and Beecher Stowe, H. *The American Woman's Home: A Guide to the
Formation and Maintenance of Economical, Healthful, Beautiful and Christian
Homes.* Watkins Glen, NY: Library of Victorian Culture American Life Founda-
tion, 1869.

Bell, David. Review of *Gender and Power in the Japanese Visual Field*. New Zealand
Journal of Asian Studies 5, no. 2 (2003): 197–201.

Bell, David. Review of *Japanese Erotic Fantasies: Sexual Imagery of the Edo Period.*
New Zealand Journal of Asian Studies 10, no. 1 (2003): 150–58.

Bell, David. "The Source and the Period Eye: New Perspectives on Japanese Visual
Culture." *New Zealand Journal of Asian Studies* 10, no. 2 (2008): 132–58.

Bell, David. "Ukiyo-e in New Zealand." *New Zealand Journal of Asian Studies* 10,
no. 1 (2008): 28–53.

Bell, Diane. *Daughters of the Dreaming.* Sydney: Allen & Unwin, 1983.

Bell, Sanford. "A Preliminary Study of the Emotion of Love between the Sexes." *American Journal of Psychology* 13, no. 3 (1902): 325–54.

Benn, Miriam. *Predicaments of Love.* London: Pluto Press, 1992.

Berger, Mark T. "Imperialism and Sexual Exploitation: A Response to Ronald Hyam's
'Empire and Sexual Opportunity.'" *Journal of Imperial Commonwealth History* 17,
no. 1 (1988): 83–99.

Berman, Patricia. "F. Holland Day and His 'Classical' Models: Summer Camp." *History
of Photography* 18 (1994): 348–67.

Bersani, Leo. *Homos.* Cambridge, MA: Harvard University Press, 1995.

Bersani, Leo. "Is the Rectum a Grave?" *October* 43 (1987): 197–222.

Bertrand, Ina. *Government and Film in Australia.* Sydney: Currency Press, 1981.

Bertrand, Ina. "Government Regulation of Film Exhibition in Australia to 1960." Ph.D.
thesis, La Trobe University, 1973.

Bevoise, Ken de. *Agents of Apocalypse: Epidemic Disease in the Colonial Philippines.* Princeton, NJ: Princeton University Press, 1995.

Bigelow, Maurice. *Sex-Education: A Series of Lectures Concerning Knowledge of Sex in Its Relation to Human Life.* New York: Macmillan, 1916.

Binet, A. "Le fetischisme dans l'amour." *Revue Philosophique* 24 (1887): 143–67, 252–74.

Blackwell, Elizabeth. *Christian Duty in Regard to Vice.* London: Moral Reform Union, 1891.

Blackwell, Elizabeth. *Counsel to Parents on the Moral Education of Their Children in Relation to Sex.* 7th ed. London: Hatchards Piccadilly, 1884.

Blackwell, Elizabeth. *Essays in Medical Sociology.* London: Ernest Bell, 1902.

Blair-Bell, William. *The Sex Complex: A Study of the Relationships of the Internal Secretions to the Female Characteristics and Function in Health and Disease.* London: Baillière, Tindall and Cox, 1916.

Blamires, David. "Some German and English Travesties of Struwwelpeter." In *Connections: Essays in Honour of Eda Sagarra on the Occasion of Her 60th Birthday,* ed. Peter Skrine, Rosemary Wallbank-Turner, and Jonathon West. Stuttgart: Hans-Dieter Heinz Akademischer Verlag, 1993.

Bland, Lucy. *Banishing the Beast: English Feminism and Sexual Morality, 1885–1914.* London: Penguin, 1995.

Bland, Lucy, and Laura Doan, eds. *Sexology in Culture: Labelling Bodies and Desires.* Cambridge: Polity Press, 1998.

Bloch, Iwan. *Sex Life in England.* New York: Gargoyle Press, 1934.

Boas, George. *The Cult of Childhood.* London: Warburg Institute, 1966.

Boritch, Helen. *Fallen Women: Female Crime and Criminal Justice in Canada.* Toronto: ITP Nelson, 1997.

Borris, Kenneth, and George Rousseau, eds. *The Sciences of Homosexualities in Early Modern Europe.* London: Routledge, 2008.

Bottomore, Stephen. "Archives Section: Morals and Moving Pictures (1910)." *Early Popular Visual Culture* 3, no. 2 (2005): 197–205.

Bottomore, Stephen. "Eugène Pirou." In *Who's Who of Victorian Cinema: A World-wide Survey,* edited by Stephen Herbert and Luke McKernan. London: British Film Institute, 1996.

Boyer, P. S. *Purity in Print: The Vice Society Movement and Book Censorship in America.* New York: Charles Scribner's Sons, 1968.

Brady, Sean, ed. *John Addington Symonds (1840–1893) and Homosexuality: A Critical Edition of Sources.* Basingstoke, UK: Palgrave Macmillan, forthcoming.

Brady, Sean. *Masculinity and Male Homosexuality in Britain, 1861–1913.* Basingstoke, UK: Palgrave Macmillan, 2005.

Bristow, Edward J. *Vice and Vigilance: Purity Movements in Britain since 1700.* Dublin: Gill and Macmillan, 1977.

Bristow, Joseph. *Sexuality.* London: Routledge, 1997.

British Parliamentary Papers, 1884–1885, XXX.1. Royal Commission on the Housing of the Working Classes.

Broinowski, Alison. *The Yellow Lady: Australian Impressions of Asia.* Melbourne: Oxford University Press, 1992.

Brown, Alyson. "Mythologies and Panics: Twentieth Century Constructions of Child Prostitution." *Children and Society* 18, no. 2 (2004): 344–54.

Brown, Alyson, and David Barrett. *Knowledge of Evil: Child Prostitution and Child Sexual Abuse in Twentieth Century England*. London: Willian, 2002.

Brown, Marilyn, ed. *Picturing Children: Constructions of Childhood between Rousseau and Freud*. New York: Ashgate, 2002.

Brown, Simon. "Early Cinema in Britain and the Smoking Concert Film." *Early Popular Visual Culture* 3, no. 2 (2005): 165–78.

Brumberg, J. J. "'Something Happens to Girls': Menarche and the Emergence of the Modern American Hygienic Imperative." *Journal of the History of Sexuality* 4, no. 1 (1993): 99–127.

Bryder, Linda. "Sex, Race and Colonialism: An Historiographical Overview." *International History Review* 20, no. 4 (1998): 806–22.

Buckingham, David, and Sarah Bragg. *Young People, Sex and the Media: The Facts of Life*. London: Palgrave, 2004.

Bullough, Vern L. *Science in the Bedroom: The History of Sex Research*. New York: Basic Books, 1994.

Burnham, J. C. "The Progressive Era Revolution in American Attitudes toward Sex." *Journal of American History* 59, no. 4 (1973): 885–908.

Burns, Stanley, and Elizabeth Burns. *Geisha: A Photographic History, 1872–1912*. Brooklyn, NY: Power House Books, 2006.

Burton, Antoinette. "From Child Bride to Hindoo Lady: Rukmabai and the Debate on Sexual Respectability in Imperial Britain." *American Historical Review* 103 (1998): 1119–46.

Burton, Richard F. *A Plain and Literal Translation of the Arabian Nights Entertainments, Now Intituled the Book of the Thousand Nights and a Night with Introduction Explanatory Notes on the Manners and Customs of Moslem Men and Terminal Essay upon the History of the Nights*. Vol. 10. London: Burton Club, 1886.

Butchart, Alexander. *The Anatomy of Power: European Constructions of the African Body*. London: Zed Books, 1998.

Butcher, John G. *The British in Malaya, 1880–1941: The Social History of a European Community in Colonial Southeast Asia*. Kuala Lumpur: Oxford University Press, 1979.

Butler, Josephine. "An Appeal to the People of England (1870)." In *The Sexuality Debates*, edited by Sheila Jeffreys. London: Routledge, 1987.

Cable, M. *The Little Darlings: A History of Child Rearing in America*. New York: Charles Scribner's Sons, 1975.

Caine, Barbara. *English Feminism, 1780–1920*. Oxford: Oxford University Press, 1997.

Calhoun, G. R. *Report of the Consulting Surgeon, on Spermatorrhoea or Seminal Weakness, and Other Diseases of the Sexual Organs*. Philadelphia: Howard Association, 1858.

Calvert, Karin. "Children in the House." In *The Children's Culture Reader*, edited by Henry Jenkins. New York: New York University Press, 1992.

Calvert, Karin. *Children in the House: The Material Culture of Early Childhood, 1600–1900.* Boston: Northeastern University Press, 1992.

Camagay, Maria Luisa. "Prostitution in Nineteenth Century Manila." *Philippine Studies* 36 (1988): 241–55.

Canguilhem, Georges. *Le normal et le pathologique.* Paris: Presses Universitaires de France, 1966.

Canguilhem, Georges. *The Normal and Pathological.* Translated by Caroline R. Fawcett. New York: Zone Books, 1989.

Carden-Coyne, Ana. *Reconstructing the Body: Classicism, Modernism, and the First World War.* Oxford: Oxford University Press, 2009.

Carpenter, Edward. *The Intermediate Sex: A Study of Some Transitional Types of Men and Women.* London: Swan Sonnenschein, 1908.

Carpenter, Edward. *My Days and Dreams: Being Autobiographical Notes.* London: Allen & Unwin, 1916.

Carter, K. C. "Infantile Hysteria and Infantile Sexuality in Late Nineteenth-Century German-Language Medical Literature." *Medical History* 27, no. 2 (1983): 186–96.

Casper, Johann Ludwig. "Ueber Nothzucht und Päderastie und deren Ermittelung Seitens des Gerichtesarztes." *Vierteljahrschrift für gerichtliche öffentliche Medizin* 1 (1852): 21–78.

Chaddock, C. G., trans. *Psychopathia Sexualis with Special Reference to Contrary Sexual Instinct: A Medico-legal Study,* by Richard von Krafft-Ebing. Philadelphia: F. A. Davis, 1920.

Chauncey, George. "From Sexual Inversion to Homosexuality: Medicine and the Changing Conceptualization of Female Deviance." *Salmagundi* 58–59 (1982–1983): 114–46.

Chauncey, George. *Gay New York: Gender, Urban Culture, and the Making of the Gay Male World, 1890–1940.* New York: Basic Books, 1994.

Chinn, Carol. *They Worked All Their Lives: Women of the Urban Poor in England, 1880–1939.* Manchester: Manchester University Press, 1988.

Choquette, Leslie. "Homosexuals in the City: Representations of Lesbian and Gay Space in Nineteenth-Century Paris." In *Homosexuality in French History and Culture,* edited by Jeffrey Merrick and Michael Sibalis. London: Harrington Park Press, 2001.

Clark, Anna. "Twilight Moments." *Journal of the History of Sexuality* 14 (2005): 139–60.

Clark, Anna. *Women's Silence, Men's Violence: Sexual Assault in England, 1770–1845.* London: Pandora, 1987.

Cleverley, John, and Denis Charles Phillips. *Visions of Childhood: Influential Models from Locke to Spock.* New York: Teachers College, 1986.

Cockington, James. *Banned: Tales from the Bizarre History of Australian Obscenity.* Sydney: ABC Books for the Australian Broadcasting Corporation, 2005.

Cocks, Harry G. *Nameless Offences: Homosexual Desire in the Nineteenth Century.* London: I. B. Taurus, 2003.

Cohen, William A. *Sex Scandal: The Private Parts of Victorian Fiction.* Durham, NC: Duke University Press, 1996.

Colligan, Colette. "A Race Born of Pederasts: Sir Richard Burton, Homosexuality, and the Arabs." *Nineteenth-Century Contexts* 25, no. 1 (2003): 1–20.

Colligan, Colette. *Traffic in Obscenity from Byron to Beardsley: Sexuality and Exoticism in Nineteenth-Century Print Culture*. New York: Palgrave Macmillan, 2006.

Comfort, Alex. *The Anxiety Makers: Some Curious Preoccupations of the Medical Profession*. London: Nelson, 1967.

Cook, Matt. *London and the Culture of Homosexuality, 1885–1914*. Cambridge: Cambridge University Press, 2003.

Coote, William A. "The Suppression of the White Slave Traffic." In *Fighting the Traffic in Young Girls*, edited by Ernest A. Bell. Chicago: G. S. Ball, 1910.

Copley, Antony. *Sexual Moralities in France, 1780–1980: New Ideas on the Family, Divorce, and Homosexuality: An Essay on Moral Change*. London: Routledge, 1989.

Corbey, Raymond. "Alterity: The Colonial Nude." *Critique of Anthropology* 8, no. 3 (1988): 75–92.

Corbey, Raymond. "Ethnographic Showcases." *Cultural Anthropology* 8, no. 3 (1993): 338–69.

Corbin, Alain. *Les filles de noce*. Paris: Aubier, 1978.

Corbin, Alain. *Women for Hire: Prostitution and Sexuality in France after 1850*. Translated by Alan Sheridan. Cambridge, MA: Harvard University Press, 1990.

Cox, Pamela. *Gender, Justice and Welfare: Bad Girls in Britain, 1900–1950*. Basingstoke, UK: Palgrave, 2003.

Crozier, Ivan. "'All the Appearances Were Perfectly Natural': The Anus of the Sodomite in Nineteenth-Century Medical Discourse." In *Body Parts: Critical Explorations in Corporeality*, edited by Christopher E. Forth and Ivan Crozier. Lanham, MD: Lexington Books, 2005.

Crozier, Ivan. "Havelock Ellis, Eonism, and the Patient's Discourse." *History of Psychiatry* 11 (2000): 125–54.

Crozier, Ivan. "The Medical Construction of Homosexuality and Its Relation to the Law in Nineteenth-Century England." *Medical History* 45, no. 1 (2001): 61–82.

Crozier, Ivan. "Nineteenth-Century British Psychiatric Writing about Homosexuality before Havelock Ellis: The Missing History." *Journal of the History of Medicine and Allied Sciences* 63 (2008): 65–102.

Crozier, Ivan. "Philosophy in the English Boudoir: Havelock Ellis, Love and Pain, and Sexological Discourses on Algophilia." *Journal of the History of Sexuality* 13 (2004): 275–305.

Crozier, Ivan. "Pillow Talk: Credibility, Trust and the Sexological Case History." *History of Science* 46 (2008): 375–404.

Crozier, Ivan. "'Rough Winds Do Shake the Darling Buds of May': A Note on William Acton's Conception of Childhood Sexuality." *Journal of Family History* 26 (2001): 411–20.

Crozier, Ivan. "The Sexual Body, 1920–Present." In *Cultural History of the Human Body*, edited by Ivan Crozier. Vol. 5. Oxford: Berg, 2010.

Crozier, Ivan. "Taking Prisoners: Havelock Ellis, Sigmund Freud, and the Politics of Constructing the Homosexual, 1897–1951." *Social History of Medicine* 13 (2000): 447–66.

Crozier, Ivan. "William Acton and the History of Sexuality: The Professional and Medical Contexts." *Journal of Victorian Culture* 5 (2000): 1–27.

Crozier, Ivan, and Gethin Rees. "Making a Space for Medical Expertise: Forensic Discussions of Sexuality Assault in Nineteenth-Century Medicine." *Law, Culture and Humanities* (forthcoming).

Cunningham, Hugh. *Children and Childhood in Western Society since 1500*. London: Longman, 1995.

Cunningham, Hugh. *Children of the Poor: Representing Childhood since the Seventeenth Century*. Oxford: Blackwell, 1991.

Daniels, Kay. "Prostitution in Tasmania during the Transition from Penal Settlement to 'Civilised' Society." In *So Much Hard Work: Women and Prostitution in Australian History*, edited by Kay Daniels. Melbourne: Fontana/Collins, 1984.

Dansel, Michel. *Le sergent Bertrand: Portrait d'un nécrophile heureux*. Paris: Albin Michel, 1991.

Darby, Robert. "The Masturbation Taboo and the Rise of Routine Male Circumcision: A Review of the Historiography." *Journal of Social History* 27 (2003): 737–57.

Darby, Robert. "Pathologizing Male Sexuality: Lallemand, Spermatorrhea, and the Rise of Circumcision." *Journal of the History of Medicine and Allied Sciences* 60, no. 3 (2005): 283–319.

Darby, Robert. *A Surgical Temptation: The Demonization of the Foreskin and the Rise of Circumcision in Britain*. Chicago: University of Chicago Press, 2005.

Darby, Robert. "William Acton's Antipodean Disciples: A Colonial Perspective on His Theories of Male Sexual (Dys)function." *Journal of the History of Sexuality* 13 (2004): 157–82.

Darwin, Charles. *The Descent of Man, and Selection in Relation to Sex*. Princeton, NJ: Princeton University Press, 1981.

Dauphiné, Claude. *Rachilde*. Paris: Mercure de France, 1991.

Davidson, Arnold I. *The Emergence of Sexuality: Historical Epistemology and the Formation of Concepts*. Cambridge, MA: Harvard University Press, 2001.

Davidson, Arnold I. "Sex and the Emergence of Sexuality." *Critical Inquiry* 14, no. 1 (1987): 16–48.

Davidson, Roger. "Dealing with the 'Social Evil': Prostitutes and Police in Western Australia, 1895–1924." In *So Much Hard Work: Women and Prostitution in Australian History*, edited by Kay Daniels. Sydney: Fontana/Collins, 1984.

Davidson, Roger, and Lesley A. Hall. *Sex, Sin and Suffering: Venereal Disease and European Society since 1870*. London: Routledge, 2001.

Davis, Julie. *Utamaro and the Spectacle of Beauty*. Honolulu: University of Hawaii Press, 2005.

Davis, Natalie Zemon. *Society and Culture in Early Modern France*. London: Duckworth, 1975.

Dean, Carolyn J. *Sexuality and Modern Western Culture*. New York: Twayne, 1996.

De Groot, Johanna. "'Sex' and 'Race': The Construction of Language and Image in the Nineteenth Century." In *Cultures of Empire: A Reader: Colonisers in Britain and the Empire in the Nineteenth and Twentieth Centuries*, edited by Catherine Hall. Manchester: Manchester University Press, 2000.

Dekkers, Midas. *Dearest Pet: On Bestiality*. Translated by Paul Vincent. New York: Verso, 2000.

DeMause, Lloyd, ed. *The History of Childhood*. London: Souvenir Press, 1976.

D'Emilio, John, and Estelle Freedman. *Intimate Matters: A History of Sexuality in America*. New York: Perennial Library, 1989.

Dennett, M. *The Sex Education of Children*. London: George Routledge and Sons, 1932.

Derrida, Jacques. *Of Grammatology*. Translated by Gayatri Chakravorty Spivak. Baltimore: Johns Hopkins University Press, 1976.

Dery, Luis C. "Prostitution in Colonial Manila." *Philippine Studies* 39, no. 4 (1991): 475–89.

Dickinson, Edward Ross. "Policing Sex in Germany, 1882–1982: A Preliminary Statistical Analysis." *Journal of the History of Sexuality* 16 (2007): 204–50.

Di Lauro, A., and G. Rabkin. *Dirty Movies: An Illustrated History of the Stag Film, 1915–1970*. New York: Chelsea House, 1976.

Doan, Laura. *Fashioning Sapphism: The Origin of the Modern Lesbian Culture*. New York: Columbia University Press 2001.

Dollimore, Jonathan. *Sexual Dissidence: Augustine to Wilde, Freud to Foucault*. Oxford: Oxford University Press, 1991.

Donovan, James M. "Combating the Sexual Abuse of Children in France, 1825–1913." *Criminal Justice History* 15 (1994): 59–95.

Downing, Lisa. "The Birth of the Beast: Death-Driven Masculinity in Monneret, Zola and Freud." *Dix-Neuf* 5 (2005): 28–46.

Downing, Lisa. "Death and the Maidens: A Century of Necrophilia in Female-Authored Textual Production." *French Cultural Studies* 14 (2003): 157–68.

Downing, Lisa. *Desiring the Dead: Necrophilia and Nineteenth-Century French Literature*. Oxford: Legenda, 2003.

Downing, Lisa, and Dany Nobus. "The Iconography of Asphyxiophilia: From Fantasmatic Fetish to Forensic Fact." *Paragraph: A Journal of Modern Critical Theory* 27 (2004): 1–15.

Drysdale, George. *The Elements of Social Science or Physical, Sexual and Natural Religion: An Exposition of the True Cause and Only Cure of the Three Primary Social Evils: Poverty, Prostitution, and Celibacy*. London: Privately printed, 1854.

Drysdale, George. *The Elements of Social Science or Physical, Sexual and Natural Religion: An Exposition of the True Cause and Only Cure of the Three Primary Social Evils: Poverty, Prostitution, and Celibacy*. London: E. Truelove, 1882.

Duggan, Lisa. *Sapphic Slashers: Sex, Violence, and American Modernity*. Durham, NC: Duke University Press, 2000.

Duggan, Lisa. "The Trials of Alice Mitchell: Sensationalism, Sexology and the Lesbian Subject in Turn-of-the-Century America." *Signs* 18 (1993): 791–814.

Eder, Franz, Lesley A. Hall, and Gert Hekma, eds. *National Histories*. Vol. 1 of *Sexual Cultures in Europe*. Manchester: Manchester University Press, 1999.

Edison, Newell. "Sex Education as a Community Problem," *Journal of Educational Sociology* 8, no. 6 (1935): 361–70.

Edmond, Gary. "The Law Set: The Legal-Scientific Production of Medical Propriety." *Science, Technology & Human Values* 26 (2001): 191–226.

Edwardes, S. M. *Crime in India*. London: Oxford University Press, 1924.

Edwards, Elizabeth, ed. *Anthropology and Photography, 1860–1920*. New Haven, CT: Yale University Press, 1992.

Egan, R. Danielle, and Gail Hawkes. "Childhood Sexuality, Normalization and the Social Hygiene Movement in the Anglophone West, 1900–1935." *Social History of Medicine* (forthcoming).

Egan, R. Danielle, and Gail Hawkes. "Girls, Sexuality and the Strange Carnalities of Advertisements: Deconstructing the Discourse of Corporate Paedophilia." *Australian Feminist Studies* 23, no. 57 (2008): 307–22.

Egan, R. Danielle, and Gail Hawkes. "The Problem with Protection: Or, Why We Need to Move towards Recognition and the Sexual Agency of Children." *Continuum Journal of Media and Cultural Studies* 23, no. 3 (2009): 389–400.

Egan, R. Danielle, and Gail Hawkes. "Producing the Prurient through the Pedagogy of Purity: Childhood Sexuality and the Social Purity Movement." *Journal of Historical Sociology* 20, no. 4 (2007): 443–61.

Egan, R. Danielle, and Gail Hawkes. *Theorizing the Sexual Child in Modernity*. New York: Palgrave Macmillan, 2010.

Eigen, Joel P. *Unconscious Crime*. Baltimore: Johns Hopkins University Press, 2003.

Eigen, Joel P. *Witnessing Insanity*. New Haven, CT: Yale University Press, 1995.

Ellenberger, Henry F. *The Discovery of the Unconscious: The History and Evolution of Dynamic Psychiatry*. New York: Basic Books, 1970.

Ellis, Havelock. *Studies in the Psychology of Sex*. Psyplexus. http://www.psyplexus. com/ellis/.

Ellis, Havelock. *The Task of Social Hygiene*. Project Gutenberg, 2007. http://www. gutenberg.org/files/22090/22090-h/22090-h.htm.

Ellis, Havelock, and John Addington Symonds. *Sexual Inversion: A Critical Edition*. Edited by Ivan Crozier. Basingstoke, UK: Palgrave Macmillan, 2008.

Eng, Lai Ah. *Peasants, Proletarians and Prostitutes: A Preliminary Investigation into the Work of Chinese Women in Colonial Malaya*. Research Notes and Discussion Paper No. 59. Singapore: Institute of Southeast Asian Studies, 1986.

Engels, Dagmar. "The Changing Role of Women in Bengal, 1890–1930." Ph.D. thesis, School of Oriental and Asian Studies, London, 1987.

Engels, Dagmar. "The Limits of Gender Ideology: Bengali Women, the Colonial State, and the Private Sphere, 1890–1930." *Women's Studies International Forum* 12 (1989): 425–37.

Engels, Friedrich F. *The Condition of the Working Class in England in 1844*. Translated by Florence K. Wischnewetzky. London: Sonnenschein, 1892.

Engelstein, Laura J. "Gender and the Juridical Subject: Prostitution and Rape in Nineteenth-Century Russian Criminal Codes." *Journal of Modern History* 60 (1988): 458–95.

Enloe, Cynthia. *Does Khaki Become You? The Militarization of Women's Lives.* London: Pluto Press, 1983.

Epaulard, Alexis. *Vampirisme: Nécrophilie, nécrosadisme, nécrophagie.* Lyon: Stock, 1901.

Esquirol, Jean-Étienne-Dominique. *Mental Maladies: A Treatise on Insanity.* Translated by E. K. Hunt. New York: Hafner, 1965.

Euler, Catherine. "'The Iron Fetters of Our Souls': Nineteenth-Century Feminist Strategies to Get Our Bodies into the Political Agenda." In *Everyday Violence in Britain, 1850–1950,* edited by S. D'Cruze. Harlow, UK: Pearson, 2000.

Evans, Raymond. "'Don't You Remember Black Alice, Sam Holt?' Aboriginal Women in Queensland History." *Hecate* 8, no. 2 (1982): 7–21.

Evans, Raymond. "'Soiled Doves': Prostitution in Colonial Queensland." In *So Much Hard Work: Women and Prostitution in Australian History,* edited by Kay Daniels. Melbourne: Fontana/Collins, 1984.

Evans, Tom, and Mary Anne Evans. *Shunga: The Art of Love in Japan.* New York: Paddington Press, 1975.

Everett, R. H. "Social Hygiene and Public Health." *Social Forces* 2, no. 1 (1923): 61–64.

Faderman, Lillian. *Surpassing the Love of Men: Friendships between Women from the Renaissance to the Present.* London: Women's Press, 1991.

Féray, Jean-Claude, and Manfred Herzer, "Homosexual Studies and Politics in the 19th Century: Karl Maria Kertbeny." *Journal of Homosexuality* 19 (1990): 23–48.

Finnegan, Frances. *Poverty and Prostitution: A Study of Victorian Prostitutes in York.* Cambridge: Cambridge University Press, 1979.

Fischer-Tiné, Harald. "'White Women Degrading Themselves to the Lowest Depths': European Networks of Prostitution and Colonial Anxieties in British India and Ceylon, ca. 1880–1914." *Indian Economic and Social History Review* 40, no. 2 (2003): 163–90.

Fishman, Sterling. "The History of Childhood Sexuality." *Journal of Contemporary History* 17, no. 2 (1982): 269–83.

Fiske, Jo-Anne. "Colonization and the Decline of Women's Status: The Tsimshian Case." *Feminist Studies* 17, no. 3 (1991): 509–35.

Foldy, Michael S. *The Trials of Oscar Wilde: Deviance, Morality, and Late-Victorian Society.* New Haven, CT: Yale University Press, 1997.

Forbes, Geraldine. "Women and Modernity: The Issue of Child Marriage in India." *Women's Studies International Quarterly* 2 (1979): 407–19.

Ford, Ruth. "Contested Desires: Narratives of Passionate Friends, Married Masqueraders and Lesbian Love in Australia, 1918–1945." Ph.D. thesis, La Trobe University, 2000.

Ford, Ruth. "Speculating on Scrapbooks, Sex and Desire: Issues in Lesbian History." *Australian Historical Studies* 106 (1996): 111–26.

Forel, August. *The Sexual Question: A Scientific, Psychological, Hygienic and Sociological Study for the Cultured Classes.* London: Rebman, 1908.

Forman, Ross G. "Randy on the Rand: Portuguese African Labour and the Discourse on 'Unnatural Vice' in the Transvaal in the Early Twentieth Century." *Journal of the History of Sexuality* 11, no. 4 (2002): 570–609.

Forth, Christopher E. *Masculinity and the Modern West: Gender, Civilization and the Body*. Basingstoke, UK: Palgrave Macmillan, 2008.

Forth, Christopher E., and Ivan Crozier, eds. *Body Parts: Critical Explorations in Corporeality*. Lanham, MD: Lexington Books, 2005.

Foucault, Michel. *Abnormal: Lectures at the Collège de France, 1974–1975*. Edited by Valerio Marchetti and Antonella Salomoni. Translated by Graham Burchell. London: Verso, 2003.

Foucault, Michel. *Discipline and Punish: The Birth of the Prison*. Translated by Alan Sheridan. London: Allen Lane, 1977.

Foucault, Michel. "Governmentality." In *The Foucault Effect: Studies in Governmentality*, edited by Graham Burchell, Colin Gordon, and Peter Miller. London: Harvester Wheatsheaf, 1991.

Foucault, Michel. *The History of Sexuality: An Introduction*. New York: Vintage, 1990.

Foucault, Michel. *The Order of Things*. Translated by Alan Sheridan. London: Routledge, 1989.

Foucault, Michel. *Power/Knowledge: Selected Interviews and Other Writings, 1972–1977*. Edited by Colin Gordon. Sussex, UK: Harvester Press, 1980.

Foucault, Michel. *La volonté de savoir*. Paris: Gallimard, 1976.

Foucault, Michel. *The Will to Knowledge*. Vol. 1 of *The History of Sexuality*. Translated by Robert Hurley. Harmondsworth, UK: Penguin, 1998.

Frances, Raelene. "A History of Female Prostitution in Australia." In *Sex Work and Sex Workers in Australia*, edited by Roberta Perkins, Garreth Prestage, and Frances Lovejoy. Kensington: University of New South Wales Press, 1994.

Frances, Raelene. *Selling Sex: A Hidden History of Prostitution*. Sydney: Allen & Unwin, 2007.

Frances, Raelene. "White Australia and the White Slave Traffic: Gender, Race and Citizenship." *International Review of Social History* 44, Supplement (1999): 101–22.

Freed, Louis Franklin. *The Problem of European Prostitution in Johannesburg*. Johannesburg: Juta, 1949.

Freedman, E. B. "Sexuality in Nineteenth Century America: Behavior, Ideology and Politics." *Reviews in American History* 10, no. 4 (1982): 196–215.

Freud, Sigmund *On Sexuality: Three Essays on the Theory of Sexuality and Other Works*. Translated by James Strachey. New York: Penguin, 1977.

Gallagher, Catherine, and Thomas Laqueur. *The Making of the Modern Body: Sexuality and Society in the Nineteenth Century*. Berkeley: University of California Press, 1987.

Gallichan, William M. *A Textbook of Sex Education for Parents and Teachers*. Boston: Small, Maynard, 1921.

Galloway, Thomas W. *Sex and Social Health*. New York: American Hygiene Association, 1924.

Garon, Sheldon. "The World's Oldest Debate? Prostitution and the State in Imperial Japan, 1900–1945." *American Historical Review* 98, no. 3 (1993): 710–32.

Gay, Peter. *The Bourgeois Experience: Victoria to Freud*. Vol. 1 of *Education of the Senses*. Oxford: Oxford University Press, 1984.

Gay, Peter, ed. *The Freud Reader*. London: Vintage, 1995.

Geddes, Patrick, and J. Arthur Thomson. *The Evolution of Sex*. London: Walter Scott, 1889.

Gibson, Mary. *Prostitution and the State in Italy, 1860–1915*. New Brunswick, NJ: Rutgers University Press, 1986.

Gilbert, A. N. "Doctor, Patient and Onanist Diseases in the Nineteenth Century." *Journal of the History of Medicine and Allied Sciences* 30, no. 3 (1975): 217–34.

Gillis, Jonathan. "Bad Habits and Pernicious Results: Thumb Sucking and the Discipline of Late-Nineteenth-Century Paediatrics." *Medical History* 40, no. 1 (1996): 55–73.

Gilman, Sander L. *Difference and Pathology: Stereotypes of Sexuality, Race, and Madness*. Ithaca, NY: Cornell University Press, 1985.

Gilman, Sander L. *Sexuality: An Illustrated History*. New York: Wiley, 1989.

Goldman, Jason. "'The Golden Age of Gay Porn': Nostalgia and the Photography of Wilhelm von Gloeden." *GLQ: A Journal of Lesbian and Gay Studies* 12, no. 2 (2006): 237–58.

Goldstein, Jan. *Console and Classify: The French Psychiatric Profession in the Nineteenth Century*. Cambridge: Cambridge University Press, 1990.

Gollaher, D. L. "From Ritual to Science: The Medical Transformation of Circumcision in America." *Journal of Social History* 28, no. 1 (1994): 5–36.

Goncourt, Edmond de. *Hokusai*. Paris, 1896.

Goncourt, Edmond de. *Utamaro: Le peintre des maisons vertes*. Paris, 1891.

Gordon, Linda. *The Great Arizona Orphan Abduction*. Cambridge, MA: Harvard University Press, 2000.

Gordon, Linda. *The Politics and History of Family Violence*. London: Virago, 1989.

Gowing, Laura. *Domestic Dangers: Women, Words and Sex in Early Modern London*. Oxford: Oxford University Press, 1996.

Graebner, William. "The Unstable World of Benjamin Spock: Social Engineering in a Democratic Culture, 1917–1950." *Journal of American History* 67, no. 3 (1980): 612–19.

Gray, G. Z. *The Children's Crusade: A History*. New York: W. Morrow Press, 1972.

Grayzel, Susan R. *Women's Identities at War: Gender, Motherhood, and Politics in Britain and France during the First World War*. Chapel Hill: University of North Carolina Press, 1999.

Gregg, Robert. "Apropos Exceptionalism: Imperial Location and Comparative Histories of South Africa and the United States." In *Inside Out, Outside In: Essays in Comparative History*. London: Macmillan, 2000.

Gregory, Samuel. *Facts and Important Information for Young Women on the Subject of Masturbation; with Its Causes, Prevention and Cure*. New York: Arno Press, 1974.

Griesinger, Wilhelm. "Vortrag zur Eröffnung der psychiatrischen Clink." *Archiv für Psychiatrie und Nervenkrankheiten* 1 (1868): 636–54.

Grinstead, Wren J. "Reading for Teachers of Sex Hygiene." *School Review* 22, no. 4 (1914): 249–55.

Groneman, Carol. "Nymphomania: The Historical Construction of Female Sexuality."
    Signs 19 (1994): 337–67.
Gronewold, Sue. *Beautiful Merchandise: Prostitution in China, 1860–1936.* New York:
    Haworth, 1982.
Grover, K. *Hard at Play: Leisure in America, 1840–1940.* Amherst: University of
    Massachusetts Press, 1992.
Guarnieri, Patrizia. *A Case of Child Murder: Law and Science in Nineteenth-Century
    Tuscany.* Cambridge: Polity Press, 1996.
Guereña, Jean Louis. "Prostitution and the Origins of the Governmental Regulatory
    System in Nineteenth-Century Spain: The Plans of the Trienio Liberal, 1820–1823."
    Journal of the History of Sexuality 17 (2008): 216–34.
Gupta, Charu. *Sexuality, Obscenity, Community: Women, Muslims and the Hindu
    Public in Colonial India.* New York: Palgrave, 2001.
Gutmann, Philipp. "Hermann Joseph Löwenstein's Dissertation: De Mentis Aberra-
    tionibus Ex Partium Sexualium Conditione Abnormi Oriundis (1823)." *History of
    Psychiatry* 15 (2004): 455–65.
Gutmann, Philipp. "On the Way to Scientia Sexualis: 'On the Relation of the Sexual
    System to the Psyche in General and to Cretinism in Particular' (1826) by Joseph
    Häussler." *History of Psychiatry* 17 (2006): 45–53.
Guy, Donna J. *Sex and Danger in Buenos Aires: Prostitution, Family, and Nation in
    Argentina.* Lincoln: University of Nebraska Press, 1991.
Guy, Donna J. "'White Slavery,' Citizenship and Nationality in Argentina." In *Nation-
    alisms and Sexualities,* edited by Andrew Parker, Mary Russo, Doris Summer, and
    Patricia Yaeger. London: Routledge, 1992.
Hacking, Ian. "Kinds of People: Moving Targets." http://www.britac.ac.uk:80/pubs/src/
    britacad06/index.cfm.
Hacking, Ian. "Making up People." In *Reconstructing Individualism: Autonomy,
    Individuality, and the Self in Western Thought,* edited by Thomas C. Heller et al.
    Stanford, CA: Stanford University Press, 1986.
Haley, Bruce. *The Healthy Body and Victorian Culture.* Cambridge, MA: Harvard
    University Press, 1978.
Hall, Lesley A. "'I Have Never Met the Normal Woman': Stella Browne and the Politics
    of Womanhood." *Women's History Review* 6 (1997): 157–82.
Hall, Lesley A. "Hauling down the Double Standard: Feminism, Social Purity and
    Sexual Science in Late Nineteenth-Century Britain." *Gender and History* 16, no. 1
    (2004): 36–56.
Hall, Lesley A. *Hidden Anxieties: Male Sexuality, 1900–1950.* Cambridge: Polity Press,
    1991.
Hall, Lesley A. "Malthusian Mutations: The Changing Politics and Moral Meaning of
    Birth Control in Britain." In *Malthus, Medicine, and Morality: "Malthusianism"
    after 1798,* edited by Brian Dolan. Amsterdam: Rodopi, 2000.
Hall, Lesley A. *Sex, Gender and Social Change in Britain since 1880.* Basingstoke, UK:
    Macmillan, 2000.
Hall, Lesley A. "Suffrage, Sex and Science." In *The Women's Suffrage Movement: New
    Feminist Perspectives,* edited by Maroula Joannou and June Purvis. Manchester:
    Manchester University Press, 1998.

Hall, Winfield Scott. *Sexual Education for Sex Problems: Sex Hygiene by the Highest Authority*. Philadelphia: International Bible Houses, 1916.

Halperin, David M. *How to Do the History of Homosexuality*. Chicago: University of Chicago Press, 2002.

Halperin, David M. *One Hundred Years of Homosexuality: And Other Essays on Greek Love*. London: Routledge, 1990.

Halperin, David M. *Saint Foucault: Towards a Gay Hagiography*. Oxford: Oxford University Press, 1995.

Hammond, Paul. *French Undressing: Naughty Postcards from 1900 to 1920*. London: Bloomsbury Books, 1988.

Hamowy, R. "Medicine and Crimination of Sin: 'Self-Abuse' in Nineteenth Century America." *Journal of Libertarian Studies* 1, no. 3 (1977): 229–70.

Hare, E. H. "Masturbatory Insanity: The History of an Idea." *Journal of Mental Science* 108 (1962): 2–25.

Harrison, Fraser. *The Dark Angel: Aspects of Victorian Sexuality*. London: Sheldon Press, 1977.

Hawes, Joseph. *Children's Health in America: A History*. New York: Twayne, 1991.

Hawkes, Gail. *Sex and Pleasure in Western Culture*. Cambridge: Polity Press, 2004.

Hawkes, Gail, and R. Danielle Egan. "Developing the Sexual Child." *Journal of Historical Sociology* 21, no. 4 (2008): 443–65.

Hayes, Jerrod. *Queer Nations: Marginal Sexualities in the Maghreb*. Chicago: University of Chicago Press, 2000.

Hearn, Jeff. *Men in the Public Eye*. London: Routledge, 1992.

Hekma, Gert. "A Female Soul in a Male Body: Sexual Inversion as Gender Inversion in Nineteenth Century Sexology." In *Third Sex, Third Gender: Beyond Dimorphism in Culture and History*, edited by Gilbert Herdt. New York: Zone Books, 1994.

Hekma, Gert. "A History of Sexology: Social and Historical Aspects of Sexuality." In *From Sappho to De Sade: Moments in the History of Sexuality*, edited by Jan Bremmer. London: Routledge, 1989.

Henriot, Christian. "'From a Throne of Glory to a Seat of Ignominy': Shanghai Prostitution Revisited (1849–1949)." *Modern China* 22, no. 2 (1996): 132–63.

Henriot, Christian. *Prostitution and Sexuality in Shanghai: A Social History, 1849–1949*. Translated by Noël Castelino. Cambridge: Cambridge University Press, 2001.

Herbert, T. W. "The Erotics of Purity: The Marble Faun and the Victorian Construction of Sexuality." *Representations* 36 (1991): 114–32.

Herschatter, Gail. *Dangerous Pleasures: Prostitution and Modernity in Twentieth-Century Shanghai*. Berkeley: University of California Press, 1997.

Herschatter, Gail. "'From a Throne of Glory to a Seat of Ignominy': Shanghai Prostitution Revisited (1849–1949): A Response." *Modern China* 22, no. 2 (1996): 164–69.

Herschatter, Gail. "The Hierarchy of Shanghai Prostitution, 1870–1949." *Modern China* 15, no. 4 (1989): 463–98.

Herzer, Manfred. "Kertbeny and the Nameless Love." *Journal of Homosexuality* 12 (1985): 1–26.

Hesselink, Liesbeth. "Prostitution: A Necessary Evil, Particularly in the Colonies. Views on Prostitution in the Netherlands Indies." In *Indonesian Women in Focus: Past and Present Notions*, edited by Elsbeth Locher-Scholten and Anke Niehof. Dordrecht: Foris, 1987.

Heywood, Colin. *A History of Childhood: Children and Childhood in the West from Medieval to Modern Times*. Cambridge: Polity Press, 2001.

Hight, Eleanor. "The Many Lives of Beato's 'Beauties.'" In *Colonialist Photography: Imag(in)ing Race and Place*, edited by Eleanor Hight and Gary Sampson. London: Routledge, 2002.

Hight, Eleanor, and G. Sampson, eds. *Colonialist Photography: Imag(in)ing Race and Place*. London: Routledge, 2002.

Higonnet, Anne. *Pictures of Innocence: The History and Crisis of Ideal Childhood*. London: Thomas and Hudson, 1998.

Himmelfarb, Gertrude. *The Idea of Poverty*. New York: Knopf, 1984.

Hirata, Lucy Cheng. "Chinese Immigrant Women in Nineteenth-Century California." In *Women in America: A History*, edited by Carol Ruth Berkin and Mary Beth Norton. Boston: Houghton Mifflin, 1979.

Hodges, F. M. "The Anti-masturbation Crusade in Antebellum American Medicine." *Journal of Sexual Medicine* 2, no. 5 (2005): 722–31.

Holt, Emmett. *The Diseases of Infancy and Childhood*. New York: Appleton, 1897.

Hopkins, E. *On the Early Training of Girls and Boys: An Appeal to Working Women*. New York: B. M. Hammett, 1884.

Horowitz, Helen Lefkowitz. *Rereading Sex: Battles over Sexual Knowledge and Suppression in Nineteenth-Century America*. New York: Vintage, 2003.

Houlbrook, Matt. *Queer London: Perils and Pleasures in the Sexual Metropolis, 1918–1957*. Chicago: University of Chicago Press, 2005.

Houlbrook, Matt. "Towards a Historical Geography of Sexuality." *Journal of Urban History* 27 (2001): 497–504.

Houlbrook, Matt, and Harry G. Cocks, eds. *Palgrave Advances in the Modern History of Sexuality*. Basingstoke, UK: Palgrave Macmillan, 2006.

Howe, J. W. *Excessive Venery Masturbation and Continence: The Etiology, Pathology and Treatment of the Diseases Resulting from Venereal Excesses, Masturbation and Continence*. New York: E. B. Treat, 1887.

Howell, Philip. "Prostitution and Racialised Sexuality: The Regulation of Prostitution in Britain and the British Empire before the Contagious Diseases Acts." *Environment and Planning D: Society and Space* 18 (2000): 321–39.

Howell, Philip. "Prostitution and the Place of Empire: Regulation and Repeal in Hong Kong and the British Imperial Network." In *(Dis)placing Empire: Renegotiating British Colonial Geographies*, edited by Lindsay J. Proudfoot and Michael M. Roche. Burlington, VT: Ashgate, 2005.

Howell, Philip. "Race, Space and the Regulation of Prostitution in Colonial Hong Kong." *Urban History* 31, no. 2 (2004): 229–48.

Howell, Philip. "Sexuality, Sovereignty and Space: Law, Government and the Geography of Prostitution in Colonial Gibraltar." *Social History* 29, no. 4 (2004): 444–64.

Hubbard, Philip. *Sex and the City: Geographies of Prostitution in the Urban West*. Aldershot, UK: Ashgate, 1999.

Hulbert, Anne. *Raising America: Experts, Parents, and a Century of Advice about Children*. London: Vintage, 2004.

Hull, Isabelle. *The Entourage of Kaiser Wilhelm II, 1888–1918*. New York: Cambridge University Press, 1982.

Hunt, Alan. *Governing Morals: A Social History of Moral Regulation*. Cambridge: Cambridge University Press, 1991.

Hunt, Lynn. "Obscenity and the Origins of Modernity, 1500–1800." In *The Invention of Pornography: Obscenity and the Origins of Modernity, 1500–1800*, edited by Lynn Hunt. New York: Zone Books, 1993.

Hunt, Lynn. "Pornography and the French Revolution." In *The Invention of Pornography: Obscenity and the Origins of Modernity, 1500–1800*, edited by Lynn Hunt. New York: Zone Books, 1993.

Hyam, Ronald. *Empire and Sexuality: The British Experience*. Manchester: Manchester University Press, 1990.

Hyam, Ronald. "Empire and Sexual Opportunity." *Journal of Imperial and Commonwealth History* 14, no. 2 (1986): 34–90.

Hyam, Ronald. "'Imperialism and Sexual Exploitation': A Reply." *Journal of Imperial and Commonwealth History* 17, no. 1 (1988): 90–99.

Hyde, H. Montgomery. *The Cleveland Street Scandal*. London: W. H. Allen, 1976.

Hyde, A. M. *A History of Pornography*. London: Heinemann, 1964.

Imber, Michael. "Toward a Theory of Curriculum Reform: An Analysis of the First Campaign for Sex Education." *Curriculum Inquiry* 12, no. 4 (1982): 339–62.

Ingleson, John. "Prostitution in Colonial Java." In *Nineteenth and Twentieth Century Indonesia: Essays in Honour of Professor J. D. Legge*, edited by David P. Chandler and M. C. Ricklefs. Clayton, Vic.: Southeast Asian Studies, Monash University, 1986.

Ingraham, Chrys. *White Weddings: Romancing Heterosexuality in Popular Culture*. 2nd ed. New York: Routledge, 2008.

Ishiguro, Keisho. *Meijiki No Porunogurafi [Pornography in the Meiji Era]*. Tokyo: Shinchosha, 1996.

Jackson, Louise A. *Child Sexual Abuse in Victorian England*. London: Routledge, 2000.

Jackson, Margaret. *The Real Facts of Life: Feminism and the Politics of Sexuality, c. 1850–1940*. London: Taylor and Francis, 1994.

James, Allison, Christopher Jenks, and Alan Prout. *Theorising Childhood*. Cambridge: Polity Press, 1998.

James, Allison, and Alan Prout. *Constructing and Reconstructing Childhood*. London: Falmer Press, 1997.

Jeffreys, Sheila. *The Spinster and Her Enemies: Feminism and Sexuality, 1880–1930*. London: Pandora Press, 1985.

Jenkins, Philip. *Moral Panic: Changing Concepts of the Child Molester in Modern America*. New Haven, CT: Yale University Press, 1998.

Jenks, Christopher. *Childhood*. London: Routledge, 1996.

Jones, Noreen. *No. 2 Home: A Story of Japanese Pioneers in Australia.* Freemantle: Fremantle Arts Centre Press, 2002.

Jordanova, Ludmilla. "Children in History: Concepts of Nature and Society." In *Children, Parents and Politics*, edited by G. Scarre. Cambridge: Cambridge University Press, 1987.

Jordanova, Ludmilla. *Sexual Visions: Images of Gender in Science and Medicine between the Eighteenth and Twentieth Centuries.* Madison: University of Wisconsin Press, 1989.

Judd, Dennis. *Empire: The British Imperial Experience from 1765 to the Present.* London: Harper Collins, 1996.

Kaplan, Morris B. "Who's Afraid of John Saul? Urban Culture and the Politics of Desire in Late Victorian London." *GLQ: A Journal of Lesbian and Gay Studies* 5 (1999): 267–314.

Katz, Jonathan Ned. *The Invention of Heterosexuality.* New York: Plume, 1996.

Kearney, Patrick J. *A History of Erotic Literature.* London: Macmillan, 1982.

Kearney, Patrick J. *The Private Case: An Annotated Bibliography of the Private Case Erotica Collection in the British (Museum) Library.* London: J. Landesman, 1981.

Keire, Mara L. "The Vice Trust: A Reinterpretation of the White Slavery Scare in the United States, 1907–1917." *Journal of Social History* 35 (2001): 5–41.

Kellogg, J. H. *Plain Facts about Sexual Life.* Burlington, Iowa: I. F. Segner, 1877.

Kendrick, Walter. *The Secret Museum.* Berkeley: University of California Press, 1996.

Kennedy, Dane. *The Highly Civilized Man: Richard Burton and the Victorian World.* Cambridge, MA: Harvard University Press, 2005.

Kennedy, Hubert. "Karl Heinrich Ulrichs: First Theorist of Homosexuality." In *Science and Homosexualities*, edited by Vernon A. Rosario. New York: Routledge, 1997.

Kennedy, Hubert. *Karl Heinrich Ulrichs: Pioneer of the Modern Gay Movement.* San Francisco: Peremptory, 2002.

Kent, Susan K. *Sex and Suffrage in Britain, 1860–1914.* Princeton, NJ: Princeton University Press, 1987.

Kincaid, James R. *Child-Loving: The Erotic Child and Victorian Culture.* New York: Routledge, 1992.

Kincaid, James R. *Erotic Innocence: The Culture of Child Molesting.* Durham, NC: Duke University Press, 1998.

Klaf, Franklin S., trans. *Psychopathia Sexualis with Especial Reference to the Antipathic Sexual Instinct: A Medico-forensic Study*, by Richard von Krafft-Ebing. London: Arcade, 1965.

Kohn, David. "Theories to Work By: Rejected Theories, Reproduction, and Darwin's Path to Natural Selection." *Studies in the History of Biology* 4 (1980): 67–170.

Krafft-Ebing, Richard von. *Psychopathia sexualis: Eine klinisch-forensische Studie.* Stuttgart: Ferdinand Enke, 1886.

Krafft-Ebing, Richard von. *Psychopathia Sexualis: With Especial Reference to Contrary Sexual Instinct: A Medico-legal Study.* Philadelphia: F. A. Davis, 1893.

Krafft-Ebing, Richard von. "Über gewisse Anomalies des Geschlechtstriebs und die klinisch-forensich Verwertung derselben als eines wahrscheinlich funktionellen

Degenerationszeichens des centralen Nervensystems." *Archiv für Psychiatrie und Nervenkrankheiten* 7 (1877): 291–312.

Kramer, Paul. "The Darkness that Enters the Home: The Politics of Prostitution during the Philippine-American War." In *Haunted by Empire: Geographies of Intimacy in North American History*, edited by Ann Laura Stoler. Durham, NC: Duke University Press, 2006.

Kumar, Satish M. "'Oriental Sore' or 'Public Nuisance': The Regulation of Prostitution in Colonial India, 1895–1889." In *(Dis)placing Empire: Renegotiating British Colonial Geographies*, edited by Lindsay J. Proudfoot and Michael M. Roche. Burlington, VT: Ashgate, 2005.

Kutchins, Herb, and Stuart Kirk. *Making Us Crazy: DSM—the Psychiatric Bible and the Creation of Mental Disorders*. London: Constable, 1999.

La Berge, A. F. "A.J.B. Parent-Duchâtelet: Hygienist of Paris, 1821–1936." *Clio Medica* 12 (1977): 278–301.

LaCapra, Dominic, ed. *The Bounds of Race: Perspectives on Hegemony and Resistance*. Ithaca, NY: Cornell University Press, 1991.

Ladenson, Elisabeth. *Dirt for Art's Sake: Books on Trial from "Madame Bovary" to "Lolita."* Ithaca, NY: Cornell University Press, 2006.

Lai, A. E. *Peasants, Proletarians and Prostitutes: A Preliminary Investigation into the Work of Chinese Women in Colonial Malaya*. Research Notes and Discussion Paper No. 59. Singapore: Institute of Southeast Asian Studies, 1986.

Lake, Marilyn, and Henry Reynolds,. *Drawing the Global Colour Line: White Men's Countries and the Question of Racial Equality*. Carlton, Vic.: Melbourne University Press, 2008.

Lallemand, Claude-François. *A Practical Treatise on the Causes, Symptoms and Treatment of Spermatorrhoea*. Translated by Henry J. McDougall. Philadelphia: Blanchard and Lea, 1858.

Lampard, Eric. "The Urbanizing World." In *The Victorian City: Images and Realities*, edited by Harold J. Dyos and Michael Woolff. 2 vols. London: Routledge, 1973.

Laqueur, Thomas. *Making Sex: Body and Gender from the Greeks to Freud*. Cambridge, MA: Harvard University Press, 1990.

Laqueur, Thomas. *Solitary Sex: A Cultural History of Masturbation*. New York: Zone Books, 2004.

Lasch, Christopher. *Haven in a Heartless World: The Family Besieged*. New York: Basic Books, 1977.

Lees, Andrew, and Lynn Hollen Lees. *Cities and the Making of Modern Europe*. Cambridge: Cambridge University Press, 2007.

Legrand. Directeur du port de commerce et Chef de la police indigène à le Consul à Haiphong, April 25, 1880, Indochine FM SG, Anciens fonds, Carton 1 Dossier A00 (16), CAOM, Aix-en-Provence.

Levine, Judith. *Harmful to Minors: The Perils of Protecting Children from Sex*. Minneapolis: Minnesota University Press, 2002.

Levine, Philippa. "Consistent Contradictions: Prostitution and Protective Labour Legislation in Nineteenth-Century England." *Social History* 19 (1994): 17–35.

Levine, Philippa. "Modernity, Medicine, and Colonialism: The Contagious Diseases Ordinances in Hong Kong and the Straits Settlements." *Positions* 6 (1998): 675–705.

Levine, Philippa. "'A Multitude of Unchaste Women': Prostitution in the British Empire." *Journal of Women's History* 15, no. 4 (2004): 159–63.

Levine, Philippa. *Prostitution, Race and Politics: Policing Venereal Disease in the British Empire.* New York: Routledge, 2003.

Levine, Philippa. "Rereading the 1890s: Venereal Disease as 'Constitutional Crisis' in Britain and British India." *Journal of Asian Studies* 55, no. 3 (1996): 585–612.

Levine, Philippa. "'Rough Usage': Prostitution, Law, and the Social Historian." In *Rethinking Social History: English Society, 1570–1920,* edited by Adrian Wilson. Manchester: Manchester University Press, 1993.

Lind, W.A.T. *Sex Irregularities of Children and Youth.* RNB Family Life Series. Sydney: Government Printer, 1916.

Lindsay, Jack. *The Roaring Twenties: Literary Life in Sydney, New South Wales in the Years 1921–6.* London: Bodley Head, 1960.

Lindsay, Norman. *My Mask: For What Little I Know of the Man behind It.* Sydney: Angus and Robertson, 1970.

Locher-Scholten, Elsbeth. "The Nyai in Colonial Deli: A Case of Supposed Mediation." In *Women and Mediation in Indonesia,* edited by Sita van Bemmelen, Madelon Djajadiningrat-Nieuwenhuis, Elsbeth Locher-Scholten, and Elly Touwen-Bouwsma. Leiden: KITLV Press, 1992.

Lombardi-Nash, Michael A., ed., *Sodomites and Urnings: Homosexual Representations in Classic German Journals.* Binghamton, NY: Harrington Park Press, 2006.

Lombroso, Cesare. "*La bête humaine* et l'anthropologie criminelle." *La Revue des revues* 4, no. 23 (1892): 260–64.

Lombroso, Cesare. *Criminal Man.* Translated by Mary Gibson and Nicole Hahn Rafter. Durham, NC: Duke University Press, 2006.

Lombroso, Cesare, and Guglielmo Ferrero. *Criminal Woman, the Prostitute, and the Normal Woman.* Translated by Nicole Hahn Rafter and Mary Gibson. Durham, NC: Duke University Press, 2004.

Lombroso, Cesare, and Guglielmo Ferrero. *La donna delinquente, la prostituta e la donna normale.* Turin: Roux, 1893.

Long, Alecia P. *The Great Southern Babylon: Sex, Race and Respectability in New Orleans, 1865–1920.* Baton Rouge: Louisiana State University Press, 2004.

Luddy, Maria. *Women and Philanthropy in Nineteenth-Century Ireland.* Cambridge: Cambridge University Press, 1995.

Luker, K. "Sex, Social Hygiene and the State: The Double-Edged Sword of Social Reform." *Theory and Society* 27, no. 2 (1998): 601–34.

Lynch, Michael. "'Here Is Adhesiveness': From Friendship to Homosexuality." *Victorian Studies* 29 (1985): 67–96.

Macdonald, Charlotte. "The 'Social Evil': Prostitution and the Passage of the Contagious Diseases Act (1869)." In *Women in History: Essays on European Women in New Zealand,* edited by Barbara Brookes, Charlotte Macdonald, and Margaret Tennant. Wellington: Allen & Unwin/Port Nicholson Press, 1986.

Macdonald, Charlotte. *A Woman of Good Character: Single Women as Immigrant Set-tlers in Nineteenth-Century New Zealand*. Wellington: Allen & Unwin, 1990.

Mackey, Thomas C. *Red Lights Out: A Legal History of Prostitution, Disorderly Houses and Vice Districts, 1780–1917*. London: Taylor and Francis, 1987.

MacPherson, Kerrie L. "Caveat Emptor! Attempts to Control the Venereals in Nineteenth Century Hong Kong." In *New Countries and Old Medicine: Proceedings of an International Conference on the History of Medicine and Health*, edited by Linda Bryder and Derek A. Dow. Auckland: Pyramid Press, 1995.

MacPherson, Kerrie L. "Conspiracy of Silence: A History of Sexually Transmitted Diseases and HIV/AIDS in Hong Kong." In *Sex, Disease, and Society: A Comparative History of Sexually Transmitted Disease and HIV/AIDS in Asia and the Pacific*, edited by Milton Lewis, Scott Bamber, and Michael Waugh. Westport, CT: Greenwood Press, 1997.

Mahood, Linda. *Policing Gender, Class and Family: Britain, 1850–1940*. London: UCL Press, 1995.

Maines, Rachel P. *The Technology of Orgasm: "Hysteria" the Vibrator, and Women's Sexual Satisfaction*. Baltimore: Johns Hopkins University Press, 1998.

Mak, Geertje. "Sandor/Sarolta Vay, from Passing Woman to Sexual Invert." *Journal of Women's History* 16 (2004): 54–77.

Maloka, Tshidiso. "*Khomo Lia Oela*: Canteens, Brothels and Labour Migrancy in Colonial Lesotho, 1900–40." *Journal of African History* 38 (1997): 101–22.

Manderson, Lenore. "Colonial Desires: Sexuality, Race, and Gender in British Malaya." *Journal of the History of Sexuality* 7, no. 3 (1997): 372–88.

Manderson, Lenore. "Migration, Prostitution and Medical Surveillance in Early Twentieth-Century Malaya." In *Migrants, Minorities and Health: Historical and Contemporary Studies*, edited by Lara Marks and Michael Worboys. London: Routledge, 1997.

Manderson, Lenore. *Sickness and the State: Health and Illness in Colonial Malaya, 1870–1940*. Cambridge: Cambridge University Press, 1996.

Mangan, J. A., and James Walvin, eds., *Manliness and Morality: Middle-Class Masculinity in Britain and America, 1800–1940*. New York: St. Martin's Press, 1987.

Manvell, Roger. *The Trial of Annie Besant and Charles Bradlaugh*. London: Elek, 1976.

Marcus, Sharon. *Between Women: Friendship, Desire, and Marriage in Victorian England*. Princeton, NJ: Princeton University Press, 2007.

Marcus, Steven. *The Other Victorians: A Study of Sexuality and Pornography in Mid-Nineteenth-Century England*. London: Corgi Books, 1970.

Marshall, John. "Pansies, Perverts and Macho Men: Changing Conceptions of Male Homosexuality." In *The Making of the Modern Homosexual*, edited by Kenneth Plummer. London: Hutchinson, 1981.

Martens, Jeremy C. "'Almost a Public Calamity': Prostitutes, 'Nurseboys,' and Attempts to Control Venereal Diseases in Colonial Natal, 1886–1890." *South African Historical Journal* 45 (2001): 27–52.

Martinez, Julia. "The Chinese Trade in Women and Children from Northern Vietnam." In *The Trade in Human Beings for Sex*, edited by P. Legros, J. Le Roux, and G. Faure. Bangkok: IRASEC, forthcoming.

Martinez, Julia. "*La Traite des Jaunes*: Trafficking in Women and Children across the China Seas." In *Many Middle Passages: Forced Migration and the Making of the Modern World*, edited by Cassandra Pybus, Markus Rediker, and Emma Christopher. Berkeley: University of California Press, 2007.

Mason, D. "Masturbation, Little Suck-a-Thumb and Struwwelpeter." *Udolpho* 32 (1998): 24–32.

Mason, Michael. *The Making of Victorian Sexual Attitudes*. Oxford: Oxford University Press, 1994.

Mason, Michael. *The Making of Victorian Sexuality*. Oxford: Oxford University Press, 1994.

Masson, Jeffrey. *The Assault on Truth: Freud's Suppression of the Seduction Theory*. Harmondsworth, UK: Penguin, 1985.

Matthews, Jill Julius. "Blue Movies in Australia: A Preliminary Study." *National Film and Sound Archive Journal* 2, no. 3 (2007): 1–12.

Matus, Jill. *Unstable Bodies: Victorian Representations of Sexuality and Maternity*. Manchester: University of Manchester Press, 1995.

Maxwell, Anne. *Colonial Photography and Exhibitions: Representations of the "Native" and the Making of European Identities*. London: Leicester University Press, 1999.

May, Dawn. *Aboriginal Labour and the Cattle Industry: Queensland from White Settlement to the Present*. Cambridge: Cambridge University Press, 1994.

Mayall, Berry. *Towards a Sociology for Childhood: Thinking from Children's Lives*. Buckingham, UK: Open University Press, 2002.

McBride, Theresa. "Public Authority and Private Lives: Divorce after the French Revolution." *French Historical Studies* 17 (1992): 747–60.

McCalman, Iain. "Unrespectable Radicalism: Infidels and Pornography in Early Nineteenth-Century London." *Past and Present* 104 (1984): 74–110.

McClintock, Anne. "Family Feuds: Gender, Nationalism, and the Family." *Feminist Review* 44 (1993): 61–80.

McClintock, Anne. *Imperial Leather: Race, Gender and Sexuality in the Colonial Contest*. New York: Routledge, 1995.

McClintock, Anne. "Screwing the System: Sexwork, Race and the Law." *Boundary 2*, 19, no. 2 (1992): 70–95.

McCormick, Leanne. "Sinister Sisters? The Portrayal of Ireland's Magdalene Asylums in Popular Culture." *Cultural and Social History* 2 (2005): 374–79.

McGarry, Molly. "Spectral Sexualities: Nineteenth-Century Spiritualism, Moral Panics, and the Making of U.S. Obscenity Law." *Journal of Women's History* 12 (2000): 8–29.

McGrath, Ann. "'Black Velvet': Aboriginal Women and Their Relations with White Men in the Northern Territory, 1910–1940." In *So Much Hard Work: Women and Prostitution in Australian History*, edited by Kay Daniels. Sydney: Fontana/Collins, 1984.

McGrath, Ann. *Born in the Cattle: Aborigines in Cattle Country*. Sydney: Allen & Unwin, 1987.

McIntosh, Mary. "The Homosexual Role." *Social Problems* 16 (1968): 182–92.

McLaren, Angus. *Birth Control in Nineteenth-Century England*. London: Croom Helm, 1978.

Mendelson, George. "Homosexuality and Psychiatric Nosology." *Australian and New Zealand Journal of Psychiatry* 37 (2003): 678–83.

Merrick, Jeffrey, and Michael Sibalis, eds. *Homosexuality in French History and Culture*. London: Harrington Park Press, 2001.

Merriman, John. "Urban Space and the Power of Language: The Stigmatization of the Faubourg in Nineteenth-Century France." *Social Science Information* 38 (1999): 329–51.

Mesch, Rachel. *The Hysteric's Revenge: French Women Writers at the Fin de Siècle*. Nashville, TN: Vanderbilt University Press, 2006.

Meschling, Jay. "Advice to Historians on the Advice to Mothers." *Journal of Social History* 9, no. 1 (1975): 44–63.

Metraux, Ruth. "Parents and Children: An Analysis of Contemporary German Child-Care and Youth-Guidance Literature." In *Childhood in Contemporary Cultures*, ed. Margaret Mead and Martha Wolfenstein. Chicago: University of Chicago Press, 1955.

Michéa, Claude François. "Des déviations de l'appétit vénérien." *Union Medicale*, July 1849, 338–39.

Mihalopoulos, Bill. "The Making of the Prostitutes: The *Karayuki-San*." *Bulletin of Concerned Asian Scholars* 25 (1993): 41–56.

Miners, Norman. *Hong Kong under Imperial Rule, 1912–1941*. Hong Kong: Oxford University Press, 1987.

Miners, R. J. "State Regulation of Prostitution in Hong Kong, 1857 to 1941." *Journal of the Hong Kong Branch of the Royal Asiatic Society* 24 (1984): 143–61.

Ming, Hanneke. "Barracks-Concubinage in the Indies, 1887–1920." *Indonesia* 35 (1983): 70–71.

Mitchison, Rosemary, and Leah Leneman, *Sexuality and Social Control: Scotland, 1660–1780*. Oxford: Blackwell, 1989.

Moll, Alfred. *Handbuch der Sexualwissenschaften mit besonderer Berücksichtigung der Kulturgeschichtlichen Beziehungen*. Leipzig: F.C.W. Vogel, 1912.

Moll, Alfred. *The Sexual Life of the Child*. Books Reborn. http://www.ipce.info/booksreborn/moll.

Monet, Paul. *Les jauniers, histoire vraie*. Paris: Gallimard, 1930.

Moore, C. "'A Precious Few': Melanesian and Asian Women in Northern Australia." In *Gender Relations in Australia: Domination and Negotiation*, edited by Kay Saunders and Raymond Evans. Sydney: Harcourt Brace and Jovanovich, 1992.

Moran, Jeffrey P. "Modernism Gone Mad: Sex Education Comes to Chicago, 1913." *Journal of American History* 83, no. 2 (1996): 481–513.

Moreau de Tours, P. *Des aberrations du sens génésique*. Paris: J. B. Baillière et fils, 1877.

Morgan, S. "Faith, Sex and Purity: The Religio-feminist Theory of Ellice Hopkins." *Women's History Review* 9, no. 1 (2000): 13–34.

Morrow, P. A. *A Plea for Sanitary and Moral Prophylaxis: Purity Series No. 6*. Sydney: William Brooks, n.d.

Mort, Frank. *Dangerous Sexualities: Medico-moral Politics in England since 1830*. 2nd ed. London: Routledge, 2000.

Moscucci, Ornella. *The Science of Woman: Gynaecology and Gender in England, 1800–1929*. Cambridge: Cambridge University Press, 1990.

Mosse, George L. *Nationalism and Sexuality: Respectability and Abnormal Sexuality in Modern Europe*. New York: H. Fertig, 1985.

Mostow, Joshua. "The Gender of Wakashu and the Grammar of Desire." In *Gender and Power in the Japanese Visual Field*, edited by Joshua Mostow, Norman Bryson, and Maribeth Graybill. Honolulu: University of Hawaii Press, 2003.

Mumm, Susan. "'Not Worse than Other Girls': The Convent-Based Rehabilitation of Fallen Women in Victorian Britain." *Journal of Social History* 29 (1996): 527–46.

Murnane, Mary, and Kay Daniels. "Prostitutes as 'Purveyors of Disease': Venereal Disease Legislation in Tasmania, 1868–1945." *Hecate* 5, no. 1 (1979): 5–21.

Musgrave, P. W. "Morality and the Medical Department: 1907–1974." *British Journal of Educational Studies* 25, no. 2 (1977): 136–54.

Myers, Tamara. *Caught: Montreal's Modern Girls and the Law, 1869–1945*. Toronto: University of Toronto Press, 2006.

Nead, Lynda. "Strip: Moving Bodies in the 1890s." *Early Popular Visual Culture* 3, no. 2 (2005): 135–50.

Nead, Lynda. *Myths of Sexuality: Representations of Women in Victorian Britain*. Oxford: Blackwell, 1988.

Nead, Lynda. *Victorian Babylon: People, Streets and Images in Nineteenth-Century London*. New Haven, CT: Yale University Press, 2000.

Nelson, James. *Publisher to the Decadents: Leonard Smithers in the Careers of Beardsley, Wilde, Dowson*. University Park: Pennsylvania State University Press, 2000.

Neuman, Richard P. "Masturbation, Madness, and the Modern Concepts of Childhood and Adolescence." *Journal of Social History* 8, no. 3 (1975): 1–27.

Newton, Esther. "The Mythic Mannish Lesbian: Radclyffe Hall and the New Woman." *Signs* 9 (1984): 557–75.

Noble, Marianne. *The Masochistic Pleasures of Sentimental Literature*. Princeton, NJ: Princeton University Press, 2000.

Nobus, Dany. "Locating Perversion, Dislocating Psychoanalysis." In *Perversion: Psychoanalytic Perspectives/Perspectives on Psychoanalysis*, edited by Dany Nobus and Lisa Downing. London: Karnac, 2006.

Nordau, M. *Degeneration*. Translated by George L. Mosse. Lincoln: University of Nebraska Press, 1993.

Norgaard, Erik. *With Love: The Erotic Postcard*. London: MacGibbon and Kee, 1969.

Norton, Rictor. *Mother Clap's Molly House: The Gay Subculture in England, 1700–1830*. London: Gay Men's Press, 1992.

Norton, Rictor. "Recovering Gay History from the Old Bailey." *London Journal* 30, no. 1 (2005): 39–54.

Noyes, John. *The Mastery of Submission: Inventions of Masochism*. Ithaca, NY: Cornell University Press, 1997.

Nye, Robert. "The History of Sexuality in Context: National Sexological Tradition." *Science in Context* 4, no. 2 (1991): 387–406.

Nye, Robert. "The Medical Origins of Sexual Fetishism." In *Fetishism as Cultural Discourse*, edited by Emily Apter and William Pietz. Ithaca, NY: Cornell University Press, 1993.

Nye, Robert. "Sex and Sexuality in France since 1800." In *National Histories*. Vol. 1 of *Sexual Cultures in Europe*, edited by Franz Eder, Lesley A. Hall, and Gert Hekma. Manchester: Manchester University Press, 1999.

O'Brien, Anne. "Missionary Masculinities, the Homoerotic Gaze and the Politics of Race: Gilbert White in Northern Australia, 1885–1915." *Gender and History* 20, no. 1 (2008): 68–86.

Oldenburg, Veena Talwar. "Lifestyle as Resistance: The Case of the Courtesans of Lucknow, India." *Feminist Studies* 16 (1990): 259–88.

Oldenburg, Veena Talwar. *The Making of Colonial Lucknow, 1856–77*. Princeton, NJ: Princeton University Press, 1984.

O'Malley, Andrew. *The Making of the Modern Child*. London: Routledge, 2003.

Oosterhuis, Harry. *Stepchildren of Nature: Krafft-Ebing, Psychiatry, and the Making of Sexual Identity*. Chicago: University of Chicago Press, 2000.

Oram, Alison. "Cross-Dressing and Transgender." In *The Modern History of Sexuality*, edited by Harry G. Cocks and Matt Houldbrook. Basingstoke, UK: Palgrave Macmillan, 2006.

Ordover, Nancy. *American Eugenics: Race, Queer Anatomy, and the Science of Nationalism*. Minneapolis: University of Minnesota Press, 2003.

Ouellette, William. *Fantasy Postcards*. London: Sphere, 1976.

Parent-Duchâtelet, Alexandre Jean Baptiste. *De la prostitution dans la ville de Paris, considérée sous le rapport de l'hygiène publique, de la morale et de l'administration*. Paris: Baillière, 1836.

Parent-Duchâtelet, Alexandre Jean Baptiste. *De la prostitution dans la ville de Paris, considérée sous le rapport de l'hygiène publique, de la morale et de l'administration*. Paris: Baillière, 1837.

Parker, Kunal M. "'A Corporation of Superior Prostitutes': Anglo-Indian Legal Conceptions of Temple Dancing Girls, 1900–1914." *Modern Asian Studies* 32, no. 3 (1998): 559–60.

Parker, Valerie. "Social Hygiene and the Child." *Annals of the American Academy of Political and Social Science* 121 (1925): 46–52.

Peakman, Julie. *Mighty Lewd Books: The Development of Pornography in Eighteenth-Century England*. Hampshire, UK: Palgrave Macmillan, 2003.

Peakman, Julie, ed. *Sexual Perversions, 1670–1890*. Basingstoke, UK: Palgrave Macmillan, 2009.

Pearsall, Ronald. *Public Purity, Private Shame: Victorian Sexual Hypocrisy Exposed*. London: Weidenfeld and Nicolson, 1976.

Pearsall, Ronald. *The Worm in the Bud: The World of Victorian Sexuality*. London: Weidenfeld and Nicolson, 1969.

Peers, Douglas M. "Soldiers, Surgeons and the Campaigns to Combat Sexually Transmitted Diseases in Colonial India, 1805–1860." *Medical History* 42 (1998): 137–60.

Petrow, Stefan. *Policing Morals: The Metropolitan Police and the Home Office, 1870–1914*. Oxford: Clarendon Press, 1994.

Phillips, Richard. "Heterogeneous Imperialism and the Regulation of Sexuality in British West Africa." *Journal of the History of Sexuality* 14 (2005): 291–315.

Phillips, Richard. "Imperialism and the Regulation of Sexuality: Colonial Legislation on Contagious Diseases and Ages of Consent." *Historical Geography* 28 (2002): 339–62.

Pick, Daniel. *Faces of Degeneration: A European Disorder, c. 1848–1918*. Cambridge: Cambridge University Press, 1989.

Piddington, Marion. *Tell Them! or The Second Stage of Mothercraft: A Handbook of Suggestions for the Sex Training of the Child*. Sydney: Moore's Book Shop, 1926.

Pinchbeck, Ivy, and Margaret Hewitt. *Children in English Society*. 2 vols. Routledge, 1969.

Pivar, David J. "The Military, Prostitution, and Colonial Peoples: India and the Philippines, 1885–1917." *Journal of Sex Research* 17, no. 3 (1981): 256–69.

Pivar, David J. *Purity Crusade: Sexual Morality and Social Control, 1868–1900*. Westport, CT: Greenwood Press, 1973.

Ploss, Hermann. *Das Weib, in der Natur- und Völkerkunde* [*Woman in Natural History and Folklore*]. 2 vols. Leipzig: Griebens, 1884.

Plummer, K., ed. *The Making of the Modern Homosexual*. London: Hutchinson, 1981.

Pollock, Linda. *Forgotten Children: Parent-Child Relations from 1500 to 1900*. Cambridge: Cambridge University Press, 1983.

Porter, Roy, and Marijke Geswijt-Hofstra, eds. *Cultures of Neurasthenia*. Amsterdam: Rodopi, 2000.

Porter, Roy, and Lesley A. Hall. *The Facts of Life: The Creation of Sexual Knowledge in Britain, 1650–1950*. New Haven, CT: Yale University Press, 1995.

Porter, Roy, and Sylvana Tomeselli, eds. *Rape*. Oxford: Blackwell, 1986.

Posel, Ros. "'Continental Women' and Durban's 'Social Evil,' 1899–1905." *Journal of Natal and Zulu History* 12 (1989): 1–13.

Postman, Neil. *The Disappearance of Childhood*. London: Vintage, 1994.

Praz, Mario. *The Romantic Agony*. 2nd ed. Translated by A. Davis. Edited by F. Kermode. Oxford: Oxford University Press, 1970.

Pritchard, David. *Oscar Wilde*. New Lanark, UK: Geddes & Grosset, 2001.

Proschan, Frank. "'Syphilis, Opiomania and Pederasty': Colonial Constructions of Vietnamese (and French) Social Diseases." *Journal of the History of Sexuality* 11, no. 4 (2002): 610–36.

Prosser, Jay. *Second Skins: The Body Narratives of Transsexuality*. New York: Columbia University Press, 1998.

Qvortrup, Jens, ed. *Studies in Modern Childhood: Society, Agency, Culture*. London: Palgrave Macmillan, 2005.

Rachilde. *La marquise de Sade*. Paris: Gallimard, 1996.

Rachilde. *Monsieur Vénus*. Paris: Flammarion, 1926.

Raffi, Gilles. "Haiphong, origines, conditions et modalités du développement jusqu'à 1921." Doctoral thesis, Université de Provence, 1994.

Raj, M. Sundra. *Prostitution in Madras: A Study in Historical Perspective.* Delhi: Konark, 1993.

Ramseyer, J. Mark. "Indentured Prostitution in Imperial Japan: Credible Commitments in the Commercial Sex Industry." *Journal of Law, Economics and Organisation* 7 (1991): 89–116.

Rebman, F. J., trans. *Psychopathia Sexualis with Especial Reference to Antipathic Sexual Instinct: A Medico-legal Study,* by Richard von Krafft-Ebing. London: Rebman, 1901.

Reiger, Kereen. *The Disenchantment of the Home: Modernizing the Australian Family.* Melbourne: Oxford University Press, 1985.

Renz, Carl, and Mildred Renz. *Big Problems on Little Shoulders.* New York: Macmillan, 1935.

Robertson, Stephen. *Crimes against Children: Sexual Violence and Legal Culture in New York City, 1880–1960.* Chapel Hill: University of North Carolina Press, 2005.

Robertson, Stephen. "What's Law Got to Do with It? Legal Records and Sexual Histories." *Journal of the History of Sexuality* 14 (2005): 161–85.

Robie, Walter. *Sex and Life: What the Experienced Should Teach and What the Inexperienced Should Learn.* Boston: Gorham Press, 1920.

Robinson, M. E. "The Sex Problem." *Journal of International Ethics* 21, no. 3 (1911): 326–39.

Rodriguez, Suzanne. *Wild Heart. A Life: Natalie Clifford Barney's Journey from Victorian America to Belle Epoque Paris.* New York: Ecco, 2002.

Rosario, Vernon A. *The Erotic Imagination: French Histories of Perversity.* New York: Oxford University Press, 1997.

Rosario, Vernon A. "On Sexual Perversion and Transsensualism." In *Perversion: Psychoanalytic Perspectives/Perspectives on Psychoanalysis,* edited by Dany Nobus and Lisa Downing. London: Karnac, 2006.

Rosario, Vernon A., ed. *Science and Homosexualities.* New York: Routledge, 1997.

Rose, Nikolas. *Governing the Soul.* London: Routledge, 1989.

Ross, Ellen. *Love and Toil: Motherhood in Outcast London.* Oxford: Oxford University Press, 1993.

Rousseau, Jean-Jacques. *The Emile of Jean Jacques Rousseau.* London: Heinemann, 1963.

Rowbotham, Sheila. *Edward Carpenter: A Life of Love and Liberty.* London: Verso, 2008.

Rule, Pauline. "Prostitution in Calcutta, 1860–1940: The Pattern of Recruitment." In *Class, Ideology and Women in Asian Societies,* edited by Gail Pearson and Lenore Manderson. Hong Kong: Asian Research Service, 1987.

Rupp, Leila J. "Loving Women in the Modern World." In *Gay Life and Culture: A World History,* edited by Robert Aldrich. London: Thames and Hudson, 2006.

Sachiko, Sone. "Karayuki-San of Asia, 1868–1938: The Role of Prostitutes Overseas in Japanese Economic and Social Development." MPhil thesis, Murdoch University, 1980.

Said, Edward. *Orientalism: Western Conceptions of the Orient*. London: Penguin, 1995.

Sanchez-Eppler, Karen. *Dependent States: The Child's Part in Nineteenth-Century American Culture*. Chicago: University of Chicago Press, 2005.

Sanger, Margaret. *What Every Boy and Girl Should Know*. New York: Brentano's, 1927.

Sardar, Tanika. "Rhetoric against the Age of Consent: Resisting Colonial Reason and the Death of a Child-Wife." *Economic and Political Weekly*, September 4, 1993, 1869–78.

Sass, H., and S. Herpertz. "Personality Disorders." In *A History of Clinical Psychiatry: The Origin and History of Psychiatric Disorders*, edited by German E. Berrios and Roy Porter. London: Athlone Press, 1999.

Schafer, Sylvia. *Children in Moral Danger and the Problem of Government in Third Republic France*. Princeton, NJ: Princeton University Press, 1997.

Schiebinger, Londa. "Skeletons in the Closet: The First Illustrations of the Female Skeleton in Eighteenth- Century Anatomy." *Representations* 14 (1986): 42–82.

Scully, Eileen P. "Prostitution as Privilege: The 'American Girl' of Treaty-Port Shanghai, 1860–1937." *International History Review* 20 (1998): 855–83.

Sedgwick, Eve Kosofsky. *Epistemology of the Closet*. Berkeley: University of California Press, 1990.

Seitler, Dana. "Queer Physiognomies; or, How Many Ways Can We Do the History of Sexuality?" *Criticism* 46 (2004): 71–102.

Sekula, Alan. "The Body and the Archive." *October* 39 (1986): 3–64.

Sengoopta, Chandak. "The Modern Ovary: Constructions, Meanings, Uses." *History of Science* 38 (2000): 426–85.

Sengoopta, Chandak. *The Most Secret Quintessence of Life: Sex, Glands, and Hormones, 1850–1950*. Chicago: University of Chicago Press, 2006.

Shapiro, Anne-Louise. "Paris." In *Housing the Workers*, edited by M. Daunton. Leicester: Leicester University Press, 1990.

Shimizu, Hiroshi. "Karayuki-San and the Japanese Economic Advance into British Malaya, 1870–1920." *Asian Studies Review* 20, no. 3 (1997): 107–32.

Shortland, Michael. "Courting the Cerebellum: Early Organological and Phrenological Views on Sexuality." *British Journal of the History of Science* 20 (1987): 173–99.

Shumsky, Neil L. "Tacit Acceptance: Respectable Americans and Segregated Prostitution, 1870–1910." *Journal of Social History* 19 (1986): 665–79.

Sigel, Lisa Z. *Governing Pleasures: Pornography and Social Change in England, 1815–1914*. New Brunswick, NJ: Rutgers University Press, 2002.

Singy, Peter. "The History of Masturbation: An Essay Review." *Journal of the History of Medicine and Allied Sciences* 59, no. 1 (2004): 112–21.

Sinn, Elizabeth. "Chinese Patriarchy and the Protection of Women in 19th-Century Hong Kong." In *Women and Chinese Patriarchy: Submission, Servitude and Escape*, edited by Maria Jaschok and Suzanne Miers. Hong Kong: Hong Kong University Press, 1994.

Sissons, C. "Karayuki-San: Japanese Prostitutes in Australia, 1887–1916—I." *Historical Studies* 17, no. 68 (1977): 323–41.

Sissons, C. "Karayuki-San: Japanese Prostitutes in Australia, 1887–1916—II." *Historical Studies* 17, no. 69 (1977): 474–88.

Skultans, Vieda. *Madness and Morals: Ideas on Insanity in the Nineteenth Century.* London: Routledge, 1975.

Slater, Stefan. "Pimps, Police and Filles de Joie: Foreign Prostitution in Interwar London." *London Journal* 32 (2007): 53–74.

Sloan, Phillip R. "Performing the Categories: Eighteenth-Century Generation Theory and the Biological Roots of Kant's A Priori." *Journal of the History of Philosophy* 40 (2002): 229–53.

Smith, F. B. "Ethics and Disease in the Later Nineteenth Century: The Contagious Diseases Acts." *Historical Studies* 15, no. 57 (1971): 118–35.

Smith, F. B. "Labouchere's Amendment to the Criminal Law Amendment Act." *Historical Studies* 17 (1976): 165–73.

Smith-Rosenberg, Carroll. "Discourses of Sexuality and Subjectivity: The New Woman, 1870–1936." In *Hidden from History: Reclaiming the Gay and Lesbian Past*, edited by Martin Duberman, Martha Vicinus, and George Chauncey. New York: New American Library, 1989.

Smith-Rosenberg, Carroll. *Disorderly Conduct: Vision of Gender in Victorian America.* New York: Knopf, 1985.

Smith-Rosenberg, Carroll. "The Female World of Love and Ritual." *Signs* 1 (1975): 1–29.

Somerville, Siobhan. "Scientific Racism and the Emergence of the Homosexual Body." *Journal of the History of Sexuality* 5, no. 2 (1994): 243–66.

Somerville, Siobhan. "Scientific Racism and the Invention of the Homosexual Body." In *Sexology in Culture: Labelling Bodies and Desires*, edited by Lucy Bland and Laura Doan. Cambridge: Polity Press, 1998.

Sommerville, C. John. *The Rise and Fall of Childhood.* Beverly Hills, CA: Sage, 1982.

Spencer, H. *The Principles of Sociology.* 3rd ed. London: Williams and Norgate, 1876.

Spitz, René A. "Authority and Masturbation: Some Remarks on a Bibliographical Investigation." *Psychoanalytical Study of the Child* 7 (1952): 490–27.

Spongberg, Mary. *Feminizing Venereal Disease: The Body of the Prostitute in Nineteenth-Century Medical Discourse.* London: Palgrave Macmillan, 1997.

Spree, R. "Shaping the Child's Personality: Medical Advice on Child-Rearing from the Late Eighteenth to the Early Twentieth Century in Germany." *Social History of Medicine* 5, no. 2 (1992): 16–35.

Steakley, James. *The Homosexual Emancipation Movement in Germany.* New York: Arno Press, 1975.

Stearns, Peter. *Anxious Parents: A History of Modern Childrearing in America.* New York: New York University Press, 2003.

Stengers, Jean, and Anne Van Neck. *Masturbation: The History of a Great Terror.* New York: Palgrave Macmillan, 2001.

Stepansky, Paul E. "A Footnote to the History of Homosexuality in Britain: Havelock Ellis and the Bedborough Trial of 1898." In *Essays in the History of Psychiatry,* ed. Edwin R. Wallace and Lucius C. Pressley. Columbia, SC: Wm. S. Hall Psychiatric Institute, 1980.

Stolberg, Michael. "The Crime of Onan and the Laws of Nature. Religious and Medical Discourses on Masturbation in the Late Seventieth and Early Eighteenth Centuries." *Paedagogica Historica* 39, no. 6 (2003): 701–17.

Stolberg, Michael. "An Unmanly Vice: Self-Pollution, Anxiety and the Body in the Eighteenth Century." *Social History of Medicine* 13, no. 1 (2000): 1–22.

Stoler, Ann Laura. *Carnal Knowledge and Imperial Power: Race and the Intimate in Colonial Rule*. Berkeley: University of California Press, 2002.

Stoler, Ann Laura. "Making Empire Respectable: The Politics of Race and Sexual Morality in Twentieth-Century Colonial Cultures." In *Imperial Monkey Business: Racial Supremacy in Social Darwinist Theory and Colonial Practice*, edited by Jan Breman. Amsterdam: VU University Press, 1990.

Stoler, Ann Laura. *Race and the Education of Desire: Foucault's "History of Sexuality" and the Colonial Order of Things*. Durham, NC: Duke University Press, 1995.

Stone, Laurence. *The Family, Sex and Marriage in England, 1500–1800*. London: Harper and Row, 1979.

Stopes, Marie. *Sex and the Young*. London: G. P. Putnam's Sons, 1926.

Storch, Robert D. "Police Control of Street Prostitution in Victorian London: A Case Study of Police Action." In *Police and Society*, edited by David H. Bayled. Beverley Hills, CA: Sage, 1976.

Strachey, Lytton. *Eminent Victorians*. London: Chatto and Windus, 1918.

Strachey, Lytton. "Macaulay." *Portraits in Miniature and Other Essays*. London: Chatto & Windus, 1931.

Strachey, Lytton. *Queen Victoria*. London: Chatto and Windus, 1921.

Strain, Frances. *New Patterns in Sex Teaching: The Normal Sex Interests of Children and Their Guidance from Infancy to Adolescence*. New York: D. Appleton-Century, 1934.

Strong, B. "Ideas of the Early Sex Education Movement in America, 1890–1920." *History of Education Quarterly* 12 (1972): 129–61.

Sullivan, Nikki. *A Critical Introduction to Queer Theory*. Edinburgh: Edinburgh University Press, 2003.

Sulloway, Frank J. *Freud, Biologist of the Mind: Beyond the Psychoanalytic Legend*. Cambridge, MA: Harvard University Press, 1992.

Summers, Anne. "'The Constitution Violate': The Female Body and the Female Subject in the Campaigns of Josephine Butler." *History Workshop Journal* 48 (1999): 1–15.

Swanson, Maynard. "The Sanitation Syndrome: Bubonic Plague and Urban Native Policy in the Cape Colony, 1900–1909." *Journal of African History* 18 (1977): 408–10.

Symonds, John Addington. *A Problem in Greek Ethics Being an Inquiry into the Phenomenon of Sexual Inversion Addressed Especially to Medical Psychologists and Jurists*. London: Privately printed, 1901.

Symonds, John Addington. *A Problem in Modern Ethics*. London: Privately printed, 1896.

Symonds, John Addington. *A Problem in Modern Ethics Being an Inquiry into the Phenomenon of Sexual Inversion. Addressed Especially to Medical Psychologist and Jurists*. London: Charles R. Dawes ex Libris, 1896.

Szretzer, Simon, Robert Nye, and Frans van Poppel. "Fertility and Contraception during the Demographic Transition: Qualitative and Quantitative Approaches." *Journal of Interdisciplinary History* 34, no. 2 (2003): 141–54.

Taithe, Bertrand. "Consuming Desires: Female Prostitutes and 'Customers' at the Margins of Crime and Perversion in France and Britain, c. 1836–85." In *Gender and Crime in Modern Europe,* edited by Margaret L. Arnot and Cornelie Usborne. London: UCL Press, 1999.

Tatar, Maria. *Lustmord: Sexual Murder in Weimar Germany.* Princeton, NJ: Princeton University Press, 1995.

Taylor, Clare L. *Women, Writing and Fetishism, 1890–1950: Female Cross-Gendering.* Oxford: Oxford University Press, 2003.

Temkin, Oswei. *The Double Face of Janus and Other Essays in the History of Medicine.* Baltimore: Johns Hopkins University Press, 1977.

Terami-Wada, Motoe. "Karayuki-San of Manila: 1880–1920." *Philippine Studies* 34 (1986): 287–316.

Terry, Jennifer. *An American Obsession: Science, Medicine, and Homosexuality in Modern Society.* Chicago: University of Chicago Press, 1999.

Thomas, Nicholas. "Colonial Conversions: Difference, Hierarchy, and History in Early Twentieth-Century Evangelical Propaganda." In *Cultures of Empire: A Reader: Colonisers in Britain and the Empire in the Nineteenth and Twentieth Centuries,* edited by Catherine Hall. Manchester: Manchester University Press, 2000.

Thompson, Edward P. *Customs in Common.* London: Merlin, 1991.

Tissot, S. *Onanism: Treatise on the Diseases Produced by Onanism.* New York: Collins and Hannay, 1832.

Tomoko, Yamazaki. *Sandakan Brothel No. 8.* Translated by Karen Colligan-Taylor. New York: M. E. Sharpe, 1999.

Trumbach, Randolph. "Sex, Gender, and Sexual Identity in Modern Culture: Male Sodomy and Female Prostitution in Enlightenment London." In "The State, Society, and the Regulation of Sexuality in Modern Europe." Special issue. Part 1. *Journal of the History of Sexuality* 2, no. 2 (1991): 186–203.

Tucker, Anne, ed. *The History of Japanese Photography.* New Haven, CT: Yale University Press in association with the Museum of Fine Arts, Houston, 2003.

Turner, Bryan. *The Body and Society: Explorations in Social Theory.* 2nd ed. London: Sage, 1996.

Van der Meer, Theo. "Sodomy and Its Discontents: Discourse, Desire and the Rise of a Same-Sex and Proto-Something in the Early Modern Dutch Republic." *Historical Reflections* 33 (2007): 41–67.

Van Heyningen, Elizabeth B. "The Social Evil in the Cape Colony, 1868–1902: Prostitution and the Contagious Diseases Acts." *Journal of South African Studies* 10, no. 2 (1984): 170–97.

Van Onselen, Charles. "Prostitutes and Proletarians, 1886–1914." In *New Babylon.* Vol. 1 of *Studies in the Social and Economic History of the Witwatersrand, 1886–1914.* New York: Longman, 1982.

Varley, Henry. *Private Address to Boys and Youths: On an Important Subject Containing Invaluable Information.* London: Office of the Christian Commonwealth, 1884.

Vaughan, Megan. *Curing Their Ills: Colonial Power and African Illness*. Cambridge: Cambridge University Press, 1991.

Vicinus, Martha. *Intimate Friends: Women Who Loved Women, 1778–1928*. Chicago: University of Chicago Press, 2004.

Vicinus, Martha. *Suffer and Be Still: Women in the Victorian Age*. Bloomington: Indiana University Press, 1972.

Vicinus, Martha. "They Wonder to Which Sex I Belong: The Historical Roots of the Modern Lesbian Identity." In *Homosexuality: Which Homosexuality?* edited by Dennis Altman, Carole Vance, Martha Vicinus, and Jeffrey Weeks. London: GMP, 1989.

Waddams, Stephen M. *Sexual Slander in Nineteenth-Century England: Defamation in the Ecclesiastical Courts, 1815–55*. Toronto: University of Toronto Press, 2000.

Wagner, David. *The New Temperance: The American Obsession with Sin and Vice*. Boulder, CO: Westview Press, 1997.

Walkowitz, Judith R. *City of Dreadful Delight: Narratives of Sexual Danger in Late-Victorian London*. Chicago: University of Chicago Press, 1992.

Walkowitz, Judith R. "The Making of an Outcast Group: Prostitutes and Working Women in Nineteenth-Century Plymouth and Southampton." In *A Widening Sphere: Changing Roles of Victorian Women*, edited by Martha Vicinus. Bloomington: Indiana University Press, 1977.

Walkowitz, Judith R. *Prostitution and Victorian Society: Women, Class and the State*. Cambridge: Cambridge University Press, 1980.

Walkowitz, Judith R., and Daniel J. Walkowitz. "'We Are Not Beasts of the Field': Prostitution and the Poor in Plymouth and Southampton under the Contagious Diseases Acts." *Feminist Studies* 1 (1973): 73–106.

Walsh, J. J., and J. A. Foote. *Safeguarding the Children's Nerves: A Handbook of Mental Hygiene*. Philadelphia: J. B. Lippincott, 1924.

Walters, Roger G. *Primers for Prudery: Sexual Advice for Victorian America*. Baltimore: Johns Hopkins University Press, 2000.

Ware, Vron. *Beyond the Pale*. London: Verso, 1992.

Warren, James Francis. *Ah Ku and Karayuki-San: Prostitution in Singapore, 1870–1940*. Oxford: Oxford University Press, 1993.

Warren, James Francis. "Prostitution and the Politics of Venereal Disease: Singapore, 1870–98." *Journal of Southeast Asian Studies* 21 (1990): 360–83.

Waters, Chris. "Sexology." In *Palgrave Advances in the Modern History of Sexuality*, ed. Matt Houlbrook and Harry G. Cocks. Basingstoke, UK: Palgrave Macmillan, 2006.

Watson, John. *The Psychological Care of the Infant and Child*. New York: W. W. Norton, 1978.

Watson, John. "Psychology as the Behaviorist Views It." Classics in the History of Psychology. http://psychclassics.asu.edu/Watson/views.htm.

Weeks, Jeffrey. *Coming Out: Homosexual Politics in Britain, from the Nineteenth Century to the Present*. London: Quartet Books, 1977.

Weeks, Jeffrey. *Making Sexual History*. Cambridge: Polity Press, 2000.

Weeks, Jeffrey. *Sex, Politics and Society: The Regulation of Sexuality since 1800*. 2nd ed. London: Longman, 1989.

Weeks, Jeffrey. *Sexuality and Its Discontents: Meaning, Myths and Modern Sexualities*. London: Routledge and Kegan Paul, 1985.

Welsh, D. A. *The Massacre of the Innocents*. Sydney: Workers' Educational Association of New South Wales, 1917.

Werth, Paul W. "Through the Prism of Prostitution: State, Society and Power." *Social History* 19 (1994): 1–15.

Westney, D. Eleanor. *Imitation and Innovation: The Transfer of Western Organizational Patterns to Meiji Japan*. Cambridge, MA: Harvard University Press, 1987.

Westphal, Carl. "Die conträre Sexualempfindung: Symptom eines neuropathischen (psychopathischen) Zustandes." *Archiv für Psychiatrie und Nervenkrankheiten* 2 (1869): 73–108.

Whitbread, Helena, ed. *I Know My Own Heart: The Diaries of Anne Lister (1791–1840)*. London: Virago, 1988.

White, Jerry. *Rothschild Buildings: Life in an East End Tenement Block, 1887–1920*. London: Routledge, 1980.

White, Luise. *The Comforts of Home: Prostitution in Colonial Nairobi*. Chicago: University of Chicago Press, 1990.

Whitehead, Judy. "Bodies Clean and Unclean: Prostitution, Sanitary Legislation, and Respectable Femininity in Colonial North India." *Gender and History* 7, no. 1 (1995): 41–63.

Wickes, Frances. *The Inner World of Childhood: A Study in Analytic Psychology*. New York: D. Appleton, 1927.

Wiener, Martin. *Men of Blood: Violence, Manliness and Criminal Justice in Victorian England*. Cambridge: Cambridge University Press, 2004.

Williams, Linda. *Hard Core: Power, Pleasure, and the "Frenzy of the Visible."* Berkeley: University of California Press, 1989.

Wilson, Elizabeth. *The Sphinx in the City: Urban Life, the Control of Disorder, and Woman*. Berkeley: California University Press, 1991.

Wittig, Monique. *The Straight Mind and Other Essays*. Boston: Beacon Press, 1992.

Wohl, Anthony S. *Endangered Lives: Public Health in Victorian Britain*. Cambridge, MA: Harvard University Press, 1983.

Wood, Thomas, Marian Lerrigo, and Thurman Rice. *Sex Education: A Guide for Teachers and Parents*. New York: Thomas Nelson and Sons, 1937.

Woodward, S. *Hints for the Young in Relation to the Health of Body and Mind*. New York: Arno Press, 1974.

Woollacott, Angela M. "'Khaki Fever' and Its Control: Gender, Class, Age and Sexual Morality on the British Homefront in the First World War." *Journal of Contemporary History* 29 (1994): 25–47.

Woollen, Geoff. "Une nouvelle de Camille Lemonnier: De 'Jacques l'Éventreur' à *La bête humaine*." *Les Cahiers naturalistes* 69 (1995): 167–77.

Woollen, Geoff, ed. *Zola: "La bête humaine": Colloque du centenaire à Glasgow*. Glasgow: Glasgow University Press, 1995.

Yeoh, B.S.A. *Contesting Space: Power Relations and the Urban Built Environment in Colonial Singapore*. Kuala Lumpur: National University of Singapore, 1996.

Zelizer, Vivienne. *Pricing the Priceless Child: The Changing Social Value of Children*. Princeton, NJ: Princeton University Press, 1985.

Zola, Emile. *La bête humaine*. Vol. 6 of *Œuvres completes*. Paris: Cercle du livre précieux, 1967.

Zola, Emile. "Préface au roman d'un inverti-né." In *Nos ancêtres les pervers: La vie des homosexuels au dix-neuvième siècle*, edited by Pierre Hahn. Paris: Olivier Orban, 1979.

Zornado, Joseph. *Inventing the Child: Culture, Ideology, and the Story of Childhood*. New York: Garland, Brown, 2001.

CONTRIBUTORS

Chiara Beccalossi is a postdoctoral research fellow at the Centre for the History of European Discourses, University of Queensland, Australia, and author of the forthcoming *Female Sexual Inversion: Same-Sex Desires in Italian and British Sexology*.

Sean Brady is lecturer in modern British history at Birkbeck College, University of London. His research interest focuses on gender, sexuality, politics, and religion in nineteenth- and twentieth-century Britain. He is the author of *Masculinity and Male Homosexuality in Britain, 1861–1913*, co-editor of the forthcoming *What Is Masculinity? Historical Dynamics from Antiquity to the Contemporary World*, and editor of the forthcoming *Masculinities in History* and *John Addington Symonds (1840–1893) on Homosexuality: A Critical Edition of Sources*. He is convening editor of Palgrave Macmillan's series "Genders and Sexualities in History."

Ivan Crozier is a Senior Lecturer in the Science Studies Unit at the University of Edinburgh and is currently writing a book on culture-bound syndromes in psychiatry.

Lisa Downing is professor of French discourses of sexuality and director of the Centre for the Interdisciplinary Study of Sexuality and Gender in Europe at the University of Exeter in the United Kingdom. She is the author of *Desiring the Dead: Necrophilia and Nineteenth-Century French Literature* and *The Cambridge Introduction to Michel Foucault* and is the author or co-editor of numerous other publications in the fields of sexuality and

gender studies, modern critical theory, and modern French film and literature.

R. Danielle Egan is an associate professor of gender and sexuality studies at
St. Lawrence University in Canton, New York. Her research interests cover
areas such as the sex industry and childhood sexuality in medical reform and
academic discourse from the mid-nineteenth to early-twentieth centuries. Her
current project, with Gail Hawkes, is on the anti-sexualization campaign and
contemporary cultural panics on childhood sexuality in the Anglophone West.
She has published extensively in these fields, including *Dancing for Dollars
and Paying for Love: The Relationships between Exotic Dancers and their
Regulars*, and *Theorizing the Sexual Child in Modernity* (co-authored with
Gail Hawkes).

Ruth Ford is senior lecturer in history at La Trobe University, Australia. She
is the author of "Filthy, Obscene and Mad: Engendering Homophobia in
Australia, 1940s–1960s" in *Homophobia: An Australian History* and "The
Man-Woman Murderer: Sex Fraud, Sexual Inversion and the Unmentionable
Article in 1920s Australia" in *Gender and History*. She is currently complet-
ing a monograph titled *Secret Lives: Passionate Friends and Lesbian Love in
Australia, 1920s–1950s.*

Raelene Frances is professor of history and dean of arts at Monash Univer-
sity, Australia. She has published on the history of work, women's history,
Aboriginal/European contact history, and religious and community history
and has also co-edited several collections of essays on Australian and New
Zealand history. Her publications include *Selling Sex: A Hidden History of
Prostitution, White Slaves/White Australia: Prostitution and the Making
of Australian Society, Women and the Great War* (co-authored with Bruce
Scates), *Women at Work from the Gold Rushes to World War II* (co-authored
with Bruce Scates), and *The Politics of Work.*

Gail Hawkes is a senior lecturer in sociology at the School of Behavioural,
Cognitive and Social Sciences, University of New England, Australia. She has
published extensively on sexuality and childhood sexuality. Her publications include *A Sociology of Sex and Sexuality, Sex and Pleasure in Western Culture*, and
Theorizing the Sexual Child in Modernity (co-authored with R. Danielle Egan).

Louise A. Jackson is a senior lecturer in the School of History, Classics and
Archaeology, University of Edinburgh. Her publications include *Child Sexual*

Abuse in Victorian England; Women Police: Gender, Welfare and Surveillance in the Twentieth Century; and, with S. D'Cruze, *Women, Crime and Justice in England since 1660.*

Chad Parkhill is a Ph.D. student at the University of Queensland, Australia. His dissertation is an interdisciplinary examination of constructs of contemporary heterosexuality. His work will appear in *Pornography and Philosophy* and *Error: Information, Control, and the Cultures of Noise.*

Elizabeth Stephens is a research fellow at the Centre for the History of European Discourses, University of Queensland, Australia. She has published widely in the areas of queer theory, gender studies, and poststructuralism. Her publications include *Queer Writing: Homoeroticism in the Fiction of Jean Genet* and the forthcoming *Anatomy as Spectacle: Public Exhibitions of the Body from the Nineteenth Century to the Present.*

INDEX

Acton, William, 108, 126
age of consent, 91, 92, 93–4, 95, 96,
    100, 129
AIDS, 38
Aldrich, Robert, 53
anal sex, *see* sodomy
Aristotle, 36
Arthurnot, F. F., 175
Augiéras, François, 53
Australian Aboriginals, 56–7

Baker Brown, Isaac, 117
Bakshi, Parminder, 58
Bancroft, H. H., 6–7
Barret-Ducroq, Françoise, 24
Bat' d'Af (*Bataillons d'Afrique*), 54
Baudelaire, Charles, 11
BDSM, 42
    see also sadomasochism
Bersani, Leo, 40
Binet, Alfred, 69, 114–15
birth control, 102–4
bisexuality, 119
Blackwell, Elizabeth, 130
Blair-Bell, William, 117
Bloch, Iwan, 7, 48
Brady, Sean, 20

brothels, 87, 89, 106, 108, 148, 154,
    157–8, 161–4, 176
Buret, Eugène, 85
Burton, Sir Richard, 6, 59, 175
Butler, Josephine, 13–14, 87–8

Carlile, Richard, 36
Carpenter, Edward, 14, 16, 57–60
Casper, Johann Ludwig, 17, 30, 112
Ceylon (Sri Lanka), 58–60
Charcot, Jean-Martin, 114
Chauncey, George, 20, 50
Chéreau, Achille, 117
Choquette, Leslie, 53
Christianity, 3
city, sex and, 23–4
clitoridectomy, 117, 127
Cocks, Harry, 20
Comfort, Alex, 8
Comstock Law, 11, 186
Conrad, Joseph, 59
Contagious Diseases Acts, 13–14, 22,
    87–8, 106–7, 157–9
contraception, 2–3
Cook, Matt, 20
Copley, Antony, 50, 51
Corbin, Alain, 24

www.ingramcontent.com/pod-product-compliance
Lightning Source LLC
Chambersburg PA
CBHW081429270326
41932CB00019B/3142